The Tale of al-Barrāq Son of Rawḥān and Laylā the Chaste

A British Academy Monograph

British Academy Monographs showcase work arising from:

British Academy Postdoctoral Fellowships
British Academy Newton International Fellowships

The Tale of al-Barrāq Son of Rawḥān and Laylā the Chaste

A Bilingual Edition and Study

Marlé Hammond

Published for THE BRITISH ACADEMY
by OXFORD UNIVERSITY PRESS

Oxford University Press, Great Clarendon Street, Oxford OX2 6DP

First edition published in 2020

British Library Cataloguing in Publication Data
Data available

Library of Congress Cataloging in Publication Data
Data available

Typeset by
KSPM, Neville Lodge, 8 Wood Road, Codsall, Wolverhampton

Printed in Great Britain by
TJ International, Padstow, Cornwall

ISBN 978-0-19-726668-7

Contents

Preface

This monograph was born of a mistake; it represents an attempt to set the record straight. In my doctoral dissertation on classical Arabic women's poetry, I began my timeline of ancient Arabic women's writing with a certain Laylā bt. Lukayz, who was said to have lived in the fifth century, CE. Whilst I acknowledged that the famous poem ascribed to her may well have been apocryphal, I did not doubt its ancient provenance.[1] Now, after devoting years of research trying to track her down, trying to find a trace of her in the classical sources, I have come to the conclusion that she is a fictional character, a fabrication of the literary imagination of the Ottoman era. She is not a poet but rather the heroine of a story which is make-believe, the tale which is the subject of this volume. Overreliance on early modern scholars, and specifically the figure of Louis Cheikho (1859–1927), who, having come across her story, packaged it as history for his reader, had led me to believe that Laylā bt. Lukayz, however legendary, was at least authentically ancient. Her poems helped to shape my assumptions about the role that women played in the production of poetry in pre-Islamic times. This role is largely seen as one of mourning the deaths of fallen warriors, or inciting men to war, either to seek revenge or to defend tribal honour. Laylā's legend thus conforms to our expectations and reinforces our impressions about women's verse. Yet it should not.

Here I would like to caution against overreaction. Just because Laylā's story is 'untrue', and just because the whole corpus of

[1] Martha Latané Hammond, 'The Poetics of S/Exclusion: Women, Gender and the Classical Arabic Canon' (PhD thesis, Columbia University, 2003). See pages 12n and 18.

ancient Arabic poetry is likewise mired in legend, does not mean that we should, as Ṭāhā Ḥusayn famously suggested, doubt everything. Moreover, we certainly should not doubt that women made important contributions to Arabic literature in its formative period. What we do need to do, however, is to sort the wheat from the chaff. Early modern scholars rightly wished to celebrate Arab women's achievements in the literary realm, and they produced many biographical dictionaries and anthologies rejoicing in this legacy, from Zaynab Fawwāz' *al-Durr al-manthūr* (Scattered Pearls, 1894–5), to Cheikho's *Riyāḍ al-adab fī marāthī shawāʿir al-ʿArab* (Literary Gardens of the Laments of Arabic Women Poets, 1897), to Bashīr Yamūt's *Shāʿirāt al-ʿArab* (Female Poets of the Arabs, 1934). Subsequent scholars, such as ʿAbd A. Muhannā, in his *Muʿjam al-nisāʾ al-shāʿirāt* (Dictionary of Women Poets, 1990), have returned to these early modern sources and have given them more or less the same weight they give the classical sources, despite the fact that, during the Arab Renaissance or *Nahḍa*, there was a lot of confusion and *naïveté* about the newly rediscovered ancient corpus of poetry.

Some of that confusion persists, and there are many unanswered questions that loom over this monograph: Who invented the tale? Where exactly did it emerge? When precisely was it composed? I may be proven wrong if earlier manuscripts are unearthed, but I believe that the tale dates from the latter half of the seventeenth century. Whilst I find that linguistic analysis of the text yields few clues that could help us to date it, formal analysis of its narrative structures and literary themes does help to situate the text within Arabic literary history. Its peculiar reworking of the ʿUdhrī love tale, for example, would indicate that the tale is post-Umayyad at the very least. Its resemblance to the popular *sīra* would, on the other hand, suggest a much later origin, perhaps one emanating from the twelfth century or beyond. Moreover, the parallels between the eighteenth-century European trends of representing women as hapless victims and the tale's knight-in-shining-armour-rescues-damsel-in-distress storyline, parallels which are indicative of cross-fertilisation, lead me to conclude that the manuscript whose copying dates from 1719, namely 1194 Adab at Dār al-Kutub in Cairo, must be one of the earliest. Indeed, if I am right that the storyline has its origins in the European fairy tale, then 1697, the publication date of Charles Perrault's *Histoires et contes du temps passé* (Tales of Olden Times), is perhaps a very significant milestone. As there is no trace of the tale in the bibliographical lexicon, *Kashf al-ẓunūn ʿan asāmī l-kutub wa-l-funūn* (The Lifting of Doubts on the Names of Books and the Arts), by Kâtip Çelebi (a.k.a. Ḥājjī Khalīfa d. 1657), the mid-seventeenth century does seem like a reasonable vanishing point. Nevertheless, I have to admit that dating the *Tale of al-Barrāq Son of Rawḥān and Laylā the Chaste* is an extremely difficult exercise, especially given that the broad period of time from which it originates falls within the pre-modern era often dubbed the 'Period of Decline', which is notoriously understudied. In any case, the historical moment upon which the book concentrates is not the point of origin of the tale, which could in theory be any time before the copying of the earliest manuscript in 1719 CE, but rather its absorption into literary history in the latter half of the nineteenth century and its fictional evolution in the first half of the twentieth.

As to the question of where the story emerged, this, too, remains a mystery, but we see from its early evolution that we may identify two branches of the tale: a Christian version which was propagated in the Levant, and a non-Christian version which seems to have centred on Egypt. Then there is the question of authorship: did the tale arise from folklore, or was it simply self-consciously fabricated in one go by an anonymous author? My belief is that the prose sections, that is the narrative framework, were created by an individual who may have drawn on a set of pre-existing poems or songs, but that the latter, if they were pre-existing, were not very old. If the poetry was drawn from folklore, in other words, it was recent not ancient. Given the tale's odd combination of elements that are both alien to and cliché within Arabic literature, it would not surprise me if the 'original' author was either a non-Arab or a polyglot, someone who was versed in the Arabic literary tradition but who had internalised foreign paradigms.

Whilst in the following pages an attempt is made to situate the *Tale of al-Barrāq Son of Rawḥān and Laylā the Chaste* within the context of Arabic literary history by comparing it with known genres, this attempt is hampered somewhat by what is essentially the text's atypical and unrepresentative nature. Nothing else like it exists, to my knowledge. The text, in my view, seems like an 'imposter'. In fact, before I tracked down the eighteenth-century sources of the narrative, I had speculated that it was a nineteenth-century orientalist fabrication. Scholarly investigations of 'post-classical', 'pre-modern', or, more specifically, Ottoman Arabic literature, with the exception of studies of the popular epic or *sīra*, have not proven to be particularly relevant. I have therefore tried to supplement my readings about Arabic literature with readings about social and cultural history, works such as Bruce Masters' *The Arabs of the Ottoman Empire, 1516–1918* (2013), Nelly Hanna's *In Praise of Books: A Cultural History of Cairo's Middle Class, Sixteenth to the Eighteenth Century* (2003), and Dana Sajdi's *The Barber of Damascus: Nouveau Literacy in the Eighteenth-Century Ottoman Levant* (2013). These books allow one to envision the milieu in which the text was born, one in which changes to political and material cultures brought about transformations in the relationships between the elites and the masses, authors and audiences, and the oral and the written.

This leads me to a further set of urgent questions. How do I hope this tale and its analysis may contribute to a field into which it does not easily fit? How can it change our understanding of Arabic literature when it cannot be viewed as representative? Why lift the tale out of its relative obscurity, much less share it with an English-reading audience? Why draw attention to the mistakes of nineteenth- and twentieth-century scholars and intellectuals? What is to be gained by making the likes of Louis Cheikho look foolish?

The answer lies in the sheer enjoyment of playing detective. The mystery behind the tale absolutely fascinates me. Moreover, what I found during my investigations is that I could relate the disparate textual clues to pre-existing trends and debates. In particular I could link the tale and its metamorphoses to the rise of early modern – or rather late 'pre-modern' – Arabic narrative fiction. Indeed, the mere existence of the tale goes some way toward debunking the somewhat outdated yet persistent orientalist contention that pre-modern Arabs 'lacked' sustained fictional narrative. Moreover, the misinterpretation and misrepresentation of the tale as history sheds light on processes of reception and consumption. The 'disconnect' between the signs of fiction embedded in the text and the historicising tendencies found in the way that it was framed by those who redacted and studied it suggests that the culture that produced it and transmitted it was heterogeneous and volatile rather than set in its ways and bogged down in tradition. Many aspects of the mystery behind the tale remain unsolved, of course, but I think I have compiled a convincing and revealing case file. Perhaps someone, someday, will feel compelled to add to it.

Acknowledgements

Many institutions and individuals have contributed directly to the project resulting in this monograph. I would like to thank first of all the British Academy for its support of both my Postdoctoral Research Fellowship (2007–10), entitled 'Sisters and Singing-Girls: Representations of Ancient Women Poets in Modern Arabic Literature and Film', as well as my Mid-Career Research Fellowship (2017–18), namely 'From Fiction to Fact: The Curious Evolution of an Arabic Epic'. It has furthermore enabled me to share the results of my research by publishing this book through its monograph scheme. Geetha Nair has been particularly supportive in this regard. I am also grateful to St John's College and the Oriental Institute of Oxford University for hosting my British Academy Postdoctoral Fellowship. I could not have benefited from a more nurturing research environment. As my then mentor, Geert Jan van Gelder proved to be a constant source of invaluable information and advice. Robin Ostle also deserves special mention for his encouragement of my career and my ventures into modern topics. Thanks are also due to Jonathan Rodgers, Head of the Near Eastern division of the University of Michigan Library, who, in 2009, helped me identify Aloys Sprenger's 'Notes on Alfred von Kremer's edition of Wáqidy's Campaigns', what turned out to be a crucial article.

More recently I have profited from the support of my close colleagues at SOAS University of London. Wen-chin Ouyang, Stefan Sperl, and Hugh Kennedy have all had a role in the promulgation of this volume. Wen-chin, especially, has provided me with constructive feedback on drafts of the chapters that follow. Karima Laachir helped me think through the narrative's indebtedness to the 'western' fairy tale and the role of multilingualism in traversing literary boundaries, and I am greatly indebted to her. Mohamed

Said, too, kindly assisted me with some linguistic matters, including the transcription of the Arabic text. I would also like to thank colleagues further afield, namely Adam Talib and Pernilla Myrne – Adam for some insightful corrections he made to early portions of the translation, and Pernilla for graciously sharing her resources and know-how on a research trip to the Bāb al-Khalq branch of Dār al-Kutub in Cairo in November 2018.

Thanks are due as well to the anonymous 'Final Reader', appointed by the British Academy, to review the manuscript of the book that I submitted in January 2019. This person's main criticism was that I was in danger of presenting the material in an 'ahistorical vacuum' and that I should make more of an effort to analyse the text for possible clues as to its historical context. In response I have attempted to firm up my theories about the tale's origins. The staff at Keystroke Project Management, particularly copy-editor Sarah Pearsall, who handled the manuscript with care and attention, deserve my thanks as well.

Last but not least, I need to convey my heartfelt gratitude once again to Geert Jan van Gelder, who graciously agreed to subject my translation of the tale to his scrutiny. He spotted many problems and, as is his wont, spelled out the solutions. His mastery of the Arabic lexicon and grammar – down to the permissible poetic licences, coupled with his keen metrical sense, put me to shame. The experience has made me appreciate just how important it is that we train our classicists or 'pre-modernists' to scan verse. Often it was the violation of a poem's metre that alerted him that I had misvocalised and misread a word. He was not able to iron out all the wrinkles, but I am now confident that the translation roughly represents the semantic content of the Arabic text. Arabic readers will be able to judge this for themselves.

Abbreviations

b.	ibn (son of . . .)
bt.	bint (daughter of . . .)
EAL	*Encyclopedia of Arabic Literature*
EI[1]	*Encyclopaedia of Islam*, 1st edition
EI[2]	*Encyclopaedia of Islam*, 2nd edition
EI[3]	*Encyclopaedia of Islam*, THREE
IJMES	*International Journal of Middle East Studies*
JAL	*Journal of Arabic Literature*
MEL	*Middle Eastern Literatures*

A Note on Transliteration and Terminology

Throughout this monograph, I have followed the *IJMES* transliteration guidelines, except that I have employed full transliteration (i.e. macrons and dots) for names and titles and not merely for technical terms. I have avoided transliterating lengthy chunks of text, opting instead to cite the original Arabic.

More problematic is the question of what categorical label I should attach to the story that is presented, translated, and analysed here. Could we call it an 'epic'? A 'romance'? A 'novel'? Or is it simply a 'tale' or a 'story' that eludes classification? This crisis in terminology stems not only from the inadequacy of western terms to capture Arabic genres – what is, for example, the equivalent of the *sīra*? It also derives from the lack of consistency in the application of Arabic terms to the narrative. Sometimes it is called *sīra*, sometimes *qiṣṣa*, sometimes merely 'an account of what happened' (*dhikr mā jarā*). Perhaps rather than pinning it down precisely, we could look at the tale's prosimetrical consistency, its relative length, and its concern with charting a foundational myth of a people, and declare it to be a narrative on the 'epic spectrum'.

Lastly, I need to address the thorny issue of the labels by which we periodise Arabic literature. I myself am not particularly bothered by the ambiguity and imprecision of the application of various Eurocentric terms – like 'classical' and 'medieval' – to periods of Arabic literature, but I am very aware that some of my colleagues are. Indeed, Thomas Bauer, in his animated review of the Cambridge History of Arabic Literature's *Arabic Literature in the Post-Classical*

Period (2006),[1] edited by Roger Allen and D.S. Richards, rails against the editors' use of several such terms, including 'post-classical'. While there is much truth in Bauer's criticisms of this qualifier, including the notion that it is potentially polemically biased against the literature it describes, I find the designation beneficial. Whereas before we only had the binary division of classical and modern, in which literature from the thirteenth to the eighteenth century was either ignored completely or subsumed under the rubric of 'classical', now we have a comparatively neutral term to refer to literature of what was once pejoratively called the period of decline or *ʿaṣr al-inḥiṭāṭ*. The hint of negativity in the term 'post-classical' enables us to avoid a complete epistolary rupture with previous generations of scholars, at the same time that it opens up a neglected, and in many ways intriguing, corpus to new avenues of enquiry. In the following chapters, I sometimes use 'classical' to refer to Arabic literature of the sixth to the thirteenth century, 'post-classical' to refer to that of the thirteenth through to the *Nahḍa* or Arab Renaissance in the eighteenth or nineteenth century, and 'modern' to refer to texts written during the *Nahḍa* and beyond. I also use the term 'pre-modern' to indicate either the whole of the 'classical' and 'post-classical' tradition or the very late 'post-classical' tradition, in other words literature on the cusp of the Renaissance. This is not to say that I do not also sometimes draw on more precise vocabulary, in instances where I can, but that the ambiguity of these general terms suits me given the unanswered questions that surround the geographical and chronological circumstances behind the origins and evolution of the tale.

[1] Thomas Bauer, 'In Search of "Post-Classical Literature": A Review Article', *Mamlūk Studies Review* 11.2 (2007), 137–67.

A Note on the Manuscripts and Published Editions

To date I have tracked down seven manuscripts and three published editions of the tale. Of the seven manuscripts I have consulted five, namely:

- Ahlwardt 9747 (Berlin), copied in 1854, 77v–141v. Part of Sprenger 1215.
- Arabe 5833 (Paris), copied in 1797, 107v–131.
- Ms. Or. Oct. 1383 (Berlin), copied in early 1824, 87–147.
- Or. 2676 (Leiden), undated, 155v–231.
- 5984 Adab (Dār al-Kutub, Cairo), copied in 1927, 2–119. A copy of 1194 Adab, below.

There are two further manuscripts:

- 1194 Adab (Dār al-Kutub, Cairo), copied in 1719.
- 6375 Adab (Dār al-Kutub, Cairo), undated [?].

Despite the fact that I made a research trip to Cairo in November 2018, I was unable to see the last two, as their microfilms were missing from the Bāb al-Khalq branch of Dār al-Kutub. Nevertheless, I have been able to consult them indirectly. These two manuscripts form the basis for the most recent published edition of the tale – the ʿAṭiyya edition listed below, a volume which I have been able to read. Moreover, 5984 Adab, a manuscript I did review in Cairo, is a copy of 1194 Adab.

Of the three published versions of the tale, one is serialised in a periodical and two are in book form. They are as follows:

- Anonymous, 'Riwāyat al-Barrāq b. Rawḥān', *Ḥadīqat al-akhbār* 1.39–1.48 (2 October 1858–4 December 1858).

- Iskandar Abkāriyūs, 'Ḥarb al-Barrāq', *Tazyīn nihāyat al-arab fī akhbār al-ʿArab* (Beirut: Al-Maṭbaʿa al-Waṭaniyya, 1867), 211–300.
- Aḥmad ʿAṭiyya (ed.),[1] *Kitāb al-Jamhara fī ayyām al-ʿArab li-l-ḥāfiẓ ʿUmar b. Shabba al-Baṣrī al-mutawaffā sanat 262 hijrī* (Ismailiyah: Maktabat al-Imām al-Bukhārī, 2015), 69–183.

Having compared the structures and contents of the different versions of the narrative, I identified a branch of the tale, which I call the Christian version. I call it that not only because the chief protagonist of the story is Christian in this version, but also because it was propagated by Christian scholars during the Arab *Nahḍa* or 'Renaissance'. The Christian versions are:

- Ahlwardt 9747
- Ms. Or. Oct. 1383
- *Ḥadīqat al-akhbār*
- Abkāriyūs

As the Christian version of the tale ultimately predominated, and as it has a better story arc, I decided to translate it over and above the non-Christian version. I based the transcription and the translation on the more legible of the Christian manuscripts (Ahlwardt 9747), adding flourishes from the less legible one (Ms. Or. Oct. 1383), which was more detailed. Then, when I came upon curiosities in the text, such as unfamiliar words, I read all the manuscripts and published sources in conjunction with one another to determine the most probable 'intended' meaning.

[1] It has recently come to my attention that Aḥmad ʿAṭiyya published an edition of al-Barrāq's *dīwān* in 2017. I have not yet been able to consult this book.

A Note on the Attribution of the Text to ʿUmar b. Shabba

The Cairo manuscripts, as well as some Cairo-based modern scholars who must have had exposure to them, attribute the work to the third-/ninth-century scholar and transmitter Abū Zayd ʿUmar b. Shabba.[1] Likewise Aḥmad ʿAṭiyya, the editor of *Kitāb al-Jamhara*, presents ʿUmar b. Shabba as the likely author of his book. Were this attribution to be correct, that would undermine two of the premises of this monograph, the first being that the tale is a work of anonymous fiction, and the second that it is a product of the Ottoman Empire. I am confident, however, that the attribution is incorrect. This is because ʿUmar b. Shabba is a transmitter with whom I am rather intimately acquainted, given that he figures as an important source of reports (*akhbār*) in a compendium which I, as a scholar of classical Arabic women's writing, have studied closely, namely *Balāghāt al-nisāʾ* (The Eloquent Sayings of Women) by Aḥmad b. Abī Ṭāhir Ṭayfūr (d. 280/893).[2] This is the section of his voluminous *Kitāb al-manthūr wa-l-manẓūm* (The Book of Prose and Verse) which is devoted to the statements of women. As the lives and careers of these two illustrious figures would have crossed paths in Baghdad in the third/ninth century, it seems improbable that ʿUmar b. Shabba would have been knowledgeable enough to compose a book including the entire legend of al-Barrāq b. Rawḥān and Laylā

[1] See S. Leder, 'ʿUmar b. Shabba', *EI*².

[2] See F. Rosenthal, 'Ibn Abī Ṭāhir Ṭayfūr', *EI*². Some reports attributed to Abū Zayd ʿUmar b. Shabba begin on the following pages in Ibn Abī Ṭāhir Ṭayfūr, *Balāghāt al-nisāʾ* (Beirut: Dār al-Ḥadātha, 1987): 61, 134, 136, 143–4, 147, 153, 212, 257–8, 261, 264, 271–2, 274, 284–5, 288, 292, 294, and 314.

the Chaste and yet not have shared a report or two about Laylā with Ibn Ṭayfūr for his treatise on eloquent women. Moreover, had ʿUmar b. Shabba authored the narrative, it would probably take the form of a pastiche of different *akhbār*, rather than one single continuous account.

Key Dates

483 Erroneous estimated death date of Laylā bt. Lukayz. Approximate setting of the tale.

622 *Hijra* from Mecca to Medina. Start of the Islamic calendar. End of pre-Islamic era.

632 Death of Muḥammad.

661 Start of the Umayyad Caliphate. Emergence of the ʿUdhrī love tale.

750 End of the Umayyad Caliphate in the eastern Islamic world. Rise of the Abbasids.

878 Death of ʿUmar b. Shabba, to whom some manuscripts incorrectly attribute the tale.

893 Death of Ibn Ṭayfūr. No mention of Laylā in his *Balāghāt al-nisāʾ* (Eloquent Sayings of Women) despite numerous reports transmitted on the authority of ʿUmar b. Shabba.

900s Approximate date of Abū Zayd al-Qurashī's *Jamharat ashʿār al-ʿArab* (The Collection of the Arabs' Poetry) to which manuscripts of the tale are appended.

972 Death of Abū al-Faraj al-Iṣfahānī. No mention of Laylā or al-Barrāq in his voluminous *Kitāb al-aghānī* (Book of Songs).

1100s References to the *Epic of ʿAntar* begin to appear in the literature.

1258 Sacking of Baghdad. End of the Abbasid Caliphate. Rough dividing line between 'classical' and 'post-classical' Arabic literature.

1466 Date of earliest extant manuscript of the *Epic of ʿAntar*.

1517 Fall of the Mamlūks. Beginning of Ottoman era.

1657 Death of Kâtip Çelebi. His encyclopaedic bibliography of books in the Islamic world makes no mention of Laylā or al-Barrāq.

1697 Publication of Charles Perrault's *Histoires et contes du temps passé* (Tales of Olden Times). Collection includes 'Sleeping Beauty' and 'Cinderella'.
1704 Start date of the publication of Antoine Galland's French translation of the *Thousand and One Nights*.
1712 End date of the publication of Antoine Galland's French translation of the *Thousand and One Nights*.
1719 Copying of 1194 Adab.
1728 Muslim Turkish book printing begins in Istanbul.
1797 Copying of Arabe 5833.
1798 Napoleon's conquest of Egypt.
1812 Start date of the publication of the Grimm Brothers' *Kinder- und Hausmärchen* (Children's and Household Tales).
1820 Founding of Būlāq Press in Cairo.
1824 Copying of Ms. Or. Oct. 1383.
1854 Copying of Ahlwardt 9747.
1857 End date of the publication of the Grimm Brothers' *Kinder- und Hausmärchen* (Children's and Household Tales).
1858 Tale serialised in Lebanese periodical *Ḥadīqat al-akhbār*.
1867 Book by Iskandar Abkāriyūs containing tale published.
1890 Publication of Louis Cheikho's *Kitāb shuʿarāʾ al-Naṣrāniyya* (Book of Christian Poets), vol. 1, which assigns a death date of 483 to Laylā.
1894 Publication of Zaynab Fawwāz' biographical dictionary of women *al-Durr al-manthūr* (Scattered Pearls). Contains no mention of Laylā bt. Lukayz.
1909 Publication of ʿAbd al-Raḥmān Shukrī's poem 'Kisrā wa-l-asīra' (Chosroes and the Captive).
1913 Publication of what is traditionally considered the first Arabic novel, Muḥammad Ḥusayn Haykal's *Zaynab*.
1927 Copying of 5984 Adab.
1937 Screening of Bahīja Ḥāfiẓ film *Laylā bt. al-ṣaḥrāʾ* (Laylā, Daughter of the Desert).
1937 Release of Asmahān's recording of song adaptation of Laylā's 'torture' poem.
1944 *Laylā bt. al-ṣaḥrāʾ* rereleased as *Laylā al-badawiyya* (Laylā the Bedouin).

1954 ʿĀdil al-Ghaḍbān's novel *Laylā al-ʿafīfa* (Laylā the Chaste) is published.
1974 Airing of Lebanese television serial entitled 'Laylā wa-l-Barrāq' (Laylā and al-Barrāq).
1999 Date of Suad al-Attar's 'Inspiration from a Poem', an etching and aquatint featuring a verse of Laylā bt. Lukayz.
2000 'Inspiration from a Poem' acquired by the British Museum.
2015 Aḥmad ʿAṭiyya publishes edition of 1194 Adab and 6375 Adab. Book attributed to ʿUmar b. Shabba.
2017 Aḥmad ʿAṭiyya publishes *Dīwān al-Barrāq b. Rawḥān* (The Collected Poems of al-Barrāq b. Rawḥān).
2017 Founding of https://martha-hammond-msds.squarespace.com, a website devoted to the persona of Laylā bt. Lukayz.

1
From Fiction to History and Back: The Tale, Its Versions and Its Afterlives

> The unfortunate, persecuted maiden! The subject is as old as the world . . .
>
> Mario Praz[1]

Introduction

What I call the *Tale of al-Barrāq Son of Rawḥān and Laylā the Chaste* in fact has no fixed title. Before the second half of the nineteenth century it did not circulate independently as a discrete text.[2] Rather it formed a lengthy chapter in a collection of heroic tales interspersing prose and verse passages and set in a pseudo-pre-Islamic Arabian environment. Despite its occasional and almost certainly spurious attribution to the third-/ninth-century transmitter ʿUmar b. Shabba, it is safe to say that the collection of tales has no identifiable author.[3] In addition to the legend of al-Barrāq, the collection includes the story of Kulayb and his consolidation of power over the Yemen and

[1] Mario Praz, *The Romantic Agony*, 2nd edn (Oxford and New York: Oxford University Press, 1970), 97.
[2] Perhaps the first time that it appears as a discrete legend is in the 1858 version which was serialised in the Lebanese periodical *Ḥadīqat al-akhbār*.
[3] Aḥmad ʿAṭiyya, editor of *Kitāb al-jamhara fī ayyām al-ʿArab*, attributes his book to ʿUmar b. Shabba. This attribution comes from the two Cairo manuscripts he consulted.

the story of the War of the Basūs.[4] Often it is appended to copies of Abū Zayd Muḥammad b. Abī al-Khaṭṭāb al-Qurashī's *Jamharat ashʿār al-ʿArab*,[5] which is a fourth-/tenth-century anthology of forty-nine pre- and early Islamic poems.[6] Our tale, which, as a relatively lengthy semi-poetic heroic narrative could variously be described as a short 'epic' or 'romance' (*sīra*),[7] seems to have originated much later than this anthology, perhaps as late as the beginning of the eighteenth century, and it was widely circulated in the nineteenth century. Thus far I have tracked down ten sources of the tale, three publications and seven manuscripts.[8] It is narrated by a certain Dhuʾayb b. Nāfiʿ,[9] who remains an obscure and mysterious figure.[10]

The text itself exhibits many characteristics of what some have called 'Middle Arabic Literature', or that literature that straddles the divide between high and low literature. If we look at the ten criteria laid out by Aboubakr Chraïbi,[11] we find that the *Tale of*

[4] As Kulayb features centrally in both of these tales one may get a sense of their content from G. Levi Della Vida, 'Kulayb b. Rabīʿa', *EI*[2].

[5] Abū Zayd al-Qurashī, *Jamharat ashʿār al-ʿArab* (Beirut: Dār Ṣādir/Dār Bayrūt, 1963).

[6] Ch. Pellat, 'Abū Zayd al-Ḳura<u>sh</u>ī', *EI*[2].

[7] None of these terms fits our tale precisely. Unlike the epic, our tale is composed partly in prose. Moreover, its style is not grandiose. But like the epic it focuses on the actions of a heroic individual fighting in tribal wars whose actions bear on the fate of the community. The romance, too, has characteristics in common with our tale. It allows for prose and emphasises themes of chivalry and civility. For more on the 'epic', the 'chivalric romance', and the distinction between them, see M.H. Abrams and Geoffrey Galt Harpham, *A Glossary of Literary Terms*, 11th edn (Stamford, CT: Cengage Learning, 2014), 44 and 97–9. The Arabic term *sīra*, though largely applicable, could be misleading. Our tale is shorter than a typical *sīra*, and it is not composed in rhymed prose or *sajʿ*.

[8] See 'A Note on the Manuscripts and Published Editions', above.

[9] Note that not all of the tales in the collection are narrated by Dhuʾayb b. Nāfiʿ.

[10] ʿAṭiyya speculates as to his identity (*Kitāb al-jamhara*, 30–3), looking for him among known transmitters for ʿUmar b. Shabba, who are called Ibn Nāfiʿ, but none of them are known as Dhuʾayb. Given that the text probably originates much later than the life of ʿUmar b. Shabba, this seems like a pointless exercise.

[11] Aboubakr Chraïbi, *Arabic Manuscripts of the Thousand and One Nights* (Paris: Espaces & Signes, 2016), 63. Chraïbi suggests that eight of his criteria should be met for a work to count as 'Middle Literature'. For more on the concept of 'Middle Arabic Literature', see Chraïbi's article, 'Classification des traditions narratives

al-Barrāq Son of Rawḥān and Laylā the Chaste meets several of them. I will not list all of Chraïbi's criteria here. Suffice it to say that the tale conforms to the profile of Middle Literature by virtue of the fact that it is a medium-length prosimetrical love story which is set in a specific place – Arabia and adjacent lands – and at a specific point in time – before the rise of Islam. On the other hand, it departs from the paradigm in that it is not described as 'marvellous' (*ʿajīb*) or 'strange' (*gharīb*) in its title or content – in other words, it has no fantastical elements, and the hero is not a merchant or a merchant's son. But perhaps the most striking disqualification of the label 'Middle Arabic Literature' is that the tale is not composed in 'Middle Arabic'. It is composed, rather, in straightforward *fuṣḥā*, violating few if any of the rules of grammar apart from its treatment of the *hamza*. Nevertheless, the language used is syntactically very simple and lexically very repetitive, thus it does not come across as 'high' literature.[12]

Here, in this chapter, I introduce the tale by familiarising the reader with its content and contexts. A short synopsis is followed by an assessment of the discrepancies between two main branches of the tale. I go on to explore the nature of fiction in pre-modern Arabic literature. In a section entitled, 'From Fiction to History', having explored the fictional status of the tale by drawing attention to its imaginary components, I explain how it came to be understood as history by scholars in the nineteenth century. Then, in 'Storytelling and Hybridity', I consider the generic make-up of the tale and show that it stems from the intersection of three literary matrices – two 'endemic' (the popular *sīra* and the ʿUdhrī love tale) and one 'western' (the damsel-in-distress-type fairy tale). I argue that the foreign plotline was one of the reasons for the tale's misrecognition as

arabes par "conte-type": Application à l'étude de quelques rôles de poète', *Bulletin d'Études Orientales* 50 (1998), 29–59.

[12] Perhaps one could equate it with – or rather compare it to – the 'simple prose' style that Peter Heath describes as one of those to be found in the popular epic. See his 'Styles in Premodern Arabic Popular Epics', in Bilal Orfali (ed.), *In the Shadow of Arabic: The Centrality of Language to Arabic Culture* (Leiden and Boston: Brill, 2011), 413–31. That style is generally rhymed, however.

history. In 'From History Back to Fiction', I explore twentieth-century literary and cinematic adaptations of the tale and their reception as historical fiction. I conclude with reflections on what the story can teach us about the nature of Arabic fiction and its historical permutations.

Synopsis

Our narrator, Dhuʾayb b. Nāfiʿ, relates the tale of a young and brave warrior, al-Barrāq b. Rawḥān, who is in love with his first cousin, Laylā bt. Lukayz, and hopes to marry her. Laylā is renowned for her beauty, and an Arab king makes a marriage proposal to her father. Much to al-Barrāq's chagrin, Laylā's father agrees to the engagement. When Laylā is sent as part of a convoy to the Arab king, she is kidnapped *en route* by a half-Arab half-Persian middleman called Burd who plans to pass her on to a Persian king named Shahrmayh. Whilst in captivity, Laylā utters a poem in which she describes the torture and suffering she endures and calls upon her kinsmen to rescue her. It begins:

> If only al-Barrāq had an eye to see
> The agony and distress I endure
>
> My brothers, Kulayb, ʿUqayl
> Junayd, help me weep
>
> Woe upon you, your sister has been tortured
> Awfully morning and night
>
> They fettered me, shackled me, and beat
> My chaste surface with a stick (2:105)

Laylā's poem is overheard by a sympathetic servant who conveys it to al-Barrāq through a series of messengers. When al-Barrāq hears Laylā's words, he rallies his people to war. Under al-Barrāq's fearless leadership, the Arab armies come close to defeating the Persians and their Arab allies, but then the Persians call in reinforcements from as far away as India and China, and the vastly outnumbered

Arab troops withdraw to regroup, leaving al-Barrāq on his own in enemy territory. Through a combination of military prowess and ruse, al-Barrāq on his own succeeds in killing both Burd and Shahrmayh, and he rescues Laylā. Al-Barrāq and Laylā wed, and it is discovered that she is a virgin – she has successfully warded off sexual violation during her captivity – hence she is known as Laylā 'the Chaste'.

Interestingly, some versions of the epic identify the hero al-Barrāq as a Christian.[13] These versions have more complex narrative structures with a stronger story arc. The non-Christian versions begin somewhat randomly with the slaying of al-Ḥārith b. ʿAbbād, an incident which sparks a blood feud amongst the Arab tribes. Hence the action builds on an act of murder and tracks the trajectory of blood vengeance as it spirals out of control. The Christian versions, on the other hand, open with a genealogical introduction of the Arabs, then they introduce the characters of al-Barrāq b. Rawḥān and Laylā bt. Lukayz and gradually develop a portrait of al-Barrāq as a warrior and of his bond with his cousin Laylā. Lukayz' decision to marry her off to an Arab king is controversial among al-Barrāq's kinship group and forms the subject of a lengthy polyphonic poetic disputation. The Christian versions also feature the slaying of al-Ḥārith b. ʿAbbād, but it occurs only after the love story has been established. The blood feud is in this sense secondary to the love story. As the non-Christian versions may antedate the Christian versions – it is hard to say exactly because not all of the known manuscripts are dated – and as the Christian version of the tale was propagated by Christian scholars and writers in the nineteenth century, it is tempting to see these additional elements in the Christian version as being a deliberate attempt to Christianise an otherwise non-Christian tale, to claim a Christian legacy in Arabic literature.[14]

[13] These are, first of all, the manuscripts Ahlwardt 9747 and Ms. Or. Oct. 1383 – both in Berlin. Then we have the serialisation in *Ḥadīqat al-akhbār* as well as the Abkāriyūs rendition. See 'A Note on the Manuscripts and Published Editions', above.

[14] On the trend amongst Christian Arabs to situate themselves at the centre of the Arabic linguistic and literary tradition both during the *Nahḍa* and in the period

However, because the non-Christian version begins rather abruptly, it may be that the opposite occurred – the beginning of the tale may have been chopped off in an attempt to de-Christianise it. It is worth noting in this regard that the Christian content of the tale comes at the beginning of the text and there is no real effort to sustain it. Although the tale is supposedly set in a pagan environment, the characters behave and speak more or less as Muslims and definitely as monotheists. The characters do not pray, but they speak of God and his sanctuary and they go on pilgrimage. The treatment of religion is one of the epic's 'timeless' aspects.

The tale has little if any historical value. There are no dates or identifiable events, no battle names, apart from perhaps one.[15] There is hardly even a temporal setting, but for the recurrence of the phrase, 'the fiery ardour of the Jāhiliyya overtook him' (أخذته حمية الجاهلية). Days of the week and months, much less years, are never specified. Moreover, the character who should be the most historically identifiable – the Persian king who threatens Laylā with forced marriage or rape – appears to be a figment of the storyteller's imagination. King Shahrmayh does not seem to have existed. This is very much a narrative that takes place in what Bakhtin calls 'adventure time'. The heroes do not age, and time is only measured in the context of each individual adventure. Perhaps in this way our tale, especially its Christian version, resembles the ancient Greek novel that Bakhtin describes:

> This Greek romance-time does not have even an elementary biological or maturational duration. At the novel's outset the heroes meet each other at a marriageable age, and at the same marriageable age, no less fresh and handsome, they consummate the marriage at the novel's

preceding it, see Abdulrazzak Patel, 'The Reintegration of Pre-modern Christians into the Mainstream of Arabic Literature and the Creation of an Inter-Religious Cultural Space', *The Arab* Nahḍah*: The Making of the Intellectual and Humanist Movement* (Edinburgh: Edinburgh University Press, 2013), 36–74.

[15] It is telling that in the index of battle days (الأيام والوقعات) found in ʿAṭiyya's *Kitāb al-jamhara*, only one of the battles listed, *waqʿat Mutūn*, is found in the pages dedicated to the epic of al-Barrāq b. Rawḥān. See ʿAṭiyya, *Kitāb al-jamhara*, 506. Note that Mutūn appears as Manwar or Manūr in Ahlwardt 9747.

> end. Such a form of time, in which they experience a most improbable number of adventures, is not measured off in the novel and does not add up; it is simply days, nights, hours, moments clocked in a technical sense within the limits of each separate adventure. This time – adventure-time, highly intensified but undifferentiated – is not registered in the slightest way in the age of the heroes. We have here an extratemporal hiatus between two biological moments – the arousal of passion, and its satisfaction.[16]

Despite its atemporality, it has been suggested that the tale has tremendous value in filling in gaps in our knowledge about the earliest years of Arabic poetry, and that it therefore has much to contribute to our knowledge of literary history. Listen to the editor of *Kitāb al-jamhara fī ayyām al-ʿArab*, which is the published edition of the collection of pre-Islamic tales based on two (non-Christian) manuscripts at Dār al-Kutub in Cairo:

> In this regard, the value of the manuscript we have before us is clear, because it sheds light on a tremendous amount of poetic material that was produced by the Jāhiliyya environment and its associated events. Furthermore, it depicts for us the days and the battles that were tied to this poetry, as if it is the historical element of the literary event.[17]

This view that the text creates a historical picture is founded perhaps on a naïve acceptance of the attribution of the text to ʿUmar b. Shabba. However, in my opinion, the only literary-historical value the text has relates to its form and not its content: it is a hybrid of written and oral literature. It connects the tradition of the *sīra*, as well as that of the ʿUdhrī love tale, to that of the modern novel. It represents an important 'step' in Arabic literary history, but it does not relate to the origins of that history but rather to its 'post-classical' or 'pre-modern' stage. The text represents a 'young' epic – one which delves further back in time, showing a predilection

[16] Mikhail M. Bakhtin, 'Forms of Time and Chronotope in the Novel', in *The Dialogic Imagination: Four Essays*, trans. Michael Holquist (Austin: University of Texas Press, 1981), 90.
[17] ʿAṭiyya, *Kitāb al-jamhara*, 7.

for ancestors which is known in folklore,[18] but one which has yet to accrue elements of the fantastical.[19] Our epic is highly formulaic and contains some folkloric motifs, but it by and large remains within the realm of the plausible. Its resemblance to a fairy tale – of the knight-in-shining-armour-rescues-damsel-in-distress variety – makes it, to my mind, obviously fictional. It is not only untrue, but actively made up, even if it is not known by whom. However, the fairy-tale, of this particular sexist type,[20] is unfamiliar in Arabic literature; hence it did not strike scholars of Arabic literature as such. This is not to say that they accepted it at face value, or that they considered it an accurate portrayal of historical events, but rather that they were willing to accept it as largely true. It is worth bearing in mind that this nineteenth-century acceptance of a fictional account as history was contemporaneous with efforts to record the oral popular epics in writing,[21] as well as with the publication of Arabic print

[18] In his study of *chansons de geste*, Howard Bloch claims that the songs 'were composed in reverse chronology pointed always toward the origin of the family line . . . The earlier a character or event can be situated within the global cycle, the later, generally speaking, the date of its addition to the whole'. See his *Etymologies and Genealogies: A Literary Anthropology of the French Middle Ages* (Chicago and London: University of Chicago Press, 1984), 94.

[19] In his essay 'Transformations of the Wondertale', Vladimir Propp states that 'A fantastic treatment of a wondertale component is older than its rational treatment.' See his *Theory and History of Folklore*, trans. Ariadne Y. Martin and Richard P. Martin (Minneapolis: University of Minnesota Press, 1984), 88. This suggests to me that fantastical elements are a sign of ancient provenance, and that therefore, a story that lacks fantastical elements would tend to be younger than one which has them. However, Propp also suggests that there are kinds of stories, such as fables, which feature 'realism' although they date from 'time immemorial'. Ibid., 80.

[20] Here I am thinking of the Cinderellas, the Snow Whites, and the Rapunzels – those narratives popularised by Disney in the twentieth century which feature helpless heroines rescued by handsome and fearless men. For a treatment of the Arabic fairy tale which presumes a much broader definition, see I. Lichtenstaedter, 'Folklore and Fairy-Tale Motifs in Early Arabic Literature', *Folklore* 51.3 (1940), 195–203.

[21] As Konrad Hirschler has pointed out, there is ample evidence to suggest that certain popular epics were in fact recorded in writing in the medieval period. See his *The Written Word in the Medieval Arabic Lands: A Social and Cultural History of Reading Practices* (Edinburgh: Edinburgh University Press, 2012), 175–6. Nevertheless, few manuscripts from this early period survive, and there is definitely an upsurge of epic-writing activity in the late pre-modern era. According to Bridget Connelly,

editions of the *Thousand and One Nights*.[22] Endemic forms of fiction, in this period, were explicitly fantastical, magical or strange. Yet here was a 'traditional' Arabic narrative related in a 'realist' mode.

Fiction in Classical Arabic Literature

Classical Arabic literature, we are often told, has little to offer in the way of fiction. In fact, one can count substantial works of originally-authored fiction on one hand. In particular what is missing is 'sustained' narrative fiction or drama, the long story fabricated for its own sake by a creative individual. Indeed, the following remarks made by Gustave von Grunebaum in the 1940s – as outdated as they should theoretically be – still ring true on a practical level:

> Arabic literary theory does not provide for fiction. The concepts of plot and action are lacking. It is a rather strange fact that Arabic literature, so rich in anecdotal material, so eager to seize upon the unusual word or deed, never did seriously turn toward the large-scale narrative or the drama. Except for parables and short stories, many of which are borrowings from foreign literatures or more or less accurate retracings of true incidents, the Arab Muslim disdained literary invention.[23]

Yes, it is admitted, there is folkloric fiction, anonymously-authored tales such as the aforementioned *Nights*, and the *sīra* epics recounting the fantastical adventures of poet-warriors. But there is a sense in which these texts evolve on their own, independent from

most manuscripts of the *Sīrat Baybars* date from the eighteenth century, while most manuscripts of *Sīrat ʿAntar* and the *Sīrat Banī Hilāl* date from the nineteenth century. See her *Arab Folk Epic and Identity* (Berkeley: University of California Press, 1986), 8.

[22] Wen-chin Ouyang, 'Introduction', in Wen-chin Ouyang and Paolo Lemos Horta (eds), *The Arabian Nights: An Anthology* (London: Everyman's Library, 2014), xiv.

[23] Gustave E. von Grunebaum, *Medieval Islam: A Study in Cultural Orientation*, 2nd edn (Chicago and London: University of Chicago Press, 1953), 287. The book was originally published in 1946 and developed out of a series of lectures delivered in 1945.

authorial intervention, gradually evolving over time, accruing elements by osmosis. They are not only anonymous, but folkloric, and their fictive elements are seen as accidental distortions of collective takes on reality. But what if we were to put an author back into the equation? What if we were to come across a story which is deliberately concocted? Von Grunebaum accedes that one can find a certain fictional genre in the ʿUdhrī love tale, but he suggests that it never developed into anything 'elaborate' because no one ever had the idea to connect the pieces together:

> The sad adventures of romantic lovers were told, grouped around and interspersed with verse ascribed with varying justification to the protagonists. Novelettes of this kind can be traced as early as the sixth century and they remain in vogue throughout the Middle Ages. But, while several littérateurs concerned themselves with collecting and retelling them, no one thought of choosing the anonymous reports and records as the basis of elaborate narrative.[24]

The orientalist impetus of von Grunebaum's remarks is striking: 'the Arab Muslim *disdained* literary invention', 'no one thought of' piecing together a lengthy (fictional) narrative. Yet we have before us the *Tale of al-Barrāq Son of Rawḥān and Laylā the Chaste* – proof that, to the contrary, someone did have this idea of building an elaborate narrative, not with pre-existing accounts of historical personages but rather with characters who were conjured up and modelled on literary precedents. The text was authored as fiction, and it was probably meant to be received as such. So why was it received instead as history, and was it always received in this way?

It is useful, in this regard, to consider the words of Stefan Leder, in his seminal essay, 'Conventions of Fictional Narration in Learned Literature', where he muses:

> Were narratives, which we may classify as fictional according to our analytical standards, ever perceived, and admitted, as fiction in their original context? Where was in pre-modern Arabic literature any conscious use of fiction as a medium of literary expression, and

[24] Ibid., 287–8.

> where can we find indications whether it was ever understood as such?
>
> A narrative which we may identify as containing fictive elements cannot readily be considered a clue to the existence of fictional literature in the common sense of the term. Fiction is determined by conventions of literary communication. Fictional literature is not only constituted by the existence of fictive contents, but requires a system of textual and extra textual signs pointing to its fictional character.[25]

In the case of the *Tale of al-Barrāq Son of Rawḥān and Laylā the Chaste*, there are plenty of textual signs pointing to its fictional character, but the extra-textual signs are misleading, and the extra-textual signs come to interfere in the narrative, historicising what were originally intended as obviously fictional elements.

From Fiction to History

Perhaps no figure is more responsible for the reception of the legend of al-Barrāq b. Rawḥān and Laylā bt. Lukayz as history than the nineteenth-century Lebanese scholar Louis Cheikho (1859–1927).[26] He produced two works of scholarship that were pivotal in this regard: *Kitāb shuʿarāʾ al-Naṣrāniyya* (Book of Christian Poets, Beirut, 1890) and *Riyāḍ al-adab fī marāthī shawāʿir al-ʿArab* (Literary Gardens of the Laments of Arabic Women Poets, Beirut, 1897). Many modern

[25] Stefan Leder, 'Conventions of Fictional Narration in Learned Literature', in Stefan Leder (ed.), *Story-Telling in the Framework of Non-Fictional Arabic Literature* (Wiesbaden: Harrassowitz, 1998), 35. This thesis that the existence of fiction is predicated on an act of communication by which a text must be received as imaginary also informs T. Herzog's argument in his probing article, '"What They Saw with Their Own Eyes . . .": Fictionalization and "Narrativization" of History in Arabic Popular Epics and Learned Historiography', in S. Dorpmueller (ed.), *Fictionalizing the Past: Historical Characters in Arabic Popular Epic* (Leuven: Peeters, 2012), 25–43.

[26] A short biography and profile of his career may be found in Yūsuf Asʿad Dāghir, *Maṣādir al-Dirāsa al-Adabiyya*, vol. 2: *al-Fikr al-ʿArabī al-Ḥadīth fī Siyar Aʿlāmihi*, part 1: *al-Rāḥilūn (1800–1955)* (Lebanon: Jamʿiyyat Ahl al-Qalam, 1956), 515–24.

sources on Laylā bt. Lukayz cite these two books.[27] In his *Book of Christian Poets*, Cheikho does two things to historicise the tale. First, he assigns a death date to Laylā of approximately 483 CE.[28] His attempt to locate her precisely in pre-Islamic history would seem to lend a certain authenticity to her persona. Second, he refers to the character of Shahrmayh as 'a son of Kisrā'.[29] Kisrā is the Arabicisation of the Persian Khusraw – the name of two Sāsānid monarchs in particular: Kisrā Anūshirwān (531–79 CE) and Kisrā Aparwīz (591–628 CE) – which became the name by which Arabs referred to all the Sāsānid kings. He thereby takes an unrecognisable fictional figure and transforms him into a familiar, historically plausible one, albeit one which is vague and non-specific. Another liberty that Cheikho seems to have taken with his source materials is that he identifies Laylā as a Christian, hence justifying her inclusion in his *Book of Christian Poets*.[30] There is no reference in any of the primary sources to Laylā's religion, though, like the other characters, she speaks like a monotheist.

Cheikho's casual attitude toward the material does not end there. The sources that he lists at the end of her entry[31] as well as at the end of al-Barrāq's entry[32] do not pan out. For example, he suggests that he draws on Ibn al-Kalbī's *Jamharat al-nasab*, but he seems to have confused this for the actual source – a set of tales attributed

[27] See, for example, Khayr al-Dīn al-Ziriklī, *al-Aʿlām*, 2nd printing, vol. 6 (Cairo: al-Mu'allif, 1955), 117; and ʿUmar Riḍā Kaḥḥāla, *Aʿlām al-nisāʾ fī ʿālamay al-ʿArab wa-l-Islām*, 2nd printing, vol. 4 (Damascus: al-Maṭbaʿa al-Hāshimiyya, 1959), 336–7.

[28] Louis Cheikho, *Kitāb shuʿarāʾ al-Naṣrāniyya* (Book of Christian Poets), vol. 1 (Beirut: Maṭbaʿat al-Ābāʾ al-Mursalīn al-Yasūʿīyīn, 1890), 148. As far as I can tell he drew this date out of thin air.

[29] Ibid., 148.

[30] Cheikho is known for labelling ancient Arabic poets as Christian on the basis of scanty evidence.

[31] At the end of Laylā's entry, Cheikho states: 'We have gotten this biography from a manuscript collection of ancient poetry, from the *History of the Arabs* (Tārīkh al-ʿArab), and from the *Classes of the Poets* (Ṭabaqāt al-shuʿarāʾ).' Ibid., 150.

[32] At the end of al-Barrāq's entry, Cheikho states, 'In our summary of this biography we have relied on *Kitāb jamharat ansāb al-ʿArab* by al-Kalbī, *Tārīkh al-ʿArab* by Iskandar Abīkāriyūs, *Kitāb ṭabaqāt al-shuʿarāʾ*, and a manuscript collection of ancient poetry.' Ibid., 147.

to the aforementioned Dhuʾayb b. Nāfiʿ and appended to al-Qurashī's *Jamharat ashʿār al-ʿArab*. Cheikho's false lead caused the historian of Arab-Byzantine relations, Irfan Shahîd, much consternation:

> It is regrettable that the indefatigable Cheikho did not document this important reference accurately and in detail. He asserts twice, and in unambiguous terms, that he derived his account from the *Jamharat al-Nasab* of Hishām al-Kalbī (*Shuʿarāʾ*, 141, 144). But the *Jamharat* as studied by W. Caskel has no reference in its Register to the poet al-Barrāq (nor to his patronymic or teknonymic). Cheikho must have derived his information from some manuscript of the *Jamharat* at his disposal or from a medieval Arabic text which quoted Hishām as the source for its account of al-Barrāq.[33]

By the time Cheikho publishes the *Gardens of the Laments* in 1897, he cites his sources with precision and accuracy,[34] but he still does not question their historical value, and he presents the life of Laylā bt. Lukayz as history rather than fiction, despite the fact that his sources are all relatively recent and she does not have an ancient presence in the literature.

Also worthy of mention is Iskandar Abkāriyūs (1826–85). He authored what were two key sources for Cheikho. The first was *Rawḍat al-adab fi ṭabaqāt shuʿarāʾ al-ʿArab* (The Literary Garden of the Classes of Arab Poets, Beirut, 1858), a kind of biographical dictionary of poets. (Cheikho abbreviates the title to *Ṭabaqāt al-shuʿarāʾ* [The Classes of the Poets] and makes no reference to Abkāriyūs, which may cause one to confuse it with *Ṭabaqāt fuḥūl al-shuʿarāʾ* [The

[33] Irfan Shahîd, *Byzantium and the Arabs in the Fifth Century* (Washington, DC: Dumbarton Oaks, 1989), 427n. It is curious that Shahîd, despite his awareness of the unreliability of Cheikho's reference, still relies on his account as his sole evidence of the existence of Christianity in South Arabia in the fifth century. Ibid., 427–9.

[34] He lists (1) *Kitāb al-raqāʾiq fī majmūʿ al-shiʿr al-jāhilī al-rāʾiq* (which he identifies as one of the manuscripts in our eastern library), (2) *Tārīkh al-ʿArab* by Iskandar Abkāriyūs (this is actually *Tazyīn nihāyat al-arab*), (3) Ms. De Mr Hartmann à Berlin (Ms. Or. Oct. 1383), (4) Ms. de la Bibl. Royale de Berlin, Sprenger 1215 (Ahlwardt 9747), (5) Ms. De Londres Add. 18,528 (this manuscript contains only a passing reference to al-Barrāq). See Louis Cheikho, *Riyāḍ al-adab fī marāthī shawāʿir al-ʿArab* (Beirut: Catholic Press, 1897), 2.

Classes of Stallions among the Poets] by Ibn Sallām al-Jumaḥī.) In his ten-page entry on al-Barrāq b. Rawḥān, Abkāriyūs states that he is a poet of the second class,[35] as are, for example, al-Khansāʾ and al-Shanfarā. The second work is entitled *Tazyīn nihāyat al-arab fī akhbār al-ʿArab* (The Adornment of the Ultimate Aim in the Accounts of the Arabs, Beirut, 1867).[36] This book, which Cheikho refers to simply as *Tārīkh al-ʿArab* (History of the Arabs), contains a version of the al-Barrāq b. Rawḥān legend.[37]

Louis Cheikho and his predecessor Iskandar Abkāriyūs are not the only scholars to imbue the legend with a certain truth value. One finds the pre-eminent scholar and historical novelist Jurjī Zaydān (1861–1914) also lending partial credence to the tale. Zaydān does not approach the text naïvely, but rather he situates it within the narrative genre of the *sīra*, that is the romance or epic, comparing it to its more famous counterpart, the *Sīrat ʿAntar* (The Romance of ʿAntar), which is supposedly based on the life of the pre-Islamic poet ʿAntara b. Shaddād. In his *Tārīkh adab al-lugha l-ʿArabiyya* (History of the Literature of the Arabic Language, Cairo, 1912),[38] Zaydān compares the two narratives and determines that the

[35] Iskandar Abkāriyūs, *Rawḍat al-adab fī ṭabaqāt shuʿarāʾ al-ʿArab* (Beirut: Maṭbaʿat Bayrūt, 1858), 49–59.

[36] Maria Nallino, commenting on the book as a source for al-Qurashī's *Jamharat ashʿār al-ʿArab*, which it also contains, calls it 'useless'. She writes: 'L'edizione incorporata nel *Tazyīn al-nihāyah* di Iskandar Abkāriyūs è anch'essa senza valore, sia per il cattivo stato del manoscritto che le servi di base, sia per la sostituzione di alcune delle *qaṣīde* originarie con altre che non apparentgono alla *Ǵamharah*.' See her 'Le varie edizioni a stampa della Ǵamharat aš'ār al-'Arab', *Rivista degli studi orientali* 13.4 (1933), 341. Curiously, the *Tazyīn* represents an expanded edition of *Nihāyat al-arab fī akhbār al-ʿArab*, which Abkāriyūs also authored, and which was published in Marseilles in 1852. This earlier book also includes some of the poetry of the *Jamhara*, but it makes no reference to al-Barrāq or Laylā. Perhaps Abkāriyūs revisited and expanded upon this earlier work because he came across a new manuscript of the *Jamhara* which contained a version of the tale.

[37] See 'A Note on the Manuscripts and Published Editions', above.

[38] According to Michael Allan, this work is comprised of a series of articles originally published in the journal *al-Hilāl* between 1894 and 1895. See his *In the Shadow of World Literature: Sites of Reading in Colonial Egypt* (Princeton and Oxford: Princeton University Press, 2016), 83.

language of the tale of al-Barrāq, which he assumed was transmitted on the authority of the third-/ninth-century ʿUmar b. Shabba,[39] is more correct and closer to the style that was prevalent in early Islam and that the tale contains less exaggeration than the *Sīrat ʿAntar*. He therefore concludes that it was written down before *Sīrat ʿAntar* by more than a century – its earlier provenance meaning that it contains fewer distortions than tales preserved through oral folklore.[40] As I have put it elsewhere, Zaydān 'clearly places it under the rubric of "story" rather than "history"', but 'finds that the tale of al-Barrāq, and the other legends appended to the *Jamhara*, are among those Arabic heroic narratives (الروايات الحماسية العربية) that mediate between history and fiction'.[41]

Orientalist scholars are largely silent about the legend of al-Barrāq and Laylā. However, the Austrian Aloys Sprenger (1813–93) provides a revealing summary and assessment of the legend in an article entitled 'Notes on Alfred von Kremer's edition of Wáqidy's Campaigns' (Second Notice) from 1856. While Sprenger does not present the tale as historically accurate, he does see it as representative of what he calls the 'epos of the Arabs' or as emblematic of Arabic epic poetry. In a lengthy description of the tale as it appears in a manuscript he owns (Sprenger 1215, corresponding to Ahlwardt 9747), he writes:

> I possess an Arabic MS. which has the title of Jamharat al-ʿArab and contains seven times seven ancient poems (the first being the Moʿallaqát) and also episodes from the early history of the Arabs in a poetical garb.
>
> The first episode is the story of Barráq (Persian authors call him Majnún) and Laylà. She was the youngest and handsomest daughter of an Arab chief and had two sisters. The eldest of them Soʿdà was

[39] Zaydān must have been aware of the manuscript/s edited by ʿAṭiyya. See 'A Note on the Manuscripts and Published Editions', above.

[40] Jurjī Zaydān, *Tārīkh adab al-lugha l-ʿArabiyya*, vol. 2 (Cairo: Dār al-Hilāl, 1912), 294.

[41] Marlé Hammond, '"If Only al-Barrāq Could See . . .": Violence and Voyeurism in an Early Modern Reformulation of the Pre-Islamic Call to Arms', in Hugh Kennedy (ed.), *Warfare and Poetry in the Middle East* (London: I.B. Tauris, 2013), 222. On this particular point see Zaydān, *Tārīkh adab*, 293.

married to Thaʿlabah, the Lame, King of Petra, and the second to Shabyb, a chief of the Tay Arabs. Barráq, the hero of the story, fell in love with the youngest.

When Barráq was young he used to go out to the pasture grounds, milk the camels and carry the milk to the Christian hermit, who instructed him in reading the gospel, for our hero was a Christian.

He had hardly obtained the age of twenty-five when the celebrated war broke out between the Arab tribes of Mesopotamia and the Syrian desert, and afforded Barráq an opportunity of giving proofs of his bravery. Without following the original in the historical details of this war, I content myself with saying, that he surpassed all other warriors in courage and attained the title of Father of Victory. [. . .]

Lokayz, the father of Laylà, was a friend of ʿAmr b. Morrah, the Laird of Çahbán, and used now and then to spend a few days in his castle. The beauty and soft feminine character of Laylà had become known all over the desert, and were the theme of conversation among the Arabian chiefs. One day as Lokayz was staying with the Laird, he demanded his daughter in marriage. Lokayz had not the courage to refuse him, but he did not give him a promise.

The rivalry of these two lovers is the plot of the story which throughout is with great art connected with the political history of the time to heighten its interest. It is not my intention here to give the outline of it, but I wish to call the attention of the reader to the method of treating the subject, which is peculiar to the Arabs and constitutes their epos. The narrative is in prose, whose only charm is its great simplicity, and it forms only a small proportion of the work. The greater part of the story consists of speeches, disputations, and monologues, which are all in verse and not without poetical beauty. They are always dignified and contain noble passions, and much wisdom.

Compositions of this description seem at all times to have been popular among the Arabs. The earliest and most beautiful specimen is the Book of Job. [. . .][42]

[42] A. Sprenger, 'Notes on Alfred von Kremer's edition of Wáqidy's Campaigns' (Second Notice), *Journal of the Asiatic Society of Bengal* 25.3 (1856), 199–200.

Thus, while Sprenger does not present the story itself as 'true', he does imbue it with a cultural authenticity. He, like his Arab counterparts, implies that the legend is ancient, and he erroneously asserts that al-Barrāq is the Arabic equivalent of the Persian Majnūn.[43] His hasty observation that the story is deftly interwoven with political history suggests that he sees some historical validity in the tale.

Matti Moosa, an Iraqi-born US scholar, in his book *The Origins of Modern Arabic Fiction*, identifies the collection of tales, which he calls *al-Jamhara* and, like Zaydān, ascribes to the ninth-century transmitter ʿUmar b. al-Shabba, as 'probably the first anthology which contained some stories of the Arabs and their wars with the neighbouring nations before the advent of Islam'.[44] Whilst he does not offer an opinion on the veracity of these tales, he does not accept them as fiction per se. He writes: 'Such can hardly be considered the ancestors of modern Arabic fiction. They are completely different not only from each other but also from recent fiction, particularly the short story, in their scope, in relation to the environment, and in their form.'[45]

It is important to acknowledge that all pre-Islamic Arabic poets are in some sense legendary, and it is impossible to ascertain their historical veracity. Indeed, many orientalist scholars as well as some Arab ones, most notably Ṭāhā Ḥusayn (1889–1973),[46] suggested that the vast majority of the pre-Islamic poetic corpus was suspect, and probably a fabrication of a later era. The difference between the status of Laylā bt. Lukayz and al-Barrāq b. Rawḥān and the status of poets like Imruʾ al-Qays and Labīd is that, in the latter cases, while we cannot confirm their historical existence, we can confirm that their legend is ancient. Their legends were already in circulation by

[43] The Arabic equivalent of the Persian Majnūn is, rather, Qays b. al-Mulawwaḥ, known as Majnūn Laylā or Laylā's Madman. See Ch. Pellat, J.T.P. de Bruijn, B. Flemming and J.A. Haywood, 'Madjnūn Laylā', *EI*².

[44] Matti Moosa, *The Origins of Modern Arabic Fiction*, 2nd edn (Boulder, CO and London: Lynne Rienner, 1997), 1.

[45] Ibid., 1.

[46] See his *Fī al-adab al-Jāhilī* (Cairo: Maṭbaʿat al-Iʿtimād, 1927).

the time their verses were recorded in the ninth and tenth centuries, CE. The legend of al-Barrāq Son of Rawḥān and Laylā 'the Chaste', on the other hand, is absent from this classical tradition. Thus far I have not been able to find a source that predates the eighteenth century.

It is interesting to note that the late nineteenth-century writer Zaynab Fawwāz (1850–1914) does not include an entry on Laylā bt. Lukayz in her seminal biographical dictionary of famous female historical figures, *al-Durr al-manthūr fī ṭabaqāt rabbāt al-khudūr* (Scattered Pearls among Mistresses of the Women's Quarters, 1894). As chastity is one of the feminine virtues she often celebrates,[47] one would think she would devote some attention to a poet dubbed 'Laylā the Chaste'. From this fact we may make one of the following inferences: either Fawwāz had not heard of her, because she was unaware of the Abkāriyūs text, the serialisation in *Ḥadīqat al-akhbār*, and Cheikho's *Book of Christian Poets* – his *Gardens of the Laments* was not published until 1897 – and because the tale was not circulating in the culture at large, or, she had heard of Laylā but thought of her as fictional, and thus excluded her. The majority of entries are on what I would call historical figures, although she does include biographies of the legendary heroines of the ʿUdhrī love tales such as Laylā l-ʿĀmiriyya, ʿAfrāʾ, and Buthayna. In fact, it turns out that she was probably just being a careful scholar, assuming that Laylā did not exist because she had found no reference to her in her literary and historical sources, which she lists in her introduction. It is likely that she knew of Iskandar Abkāriyūs' *Tazyīn nihāyat al-arab* but that she considered it a collection of folkloric tales rather than a historical source. I say that she was probably aware of him because she does include in her list of sources a book by his son, Yūḥannā Abkāriyūs, entitled *Qaṭf al-zuhūr fī tārīkh al-duhūr* (Picking Flowers across the History of the Ages).[48]

[47] Marilyn Booth, 'Exemplary Lives, Feminist Aspirations: Zaynab Fawwāz and the Arabic Biographical Tradition', *JAL* 26.1–2 (1995), 137.
[48] Zaynab Fawwāz, *al-Durr al-manthūr fī ṭabaqāt rabbāt al-khudūr* (Cairo: Hindāwī, 2012), 9.

If one feminist pioneer, writing between 1891 and 1894,[49] dismisses Laylā bt. Lukayz as a fictional or folkloric construct or at the very least ignores her presence altogether, another feminist pioneer, writing in 1911 or thereabouts, champions her as a historical figure, albeit one of timeless significance. Malak Ḥifnī Nāṣif (1886–1918), in an essay entitled 'The Arab Woman – Yesterday and Today', finds historical parallels between a young Libyan woman taken captive by the Italians and rescued by her tribe after uttering an insult at her captors, and our Laylā:

> How similar is today's Arab woman to her sister from yesterday? Laylā bt. Lukayz said, calling on her people to release her from captivity:
>
> غللوني قيدوني ضربوا
> ملمس العفة مني بالعصا
>
> They fettered me, shackled me, and beat
> My chaste surface with a stick[50]

It is tempting to attribute the difference in attitude toward our subject as the result of the influence of Louis Cheikho – to assume that Nāṣif was aware of his so-called scholarship and that Fawwāz was not; but Nāṣif must have had some other source that she cited, because this line of verse is omitted from Cheikho's edition.[51] Hence the reception of the tale as history must have extended beyond

[49] Fawwāz states that she began composing her dictionary in October of 1891. *Al-Durr al-manthūr*, 8.

[50] Malak Ḥifnī Nāṣif, 'al-Mar'a al-ʿArabiyya amsi wa-l-yawm', in Majd al-Dīn Ḥifnī Nāṣif (ed.), *Āthār Bāḥithat al-Bādiya* (Cairo: al-Mu'assasa al-Miṣriyya al-ʿĀmma, 1962), 290.

[51] Cheikho, *Shuʿarā' al-Naṣrāniyya*, 149. Bichr Farès suggests that Cheikho removes the reference to the *malmas al-ʿiffa* out of prudishness. I have translated the phrase as 'chaste surface' but it means something more like 'touching-place of chastity'. In other words, he thinks that Cheikho was deliberately censoring the phrase. See Bichr Farès, *L'honneur chez les Arabes avant l'Islam* (Paris: Librairie d'Amérique et d'Orient Adrien-Maisonneuve, 1932), 75n. I would be inclined to agree, but Farès' assertion is confused by the fact that he conflates lines 4 and 6 of the poem. Farès assumes that Cheikho distorts line 6, but in actuality he cuts out line 4.

Cheikho. Indeed, a feature on the tale that was published in a literary magazine in 1910 suggests both that it circulated widely as an account which was deemed historical and that it flourished independently of Cheikho's Christianising influence.[52]

Storytelling and Hybridity

The *Tale of al-Barrāq Son of Rawḥān and Laylā the Chaste*, as I have demonstrated above, is not a 'true' history but a fictional fabrication. In many ways it constitutes its own genre. It represents a hybrid text, informed by three different narrative paradigms. Two of these paradigms, namely the popular *sīra* and the ʿUdhrī love narrative, are very familiar in Arabic literature, and one – the story of the damsel-in-distress – is seemingly more alien. Before I elaborate on the influences of these three paradigms, let me first consider the environment in which this new genre emerged.

Yuri Lotman's notion of the 'boundary' helps us to contemplate the processes by which new genres develop. In Lotman's universe, different cultures are likened to different semiospheres or realms in which signs have certain meanings. Innovations then occur at the site where two semiospheres collide or overlap, which he calls the 'boundary'. What is made at the boundary is not seen as 'foreign' but rather as 'ours', since 'foreign' meanings are transferred to 'our' system of signs. Lotman writes:

> The notion of boundary is an ambivalent one: it both separates and unites. It is always the boundary of something and so belongs to both frontier cultures, to both contiguous semiospheres. The boundary is bilingual and polylingual. The boundary is a mechanism for translating texts of an alien semiotics into 'our' language.[53]

[52] See 'Fī ḥadāʾiq al-ʿArab: Laylā l-ʿafīfa wa-l-Barrāq', *al-Zuhūr* 1.4 (June 1910), 166–8. In this summary of the tale, there is a reference to Laylā's torture poem as 'her famous *qaṣīda*', as if the reader would be expected to be familiar with it. Moreover, there is no mention of Christianity. The feature presents the material as historical when it states that al-Barrāq died 'about a century and a half before Islam'.
[53] Yuri M. Lotman, 'The Notion of Boundary', in *Universe of the Mind* (London: I.B. Tauris, 2001), 136.

No matter how indebted a new form or genre may be to a 'foreign' source, its re-encoding according to 'native' principles ensures that it is received as 'our' text. He explains:

> Something similar can be seen when the texts of one genre invade the space of another genre. Innovation comes about when the principles of one genre are restructured according to the laws of another, and this 'other' genre organically enters the new structure and at the same time preserves a memory of its other system of encoding.[54]

One could argue that the Arabic-speaking, or rather Arabic-reading world in the seventeenth, eighteenth, and nineteenth centuries was one big boundary. With the Ottoman Empire's multicultural vibrancy,[55] the European colonial powers' rising influence, and the prevalence of emerging nationalisms, semiospheres, big and small, continental and local, were interpenetrating with intensity. As such, it was a time of tremendous cultural effervescence, culminating in what is known as the Arab renaissance or *Nahḍa*.[56]

In this environment, the damsel-in-distress storyline passes into Arabic literary history unrecognised as a fictional paradigm. It is, or at least *was* at the time of its absorption into Arabic culture, 'European' in origin, drawing on popular folktales, chivalric

[54] Ibid., 137.

[55] An informative and fascinating study of reading practices in the multi-ethnic and multilingual Ottoman Empire that elucidates mechanisms of cross-fertilisation may be found in Johann Strauss, 'Who Read What in the Ottoman Empire?', *MEL* 6.1 (2003), 39–76.

[56] Here, I am extending the *Nahḍa* a bit further back in time than is typical. Traditionally it is described as beginning in the mid-nineteenth century. See, for example, P. Starkey, 'al-Nahḍa', *EAL*, 573–4. Recent scholarship has tended to shift the start date of the *Nahḍa* a bit earlier, as early as the eighteenth century. See Peter Hill, 'Revisiting the Intellectual Space of the *Nahḍa* (Eighteenth-Twentieth Centuries)', *Les carnets de l-Ifpo: La recherche en train de se faire à l'Institut français du Proche-Orient* (Hypotheses.org), 5 June 2014. Other interventions on the *Nahḍa* include: Tarek el-Ariss, 'Let There Be Nahḍah!', *Cambridge Journal of Postcolonial Literary Inquiry* 2.2 (2015), 260–6; Muhsin al-Musawi, 'The Republic of Letters: Arab Modernity?' Parts I and II, *Cambridge Journal of Postcolonial Literary Inquiry* 1.1 (2014), 265–80, and 2.1 (2015), 115–30; and Stephen Sheehi, 'Towards a Critical Theory of al-Nahḍah: Epistemology, Ideology and Capital', *JAL* 43.2–3 (2012), 269–98.

romances, and fictional narrative in general – for by the end of the eighteenth century, the theme of the 'persecuted maiden' had become firmly entrenched in European novels and operas. Mario Praz, in *The Romantic Agony*, described this figure of the persecuted maiden who, from the late eighteenth century onwards, becomes ubiquitous in the European Romantic imagination.[57] According to Christopher Booker, she was 'the beautiful virtuous heroine whose chief role in the fantasies of so many authors was to be portrayed as imprisoned, persecuted, ill-treated or murdered; or just wasting away through consumption to a tragically early death . . .'[58] This, basically 'European', damsel-in-distress model had probably been transposed onto pre-existing Arabic genres, namely the *sīra shaʿbiyya* and the ʿUdhri love tale, at some point in the latter half of the seventeenth century, blending with them to create a peculiar hybrid. In the eighteenth century, as the damsel-in-distress flourished as a fictional paradigm in Europe, it made some inroads in the Arabic-reading world, but as a singular historical account rather than a fictional genre.

A perusal of Hasan El-Shamy's *Folk Traditions of the Arab World: A Guide to Motif Classification* is telling in this regard. Under the entry 'damsel', one finds the descriptors 'as wager', 'poisonous', and 'serpent'.[59] There is nothing there – nor is there in the Stith Thompson Index[60] – about distress or the necessity of rescue. El-Shamy's entry on 'maiden' is much longer and contains references to abduction (motif R10.1) and rescue (motif R111),[61] but the index does not lead us to very many stories classified under these headings.[62] Nevertheless, the figure of the persecuted maiden or

[57] Mario Praz, *The Romantic Agony*. See, especially, chapter III, 'The Shadow of the Divine Marquis', 95–195.
[58] Christopher Booker, *The Seven Basic Plots* (London: Continuum, 2004), 386.
[59] Hasan M. El-Shamy, *Folk Traditions of the Arab World: A Guide to Motif Classification* (Bloomington and Indianapolis: Indiana University Press, 1995), 2:118.
[60] Stith Thompson, *Motif-Index of Folk-Literature* (Copenhagen: Rosenkilde and Bagger, 1958), 6:187.
[61] El-Shamy, *Folk Traditions*, 2:302–3.
[62] Ibid., 1:329–30.

the damsel-in-distress is not entirely unknown in Arabic literature. Many will be familiar with the story of Qamar al-Aqmār, the handsome Persian prince from the *Arabian Nights* who, astride a magic horse, rescues a Yemeni princess called Shams al-Nahār from both an ugly sage and a king determined to marry her against her will. Like Laylā, Shams al-Nahār needs rescuing, and it is a handsome young man who comes to her aid and, in the end, marries her.[63]

Another folktale with a heroine whose predicament has parallels with Laylā's is the story of a certain ʿUfayra bt. ʿAbbād[64] of the Jadīs tribe. ʿImlīq, the tyrannical king of Ṭasm, has ruled that no member of the Jadīs should marry a virgin, and he has all the brides-to-be from that tribe brought to him for deflowering. ʿUfayra is one such victim. After he has violated her and released her, she goes to her people, bleeding and with clothes torn, shaming them with a few lines of *rajaz* verse, beginning with:

لا أحدٌ أذلّ من جديس
أهكذا يُفعل بالعروس

No one is more humiliated than the Jadīs.
Is this what is done to a bride?

She then recites a poem of incitement to them, and the men of the tribe exact their revenge.[65] The figure of the damsel-in-distress, then, exists in pre-modern Arabic literature, but it is nowhere near as prevalent as it is in the European literary imagination. Other

[63] See 'The Magic Tale of the Ebony Horse', in Ouyang and Horta, *The Arabian Nights*, 859–92.

[64] She is also known as ʿUfayra (or ʿAfīra) bt. ʿAfār (or ʿIfār or Ghifār).

[65] The story is found in Ibn al-Athīr, *al-Kāmil fī l-Tārīkh*, ed. Abū l-Fidāʾ ʿAbd Allāh al-Qāḍī (Beirut: Dār al-Kutub al-ʿIlmiyya, 1987), 271–3, as well as many other sources, including Muḥammad ibn Ḥabīb, *Asmāʾ al-mughtālīn*, in ʿAbd al-Salām Hārūn (ed.), *Nawādir al-makhṭūṭāt* (Cairo: Maṭbaʿat Lajnat al-Taʾlīf wa-l-Tarjama wa-l-Nashr, 1951–5) 2:118–20, and al-Iṣfahānī, *Kitāb al-aghānī* (Cairo: Dār al-Kutub, 1927–), 11:165–6. I am indebted to Geert Jan van Gelder for drawing my attention to this tale. An English version of it, and translations of two poems attributed to ʿUfayra – here known as ʿAfīra – may be found in Abdullah al-Udhari, *Classical Poems by Arab Women: A Bilingual Anthology* (London: Saqi, 1999), 28–33. Al-Udhari identifies her as a third-century poet.

feminine prototypes, such as the warrior women of the *sīra* epics, and the chaste but not entirely victimised beloveds of the ʿUdhrī love tales, are more predominant.

If, then, this damsel-in-distress storyline is alien and imported, other components of the *Tale of al-Barrāq Son of Rawḥān and Laylā the Chaste* are familiar and indigenous, and they can be traced back to those narrative traditions that are mentioned above, namely the popular epic and the ʿUdhrī love narrative. If one speaks of 'wordplay' in the study of poetry and of 'motif-play' in the study of folktales, here in the study of the formation of lengthy narratives, one could speak of 'genre-play'.[66] For our tale mixes and matches not just words or motifs, but constellations of interrelated ideas associated with different genres. In other words, it borrows independent sets of characteristics from three different genres. From the 'alien' or 'foreign' genre of the western fairy tale, it takes the components of its overarching plot: the premise of youngsters in love, the abduction of the beautiful maiden, her rescue by the handsome knight, and the happily-ever-after resolution. Overlaid on this network of components are sets of characteristics emanating from other indigenous genres.

From the popular epic[67] it takes its attention to Arab genealogy and its heroic narrative format with its episodic battle scenes. Like the epic of al-Muhalhil b. Rabīʿa the text begins with the family tree branching out from Nizār, the first of the Arabs. Al-Barrāq is inserted into this lineage as a relative of al-Muhalhil. The plot moves from one extraordinary event to another and from one battle scene to another. As Sprenger suggests in his estimation of the tale quoted

[66] I am indebted to Wen-chin Ouyang for suggesting this line of enquiry.

[67] For an overview of the popular epic, see G. Canova, 'Sīra Literature', *EAL*, 726–7; and P. Heath, 'Sīra Shaʿbiyya', *EI*[2]. See also Dwight F. Reynolds, *Arab Folklore: A Handbook* (Westport, CT and London: Greenwood Press, 2007), 52–67. Important monographs on popular epics include: M.C. Lyons, *The Arabian Epic* (Cambridge: Cambridge University Press, 1995); Connelly, *Arab Folk Epic and Identity*; Peter Heath, *The Thirsty Sword: Sīrat ʿAntar and the Arabic Popular Epic* (Salt Lake City: University of Utah Press, 1996); Susan Slyomovics, *The Merchant of Art* (Berkeley and London: University of California Press, 1987); and Dwight Reynolds, *Heroic Poets, Poetic Heroes* (Ithaca, NY: Cornell University Press, 1995).

extensively above, there is an intermixing of prose narrative and poems, uttered by the protagonists and revealing their emotional states, their objectives, and their intentions. Perhaps these poems are meant to be sung by the narrator or *rāwī* as would happen in popular epic.[68] The text is in standard Arabic, not dialect, but it is composed in a simple, low-brow, and repetitive style.

This song-cycle structure, the alternation of prose narrative and verse monologues, is to be found in the ʿUdhrī love tale as well,[69] but the ʿUdhrī love tale makes other unique contributions to the new genre that the *Tale of al-Barrāq Son of Rawḥān and Laylā the Chaste* represents, namely, the premise that the male and female protagonists are first cousins in love, and themes of religiosity and chastity. But these echoes of the ʿUdhrī love tale come with two new twists. The first is that, in the ʿUdhrī love tale, which is generally set in the early Islamic or Umayyad era, the religion featured in the tale is Islam. It is not uncommon for the lover to undertake the hajj and there are many references to Islamic law, and licit and illicit behaviours. In the story of al-Barrāq b. Rawḥān, however, which

[68] One of the complaints the 'Final Reader' had about the January 2019 manuscript of this monograph was that I hint at a relationship between the tale and traditions of oral literature but that I do not expand or elaborate on this or talk about the tale's potential performance context. I agree that this is a shortcoming, but as I have no direct evidence that the tale was performed musically in either public or private settings before the film adaptation in the twentieth century, and as the tale is not characterised by colloquialisms, I have decided not to go down this route. However, as Walter Armbrust argues, the practice of silent reading in this part of the world, which is characterised by audio-centrism, is a modern phenomenon, and in earlier eras texts were meant to be read aloud. See his 'Audiovisual Media and History of the Arab Middle East', in Israel Gershoni, Amy Singer and Y. Hakan Erdem (eds), *Middle East Historiographies: Narrating the Twentieth Century* (Seattle and London: University of Washington Press, 2006), 288–313. One can therefore expect recitations before small audiences, such as family members or students, to have occurred. But this would be true of practically any text.

[69] On the ʿUdhrī love tale, see Renate Jacobi, 'ʿU<u>dh</u>rī', *EI*². See also two contributions to Friederike Pannewick (ed.), *Martyrdom in Literature: Visions of Death and Meaningful Suffering in Europe and the Middle East from Antiquity to Modernity* (Wiesbaden: Harrassowitz, 2004): Renate Jacobi's 'The ʿUdhra: Love and Death in the Umayyad Period', 137–48, and Stefan Leder's 'The Udhri Narrative in Arabic Literature', 162–89.

is set in the pre-Islamic era, the hero is made a Christian, at least this would seem to be the case in the Christian version of the tale. The second twist involves sexuality. In the ʿUdhrī love tale there is no sex outside of marriage. The female beloved is married off; hence it is understood that she has sex with her husband, but the relationship with the lover remains chaste and their relationship unconsummated. Here the story ends with the consummation of the relationship between lover and beloved and a celebration of the beloved's ability to remain chaste despite the threat of rape. There is a shift of emphasis from a preoccupation with chastity to a preoccupation with virginity.

This combination and reformulation of genres brings about a diminished agency for the female characters, perhaps reflecting its origins in the 'symbolic language' of the European fairy-tale genre.[70] Women in the popular epic are not passive but active figures – often warriors. Remke Kruk's *The Warrior Women of Islam*[71] details the stories of several of these warrior women, such as Dhāt al-Himma – when they get into trouble, they fight their way out of it. They are nothing if not active. Women in the ʿUdhrī love tale are a bit more passive – beloved much more than lover, but a theme of parity ensures that they are somehow on a par with the lover. She is his *tirb* – that is the beloved and her lover are the same age, and their activities are often conjugated in the third-person dual. He dies of love, then she dies of love. They love in tandem. They are cousins and equals.

Women in this new, damsel-in-distress hybrid are neither active nor equal. To the contrary their passivity is almost total, and their lowly vulnerable status emphasised. As Laylā herself states when

[70] Marina Warner notes: 'The term "fairytale" is often used as an epithet – a fairytale setting, a fairytale ending – for a work that is not in itself a fairy tale, because it depends on elements of the form's symbolic language.' See her *Once Upon a Time: A Short History of Fairy Tale* (Oxford: Oxford University Press, 2014), xviii. See also Warner's *The Beast to the Blonde: On Fairy Tales and Their Tellers* (London: Vintage, 1995). Reading these two books I realise that my working definition of fairy tale is quite narrow and that I am really talking only about the damsel-in-distress sub-type.

[71] Remke Kruk, *The Warrior Women of Islam: Female Empowerment in Arabic Popular Literature* (London and New York: I.B. Tauris, 2014).

she learns of her father's decision to marry her off to someone other than al-Barrāq:

ما حيلتي فيما يراه أبي وهل
يأتي المعالي واقف في الأسفل
انّ النساء اذلة مستورة
يعرفن بالرأي الضعيف الأعزل

What power do I have over what my father thinks?
Does someone who stands at the bottom reach the heights?

Women are lowly and secluded [*mastūra*]
Known for their weak and unarmed opinion. (2:26)

Utterly oppressed, she is. Note the juxtaposition of the word for 'lowly' or 'abased' (*adhilla*) and the word for 'secluded' (*mastūra*) which seems like an alien association between seclusion and oppression, perhaps reflecting its imported 'European' content.

The theme of the 'persecuted maiden' transferred easily onto Arab women in orientalist discourses. Indeed, Arab woman, in the European imagination, becomes 'persecuted maiden' *par excellence*. But, as a literary trope, it was alien to Arabic culture, not altogether unknown, but much less predominant than other female character types and hardly figuring as the premise for a lengthy narrative.[72] The Arab damsel-in-distress is essentially new, a cultural fabrication, borrowed from European narratives and transposed onto the *sīra shaʿbiyya* and ʿUdhrī love tale models. The familiar codes masked the 'foreign' or 'alien' elements, and its lack of fantastical elements, which was in fact a sign that it was of recent provenance, meant that it was understood not as a piece of fiction, such as the *sīra shaʿbiyya* and the ʿUdhrī love tale, but as history, and literary history at that.

[72] There are certainly episodes in Arabic literary narratives where heroes rescue damsels – one thinks of ʿAntar rescuing his beloved ʿAbla, for example. See Anonymous, *The Romance of Antar*, trans. Terrick Hamilton, ed. W.A. Clouston (Milton Keynes: Dodo Press, n.d.), 64–6 and 74–8.

From History Back to Fiction

No sooner does our tale become accepted or misrecognised as history than it feeds into modern fiction, more specifically the historical novel and other outlets of cultural expression, such as poetry, music, and cinema. We can trace this trend back to 1909, when a young Egyptian poet called ʿAbd al-Raḥmān Shukrī (1886–1958) published his first collection of poetry, *Ḍawʾ al-fajr* (The Light of Dawn). The poem which inaugurates the collection is called *'Kisrā wa-l-asīra'* or 'Chosroes and the Captive' and it is subtitled 'Qiṣṣa' or 'A Story'. This twenty-eight-line narrative poem tells the story of an Arab maiden who wards off the sexual violations of a Persian tyrant. Shukrī, a 'stern moralist',[73] addresses the poem to young women – it opens *'yā fatāt al-ḥayy'* or 'O girls of the neighbourhood/tribe' – and indirectly calls on them to guard their virtue like the heroine of the poem. Shukrī does not name her; nevertheless, the reference to Laylā bt. Lukayz is quite specific, for he quotes a line of her verse – the same line as Malak Ḥifnī Nāṣif, in fact. He does so towards the end of the poem, where the line serves as a call to arms:

إيه لله عفاف مخلص
لك ما سيم الخنى إلا أبى
ثم قالت قولة في أسرها
تبعث الغلّ وتهفو بالوغى
قيّدوني، غلّلوني، ضربوا
ملمس العفة مني بالعصا
فأتاها نبأ من قومها
أنهم عافوا لذاذات الكرى
أو تجول الحرب في ميدانها
كمجال الطيش في عهد الصبا
أو يكون السيف في أعدائهم
مُعْمَلاً يودي بهامٍ وطلا

[73] M.M. Badawi, 'Shukrī the Poet – a Reconsideration', in R.C. Ostle (ed.), *Studies in Modern Arabic Literature* (Warminster: Aris & Phillips, 1975), 21.

My God what sincere chastity
You have – no obscenity was imposed on you without being refused

Then she uttered a statement in her captivity
Spreading rancour and fomenting battle

'They fettered me, they shackled me, they beat
My chaste surface with a stick'

So news came to her from her people
That they would shun the pleasures of sleep

Unless war would run through its field
Like the current of recklessness in the age of youth

Or that the sword on their enemies
Be brought to bear, causing necks and heads to perish[74]

One cannot help but wonder if the poem has political allegorical dimensions whereby the young female captive represents Egypt[75] and Chosroes, a foreign monarch who invades Arab lands, the British imperialists. The allegorical potential of the tale was certainly operative in the Bahīja Ḥāfiẓ film *Laylā bint al-ṣaḥrāʾ* (Laylā, Daughter of the Desert, 1937), which was banned and rereleased as *Laylā al-badawiyya* (Laylā the Bedouin, 1944). Although the film was censored ostensibly for its representation of the Persian monarch, which was seen as offensive to the modern-day Iranian regime, Ḥāfiẓ signals her equation of Chosroes with the British, when, in an effort to decrease her vilification of all things Persian, she renames the tyrannical despot 'Kingā' for the second release of the film. Thus, the make-believe Persian king Shahrmayh transforms into the historical but generic Persian Sāsānid king Kisrā or Chosroes when the tale becomes historicised, then, when it becomes re-fictionalised, he transmutes into a once-again make-believe but this time etymologically English king, Kingā.

[74] ʿAbd al-Raḥmān Shukrī, *Ḍawʾ al-fajr*, 2nd printing (Alexandria: Jurjī Gharzūzī Press, 1914 or 1915), 2–3. Translation mine.
[75] On the tendency for Egyptians to represent their country as a female figure, see Beth Baron, *Egypt as a Woman* (Berkeley: University of California Press, 2005).

That the film is highly politically-charged is evident from its history with censorship. After the film's initial release in 1937, it had a short run in the theatres before being banned by the local Egyptian authorities. It seems that the representation of a Persian king trying to force himself sexually on an Arab maiden was considered an indirect and insulting reference to Princess Fawzia's engagement to the Shah of Iran.[76] In addition to the local ban, the British and French authorities outlawed the screening of *Laylā, Daughter of the Desert* in their overseas territories; the British in Palestine and India, and the French in Syria, Lebanon, Tunisia, and Morocco.[77] It seems that the British feared a diplomatic incident with Iran. A telegram dated 18 July 1937 and signed by a certain Horace James Seymour, then His Majesty's Minister in Tehran, lays out the main objections:

> Political Director General of Ministry of Foreign Affairs made oral protest to me last night against exhibition of a film called 'Leila, daughter of the desert' which was released in Arabic in Egypt last month or in May. Film which seems a wild version of Leila Majnun legend, depicts Arabs as overthrowing Court of King Khosroes. This is unhistorical and wounding to national esteem of Persia.[78]

When the film was rereleased as *Laylā the Bedouin*, the British no longer objected to its screening. This was not a result of any changes made to the film – I should add that the polemically significant name change from Chosroes to Kingā seems to have passed unnoticed – but rather due to the fact that there was a new Iranian monarch, Muhammad Reza Pahlavi, who was not particularly bothered by

[76] www.bibalex.org/alexcinema/actors/Bahiga_Hafez.html (accessed 30 January 2018). Note that I have not tracked down any documentation for this local ban.
[77] British correspondence regarding the ban on *Laylā, Daughter of the Desert*, and the lifting of the ban on *Laylā al-badawiyya*, may be found in the following files: British Library, India Office Records, IOR/L/PJ/7/1296; British National Archives, Colonial Office, CO 323/1421/3; British National Archives, Foreign Office, FO 371/52594. Note that the first of these files also contains French correspondence about the banning of the film. A detailed description of the content of each of the files may be found in Hammond, 'If Only al-Barrāq Could See', 235, n.6.
[78] CO 323/1421/3, document 1.

the film's existence.[79] The French maintained the ban, however, at least in Morocco, and, according to Elizabeth Thompson, this was because they objected to the 'portrayal of the monarch as a playboy'.[80]

The revamped *Laylā the Bedouin* was reportedly a flop at the box office.[81] Thus, between its history with censorship and its status as a commercial failure, it would be a mistake to exaggerate the cultural impact of the film itself. However, musically the film made an enormous contribution to Arab popular culture. This is because Bahīja Ḥāfiẓ commissioned Muḥammad al-Qaṣabjī to compose a song for the film which was based on the poem Laylā utters whilst in captivity, 'If Only al-Barrāq Had an Eye to See' (*Layta li-l-Barrāqi ʿaynan*). The song was performed by both Ḥayāt Muḥammad and Ibrāhīm Ḥammūda in the film, but their performances were eclipsed by that of Asmahān whose recording was released in 1937 by Baidaphone.[82] Bahīja Ḥāfiẓ subsequently sued Baidaphone for ten thousand pounds for infringing on her intellectual property, and the courts awarded her five hundred pounds in compensation.[83] A measure of the song's success is perhaps that today, more than eighty years after its release, it has a ubiquitous presence on YouTube.[84] Maḥmūd Kāmil attributes the success of the song to its expressivity:

[79] Hammond, 'If Only al-Barrāq Could See', 217. Hammond cites FO 371/52594, document 28, 235, n.9, as evidence of the perceived change in attitude.

[80] E.F. Thompson, 'Politics by Other Screens: Contesting Movie Censorship in the Late French Empire', *Arab Media & Society* (January 2009), 6.

[81] www.bibalex.org/alexcinema/actors/Bahiga_Hafez.html (accessed 30 January 2018).

[82] Maḥmūd Kāmil, *Muḥammad al-Qaṣabjī: Ḥayātuh wa-aʿmāluh* (Cairo: al-Hayʾa l-Miṣriyya l-ʿĀmma li-l-Taʾlīfi wa-l-Nashr, 1971), 53.

[83] Ibid., 53. Apparently as a result of this court action, Asmahān's recording of the song was banned from sale in Egypt for a time. See Saʿīd al-Jazāʾirī, *Asmahān: ḍaḥiyyat al-istikhbārāt* (London: Riad El-Rayyes, 1990), 63.

[84] On 1 February 2018, I counted eighteen different uploads of Asmahān's recording of the song, collectively attracting more than 98,000 views. One also finds performances by Ibrāhīm Ḥammūda and covers by Nazik, Dorsaf Hamdani, Karima Skalli, and Lubana Al Quntar.

> With this poem, al-Qaṣabjī achieved a great degree of power in its musical expression. Every word sincerely evokes the meaning that it carries. For it envisions the feelings of a young woman (Laylā) when some evil people have violated her, imprisoned her, and exposed her to a variety of forms of torture, such that she prefers death to submitting to their desires, and she wishes her cousin who is in love with her (al-Barrāq) could see the kinds of torture and cruelty she endures!![85]

The song is a five-line extract, with some revisions, from 'If Only al-Barrāq Could See'. I quote the words of the song below:

ليت للبراق عيناً فترى
ما ألاقي من بلاء وعنا
عُذِّبت أختكم يا ويلكم
بعذاب النكر صبحاً ومسا
غلّلوني قيّدوني ضربوا
جسمي الناحل مني بالعصا
قيّدوني غلّلوني وافعلوا
كل ما شئتم جميعاً من بلا
فأنا كارهة بغيكم
ويقين الموت شيء يرتجى

1 If only al-Barrāq had an eye to see
The agony and distress I endure

2 Woe upon you, your sister has been tortured
Awfully morning and night

3 They fettered me, shackled me, and beat
My slender body with a stick

4 Fetter me, shackle me, and do
Every sort of atrocity you all want

5 For I hate your infringement
And the certainty of death is something to be desired[86]

[85] Kāmil, *Muḥammad al-Qaṣabjī*, 53.
[86] Asmahān wa-Farīd al-Aṭrash, *Farid & Asmahan* (Baidaphon Beirut compact disc, 1990).

The musical element of the song compounds the sense of anguish that pervades the poem. This occurs most noticeably at the beginning of line 3, where the words 'shackled' and 'fettered' are extremely elongated. Asmahān holds the *ū* sound in *ghallalūnī* and *qayyadūnī* for more than six seconds.[87] Ibrāhīm Ḥammūda takes this even further, holding the syllables in question for nine seconds.[88] The *ū* represents the third-person plural masculine past tense conjugation, and this *ū* precedes the first-person objective pronominal suffix *-nī*, hence the song emphasises the actions of males upon the female body. There is a sense in which in line 4, by addressing men in general and implying that they all would wish to do harm to her, the poetic persona abstracts upon her previously personalised victimisation and suggests that men in general pose a threat to women in general. The song thus projects a cynically feminist stance. With no reference to the Persian enemy, it is not about protecting 'our women' from them, but simply protecting women from men. Asmahān's performance of the song was particularly poignant in this regard, as she is rumoured to have been beaten by her brother Fuʾād.[89]

Harder to pin down chronologically is ʿĀdil al-Ghaḍbān's novel *Laylā al-ʿafīfa* (Laylā the Chaste). It seems that it was first published in March 1954 in the Iqraʾ series by Dār al-Maʿārif in Cairo. However, according to Maḥmūd Qāsim, the novel served as the basis for the scenario of the 1937 Bahīja Ḥāfiẓ film,[90] so it may have been composed

[87] Her performance may be heard, for example, at www.youtube.com/watch?v=_fd-T-tLW90 (accessed 1 February 2018).

[88] See www.youtube.com/watch?v=U0jligQj4HM (accessed 1 February 2018).

[89] On her brother Fuʾād's abusive behaviour toward her, specifically his beatings of her, see al-Jazāʾirī, *Asmahān*, 43, 75–6. The reports are based on what Asmahān told a journalist friend of hers. Sherifa Zuhur, who interviewed Fuʾād for her book, *Asmahan's Secrets: Woman, War and Song* (Austin, TX: Center for Middle Eastern Studies, 2000), stops short of suggesting an abusive relationship, describing Fuʾād as 'the voice of brotherly authority' whose 'efforts to control Asmahan failed' (25). Elsewhere she writes: 'He confronted her, now and then, blustering like a novice teenage baby-sitter' (81).

[90] Maḥmūd Qāsim, *Mawsūʿat al-aflām al-ʿArabiyya: 1927–2018*, vol. 2 (London: E-Kutub, 2017), 458–9. A replica of the 1937 film programme which is in my possession states that the film is 'historical' (*tārīkhiyya*) and 'realistic' (*wāqiʿiyya*) and 'adapted from Laylā's *dīwān*'.

as early as the 1930s. ʿĀdil al-Ghaḍbān (1905 or 1908–72) was a Cairene writer of Syrian extraction who was the editor-in-chief of the literary journal *al-Kitāb* (The Book) from 1945 to 1953. According to Elisabeth Kendall, in his journal he expressed pride in Arabic cultural heritage and felt that modern Arabic literature should build on the foundations of classical Arabic literature.[91] Al-Ghaḍbān takes the *Tale of al-Barrāq Son of Rawḥān and Laylā the Chaste* and transforms it into a modern novel. It is unclear what he used as his source or sources, but he adapts the Christian version of the tale, so he was probably familiar with the work of Cheikho and/or Abkāriyūs, or he may have read the serialisation of the tale in *Ḥadīqat al-akhbār*. Al-Ghaḍbān's version differs substantially from the epic, most notably in its privileging of prose over verse. Phenomena such as description and character development, which in the epic would normally be expressed as poetry uttered by a particular character, are here rendered or framed in prose by an omniscient narrator. A handful of poems figure centrally in the novel, including Laylā's 'If Only al-Barrāq Had an Eye to See', but otherwise the novel is not particularly prosimetrical.

The novel received a rave review by the feminist author and scholar Bint al-Shāṭiʾ. Writing in the government daily *al-Ahrām* in 1955, she enthuses over al-Ghaḍbān's ability to manipulate his sources with great skill and dexterity:

> From the Iqraʾ series I read the story *Laylā al-ʿafīfa*. Its core is taken from the literary heritage that has come down to us from the Pre-Islamic age. And the poet and writer Mister ʿĀdil al-Ghaḍbān has shaped it into a splendid piece of story-telling set amongst the pavilions of the Bedouin in the deserts of the peninsula. There grew up Laylā bt. Lukayz, the chaste Bedouin maiden, whose call to her cousin al-Barrāq still echoes across time:
>
> If only al-Barrāq had an eye to see,
> The agony and distress I endure

[91] Elisabeth Kendall, *Literature, Journalism and the Avant-Garde: Intersection in Egypt* (London and New York: Routledge, 2006), 57.

> I will not describe to the readers the technical virtuosity I found while I was reading this story of love, purity, and chivalry in the desert. Rather, what concerns me is the tribute to our artistic heritage which is full of vibrant images and rich in authentic, fertile materials. From them an inspired pen can shape narrative wonders.[92]

Bint al-Shāṭiʾ does not comment on the veracity of the novel, but she clearly sees it as historical fiction, or a piece of fiction which draws on historical reality. She suggests that Laylā's poem dates from the pre-Islamic era, and she also implies that al-Ghaḍbān's source materials are 'authentic'. Thus, even as the legend passes from history back into fiction, its status as history is reaffirmed.

Conclusion

Thus, our Laylā, who originates as a fictional character at some point during or shortly before the eighteenth century, who exists in adventure time, and who is victimised by the imaginary Persian king Shahrmayh, transforms into Laylā bt. Lukayz, the historical figure, who is imprisoned by vassals of the actual King Chosroes, and who is assigned a death date of 483 CE. She stands as one of the earliest Arab women poets whose existence is, to this day, unquestioned. The popularity of her figure, famous for maintaining her virginity despite all odds, has waned since the production of the movie, the song and the novel. Yet her legend still imprints itself on literary history, as she continues to be anthologised, celebrated, and even translated into English.[93] It is my wish that Laylā the Chaste remain a figure at the forefront of literary consciousness, but that her persona be re-contextualised as the post-classical fictional creation that it is.

[92] Bint al-Shāṭiʾ (a.k.a. ʿĀʾisha ʿAbd al-Raḥmān), 'Majmūʿāt min al-qiṣaṣ', *al-Ahrām*, 1 March 1955, p. 5. Note that she refers to the text as a *qiṣṣa* and not as a *riwāya*. Perhaps the latter term's equation with the novel was not yet firmly set in 1955.

[93] See, for example, al-Udhari, *Classical Poems*, 34–7. See also Suheil Bushrui's translation of one of her elegies in *Suad al-Attar* (London: al-Madad Foundation, 2004).

The *Tale of al-Barrāq Son of Rawḥān and Laylā the Chaste,* inasmuch as it inscribes the knight-in-shining-armour-rescues-damsel-in-distress storyline on the genres of the ʿUdhrī love tale and the popular epic, has much to teach us about the development of Arabic fiction. As what would seem to be a rare specimen of lengthy imaginary narrative emanating from the pre-modern environment, and as a text that was misrecognised as history in the modern era, it causes us to interrogate our definitions of fiction and to wonder at what other textual junctures the boundaries of fiction and reality have been so blurred. Let us revisit Stefan Leder's questions quoted earlier in this chapter and ask, 'Where was in pre-modern Arabic literature any conscious use of fiction as a medium of literary expression, and where can we find indications whether it was ever understood as such?' It would seem that our tale, featuring the imaginary King Shahrmayh, and ensconced as it is in an 'adventure chronotope' with abstracted and indistinct representations of time and place, was at least ahistorical if not downright fictional. Presumably, it was meant as make-believe and intended to be received as such. Perhaps what the existence of this text, so patently fictional in its construction and yet construed as historical in its latter-day reception, teaches us is that the fictional mode of communication was operative in certain milieus in the pre-modern Arabic literary environment and not in others. Fictionally-speaking, in other words, the Arab world was not a monolith but consisted of a variety of environments, some of which would receive the *Tale of al-Barrāq Son of Rawḥān and Laylā the Chaste* as make-believe, and some of which would receive it as truth. The fictionalising environments thus fostered the expansion of the tale into its Christian version, while the historicising environments – such as that in which Cheikho operated – fabricated extra-textual signs which would disguise the text as history.

2
The Tale of al-Barrāq Son of Rawḥān and Laylā the Chaste: A Translation

Know that the first of the Arabs was Nizār, son of Maʿadd, son of ʿAdnān, son of Udd, son of Muqawwam,[1] son of Tāriḥ, son of Yaʿrub, son of Yashjub,[2] son of Thīb, son of Ḥamal, son of Faydād, son of Ismāʿīl, son of Ibrāhīm, the Beloved of God, may peace be upon the last two of them.[3] Now Nizār had three sons: Rabīʿa, Muḍar, and Iyād, and each of the three had children and multiplied, and their peoples and tribes grew large. As for Rabīʿa, he sired many children and produced many peoples, and they are the Banū Asad, the Banū Jadīla, the Banū Duʿaym, the Banū Hīth, the Banū Ḍubayʿa, the Banū ʿIjl, the Banū Yashkur, the Banū Ḥanīfa, and the Banū Qāsiṭ, and Qāsiṭ being the father of Nimr and Wāʾil, and Wāʾil being the father of Bakr and Taghlib. Bakr branched out into the Banū ʿAlī, the Banū al-Ṣaʿb, the Banū ʿUkāba, the Banū Thaʿlaba, the Banū Qays, the Banū Saʿd, the Banū Sufyān, the Banū Dhuhl, the Banū Murra, and the Banū Shaybān. Taghlib branched out into the Banū Ghanm, the Banū ʿAmr, the Banū Ḥabīb, the Banū Jusham, the Banū Asad, the Arāqim, the Banū Zuhayr, and the Banū Mālik. For all of these are the sons of Rabīʿa b. Nizār. As for Muḍar

[1] Ahlwardt 9747: Mutawwam.
[2] Ahlwardt 9747: Yakhshub.
[3] Ismāʿīl and Ibrāhīm are prophets in Islam, hence they were singled out with the phrase, 'may peace be upon the two of them'. Note that the genealogy varies from standard accounts. See, for example, al-Masʿūdī, *Kitāb al-tanbīh wa-l-ashrāf*, ed. Michael Jan de Goeje (Leiden: Brill, 1893), 80, which provides two alternatives. As Geert Jan van Gelder has informed me, the genealogy confuses the essential distinction between North and South Arabs, because Nizār, Maʿadd, ʿAdnān and Udd belong to the North Arabs but Yaʿrub and Yashjub are descended from Qaḥṭān, the South Arab ancestor.

the Red, he branched into the Banū Ilyās, the Banū Mudrika, the Banū Khuzayma, the Banū Kināna, the Banū al-Naḍr, the Banū Mālik, the Banū Fihr, the Banū Ghālib, the Banū Luʾayy, the Banū Kaʿb, the Banū Murra, the Banū Kilāb, the Banū Quṣayy, the Banū ʿAbd Manāf, the Banū Hāshim, and the Banū Makhzūm. These are the sons of Muḍar. As for Iyād b. Nizār and his sons, they lived in Bahrain and the lands of the Persians, and I do not have their peoples and tribes memorised. The Rabīʿa lived in Greater Nejd and the surrounding land, and the Banū Muḍar lived in Mecca, Tihama, Jidda, and adjacent lands in Yemen, like al-Sullān and Daqqa and such. The chief of the Rabīʿa b. Nizār was al-Asad b. Bakr b. Murra, and he sired Rawḥān, the father of al-Barrāq, and a daughter whom he married to Lukayz b. Murra. From her Lukayz bore five sons – Ṣāf, ʿIkrima, al-Arqam, ʿUqayl, and Bujayr – and three daughters – Suʿdā, Khawla, and Laylā, the wife of al-Barrāq. Lukayz married his daughter Suʿdā to the Ghassānid king Thaʿlaba the Lame, and he married Khawla – and it is said rather that her name was Kāmila – to Shabīb b. Luhaym al-Ṭāʾī, al-Barrāq's maternal uncle, and there remained Laylā. She was called Laylā 'the Chaste', and she was the youngest of them and the one with the prettiest face, and al-Barrāq loved her deeply. In his youth al-Barrāq used to follow the camel herders and milk the camels and then bring the milk to a monk near the pastures, and from him he learned how to recite the Gospels, and he believed in his religion. Al-Barrāq was forbearing, generous, brave, dignified, and knowledgeable despite his young age. For he was not yet fifteen when war broke out between the tribe of Rabīʿa and the tribes of Iyād and Lakhm, and yet he displayed a battle-readiness and horsemanship like no one else. This is when the Rabīʿa's lands dried up, so they split up in search of fertile pastures. A man called Nawfal b. Samīr of the Taghlib and some of his people took up residence with Ḥajīb b. Wārid al-Iyādī. Ḥajīb put him up and let him shepherd in the protected ground of the *ḥimā*.[4] And

[4] A *ḥimā* is an area of ground, used as pasturage, which has protected status and has been declared off-limits to all but those who have claimed it for themselves. See J. Chelhod, 'Ḥimā', *EI*².

Ḥajīb had married [King] Maʿmar b. Sawār to his daughter, so she stayed with him for a time and then, when she wanted to visit her father and her siblings, Maʿmar sent her to them. She was accompanied by male and female slaves, camels, and assistants. They set up camp with Ḥajīb, and he honoured the camels of the king and ordered that they be kept and pastured in the protected ground. There they encountered the camels of Nawfal, and when the slaves who were with the king's camels saw Nawfal's camels, they beat them severely. Nawfal came while the slaves were beating his camels and said, 'take it easy, we will take our camels away from you', and he ordered his shepherds to get his camels out of the protected ground. Consequently, they hurried to get them out. But the camels, due to their hunger and the fertility of the pasture, overcame them and repelled the beating and driving. Then one of the king's slaves came, unsheathed his sword, and attacked the camels, wounding ten of the female riding camels. When Nawfal saw that, he tied up his female riding camel with the excess reins and attacked the slave and fought him. Then he untied his she-camel, mounted her, and cried out to his shepherds, 'Hurry up and get the camels out of the protected ground.' The young male slaves cried out until the shouting reached al-Akhnas b. Ḥajīb, who was nearby with his camels and with two men. When he heard the shouting, he made a foray with his two men, and they found the slave dead. At that they rode after Nawfal and caught up with him. Nawfal turned to them and said, 'The neighbour[5] is your neighbour and the slave is your slave, you have seen what he did and what was done to him. The matter goes back to you.' Al-Akhnas was alarmed and consulted his two friends on the matter. They said, 'this is an act which dishonours us'. Then they attacked Nawfal and took him at spearpoint. Then they left him dead.

Says Ibn Nāfiʿ: Now Nawfal's camels' shepherds carried Nawfal and delivered him to his wife al-Hayfāʾ bt. Ṣabīḥ al-Quḍāʿiyya and

[5] What I have translated here and elsewhere as 'neighbour', *jār*, refers more specifically to a person whom one has pledged to protect. See W. Montgomery Watt, 'Id̲jāra', *EI*².

informed her of his news. He had had ten of his men with him, and they wanted to attack to avenge their master. She said to them, 'Take it easy, don't do anything yet. Gather your people together and do not rush into anything until I come back to you.' Then she led her camel away, carrying her husband on its back. It was sunset, and as she knew where Ḥajīb resided, she made her camel kneel next to his residence, and then she wept for her husband. Ḥajīb leapt up from his bed, unawares, until she stopped crying, sighed, and uttered:

I cry, I cry in daylight or the darkness
For a young man, Taghlibī in origin, a lion

O how I grieve for him and what use is my grief to him
But to pit horsemen and tribes against one another

Tell Ḥajīb, 'May God blame you for a man'
'You carry the shame of all the people of Shem'

Does your son kill my husband, O son of Fāṭima?
while you drink water of false dreams?

By God I will not stop weeping and mourning for him
Until my uncles, maternal and paternal, visit you

With every straight pliant spear
And every bright-edged unbending sword

When she finished, Ḥajīb said to her, 'There, there, O freewoman of the Arabs. By God your wailing has afflicted me. Tell me what has happened.' She said, 'Do you ask me when you know very well?' He replied, 'By God, if I knew I wouldn't ask you.' So, she told him the story from beginning to end, and he said, 'May God kill me if I don't kill the one who has killed my neighbour.' Then she said, 'Your neighbour is before you, so bury him.' He answered, 'Leave him, for he has become mine and my responsibility.' She took leave of him and went off with her people to the Banū Taghlib. As for Ḥajīb, he prepared his neighbour for burial and buried him. Then he went looking for his son al-Akhnas and his two companions. He could not find them, and he was informed that they had joined their in-law King Maʿmar b. Sawār al-Lakhmī. So Ḥajīb saddled his riding beast, took his battle armour, led his horse by his side, and set out for the king seeking his son and his two companions. When he arrived at his in-law's he was greeted with the warmest reception and honour. King Maʿmar started to ask him about his son, and Ḥajīb said, 'No son of mine will go on living after he kills my neighbour.' The king said, 'I am not surrendering my neighbours to you.' Ḥajīb replied, 'By God, that would cut relations between us until the end of time.' He spoke harshly to the king and said, 'Do you choose to clothe me in shame before the Rabīʿa, the Muḍar, and the Iyād?' Then the king handed over the son and his two companions and said, 'You have more of a right to your son, so do what you will with him.' Ḥajīb then took them from the king and set out with them until he stopped them beside the grave of Nawfal b. Samīr al-Taghlibī. He proceeded to cut their necks, beginning with his son and then moving on to his two friends, and he buried them next to the grave of his neighbour. After that he returned to his tents where he could not enjoy food or drink, and he could not sleep at all. He threw himself down on his bed and uttered:

Sleep went away at night, and sleeplessness kept me up
The grief-stricken have no rest

For had he been killed on a day of war
When stabbing and cutting prevailed

Then his loss would be an easy matter
And we would choose one to kill in revenge

My son, what did you intend by killing my neighbour?
Does the iron-clad hunt and not get hunted?

My son, you killed my neighbour with intent
And your killing, O my son, is sanctioned

So, taste that which you made my neighbour swallow
And die of grief, for that is what you can expect

And cry O beautiful one and do not grow weary,
For my camels and water-bag have grown lean

My horses stand in the places where they're tied
The charge unfits them and the pursuit is split

Oh, what a pity for my son, if only
The blades had turned away from me at his killing

What a pity for those ancestors who passed away
From chief to chief they attained glory

And for one who, like the spring, rained down
His gifts in a time of drought

Oh, how long is the night I spend sleepless
As if my eye is stuffed with thorns

Says Ibn Nāfiʿ: When Nawfal's wife caught up with her people, she told them what had happened to her husband, and they suffered and grieved over him greatly. Then his brothers and his cousins – twenty-five horsemen altogether, rallied and made a raid on Ḥajīb al-Iyādī, so he in turn rallied with his sons and his tribe and they met and pursued each other. Then Mālik b. Samīr, Nawfal's brother, met Ziyād b. Ḥajīb and his sons. They attacked Mālik and killed him in revenge for their brother. After that the people fought for a while. Iyād's cavalry charged Taghlib's horsemen and they broke them, and they killed nine men among them and weakened the others by wounding them, and they returned to their people in the worst condition. Their crier cried out to the tribes of Rabīʿa in their entirety, so they rallied their horses and made a raid on Ḥajīb al-Iyādī.

Says Ibn Nāfiʿ: The foreparts of the horses appeared at sunrise so Ḥajīb and his sons and his whole people rallied and met the horses, and they fought for a while. Ḥajīb's horses were broken and they retreated, and Ḥajīb and his sons and his nephews fled – and Ḥajīb was the strongest of the Iyād – and seven horsemen from among his sons and nephews were killed. At that point the Banū Taghlib raised their swords and returned with their horses.

Says Ibn Nāfiʿ: At that the tribes of Iyād grew angry, and they gathered around Ḥajīb b. Wārid and resolved to fight the Rabīʿa. When Maʿmar b. Sawār, Ḥajīb's in-law, heard what they were up to, he mobilised his soldiers, spent a lavish amount of money on them, and ordered them to go to his in-law Ḥajīb and the tribes of Iyād. The houses of Rabīʿa met, they rallied at their campsites, and they got ready to fight the Iyād and their in-law Maʿmar b. Sawār.

War against King Maʿmar worried them, and his might terrified them. Then Maʿmar's horses and soldiers and the Banū Iyād set out for the neighbouring encampments of Lukayz b. Murra and Rawḥān b. Asad. The Rabīʿa saddled up their horses, and the cavalries met. Due to his young age, al-Barrāq b. Rawḥān knew nothing about what was happening, but he mounted his steed that day and wanted to fight with them. His eldest brother forbade him, fearing for his safety, but al-Barrāq did not desist. He said, 'Let me. For I was heedless but now I am roused from heedlessness.' When his brother saw that, he called his mother and said, 'Fetter al-Barrāq, for he wants to go out to war.' She replied, 'Let him. For shall I leave him to nurse at my breast?' So, he set out, as did his father, Rawḥān b. Asad, and his grandfather, Shabīb b. Luhaym al-Ṭāʾī. Now al-Barrāq attended this, his first battle, and he fought a hard fight, and he showed bravery like no one else. He and his people kept fighting the soldiers of King Maʿmar and the Banū Iyād for seven years until the conflict ceased, and the Rabīʿa, with al-Barrāq, were victorious over the Iyād and their in-law. Thus, they named him Abū Naṣr, 'the Father of Victory'. On this ʿAbīd b. Dūrān states:

With the youth al-Barrāq we broke the soldiers
Of the Arabs who were waiting to pounce

He was made to bear the banner of my people
What a smashing victory you have seen

What an excellent young man! We triumphed
Through the beloved son of Ibn Rawḥān

The most spectacular flash of the Banū Asad
He lights up the far and the near

How many ask after Ibn Rūḥ,[6]
Among the scarred ones, seeking help

They saw him in the valley in the early morning
On a horse, powerful, large and noble

[6] This would appear to be an abbreviation for Ibn Rawḥān.

He never gives up striking men
Or stabbing the arteries of the heart at close quarters

Until he brought the banners openly to the watering-place
The well springs sweet for drinking

We were guarding the water until
We drank the water from beneath the mounts

For fear that we turn away from our enemies
And scandalise ourselves with abasement and running away

We drank the water and their mill[7] was crushed
And the army of Maʿmar and al-Ḥajīb[8] escaped

Says Ibn Nāfiʿ: Besides being courageous, al-Barrāq was extremely generous. *Says he*: His generosity was such that [the following occurred]. A people of the ʿAdwān set out for the tribes of Wāʾil seeking their help with debts they had accumulated, for the Rabīʿa had given them three hundred riding camels. They set out for al-Barrāq b. Rawḥān and he showed them the utmost generosity, and he gave them his camels, his father's camels, and his brother's camels. Then his brother al-Junayd said, 'Easy now, you have been excessive in your giving.' But his father Rawḥān said, 'You are my son, and giving counteracts the inclinations of the wicked.' Thus al-Barrāq was known for his generosity in this, as the poem by Mālik b. Sulaym al-ʿAdwānī illustrates:

Wāʾil gave generosity to drink, overflowing
Like generous Arabs and kings

He bestowed the blood-prices. May my soul redeem him!
For the son of the noble lady has no equal

[7] *Raḥāhum*. I believe the 'mill' here refers to a tribal unit but it also evokes a state of war. Nadia Jamil explains: 'The *raḥā* – a structure described by a stationary netherstone on a central pivot (*quṭb*) about which a top-stone grinds – is a term applied to family groups and tribal units. When a group goes to battle to defend its honour, or to fulfil a covenantal oath of mutual redemption (*fidāʾ*), the raḥā becomes a "mill of war" (*raḥā ḥarb*).' See her *Ethics and Poetry in Sixth-Century Arabia* (Cambridge: Gibb Memorial Trust, 2017), 332.
[8] Ahlwardt 9747: al-Ḥalīb.

He gave us gifts of his father's sons
Young she-camels like sticks of *darīk*[9]

For life is still bright for us
After darkness due to this cheerful man

Says he: His maternal uncles in Ṭayy heard about this, and they gave the ʿAdwān multiples of his gift. Thus al-Barrāq's status became great in people's eyes, and they considered him awesome and lavished praise upon him. Meanwhile, we have already mentioned that Laylā the 'Chaste', the daughter of Lukayz b. Murra, remained in her father's home. Al-Barrāq loved her for himself and wanted to marry her. Word of her beauty and her manners spread among the Arabs to the extent that she was mentioned in kings' assemblies, and people talked about her. Her father, Lukayz b. Murra, used to go as an envoy to ʿAmr b. Dhī Ṣahbān, who would give to him lavishly and show generosity to him. One day Lukayz went to him, and ʿAmr was generous and gave him gifts. Then, in his assembly, he asked for the hand of Laylā the Chaste. Lukayz did not respond and, because he felt embarrassed by ʿAmr's generosity and blessings, he left. ʿAmr waited a few days. Then he sent Lukayz a delegation bearing lavish gifts. When they came to him, Lukayz received them with the utmost generosity. Then they asked for Laylā's hand. Lukayz said, 'I married two of my daughters without the permission of my people. As for this one, I must consult with them in the matter. If they do not agree, you will have to return to your master.' They replied, 'Do what you must, and choose for your daughter the abode of stability.'

Says Ibn Nāfiʿ: Then Lukayz withdrew to himself. He called his sons, and they came to him, and he said: 'I need to see your paternal uncle, Rabīʿa b. Murra, and his sons as well as your maternal uncle, Rawḥān, and his sons.' They brought them to him, and they sat before him, and he informed them of the king's marriage proposal and asked them their advice on the matter. Lukayz went out of his way to praise ʿAmr and to say that he would be a support

[9] I have not found a meaning for this word.

and a shelter for them when confronting great threats. Lukayz was the chief of the tribes of Wāʾil. They all looked down at the ground because they knew of al-Barrāq's desire for Laylā, and they knew that he wanted no one else, and they did not want, on his behalf, any other man near her. Rabīʿa b. Murra spoke first and said:

You married off Suʿdā and Kāmila to outsiders
They ordered you to sell them with ample money

You still have the choice possessions
From short-haired horses to freewomen's garb

This is why you have come to couple her up,
But coupling, woe upon you, is not like one seeking singularity

Forget your covetousness and get over the idea of marrying her
In the dominion of the Ghassānids or the Lakhmids

Verily if you ignore our advice on your misdeed,
You will chew your fingers over it like a loser

Lukayz said, 'I have heard what you have to say.' Then he turned to Kulayb b. Rabīʿa and said, 'Tell me what you think.' And he said:

What I say is sound, if it is useful to you
Some of this is harmful and some beneficial

I see us as if we are foxes around you
And you, a fiery pup, do not get frightened

We see someone other than Barrāq, when presented with a fearful thing
Gets scared and goes back

And if what you see disables you, uncle
Then how many a head will be cut off with swords

You will not achieve what you hope to obtain
Nor is there anything to be coveted in what the delegation brings you

Says Ibn Nāfiʿ: Kulayb's anger was intense, for he loved al-Barrāq dearly. Then Lukayz said, 'I have heard from you, now what do you think, O Rawḥān?' Rawḥān replied, 'Excuse me from this.' Lukayz answered, 'No, by God you must let your opinion be known.' So Rawḥān said:

I am your brother, and you are more entitled to being right
The questioner may get no response

But I lean toward your satisfaction
And conceal from you, conversations held in confidence

For when an advisor is generous with his counsel
And it is not accepted, then he is generous with rebuke

I accept the whole opinion as yours
Even if it is replete with calamities

Leave off my opinion, for there is no way to it
And your opinion is authorised in difficulty

Says Ibn Nāfiʿ: When Lukayz heard the words of his in-law, he said to his brother's son Nuwayra: 'Tell us what you think, Nuwayra.' So Nuwayra said:

I tell you what I think, but is it correct and accepted
While your opinion in what you claim is preferred?

For you are the one who knows the authorised opinion
And in this, those other than you err and are ignorant

On my life, even if my doubts are many
For you refuse and forsake al-Barrāq

And you prefer the favour of kings because they
Have what is preferable in the arts of favour

And even if the kings offer gifts and attainment
Al-Barrāq is more generous in battle

You may ask for an opinion, but it is of no use
The sayer is not like the doer

Then Lukayz said, 'We invited you all here to consult you, so what is with all the threats?' Then he turned away from them to listen to what al-Muhalhil had to say. Al-Muhalhil was the youngest of the brothers. Al-Muhalhil spoke harshly to his paternal uncle. He sighed angrily and said:

Who cares what I think about something of which I am ignorant?
You know what you want and what you will do

By God I have not said anything except that which I know
What you intend to do and what you comprehend is not hidden from you

If you actually wanted her to marry one of your cousins
Then it would not please you when something better came along

Wear your silk, I could not be bothered
I am content and satisfied in wool

Do not covet the favours of kings and do not rush your affair
For the worst affair is the most rushed

Ease your heart, and return what they have given you
Be content with your life, this opinion is the most becoming

Indeed, the master of ambition is the brother of failure
Abasement takes up residence only in its home

Says he: Lukayz smiled mockingly at al-Muhalhil, then he turned to the honourable one of his people and said, 'O Barrāq, this king has shown me the utmost grace and favour, and he thought of me the way one thinks of gentlemen, that they are respectful and compliant. He addressed me in his assembly, among his intimates and viziers. And I assured him of my hope in you, and my good opinion of you, and that you would not object, and that you would be ready for me to let this king be a relief to your hardships, a fortress for your protection, and a storehouse when times are tough. I did not think anyone other than you would oppose me. I have heard their response. Now would you be satisfied O my son with making your uncle look like a liar after he was believed and making him seem small after he was made important? I would not say this but for the fact that I know, O Barrāq, how you restrain yourself from doing bad things and how honourable and proud you are, and how little opposition you show to your clan.' When al-Barrāq had heard Lukayz' words, he sighed and said:

O seeker who is not granted his wishes
Be patient in what you covet

Wear assiduously that which hides your secret
And wear your chastity in what you have in mind

O venerable man whose favour is desired
You have called upon a man who is satisfied by what satisfies you

My advice to you is to follow your passion
Drop this topic that you've brought up

Honour your delegations and keep your promise
Forget what Rabīʿa said, and move on

For the bearer of truth gathers the goodness of truth
And the bearer of evil inclines towards the badness of evil

You are responsible for your kin, however you see fit
You keep the garment of your honour and its tassels clean

Honour your daughters and do with them what you wish
In the hopes of advantages and goodness

Lukayz, do not go back on your word
And I will keep an eye on those who scrutinise you

Follow your intention and do not follow Kulayb
For he responded to you with nonsense talk

Do not look at the illness that has alighted in my body
For the one who is ill will meet the one who cures him

O delegation, you have won what you came here for,
Ibn Ṣahbān has sent a delegation and we redeem it

The giver of the one hundred red [camels] is followed by
The one who gave thousands to the person who asked him for money

Do not inform ʿAmr of my talk of aberration
For I am not satisfied with disparagement to recompense him

And please convey greetings from me to Ibn Māriya
I will give the warmest of wishes

Says Ibn Nāfiʿ: When al-Barrāq finished with his poetry, his father and brothers, and Rabīʿa and his sons all got up in anger. Lukayz' children then came to him, blaming him, and said, 'O father, the anger of our paternal uncle and his sons is a formidable matter, is it not your inclination not to do it?' He replied, 'Al-Barrāq is the fruit of my heart and nothing is more important to me than he, and he has excused me due to the sharpness of his intellect and the breadth of his heart, so be under my thumb, as he has done.' Then he ordered for them the fine horses that the king had given to him, and he divided them up between them, wanting to satisfy them in this way. They said, 'We are satisfied with what satisfies them, and displeased with what displeases them.' Then they left. Lukayz went to the delegation and informed them of the situation. They said, 'There is nothing to do now but to inform the king of what is up with you and recite al-Barrāq's verse and the verse of others to him.' Then they said goodbye to him and went to the king and they informed him of the situation and recited to him the verses of the people. Then the king thanked al-Barrāq and praised him and said, 'I will reward him for his manliness and good morals.'

Says Ibn Nāfiᶜ: When al-Barrāq despaired of Laylā, passion overcame him. He waited patiently that day until night came, then he walked to Laylā's tents, and he entered upon her while she was sleeping. He woke her up, and she had been kept away from him because it was thought that he was going to propose to her, and she asked, 'What are you doing, O Barrāq?' He said, 'I came to you to visit you and bid you farewell.' Then he informed her that her father had bestowed her on the king. She sighed and grew anxious and said, 'What a long misery you have to endure!' Then she wept and turned to al-Barrāq and said to him: 'Love has afflicted me and you. Patience is a good cloak, so wrap yourself in as much patience as your passion gives you and use it to suppress your suffering.' When al-Barrāq saw the state she was in, he took pity on her and her crying made him cry. Then al-Barrāq concerned himself with leaving her, so she said to him, 'Come tonight, let us enjoy our goodbye, for tomorrow the curtain will come down and our separation will be long.' Then she uttered:

> Store up supplies for us, for there will be no return of
> Union after this separation
>
> Hold back, with bits of pleasure of saying goodbye,
> The flood of tears from your eyes
>
> Oh, compensate me tit for tat, as you see
> My eye is fixed on the grief in my tear-ducts

Al-Barrāq answered her, saying:

Be patient, do not cry in dismay
For one who invites longing is worthier of being obeyed

And lower your voice, O Laylā, for I [say]
When you conceal this voice, it spreads

But I will turn my effort away from you
In exchange for squadrons and terrains

And I will offer my night visitor tender meat
And I will give him the gift of female servants

By your Lord, all that I bear
Is nothing new

Before me my progenitor Asad b. Bakr
Had a high status with people in pride and generosity

And my father Rawḥān and my brother Ẓalīl
Their reputation has circulated and spread among people

And if al-Lukayz has been bestowed with judgement
Then we would have exactitude and abstention

I fear separation, and many a rising sun
On a morning of terror fears me

Says he: Al-Barrāq and Laylā stayed up all night bidding each other farewell. Then he left and went to his father and brothers and ordered them to pack up and go. They departed, and they stayed with the Banū Ḥanīfa, their people, and they congregated in their lands. Al-Barrāq took to consoling himself over Laylā, while his pining away for her only increased, and he uttered:

Why does my eye torture me?
My tears flowing forth as carnations and fine flour

Love planted in the gardens of my heart
A tree ripened through weeping and wailing

Whenever I say my heart has been consoled
Tears run and pour down my cheeks

May God curse the one who blames the lover
Even if he thinks there is correctness in blame

Love for Laylā and our love for Laylā's family
Increased my heart's longing and rebuke

Whoever sees me says that I am a phantom possessed
Or a sickly one content with that, afflicted

By God, there is no sickness in my body
Nor insanity, and I have committed no sin

Other than loving one with a beautiful face
And soft, dyed fingertips

And luxuriant hair, as black as the night
In imitation of the raven

Whoever sees her says she is a gazelle of a human being
Or a crescent moon whose brightness parts the clouds

Passion for her has emaciated me and afflicted me
And love has ignited a shooting star in my heart

Each day stirs in the middle of my heart
A fire of love whose flames burn ever higher

He also said:

Tell the one who has left my heart mad with love
Pasturing in the gardens of their former abodes and pacing

My love for you means that I spend the night sleepless
With tears running down my cheeks

O one with a face like a crescent moon when it appears
Beauty was created with him, so attractive

Oh, to reunite with you – may I never be without you
Far be it from the lover, for the lover is never stingy

What a difference there is between someone who sleeps in the evening
And someone who spends the evening moaning on the back of his mattress

Look between us, my friend – may I never be deprived of you
Is the sick one to be compared to the sound?

Says he: Now al-Barrāq had a beautiful singing slave-girl called Ṭarīqa whom he married to a slave-boy of his called Sarīʿ al-Aḥjaf. When the young man heard the verses of his master and learned of the strength of his longing, he thought that al-Barrāq wanted Ṭarīqa. He said to her, 'O Ṭarīqa, I see that our master speaks of affection and longing, and maybe it is for you, so why don't you make yourself beautiful and wear your finest clothes and go to him and make advances towards him, and if you find that he has a desire for you, I will divorce you and let him have you.' So Ṭarīqa dressed in her finest clothing and jewellery, went to her master, and made advances towards him. When al-Barrāq learned of her intention, he said:

Stop making advances, O Ṭarīqa
Indeed, you have become a friend to me

Noble, dear and true
Sympathetic to me in what you have said

It's out of the question, for I have a firm bond
With the noblest of human beings in all creation

Says he: So, she left him, shame-faced, and went to her husband and said to him, 'God curse your idea, you have scandalised me.' Then she told him what happened and recited the poetry to him. His worries were then laid to rest.

Says he: Then Umm al-Agharr, the sister of Kulayb b. Rabīʿa, entered upon her cousin Laylā and said, 'O Laylā, are you not suffering by what your father did to our master and our knight al-Barrāq?' She said, 'What is that?' Umm al-Agharr informed her and said:

You pay no mind yet you are not heedless
Rather you are considered rational

For your reason is still of a mind
And you're still distracted and distracting

Does Lukayz turn away al-Barrāq in
Estrangement, while you belong to him

Bakr and ʿIjl and their Shaybān
Will hock between them a riding-camel

Laylā answered her, saying:

Umm al-Agharr, do not rush to judge me
I will make it clear to you, so understand

Barrāq is our chief and our knight
A thruster of swords when surrounded by a large army

He is light and lightning and the moon that
Fills the heavens with its generous illumination

And he is the pillar of our tribe during hard times
And what every hoper hopes for

Indeed, I long for what you mention, only
The honour of a chaste one is like a woven fabric

What power do I have over what my father thinks?
Does someone who stands at the bottom reach the heights?

Women are lowly and secluded
Known for their weak and defenceless opinion

Says Ibn Nāfiʿ: Then al-Barrāq, due to his separation from Laylā, grew very ill. He hid his condition from everyone. One day during this time Kulayb b. Rabīʿa visited him to see what was up with him and he asked how he was doing, knowing full well that he could not bear being separated from Laylā. Kulayb was al-Barrāq's friend, and al-Barrāq kept nothing from him. He confessed his secret and complained of his lovesickness for her, and Kulayb felt very sad. Then Kulayb said, 'If I cannot be of use to al-Barrāq, what with the friendship and the bond of kinship that exists between us, then what good am I?' Then Kulayb left him, without a response, and went to his tents. He summoned his brothers and al-Barrāq's brothers, and the children of his uncle Lukayz, and they came to him, greeted him, and sat before him. Then Kulayb informed them of al-Barrāq's state and asked them what they thought they should do about it. ʿUqayl b. Lukayz, Laylā's brother, was the first one to speak, and he said:

> This matter is up to you, O Ibn Rabīʿa
> Decide what you want to accomplish
>
> Leave Lukayz and whoever sides with him
> Lukayz, if you judge, will not be victorious

Then Ṣāfī b. Lukayz spoke, and he said, 'O Kulayb, tell us, what is your judgement for our sister. We want no one else, even if he has few possessions. How could we, when he is the chief of the clan and when he meets every need?' Then he said:

> Do as you see fit, O one of judgement and manners
> And horses and spears and swords
>
> That one is our brother, our master and our chief
> We are satisfied with his satisfaction and not with my father's opinion
>
> Do not throw your weight behind kings, indeed they are
> People of luxuries, people of gold
>
> And we are people of the desert, we do not leave it
> And we do not pay attention to class and rank
>
> Execute your opinion and do not conceal it in conformity
> For you are worthier of us than all of the Arabs

Then ʿIkrima b. Lukayz spoke and said, 'The judgement is yours, O Kulayb. Perhaps it comes down to you and no one else.' Then he said:

> We defer to you, O Ibn Rabīʿa
> So, plan with deliberation what you choose
>
> Do not leave al-Barrāq in his adversities
> Tuck up[10] for him before unwanted attention
>
> For Barrāq is our master and our knight
> The thruster of spears and the striker of swords

[10] 'Tuck up' is a translation of (شمّر) and refers to the act of preparing one's garments for battle.

Then Bujayr b. Lukayz spoke and said, 'By God, I do not know what to indicate, for if I agree with my father, my brother perishes, and if I agree with my brother, my father's ire is raised. It is as if I am between a rock and a hard place.' Then he uttered:

I can only abstain from giving you an opinion on an issue such as this
For the opinion that I was seeking remains estranged

I owe al-Barrāq my brotherliness and protection
No matter if my tribal elder rebukes him when he wants to rebuke

I have no say in this and I
When I delve in to the matter, tire

My advice is to do something I cannot accomplish, so I
Fear what I say will be rejected and that I will be proven a liar

But if you are capable of achieving what you suggest
Then I am with you, ready and able

And if it is too difficult, then do what you will
When people make a promise, a promise is demanded

Then Arqam b. Lukayz spoke and said, 'Al-Barrāq is the light of our eyes and our chief support. Judge accordingly.' Then he said:

By your life, al-Barrāq is not remote from us
And he does not leave our burdens in desert crossings

Rather he removes the anxiety of the clan after
All kinds of calamities sent by enemies beset them

Make Lukayz be satisfied with milch-camels
Bring for him the horses of the waterless plains

Support al-Barrāq and procure things for him
For the procurer of things is not hasty

Do not invite, after that, censure
The word of a staid man will excuse you from that

And you are all cousins and brothers
Of Laylā in whom are all sorts of marvels

Then Nuwayra b. Rabīʿa spoke and said, 'You are both the most powerful of people and the most capable of overcoming obstacles.

As for Lukayz, if we give to him generously, he will have no need of kings and he won't fear poverty.' Then he said:

> If we have met to sort out our affairs
> Then who is going to destroy what we have built
>
> For we are her cousins and brothers
> Drawn together by this great army
>
> Go to Laylā and sort out her affair
> For you are each the arbiter of what you think
>
> From my uncle I have after seventy mornings
> Eight milch-camels trimmed like horses
>
> Kulayb has similar, as does Muhalhil
> So, get up, hurry to him and make an offer

Then Muhalhil b. Rabīʿa spoke and said, 'You all have got it right and got it wrong. You hit the target and you erred. Allow Kulayb to judge, and surrender the camels to him.' Kulayb said, 'Muhalhil has hit the target, present me with this, and set me a firm appointment.' They said, 'By God, yes', and they promised to complete what they had negotiated in three days.

Says Ibn Nāfiʿ: Then King ʿAmr b. Dhī Ṣahbān prepared a great gift of the most luxuriant jewellery, garments, carpets and mattresses, sapphires and rubies, horses, coats of mail, and swords, and he sent it with Maslama b. Mālik al-Ghassānī and a cohort of his court officials. The next thing they knew, Maslama had arrived at the dwelling of Rabīʿa b. Murra, father of Kulayb, and had distributed the king's gift among the people, earmarking the best and the finest for al-Barrāq.

Says he: The presents corrupted the judgement of Kulayb and his companions and lessened their resolve. Maslama and those who were with him renewed the king's marriage proposal, and Rabīʿa b. Murra gave in to them, setting an agreed date, and they returned to the king rejoicing at what they had accomplished.

Says Ibn Nāfiʿ: During these days, a slave of ʿAbbād al-Ḍubaʿī called Maʿmar b. Sawār and ʿAbbād's son al-Ḥārith took ʿAbbād's camels to drink at the Quwayra spring. Then came to the spring the camels of ʿImrān b. Nubayh al-Sadūsī, who was a wealthy man with many children. They were accompanied by one of his sons, called al-Fuḍayl, and one of his slaves. The camels clashed, and the two slaves became embroiled in a fight. The Ṭāʾī slave took a rock and struck the Wāʾilī slave on the head with it and killed him. Then al-Ḥārith, who was one of the Arabs' great marksmen, shot the Ṭāʾī slave-boy with an arrow and killed him and threw him down on the ground in front of his master. At that point al-Fuḍayl came toward al-Ḥārith, and al-Ḥārith said, 'Go back. I killed him only because he killed my slave.' Al-Fuḍayl advanced and al-Ḥārith told him to desist, but al-Fuḍayl kept advancing, so al-Ḥārith shot him with another arrow and made him follow in his slave's footsteps. Then al-Ḥārith returned to his camels and led them, thirsty, to the abodes of his father, ʿAbbād, and his brothers. They asked him, 'What happened to you?' He informed them of his story and said:

> I killed Ibn ʿImrān al-Fuḍayl and his slave
> For killing my slave Maʿmar Son of Sawār
>
> I didn't want to kill al-Fuḍayl but only
> Wanted restitution when I took my revenge
>
> I shot him with an arrow, and his death came quickly
> This was not something of my choosing
>
> Won't you help me in the battle and destruction
> Emaciating the horses in advance of hostilities

Says he: His father spat in his face and said, 'You are not welcome here, then. By God, I will hand you over to ʿImrān b. Nubayh so that he may kill you in revenge for his son, and I will not rouse my people to war against the Sadūs.' His son replied, 'Neither ʿImrān killing me in revenge for his son nor you handing me over will stave off war with the Sadūs. Face it, you are in trouble. You may as well prepare for it.'

Says he: News of the death reached ʿImrān b. Nubayh, and he charged at everyone who approached him until his son was brought to him, dead, and he took him in his arms and said:

> O eye, pour forth with tears
> For al-Fuḍayl al-Sadūsī Ibn ʿImrān

Who can console an eye that weeps from affliction?
Who can console a heart, grief-stricken and inflamed?

Ḍubayʿa has perpetrated something unbearable
Woe unto them, from a distant one whose honour is close

By God, revenge lies not with Ḥārith and his father
Nor with his brother, but with Ibn Rawḥān

I mean the young man, the chief, al-Barrāq, their knight
Or Kulayb – for he is their second knight

O Ṭayy, prepare the fine horses and bear
The white swords, for I am an avenger, distressed

The Sadūs returned from the appointment, bereft
Of a lion of its thickets, a lion of young men

Oh, how I grieve for him and grief is no use
Except when horsemen meet in combat

There's no escape from a large-scale assault led by
Naṣr, Jabr and Masʿūd Son of Faynān

And the daring knight Manṣūr and his brothers
Thrusting a spear from between every shank and stirrup

In revenge for the most glorious and the most noble
Glorified twice-over – from the Bakr and from the Kahlān

By God I will neither rest nor lose a wink
Until I see horses running in red blood

Says Dhu'ayb b. Nāfiʿ: The tribes of Sadūs gathered around ʿImrān b. Nubayh, and they said, 'Judgement is yours. Command as you wish.' He said to them, 'The Ḍubayʿa have no equal for my son, and I will not be satisfied except with Kulayb b. Rabīʿa or al-Barrāq b. Rawḥān.' They said, 'This judgement is not sound. Your son was killed by al-Ḥārith b. ʿAbbād, and you want Kulayb and al-Barrāq to compensate. This is clear hubris. Take that which would not be denied you, and leave aside oppression and criminality. Know that war against the Banū Ḍubayʿa will mire you in a war with Kulayb and his people the Arāqim, and a war with al-Barrāq and his people the Banū Ḥanīfa, and all of the Banū Shaybān. Do not make light of this, for it will happen.' So ʿImrān said:

O my two friends, bring me my horse
And my spear, for the time of pursuit is approaching

Bring me my sword and my lance, for I
Will take my revenge on the lowliest of slaves

The evilest of creatures, in appearance and in character
Foster-brother of the sordid is the progeny of ʿAbbād

Timid and cowardly in the turmoil of war
The basest of horsemen on the battle day

If only my vengeance were upon Ibn Rawḥān, my match
In him I would find a cure for my heartsickness

I will not be satisfied with the life of the family of ʿAbbād
In them there is neither enough for me nor the one I want

May God curse their tribe, evil is a tribe
Where judgement comes by ambush

O Sadūs, is there not a rightly-guided one amongst you?
With penetrating judgement, who keeps his promise

How can Naṣr be satisfied with Fuḍayl's killing
Why doesn't he drive the shaggy horses?

What is with Naṣr? And what is Jabr thinking?
I complain of their silence and I call out

They left me on my own, though I was not alone
The day of the striking of the hot iron and the stabbing of spears

Says he: When the two men, namely Naṣr b. Masʿūd and Jabr b. Ṭawra, heard him, they came to him and said, 'You are our master and we defer to you, so do as you like.' He replied, 'Be prepared for an attack.' They said, 'Whom are we attacking?' He responded, 'Kulayb and his people the Arāqim.' They said, 'We do not agree to that. Rather we will attack those upon whom our vengeance is due – the Banū Ḍubayʿa.' He reluctantly agreed with them on that.

Says he: News soon reached the Banū Ḍubayʿa of ʿImrān b. Nubayh's words and his reluctance to find an equal for his son among them, so they scoffed at this and grew very angry. About this, ʿAbbād said:

Insomnia set in and sweet sleep departed
Due to ʿImrān looking down on the noble

I see Ibn Murra still offending
With a claim of superiority over towering mountains

By God, we are not content with the action of Ḥārith
And we will bring him as promised

Let me spare our blood and yours
In what the perpetrator did unintentionally

And if you return to disputatiousness in meeting
And the stabbing of horsemen on a day of pursuit

Then let us drink from the bitter cup of war,
A cup, liver-wrenching, full to the brim

O you dazzled by war in which
Lies the extinction of souls and bodies

Your statement has reached me
A statement of the accursed, an heir to spite

Come, take retaliation, leave off destruction
And combat with spear-shafts and swords

Be wary for Naṣr and Jabr and save up all
Your kinsfolk, for I am showing you the way

Says Ibn Nāfiʿ: Then ʿAbbād al-Ḍubaʿī and the notables of his people sent word to ʿImrān b. Nubayh, apologising to him for the slaying of his son and indicating that they were unhappy about it, and they suggested to him that they settle the debt – they would surrender to him the killer of his son so that he could kill him in revenge. When their letter reached ʿImrān he wept for his son and said, 'I will not kill al-Ḥārith in exchange for my son. I will kill no one other than Kulayb or al-Barrāq.' Then he said:

By my life, my revenge is not with ʿAbbād and his son
But my revenge is in Kulayb b. Wāʾil

Or the knight al-Barrāq, the chief of his people
For he is the match in virtue and excellent qualities

But my people do not help, so I myself
Am about to inflict calamities on you

For we will kill a group of you in revenge for our slain one
Pressing the chests of horses against the rear-ends of the tribes

Do I kill one hyena of the 'Little Hyena' tribe[11] in revenge for the most magnificent
The choicest of heroes, a courageous chief

And the Kahlān will have the ugliest of reputations
No, by the lord of the excellent camels

The sons of Ḍubayʿa will surely be aware of their attack,
With every quivering well-straightened spear

And aware of every Sadūsī who is wont, in war's turmoil,
When heroes meet, to cut necks

Were it not for men not backing my words,
Then my revenge would not be on the despicable Ḍubayʿa

But soon, Ḍubayʿa, you may rejoice
In every strong man, spirited, joining the fray

Young men of good character, mighty from Sadūs
Aggressive in war, then killers

When, atop the tailbones of swift horses and atop their posteriors,
They see us, as young men holding swords,

Do not wish that your people will repel our force
Rather the bereaved's voice will announce their death

Because we are people about whose virtue you have heard
We surpass everyone else in battle

Says Ibn Nāfiʿ: When the messengers of the Banū Ḍubayʿa returned with ʿImrān's response, they prepared for strife. They started to saddle their horses, sharpen their swords, and dust their armour. In reply, al-Ḥārith b. ʿAbbād said:

[11] Ḍubayʿa means 'little hyena'.

I see Ibn Nubayh has risen above his capability
Mocking the noble and mighty

I swear on the soft earth of the valley and those who have alighted
around it
And by the hospitality of my glorious and virtuous people

ʿImrān will admit the heads of our horses
When we meet with quivering spears

Tell the Sadūs that if they want to engage us
That 'O Lord' is written sideways on the cheek

I did not seek to kill al-Fuḍayl as a start
But he did not listen to what a sayer said

Likewise, Ibn Nubayh will not stop transgressing
Until he sees from us the chests of legions

He is thrown down on the cheek, nose cleaving to the dust
Dusty wolves grab him by the teeth

He leaves disparaged and after him leave
Men of high stature, avoiding similar injury

Do not, O ʿImrān, wish for what you cannot bear
For there are snares other than what you found

Whoever from my people and your people was heedless
For he is not far from us today in his heedlessness

And you, in fear, race for al-Barrāq
My, what a pair of adversaries you have when the fight begins[12]

Al-Barrāq will attend swiftly with his people
Including Kulayb b. Wāʾil

Says Ibn Nāfiʿ: Now the two sides met in Manwar, which is a valley full of water, and they fought until the sun declined. After that they parted ways. At that point ʿImrān b. Nubayh, who was the mightiest of his people, came down and challenged an opponent to appear.

[12] *Al-tanāzul* involves the act of dismounting from riding camels in order to mount fighting horses.

So Nuwayra b. ʿAbbād, who was a brave horseman, appeared to him, and they fought for a while. ʿImrān vanquished Nuwayra and knocked him to the ground. Then he challenged someone else to appear. Thence came forth ʿĀmir b. ʿAbbād, who was the most accomplished horseman among his brothers. They fought for a while then parted in safety. Then they inclined toward one another, and stabs were exchanged between them. ʿImrān got one in first, and he caused ʿĀmir to fall down dead. The sons of ʿAbbād appeared one after another, following each other. They were nine. Only al-Ḥārith, the youngest of them, was left. When ʿImrān challenged someone to appear, al-Ḥārith mobilised his horse and wanted to go out to him. But his father called out to him, restraining him, 'Easy now, O my son, allow me, the horseman of the Sadūs, to go out to him, for you alone remain amongst your brothers, and after today I will not let you out of my sight.' Al-Ḥārith replied, 'O father, let me go to him and exact vengeance for my brothers or follow in their wake, for life has no pleasure for me now.' Then he advanced on his horse to ʿImrān, and they charged at each other for a while until stabs were exchanged. Al-Ḥārith got in first and knocked ʿImrān down dead, whereupon he rode about in the field and challenged an opponent to appear. Mālik b. ʿImrān appeared to him. They fought for a while, then al-Ḥārith attacked him and made him follow his father ʿImrān. Again al-Ḥārith challenged an opponent to appear, so Abū l-Aswad b. ʿImrān appeared, and they battled for a while, then al-Ḥārith made Abū l-Aswad follow the other two. And the sons of ʿImrān followed one another in succession, and al-Ḥārith made each follow the other. They were nine and their father the tenth. And it is said, rather, that they were ten and their father the eleventh. So, cavalry advanced on cavalry and they fought a fierce fight until sunset. ʿUqayl al-Ḍubaʿī attacked a group of Sadūs, and in this attack he killed fifteen horsemen and then went back on his way. Naṣr b. Masʿūd met him and took him captive. Naṣr was a forbearing man, so he let ʿUqayl live and did not kill him. Meanwhile, Manṣūr b. Ṭalḥa al-Sadūsī attacked the Banū Ḍubayʿa, and he was met by an attack. Night had descended upon them, so the cavalry dispersed. Then Naṣr b. Masʿūd left with his captive ʿUqayl b. Marwān, and since ʿUqayl was the chief of the Banū Ḍubayʿa, Naṣr said:

Ask the Ḍubayʿa about us on a battle day
The horses at times retreating, at times approaching

It may be that you did not meet with great effort from us,
But your horsemen witnessed me taking possession of war heroes

Do I not have ʿUqayl with me, enchained?
Anticipating abasement and humiliation

We are the valiant sons of war, known
To pursue struggle on horseback

One of us is still like a thousand when they turn away
And when they attack, we give all they have gained

Don't think the killing of ʿImrān passes you by
Not when I have excellent horses and swords

The forerunners at the line, storing strength
Chiefs and leaders, known and noble

In revenge for ʿImrān I will kill your commanders
We will be like a fire fed by wood

You will return, slaves, to the sons of a slave woman
And you will bear that which the Arabs do not bear

Do not be surprised by what our swords extinguish
And if they afflict a youth, in their ignorance they marvel

O woe unto your mothers, what will you do
When squadrons of Sadūs – woe betide you – overwhelm you?

Will you return from the dead so we can excuse you?
Or will you hold out for a war whose cold is flame?

Al-Ḥārith b. ʿAbbād answered him saying:

Ask the Sadūs whose squadrons were extinguished
By the stabbing of spears like shooting stars over their heads

If you did not meet with great effort from us, then your
Horsemen witnessed that I am allied with patience

Oh, woe unto your mother from the assembly of our chiefs
Squadrons pouring like locusts or rain

O father of ʿUqayl, do not take pride in your chiefs
For you are you, as Time overturns

If we get away safely, we will come to you
With every sword with a well-made edge

And every short-haired mare like the arrow surrounding her
From every angle a lion with nobility

Do not reckon that we, O people, will let you escape
Or that you will be able to flee when flight is needed

No, indeed, and many long-legged dancers in the sunlight
Are loved by handsome youths when they respond to the call

And ʿAbbād said to him in response:

You will drink the cup of death, O Naṣr, so just wait
For the stabbing of spearheads or the strike of a sword

Easy now, do not hurry, even if you go in safety
You will find with us a war with all ʿUqayl

We will kill your prisoners so do not turn over to us
A captive, and do not make haste to a slain one

Says Ibn Nāfiʿ: Then the Banū Ḍubayʿa, what with their chief ʿUqayl b. Marwān held captive, made al-Ḥārith b. ʿAbbād, who was thirteen years old, his substitute, and they gave him ʿUqayl's status among them. And he ordered them to carry out a raid on the Sadūs. So, they made a raid, and they took some of their camels. Then the Sadūs got on their horses and charged after their camels. Many of their horsemen at the vanguard were killed. At that point the Sadūs stopped to regroup and go after their camels. Then they reached the people. Now the Banū Ḍubayʿa had divided themselves into those who would meet the horses and those who would drive the camels, and when the Sadūs saw this they also divided themselves into two groups, those who would fight and those who would pursue the camels. They battled fiercely, and the horses charged at each other. Then Naṣr b. Masʿūd attacked ʿAbbād al-Ḍubaʿī and stabbed him with a blow that struck him down dead. Then he attacked his son al-Ḥārith. Al-Ḥārith met him and leaned against him with a thrust and killed him dead, avenging his father ʿAbbād. The two sides fought until the end of the day, and then they went their separate ways without a victor.

Says he: Then the horses that chased after the camels liberated them and returned with them. Al-Ḥārith and his men encountered them, and they took the camels. Now when the son of Naṣr b. Masʿūd heard about the slaying of his father, he rushed to his captive ʿUqayl b. Marwān and killed him, and no one was the wiser. When his people found out about it, they blamed him violently because they found the killing of a captive after keeping him in prison reprehensible. The most severe in his blame was Jabr b. Ṭawra.

Says he: When the Ḍubayʿa heard about the killing of their chief ʿUqayl, they saddled their horses and attacked the Sadūs. Meanwhile the Banū Sadūs, after the killing of ʿUqayl b. Marwān, knew that it was inevitable that the Banū Ḍubayʿa would attack them, so they prepared and were on their guard, and the Ḍubayʿa found them on their guard. The cavalries met and fought a fierce battle. And Jandal b. ʿUqayl attacked Jabr b. Ṭawra and stabbed him fatally. Masʿūd b. Manṣūr turned to Muʿammar[13] and informed him of the killing of Jabr b. Ṭawra. So Muʿammar and Masʿūd attacked Jandal and al-Ḥārith b. ʿAbbād, and they met and battled fiercely. Masʿūd stabbed Jandal, and Ḍubayʿa rescued him. Al-Ḥārith attacked Muʿammar and struck him a fatal blow. Then they dispersed and al-Ḥārith b. ʿAbbād pulled back his spear-shaft and said:

> The Sadūs have really seen me in action
> Me, the knight whose wont is cutting throats
>
> I received Naṣr, and then al-Muʿammar after him
> And I killed him against his will despite him
>
> It is inevitable that one follow another
> And that the first is necessarily followed by the last
>
> Sadūs, you acted unjustly when you killed my father
> And nine of my brothers. Extend to a tenth
>
> Don't you know that I'm surrounded by young men?
> Attacking the blades of sharp swords

[13] This Muʿammar is not identified in the text.

Says Ibn Nāfiʿ: After that the Sadūs, the clan of al-Jarrāḥ and the Banū Jadīla got together and attacked the Banū Ḍubayʿa, killing a terrific number of them, seizing their property, and taking their womenfolk captive. They had nothing left in them. The cry reached Kulayb and his brothers and all of his tribe al-Arāqim as well as his people the Banū Jusham, so they attacked and assaulted every target hard and soft, and everyone who heard the cry from the tribes of Taghlib attacked. They caught up with the people at Urayṭa, and they fought a fierce fight, and they liberated their property and their womenfolk, and nothing else of theirs was left. Then the two cavalries charged at each other, and when they retreated from one another, Manṣūr b. Ṭawra, the brother of Jabr, attacked Ṣāfī b. Lukayz and killed him. Then he attacked Manṣūr b. Riyāḥ al-Bujayrī and did the same. Then the horsemen of Jadīla attacked Kulayb, and Kulayb's brother Nuwayra and his cousins attacked. Then al-Jarrāḥ and al-Arāqim attacked. Then the clan of Bujayr and the tribe of Jusham attacked. Then the Sadūs and the Ḍubayʿa attacked. They fought a fierce fight until night formed a barrier between them, and then they went their separate ways. Nuwayra said:

The horsemen of the clan of Jadīla went after
My people, along with the horsemen of Jarrāḥ

They attacked with a force resembling the night in its breadth
And they led away female captives and young she-camels together

We jumped on our swift horses and pulled at their
Sides, and they went running

Until we caught up with them all in Urayṭa
And the millstone of war revolved yet again

So, I targeted Manṣūr and defiled his cheek with dust
I killed Jabbār and I killed Mismaʿ

I got what I intended from the Sadūs and others
And I left the land where they had alighted yesterday vacant

Then Mālik b. al-Dhaʿīr responded, saying:

> Have you not seen my people in struggle as if they are
> Lions of al-Sharā?[14] They attack and don't get frightened
>
> In their hands are fine sharp swords
> With them your heads and hands are cut off
>
> If the darkness of the night had not saved you, you would not be
> Returning to your mother, with her swollen perineum, O Nuwayra
>
> Be patient, until the horses charge
> And the Indian swords strike the skulls
>
> You have hurried to us, O Nuwayra, so be patient
> Until the day when you see the spearheads shine

Says Ibn Nāfiʿ: The schism between the two tribes grew great and expanded, and all attempts at reconciliation failed until its evil reached those who had been shielded from it, like al-Barrāq b. Rawḥān, who had been isolated among his people the Banū Ḥanīfa, and like Shabīb b. Luhaym al-Ṭāʾī, for he and his sons were also isolated. Now the tribes of Ṭayy met and descended upon the home of Shabīb – al-Barrāq's maternal uncle – and they tried to get him to cut off kinship ties between himself and the Banū Wāʾil. Shabīb hated this idea, and his soul shrank from foul things. But Ṭayy did not excuse him, so he said: 'Woe upon you. You have set me up for nothing but the enlargement of the schism between the two tribes of them and us, and by God I will not do that.' They replied: 'We see that and it is inevitable, and we are not base or lowly, we want only to have your leadership and counsel.' Shabīb reluctantly responded, and the tribes of Ṭayy and their allies the Quḍāʿa agreed to wage war against the Rabīʿa, and they joined each other and became neighbours.

Says Ibn Nāfiʿ: When the Rabīʿa heard of what the Ṭayy and their allies agreed to, and that Shabīb al-Ṭāʾī was standing with

[14] Al-sharā means 'road' and, as a proper noun, refers specifically to a road on the Mountain of Salmā 'abounding with lions'. Brave men are often called 'lions of Sharā'. See E.W. Lane, *Arabic-English Lexicon* (London: Williams & Norgate, 1863–7), *sh-r-y*.

them, the situation weighed on them. So Kulayb and his brothers, and his people the Arāqim, and all of the tribes of Rabīʿa met at al-Barrāq's and said, 'The matter is grave, and we cannot abide it.' Now al-Barrāq, due to Lukayz' wish to marry Laylā off to King ʿAmr b. Dhī Ṣahbān, had isolated himself with his people from the Banū Asad and the Banū Ḥanīfa. And when they came to al-Barrāq they saw him surrounded by a great group of his people, so they greeted them, and al-Barrāq said, 'Is there something I should know, O cousins?' Kulayb came forward and said, 'O Barrāq, the tribes of Ṭayy and Quḍāʿa have come together to make war on us, and the houses of Rabīʿa are dispersed, and you all know that we fear a precedent upon us and upon you. So, tell us what to do.' Al-Barrāq then recited a long poem including the following:

> Am I not but one of the Rabīʿa?
> I am strong when they are strong and their pride is mine
>
> I am mighty when they are generous
> And I lose out completely in their hour of loss

Then he said, 'O Kulayb, I am just a man among you. However, Lukayz b. Murra is the leader of the houses of Rabīʿa, and he is known amongst them for his standing, whereas I am just a man among them.' Kulayb was very cautious of this, and he knew that the Rabīʿa had moved away from Lukayz at the time when al-Barrāq stood up for them during the war with the Iyād, and they knew his virtues over the chiefs of the Rabīʿa.

Says he: At that point they left al-Barrāq, and he had not agreed to stand up with them. When Shabīb al-Ṭāʾī heard about Rabīʿa's meeting with his sister's son, al-Barrāq, and that they wanted him to stand up with them, and that he declined to do that due to Lukayz wishing to deny him his daughter, he sent a message to him asking him to defect to his side, and he said:

> Pass some advice to al-Barrāq from me
> Tell him that we are all marching towards you
>
> All of the tribes of Ṭayy have gathered
> And their allies have arrived for them, responding to a call to arms

Why don't you come quickly in salutation?
For I am for you victorious and an aide

Do you not remember when your Lukayz treated you harshly?
And turned his back on you? and that whole story?

Come to us, so I can marry you to a daughter
With honour in her fold, pure

Leave there, forget about them, for they
Are cutters of bonds, and you are an assistor

When the verses reached al-Barrāq, he passed them on to his father, Rawḥān, and said to him, 'Respond to your in-law.' He said, 'O my son, the letter is addressed to you and replying is your responsibility. Answer him as you see fit.' So, al-Barrāq answered his maternal uncle, saying:

By my life, I will not leave the family of my people
And depart from my courtyard or march

With them my submissiveness, when I am among them,
Is, despite enmity, a great honour

When I live together with my people
I have glory and greatness

Do I reside with them when times are easy?
And depart from them when times are hard?

And leave my clan while they are people
Whose largesse encompasses the world?

Do you not hear their spearheads
Grate your collarbones and ribs?

Hands off my people, leave them be
Even the blind man will see their actions

Says Ibn Nāfiʿ: When he finished his verses, his father Rawḥān leapt up, kissed his brow and said, 'Now, the capacity for leadership in you is complete. By God, you are the honourable leader of your people.' He had thought that al-Barrāq would join his maternal uncles due to the action of Lukayz. Then he ordered that his filly al-Shabūb[15] be brought, and he gave her to al-Barrāq. She was one of the finest of his horses; her father was a sprightly horse of the Quḍāʿa and her mother a horse of the Banū Shaybān. At that point the doubts of Kulayb and his brothers and his people vanished, and Kulayb and his father and his brothers and all of his people the Arāqim – and they were thirty-one horsemen – met with al-Barrāq and they said, 'O Barrāq, erase the doubts lingering in our souls about going to the house of the Rabīʿa and residing with them. For they have answered your call to war against the Iyād and others, and they have established your virtue, and we fear that we will set a precedent about which nations will talk until the end of eternity.'

Says he: Then al-Barrāq got up and ordered his brothers to ride to the houses of the Rabīʿa where they were crying out for their tribes and allies to help them. His father, Rawḥān, asked, 'Do you order your brothers and leave your slaves?' Al-Barrāq replied:

> As for the slaves, do not call on the messengers
> For the Banū Shaybān will not respond with spears
>
> Except to your fair-faced and noble sons when
> The fleet camels come to take them far away
>
> And receive the family of Dhuhl with a cry in the high sun
> And the family of ʿIjl is in a hurry to you today
>
> And the family of ʿImrān and the Rislān together
> Come to you urgently and in haste

Says Ibn Nāfiʿ: When al-Barrāq finished with his composition, he broke his spear-shaft, gave each of his brothers an internodal portion of it and said, 'Ride and urge on your horses, and hang necklaces on the finest of them.' The Arabs used to do this during serious situations. By it they meant to display their anxiety in calling out for help for their people against the enemy. Now al-Barrāq's brothers obeyed his order and dispersed to the different vicinities of the Rabīʿa, and each of them arrived with an internodal portion of his

[15] This name means 'A horse whose hind feet pass beyond his fore feet' (ibid.). It also means 'blaze' or 'flame'.

brother's spear-shaft and with a necklace upon his mount. So Rabīʿa felt al-Barrāq's anxiety. And the tribes of Rabīʿa came from every corner and set up neighbouring encampments. Then the chiefs of the Rabīʿa gathered around al-Barrāq and greeted him with the warmest of receptions and showed him hospitality and generosity, and they conferred leadership upon him and they handed over their powers to command and to interdict. While this was happening, Shabīb b. Luhaym al-Ṭāʾī's messengers arrived warning them and saying that the tribes of Ṭayy and Quḍāʿa had gathered around him. He singled out al-Barrāq in some verses saying:

Confer upon al-Barrāq greetings from me
A pure paternal uncle from a noble people

These tribes of Ṭayy with their Quḍāʿa
Have fanned the flames of War which is up on its feet

They have alighted in plains and lowlands and
They have stored their spears in the loftiest of hills

Brace yourself, O Barrāq and wait
The squadrons come to you from nations

Woe unto your mother from the rallying of soldiers and from
The fluttering of flags and the spilling of blood for blood

No one will come at you – only every choice man
Whose resolve is kindled in battle like a young eagle

And every spear whose gleaming tip shines forth
Like the shimmering of lightning when it flashes in the darkness

Al-Barrāq responded, saying:

I have found you, uncle, delivering some speech
About going to war in vengeance

Scaring me with soldiers I do not reckon
In every princely Arab and Persian

I have no one but a people with nobility
Rabīʿa the proud when they stand on their feet

They have left Shabīb and Wādī al-Rās and gathered
Around me with property and people and womenfolk

For the Ṭayy of the Shaybān advanced boldly
Together with the Taghlib and the elite of the Jusham

And the Wāʾilīs have got up in their entirety
From every choice man coming to you from the nations

Says Ibn Nāfiʿ: After al-Barrāq replied to his maternal uncle's letter and his messengers had departed, he called out to his people and said, 'O Banū Dhuhl, O Banū ʿIjl, O Banū Murra, O Banū al-Azd, O Banū Ḍarrār, O Banū Lakhm, O Banū Yashkur, O Banū Ḍubayʿa, O Banū al-Ḥarith, O Banū Jusham, O Banū Nimr, O Banū Qasam, O Banū ʿAbs, O Banū Mālik, O Banū Bahrān, O Banū Marwān, O Banū ʿImrān, O Banū ʿAlī, O Banū al-Jarrāḥ, you know how numerous are the tribes of Ṭayy, and how strong they are and how brave. Now let us saddle up our horses and beat them to the chase.' So, they saddled up and attacked. At the front was Nuwayra b. Rabīʿa, and al-Barrāq and Kulayb took up the rear. Kulayb was urging al-Barrāq on in waging war against his maternal uncles of Ṭayy and against all of Ṭayy and Quḍāʿa, and he said, 'O Barrāq, I adjure thee by God and kinship, may you not punish a man who lost his way, whose soul has floundered, and who has been beguiled by the attire and possessions of kings. Counsel your people and do not forsake them. For they have answered your call, and wanted your good deed, and acknowledged your virtue.' When he had gone on at length, al-Barrāq said, 'O Kulayb, you are my advisor, my friend and my confidant. And you should know that I have not cried against my clans seeking to defeat them, and know that I will wage the harshest of wars against the Ṭayy and will inflict the greatest of trials on the Quḍāʿa, but if I meet a man from among my maternal uncles I will let him live, and I will order my companion to do the same.' Kulayb, having heard al-Barrāq's words, grew very wary, and he accused al-Barrāq of paucity of advice because al-Barrāq's maternal uncles were the mightiest of the Ṭayy and they had no equals apart from their sister's sons al-Barrāq and his brothers and his cousins, and Kulayb and his brothers and his people the Arāqim and the Banū Ḥanīfa. As for the rest of the tribes, they are too weak to confront them. Then Kulayb sighed and said:

If your nearness to us
Puts bridles on us

For you, O Banū Asad b. Bakr
Want stabbing – so who will protect us?

And you, O Banū Asad, are a pillar
For this fanatical clan

You announced the death of their men to them and cried out
So, they all came with their harems

And they alighted, O Banū Asad, with you
They came lighting the lamp of war

Now you, Banū Asad – may your mothers be bereft of you!
Have betrayed your brothers

If your nearness is much for us
Wearing armour of iron

Then you will not march on
While your dogs prowl about me

Abū l-Naṣr Ibn Rawḥān, my friend,
We learned that you [pl.] were imagining

Abū l-Naṣr Ibn Rawḥān, my friend,
Has the oath of allegiance been withdrawn?

Abū l-Naṣr Ibn Rawḥān, my friend,
If we wade into war do not [pl.] attack us

Abū l-Naṣr Ibn Rawḥān, my friend,
Might showed you your kinfolk, scoffing

Abū l-Naṣr Ibn Rawḥān, my friend,
There is enough evil, so what will you do?

Did you not leave the Rabīʿa leaderless?
With provisions supplied by ignominy and the fates?

You are a gift to the whole of Ṭayy
And you were all going in peace

Due to the matter of Lukayz and the matter of Laylā
You all wanted to be forsakers

O Banū Asad, I see you from your passion,
Want to rupture ties in ignorance

O Banū Asad, you wanted the family of my uncle
To cut us off, and you had been the ones connecting us

O Banū Asad, lions are spurring you on
But you fail to turn up for battle

O Banū Asad, we put our men out for contests in battles
And you stand still in the place of attack

O Banū Asad, you have killed your clan
With this view – don't you know that?

O Banū Asad b. Bakr, how do you start
Your stabbing matches while you watch?

O Banū Asad, how can you do nothing,
When your cousin falls stabbed?

It appeared to me from my friend what appeared to me
They had a debt to al-Barrāq

It appeared to me from my friend what appeared to me
Some of the crafts of the distant ones

It appeared to me from my friend what appeared to me
As if we were not neighbours

Will you not inform my sincere friend for me?
The men of the Banū Ḥanīfa are warming by the fire

Says Ibn Nāfiʿ: When Kulayb finished with his poetry and had done with his rebuking of al-Barrāq, he turned to his father and his brothers and isolated himself with them from al-Barrāq. As for Nuwayra and al-Muhalhil, they had passed by a group of their people with al-Barrāq, and al-Ḥarith b. ʿAbbād was with the two of them. He was like an excited camel, charging at people from right and left, and al-Barrāq said:

I say to myself time and again
While the tribes' spears no doubt glisten

O my soul, be gentle in war and take pleasure
For in its cup poison stagnates

And if I do not lead horses to every lion
To eat the flesh of the enemies and be satiated

Then may my hand not acquire a black horse
And may I not live as a praised man nor live the easy life

May I not lead armies from distant lands
Nor may sharp, cutting swords shine

If I do not plunder Ṭayy together with their allies, the Quḍāʿa, as expected

Then march to the Ṭayy, emptying their lands
So that they become a wasteland devoid of inhabitants

Leave neither old man or young of the Ṭayy
Let no woman walk and no child suckle

Says Ibn Nāfiʿ: Now when al-Barrāq came close to the people he called out, 'O people, Kulayb and those of his brothers who are with him leave a gap that cannot be filled by anyone else. An idea has come to me about how we can fix your situation.' They replied, 'Judgement is yours.' So, he said, 'Select the finest of your horses and put the lightest of your men on them and send them in first. Then when they get to the middle of the encampments of the Ṭayy and Quḍāʿa, they will stab them with their swords and spears. When the people clamour and the cry is raised, they will turn the reins of their horses towards us and we will be prepared. When the people's horses, follow on their trail, we will attack them from every side.' They said, 'Yes, good idea.' Then they put their light men on their fine horses, and they ordered them to attack the encampments of the people. They stabbed them with their swords, and voices were raised. The people rushed towards them. Then al-Barrāq's horses returned as he had commanded and the people charged in their wake, and they were a great mass. Al-Barrāq's maternal uncle Shabīb cried out and said, 'This is the cunning of your sister's son. Do not attack.' So those who heard the cry stopped, and those who did not hear continued their pursuit until they were surrounded by the tribes of Rabīʿa. Each tribe attacked them with what they had, they battled for a while, and then the Ṭayy and the Quḍāʿa turned back after horrific killing. Al-Barrāq and those who were with him followed them, as did the horses of the Banū Rabīʿa, except the Banū Jusham and the whole of the clan of al-Barrāq, for they went forth under his banner at the end of the line.

Says Ibn Nāfiʿ: When the cavalries of Ṭayy and Quḍāʿa returned, defeated, with the cavalries of the Rabīʿa behind them, Shabīb al-Ṭāʾī and his brother ʿAmr attacked *en masse*, so the cavalries charged and the people consolidated, and they fought a fierce fight, and a great number of the Rabīʿa were killed until al-Barrāq and his men attacked, and they battled for a while until the end of the day. Then the warring parties went their separate ways after much killing and wounding without a clear victor.

Says Ibn Nāfiʿ: Now ʿAmr b. Luhaym al-Ṭāʾī came to his sons and said, 'O my sons, I have returned to you only for a matter which gives me pleasure and for which you are known among the tribes of the Arabs. Know that your sister's sons are the mightiest of the Rabīʿa and their horsemen. Now your sister's sons have come to you in war, like lions dreaded by the slyest of the Arabs. And they are al-Barrāq, Junayd, Ẓalīl, Sālim, ʿAmr, and their father Rawḥān. For you, O my son Naṣīr, are the equal in retaliation of al-Barrāq. And you, O my son Ghanm, are the equal of Junayd. And you, O Sālim, are the equal of Sālim. And you, O Jabr, are the equal of ʿAmr. And you, O Ṭaws, are the equal of Ẓalīl. And Muṣʿab, Ḥabīb and ʿĀmir are the equals of Nuwayra, al-Kulayb and al-Muhalhil.' When al-Barrāq heard about ʿAmr's advice to his sons and his inciting them to kill al-Barrāq and his brothers specifically, he called all his brothers together and said, 'You have learned about this man and his advice to his sons and his incitement of them against us. If one of them challenges us to appear, not one of you should appear. I will go, for perhaps I will return him safely and we won't devastate our mother with the killing of one of her brothers, causing her much wailing and lengthy grief as if she is a stranger among us. And if my maternal uncle Naṣīr challenges me to appear, then al-Furāfiṣa and his brothers – and they are seventy horsemen – will not be far behind. And if they attack after him, then you should attack after me. At first no one should attack but you, O Banū Asad. And if the Sadūs attack after them, then the Banū Ḥanīfa should attack after you.'

Says he: When the day arrived the people met, and when the two tribes faced each other, ʿAmr b. Luhaym got up and called his son Naṣīr and said, 'Appear before your sister's son, al-Barrāq, for this is your opportunity.' So Naṣīr appeared and challenged al-Barrāq to appear, so al-Barrāq appeared before him, saying:

Naṣīr called me to noble deeds
To the raising of swords and the placing of spears

O maternal uncle, nothing excites a desire in me
Except you, and you hated the whole of life

Go gently, and tell me – for you are well-informed
Are you not experienced in the war of the iron-clad?

So Naṣīr replied:

What does Abū l-Naṣr think of me?
And of my father ʿAmr, my judgement is not disappointed

The noblest and swiftest to advance and retreat
And nobler in the spear, O son of my sister, than I

I must do what you order that I do
And I must build what you want me to build

Says he: When al-Barrāq heard the words of his maternal uncle, he smiled and approached him, and their horses inclined towards one another, and neither one of them bore any ill will towards the other, and they resolved to separate peacefully. While they were doing this, al-Furāfiṣa attacked al-Barrāq. Then his brothers and the Banū Asad attacked. And when the horses ran, following one another, the whole of the Sadūs attacked, and the Banū Ḥanīfa attacked. And ʿAmr b. Luhaym attacked his in-law Rawḥān. So Nuwayra b. Rabīʿa charged at him and defeated him with a stab by which he subordinated him. He was not injured, and one of his sons rescued him after intense striking and stabbing. There was man-to-man combat, and they fought until sunset. Then each side went away without victory, and al-Barrāq said:

The chief of the two tribes called me, among us
The Banū Asad, brave in war

He leads into battle the Dhuhl and the ʿIjl,
The Banū Shaybān, horsemen of dignity

And the family of Ḥanīfa, and the Banū Ḍubayʿa
And their Arqam, and the tribe of the Banū Ḍirār

And you see the bold ones of the Banū Jusham
On the morning of terror like lions ferocious in the chase

And the people of Banū Rabīʿa, the family of my people
Called for exchanges of greetings and visits

With their maternal uncles, Ṭayy, then gave them
A lusty spear-thrust

We accompanied them on excellent short-haired horses
With pointed Indian swords

Were it not for the criers who assisted them,
In plain sight with the cry of one whose protection was sought

Then they would not have come back and charged at us
And they would have feared the blow of sharp sword-blades

What a cry! What a scandal!
Dust stirred up in the midst of lands

About the decorated noble steeds
Great horses with reins around their necks

Attacking with spears in every morning
Charging in a cloud of dust

And we visited the Banū Luhaym at high sun
And we made them descend into every shame

Spears aimed at the chest of ʿAmr
And he fell, thrown down, naked in the rank

My hands injured an army
With a strike of a doubly sharp-edged sword, slitting

The horseman of al-Jarrāḥ escaped from me
Due to the strike of a sword above the bracelet

Ask the scoundrel Ibn al-Dhaʿīr
Is he not as patient as I am in battle?

Did I not challenge him to a race, and he turned his back?
Like a ram that is about to bleat

I am the son of proud men, Nizār is my forefather
Noble, honourable, esteemed

Around me is every admirable Wā'ilī
Sound in judgement, with waist-wrapper tied

So Mālik b. al-Dhaʿīr replied saying:

ʿAlwa appeared from behind a curtain
The morning she was being carried away with the girls

With a face as bright as a flash of lightning
And hair, like the darkness of the night, under a veil

And an eye like the calf of a wild Nejdi cow
And teeth like shining pearls

We inhaled particles of musk from her
Emanating from her cheek

Leave off passion for the beauty of a young girl,
Who went on her way after a visit

But one may say also a saddled fleet horse
Giving birth to colts (*mihāran*) sired by dromedaries (*mahārī*)

Hostile parties treat the Rabīʿa as enemies
With days of raids against Nizār

The milch-donkeys giving them drink
Until they see the colour red with yellow

With it we entertained the Rabīʿa the day on which
Came to us the female revenge-seekers

They kept openly knocking on al-Barrāq's door
For how is Nuwayra a son of an ass?

He passed in stagnation, defeated and lowly
Like water, woe unto you, at rest

And he accuses his parents of being proud, and what living being
Is more deserving to his parents of every shame?

Did Kulayb not shrink back in fear,
Of my spear, loose-hipped, shitting?

And the Arāqim along with Lukayz disobeyed him
For fear of stabbing and swords with sharp blades

Says Ibn Nāfiʿ: When Kulayb heard Mālik b. al-Dhaʿīr's poetry and came upon his words 'loose-hipped, shitting', he swore not to eat or to drink to satiety until he met Mālik b. al-Dhaʿīr and humiliated him. At this point he went to al-Barrāq and apologised to him for going back upon him and for his disobedience of him. Al-Barrāq said, 'O Kulayb, no one can take away what is between us.' Then Kulayb asked him if he could borrow his horse al-Shabūb, which his father gave to him and which was the fastest of the horses of his people. Al-Barrāq handed it over to him without knowing the reason he wanted it. Then Kulayb saddled up al-Shabūb and donned his armour and set out for Mālik, without telling his people anything about it. Then, during the night, he arrived at the encampment of the Banū Jadīla, and he asked directions of a shepherd who led him to the tent of Mālik. He advanced and called out, 'O Mālik.' Mālik responded saying, 'Who's there?' Kulayb answered, 'A man from your allies the Quḍāʿa. They have been attacked tonight, and my sons spent the night in al-Ṭawy.' So Mālik saddled up and donned his weapons and rode. It was a moonlit night, and Mālik left the encampment with Kulayb, but when Mālik saw that Kulayb was not stopping or listening, he suspected him and said, 'This horse is not of the Quḍāʿa, and by God, I fear that this is Kulayb, and that this horse has a father from our horses and a mother from the horses of the Banū Asad – and maybe it's al-Shabūb.' Mālik lagged behind, and Kulayb missed the sound of the horse's footfall, so he pulled on the reins of his own horse and said, 'Perhaps you have exceeded the camels in perception.' Mālik replied, 'But I took notice of al-Shabūb and imagined Kulayb before my eyes.' Kulayb said, 'By God, I am he. So, watch out for yourself.' He then attacked him and said, 'O Mālik, where is your spear that loosened the hips of Kulayb such that he shat on his saddle?' Then Kulayb knocked Mālik off his horse, put his turban round his neck and took him captive. He left Mālik's horse, and it returned to his people. When the horse came to them in the night, they were sure that Mālik had been killed and that whoever called him was a man of Wā'il so they cried out to the people to carry out a raid and they set out for the Ṭayy and the Quḍāʿa on hard and easy ground. As for Kulayb, he travelled through the night with his captive until morning dawned, and lo he saw the dust of horses and knew they were the horses of his people. His brothers Nuwayra and al-Muhalhil had missed him and informed al-Barrāq, who had figured out that Kulayb had wanted al-Shabūb to attack Mālik in the abode of his people. So, he saddled up his horse and cried out. Then they all saddled up and went out on a raid looking for Kulayb. At this point Kulayb let Mālik go and said, 'Return to your people and inform them that it was you that kindled this fire and that its heat will overtake others.' So Mālik returned and informed his people of the matter with Kulayb, and he warned them that cavalries would be coming. They were too ashamed to retreat. Then the two parties met, and they fought a hard fight until the end of the day, when they separated after much killing and wounding. Then ʿĀmir b. al-Dhaʿīr appeared and challenged Kulayb to appear. So Kulayb appeared to him, and the two men met and fought for a long time, until the people were in awe of their bravery and self-restraint. Then the Banū al-Dhaʿīr made haste, and Mālik's brothers attacked Kulayb. There were sixteen of them from one woman and six from another. When they attacked Kulayb, Rabīʿa b. Murra and his two sons, Nuwayra and al-Muhalhil, and Lukayz and his sons attacked the Banū al-Dhaʿīr. People were attacking from both sides. The horses of the Banū al-Dhaʿīr and the Jadīlīs flew, as did the horses of the Banū Murra and the Arāqim, and they clashed for a while. When the torrent stopped, Nuwayra attacked Muqātil b. al-Dhaʿīr, and he stabbed him and knocked him down, wounded. Muqātil's brothers then rescued him, and he got back on his horse. The battle continued. Then Khuzayma attacked Mālik b. al-Dhaʿīr and knocked him down wounded. Then Mālik's brothers saved him, too, until they returned him to the back of his horse. Nuwayra then attacked Jarrāḥ b. al-Dhaʿīr, stabbed him, and knocked him down wounded. And Marwān b. al-Dhaʿīr attacked Lukayz b. Murra and knocked him down with his stabbing. So, his brother Rabīʿa and his son Kulayb rescued Lukayz and got him back on his horse. And ʿAmmār b. al-Dhaʿīr attacked al-Muhalhil and knocked him down on the ground. His brother Nuwayra and his cousin Khuzayma b. Lukayz then rescued him, and he got back on his horse. And the cavalries of the Banū Jadīla attacked, and the cavalries of the Arāqim attacked, and they fought for a long while. Then Nuwayra attacked al-Ḥārith b. al-Dhaʿīr and knocked him down dead. War between the two tribes broke out. They fought a fierce fight and then separated. Then al-Ḥārith b. ʿAbbād came forward and challenged someone to appear. Al-Ṣāmit al-Sadūsī appeared to him, and they exchanged blows. Al-Ḥārith got in first and knocked him down [dead] on the ground. Then he challenged someone to appear. So Yās, the brother of the slain one, appeared to him, and he was more courageous than his brother al-Ṣāmit. They battled for a while, then al-Ḥārith made him follow his brother. Then the cavalry of the Sadūs came running consecutively at al-Ḥārith b. ʿAbbād. They were twenty horsemen, and he killed them in duelling. They were the strongest of the Sadūs. After that, there was man-to-man combat, and they fought until the sun had almost set. Then ʿAmr b. Luhaym al-Ṭāʾī, al-Barrāq's maternal grandfather, appeared, and he challenged Rawḥān b. Asad to appear to him. He appeared and said, 'O ʿAmr, is it not enough for you – what you see between the two tribes – without you challenging me specifically to a duel?' Then they attacked each other, and they exchanged stabs. The quicker of the two was Rawḥān, and he knocked ʿAmr down, wounded. Then all of ʿAmr's sons attacked their in-law, and they showered their spears on him. But his shield was like a fortress the spearheads could not penetrate, so they threw him on the face of the earth. Then al-Barrāq and his brothers attacked, and they took their father Rawḥān. Then they put their grandfather ʿAmr on his horse and returned him to his sons safely.

Says Ibn Nāfiʿ: Now Ẓalīl b. Rawḥān was wounded by a stab that would be the death of him. When al-Barrāq learned that his brother would not be saved from this stabbing, he appeared between the two ranks and said, 'O sons of ʿAmr, by God you have devastated your sister by killing her son. Her devastation will not be cooled except by the killing of his match among you.' Then he challenged his maternal uncle Muṣʿab b. ʿAmr b. Luhaym to a duel. He appeared and al-Barrāq attacked him mercilessly, with lips contracted, and knocked him down dead. Then Naṣīr b. ʿAmr attacked al-Barrāq, and again he contracted his lips. There was no match for Naṣīr among the horsemen of the Rabīʿa except Kulayb and al-Barrāq, so they battled for a while. Then the cavalry of the Furāfiṣa attacked in the wake of their brother, Naṣīr, and the cavalry of the Banū Asad attacked after al-Barrāq, and they fought fiercely. Then the cavalry of the Sadūs attacked, and the cavalry of the Banū Ḥanīfa, and they engaged in man-to-man combat. Nuwayra fought hard, and he was brave. The people fought their battle until the night came down between them, and everyone retreated. Then Nuwayra said:

The horsemen of Ṭayy have witnessed my courage
For I am the lively hero chief

And the sons of Jadīla have witnessed me
Striking boldly in battle, raising dust

My spearheads are my tongue, when it pronounces,
Rather my word is true – I do what I say

What is a free man if not one who talks
The talk, and walks the walk?

Have the sons of al-Dhaʿīr not witnessed me in battle?
Mālik's wings are clipped, and he is cowardly

I see Ibn al-Dhaʿīr not desisting from his pronouncements
Of slander; for he is an ignoramus

And I forbid my soul to claim occasions of glory
Such as noble people possess

I do not overreach them
By my life arrogance is of no use

Lower your eyes from honour, O Mālik – that which
You attempt cannot be connived

I thought Kulayb left his honour with you
But he brought you in the open, terrors did not strike him

And we led the fine horses, lancing with spears
Outstripping each other, carrying horsemen in battle

Upon them are men who claim descent from Ḍubayʿa
With fine polished swords

They respond to the call of al-Barrāq when he summons them
He conquers what he desires and hopes

The young man al-Barrāq is the chief of his people
The tribes rally around him on the day of assembly

He extended an invitation to the two sons of Rabīʿa, and so
They shook on it

The one with the un-curried forelocks visited you in the morning
Raiding, young men on huge stallions

Squadrons of the sons of Rabīʿa whose war cry was still
– On the day they dismounted camels for horses – Wāʾil

Pulling away ʿAmr, then Ṣaʿb and Rājiḥ
And Rājiḥ and Muqātil were not saved from them

Quḍāʿa left a Wāʾilī faction alone
And what strikes hawks with fear came face-to-face with them

How many a wounded man left; his skin stuck
To high-necked lean spears

Says Ibn Nāfiʿ: Mālik wanted not to answer Nuwayra because of what Kulayb had done to him. But his brothers said to him, 'Answer the man. We are here beside you, so do not fear repercussions.' And Mālik was eloquent and said:

The Ṭayy have denied the status of Nuwayra
And they have not acknowledged his favour when engaging in battle

But ask the proud chiefs in battle –
– Their valiant ones from the families of Bakr and Wāʾil

About the wounding lion, and ʿAmr and the high-ranked
Choice part of a people, taken by quivering lances

For have your eyes witnessed our Naṣīr's deeds
And those of his brothers, you are not ignorant of this

Does the runner not step beneath his banner,
Passing by with a white sword, separating skulls?

I see you, O youth, as someone who does not attend gatherings,
Ask me – you'll find me knowledgeable about dispositions

I inform you of my noble people and their virtue
Besides their personal merits with spears

On every lean-flanked horse with compact back,
Wont to penetrate, when you conquer, in any event

And the sons of Rabīʿa know that we
Charge on the morning of terror under the dust

And in battle we strike skulls with swords
All the tribes have witnessed this from us

When the two groups of you and us meet
You see Lukayz strongly built in his joints

Ẓalīl remains unavenged and there has not been
A brave people invoking him against spirits

And if al-Barrāq shone for a while in fortune
Then he wouldn't be avenging [a son of] Rawḥān

Says Ibn Nāfiʿ: Nuwayra b. Rabīʿa wanted to respond to him, but his brother Kulayb stopped him and said, 'Easy now.' Then Naṣīr said, elegising his brother Muṣʿab:

O eye, well up with tears running from you
For a youth, the knight of the Sadūs, Ibn ʿAmr

Knight of the two armies, ours and yours
Powerful protector in every age

I was asleep, but I was wakened
By the calamity befalling the youth, my full brother and my treasure

Indeed, Barrāq began with me in plain sight
By the killing of a valiant warrior, not rabble

Prepare for wars, O family of Luhaym
O Abū l-Naṣr you will know my victory

With all of the Sadūs and the Jadīl
You will see humility among the brave men of Bakr

My eye was sleepless due to the stabbing, easy now
Sleep will return and I will exact my revenge

The Wā'ilī will see from us stabbing
And striking like burning embers

From Jadīl and the family of Jarrāḥ my people
And the Sadūs and Sunbus the family of Naṣr

They will come to you as fast as arrows
In the darkness of the night and the brightness of the dawn

I must be true to my word and my promise
And you will see in [your people] a completion of my vow

Al-Barrāq responded, elegising his brother Ẓalīl:

An eye cries and a heart is bereft and sad
For what has been buried in the earth – the gallant lion

Slumber is gone and sleep passes and has cut off
The ties of connection when wakefulness approaches

O eye, if you tear up, do not follow utter distraction
The rush of fine horses heals

In that is consolation for my brother, whilst you
Wail for the dead as your numbers decrease

Now whether you come to us with your snares
Or whether you stop, we will return to you

I do not decree that I will be victorious over you
Only God knows what is the end point for people

For every living being fills some function
And Time spares no one

Make haste! We march to do our duty
And if you stop then these horses of ours will arrive

Advance with these horses of yours, ours stand on three legs
Not curried, with matted locks growing from their haunches

If you come to us, you will be gifted quickly
With blows that will blaze on your heads

And if you stay where you are, then we will come to you,
O family of my mother's side, with short-haired horses that outstrip one another

Says Ibn Nāfiʿ: They all came together and some went against others, and they met at Dūma, which is at the border of the lands of the Anmār, and they fought a fierce fight. Naṣīr b. ʿAmr appeared, and he challenged al-Barrāq to appear. He responded immediately. As the two of them were noble matches, they battled for a while and not one of them vanquished the other. Then Naṣīr's brothers attacked al-Barrāq, and al-Barrāq's brothers rallied around him. Sālim b. Rawḥān and Gharsān b. ʿAmr b. Luhaym al-Ṭāʾī met, and they exchanged blows. Then Gharsān's sword fell on Sālim's sword and cut it in two. Then the cavalry of the Banū Farfaṣ attacked – and they were seventy horsemen – and the cavalry of the Banū Asad attacked, and the horses chased each other. Naṣīr and al-Aḥjaf engaged in a sword fight, and Naṣīr got in first with a blow that struck the other down dead. So, al-Barrāq attacked al-Ahmas, the cousin of Naṣīr, and killed him in revenge for his cousin al-Aḥjaf. *En masse* combat ensued, and the battle was fierce. Then each party went its own way without a clear victor. About this Naṣīr said:

There came to me from the Banū Rawḥān a statement
Like water in the abundant sea

That ignites a fire on the sides of a
Rainy autumnal springtime day

Abū Naṣr b. Rawḥān, take it easy
When the flames of war rage in a kindled fire

[Or] when you see a lion of the thicket
A mangler, a slayer and a breaker

A Luhaymī, a Sadūsī responding
To the call of war, a difficult response

In it you will find great misery
You call for humiliation and destruction

O son of my beautiful noblewoman, take it easy
Prepare yourself for the pouncing of a courageous lion

And don't hasten unto us O son of my sister
Horses like falcons will come

On the attack, pointing spear-tips
At war, O nephew of Naṣīr

Upon them thick-necked lions from the tribal chiefs
Energetic like the lions of al-Jafīr

Rushing O Banū Asad unto you
For in you is the goal of exciting death

You thought O Banū Asad, you thought
That we were weak and lowly

You showed hubris when we had not acted unjustly toward you
And we had not rent some of your veils

And men started to contend with us
Men who were unable to do any good or ill

You coveted, O sons of Rawḥān, a death
Like the death of your father, the great shaykh

Tell my noblewoman to cry over you
The cry of those whose lives are cut short

Al-Barrāq responded, saying:

A bad word came to me from Naṣīr
Ill-judged, causing a burning thirst for revenge

Did you not see that your banner is broken?
While our banner is the unbroken one

You called for war with us, so we answered
The caller to war with spears

Squadrons of Wā'il overcame you
With Indian swords, oh what a fate you have

We came to you with them in the morning, scattering our strikes
And we stabbed in orderliness, not scattered

Restraining you, dumbfounding you
The perseverance of charger upon charger

We thrusted our spears since you thrusted yours
By the life of your father, the stabbing was fierce

Naṣīr, in your land you are free
So, we visited on a brightly-lit morning

And we, if and when we attack, will leave you with
Nothing in the incitement of affairs

Naṣīr, from you are fine spears
And swords, what a defender you have

And when you appear in battle, the slender-waisted fling
The young men like falcons

We have been patient, Naṣīr, so come to us
By you we can cure the burning thirst in our chests

Why don't you come, why don't you come to us?
What a blessing there is to my people in marching

I am the son of proud men, one of my ancestors is Nizār
Chiefs of glory and fearsome nobility

Naṣīr frightens me at the midpoint of a day
So, ask after me, were you not in the know?

We protected the absent ones when we were present
And the absent ones were like the present

And how many horses did we meet with horses
We bestowed upon you, when departing at the frontiers

Indeed, you are familiar with us, young man
How does one question a knowledgeable one with sight?

Says Ibn Nāfiʿ: Then Naṣīr gathered the Banū Ṭayy and the Quḍāʿa, and with them he raided the lands of the Rabīʿa, and his horses drew near to the place of a man from the Banū Jusham, and they took camels. The cry was raised, and the tribes of Rabīʿa saddled their horses and raided after the camels. The first to catch up to the people were al-Barrāq and his brothers, and they retrieved the camels from Naṣīr and his people after much killing and wounding. And the squadrons of Wāʾil came like armies of ants, and the cavalries met, and they fought a fierce fight, then they went their separate ways with no clear victor.

Says he: Al-Barrāq, after this incident, longed for the sanctuary of God and so got ready, leaving Kulayb in charge of the Rabīʿa. When Naṣīr b. Shabīb, al-Barrāq's maternal uncle, heard about his departure on pilgrimage and his absence from his people, and when this spread among the tribes of Ṭayy, he met with the dignitaries of his people and they came to him urging him on. They said 'O Naṣīr, seize the opportunity with the houses of Rabīʿa after their knight and their chief has absented himself, for you will not have another chance like it.' He responded, 'What a foul deed! Are you commanding me to backbite al-Barrāq and to go in his absence and commit the worst transgression to his people? He will never hear of that from me!'

Says he: Now al-Barrāq, upon his return from the pilgrimage, was overcome with love for Laylā the Chaste and with longing for her, and he became ill upon the road for her sake. He spent the space of days without sensing that Ṭayy were trying to entice Naṣīr to raid the houses of Rabīʿa. The mother of Naṣīr had started shaming him over the slaying of her son and urging him to make war on the Rabīʿa in the absence of al-Barrāq, and he was refusing that and saying, 'By God, if I were the one who was absent, al-Barrāq wouldn't listen to a word about me, and he wouldn't raid anyone from my people, but you all want only to cloak me in shame. I will hear nothing of it, and I will not go in his absence except to do good.'

Says Ibn Nāfiʿ: The houses of Wāʾil met, and when they heard about Naṣīr's reluctance to backbite their chief al-Barrāq and his refusal to undertake what the people were ordering him to do, they thanked him for that, and they wanted to be disordered and slack until al-Barrāq came back. Some of them consulted with each other about this and resolved to do so. Kulayb warned them against this and prohibited it, but they did not listen.

Says he: Meanwhile, the mother of Naṣīr never stopped trying to entice him to deceive al-Barrāq with his people, and he would not accept. When she saw his determination to go against her, she resorted to women's wiles, and said, 'By God, I will set a trap for him that will lessen his resistance, and he won't be aware of it.' Then she loaded a slave-girl of hers upon a camel, secretly from her son, and said to her, 'advance towards the Rabīʿa, then come, and when you are where the crier can hear you, scream. And don't complain about anything to anyone who meets you until you see your master Naṣīr. And when he asks, "What's wrong?" tell him, "I rode to visit my mistress Karīma and I was met by al-Muhalhil. He made me dismount from my camel and deflowered me" – and the slave-girl was a virgin – 'then he will say, "go and inform your master Naṣīr, and tell him that we will do to his mother what we have done to you and that after today no one of his womenfolk will be safe. For he is too cowardly to make war against us although the Arabs in his people wanted to do so." When your master learns of this, he will feel mortified and attack al-Muhalhil and his brothers and their wounding will be stronger.' As instructed, the slave-girl went and returned, and when she met the people she screamed, and she was soon surrounded. But she did not inform anyone of anything until her master came. Then she recounted the lie and the defamation against al-Muhalhil. Naṣīr grew very angry at this and said, 'If that comes from them, I will ride against them and take their womenfolk captive, and I will commit the most scandalous of acts against them.' That very hour he staged a raid against the Arāqim, and the horses of Ṭayy and Quḍāʿa had gathered around him, and Ṣaram b. Shabīb advanced to the front and said:

> Come, let's get revenge on the family of al-Arqam
> With the slaying of Kulayb, then the slaying of al-Muhalhil
>
> When my eye sees Kulayb I will answer
> His deed with a sharp-edged sword

Says Ibn Nāfiʿ: So Naṣīr advanced with the Ṭayy and the Quḍāʿa and in the morning attacked the Arāqim, the people of Kulayb. They divided their property and took their women captive, and among them was Laylā the Chaste, the girlfriend of al-Barrāq. All this happened as al-Barrāq returned from the pilgrimage. Then the screaming grew loud among the tribes of Rabīʿa, so they saddled up all their horses, tame and untame, and Nuwayra with some horses went after the property and the women, whilst Kulayb was at the back of the horses. Al-Barrāq was too weak to ride due to illness and fatigue, and he hardly ate or drank. When he arrived back with his people, his illness had gotten so bad that he could barely ride. Then he heard the news, and he ordered that his horse be saddled and his war armour brought. He mounted his horse and attacked, saying:

> I will dispel all cares today
> From their capturing in the dawn of the white women of the harem
> Patiently they see my coming
> For I am al-Barrāq atop the black horse
> Today I will return the one with the smiling mouth
> Bright, arranged and orderly
> The daughter of Lukayz, the Wā'ilī, the Arqam

Says he: The steed of al-Barrāq was slack in his reins until he reached the people who had parted after killing and wounding. So, he summoned his people, and they surrounded him. Then he called out, 'O Kulayb, go straight with those from the group who are with you, and I will take those who are with me and go after the property and the womenfolk.' So Kulayb and his men went straight, and al-Barrāq and his brothers and cousins and his whole people attacked on noble horses. Naṣīr was busy with the rear-guard of the horses fighting Kulayb and his men. Then al-Barrāq reached the property and the captives, and with them were four thousand bridles. Nuwayra was busy with them, so al-Barrāq attacked them and killed some of their horsemen, and retrieved the womenfolk of his people and their property and he ordered some men to escort them back to their residences. He charged, setting out for Kulayb and his clan, and the two soldiers agreed to separate, and some cavalry pursued with spears. Al-Barrāq looked, and lo, Lukayz and his in-law Shabīb had dismounted with their swords. And Ṣaram b. Shabīb was nearby waiting to take Lukayz unawares, and his sons were heedless of him. So, he called his brother, and lo, he came and attacked Shabīb and stabbed him and knocked him down dead. Then his brothers surrounded him, and they were al-Jarrāḥ, ʿĀmila and Surʿa. The houses of Rabīʿa stood firm and did not turn back. When al-Barrāq saw the patience of his maternal uncles and their straightness towards the community he took pity on them, and he went aside, stopped his horse, and ordered his clan and the whole of his people to do the same. When Nuwayra saw that, he came to al-Barrāq appealing to him and saying, 'By God, this circumvention and heedlessness to your people and bad advice to them, O Barrāq, is exactly what Kulayb feared. Do you want to side with the chiefs of Ṭayy when they backbit you in your people, and they did not afford you protection, and they had no mercy on us and killed our men and took our property and captured our women?' Al-Barrāq was chidden and felt ashamed by the words of Nuwayra. Meanwhile Naṣīr and those around him persevered for the rest of the day until night fell and then everyone departed. Nuwayra then said:

> My two friends of the Sons of Bakr, may you be rightly-guided!
> Stop and ask the [encampment's] traces about Umm Sālim
>
> We ask them about Nuʿm[16] – where she has alighted
> As well as her tender and beautiful coevals
>
> Kept indoors in the forenoon, from the sons of Taghlib
> Taken captive by distinguished armies
>
> And the Ṭayy met, as did the Quḍāʿa and their
> Allies, atop grand and tall horses
>
> They came in an army with its countless hordes
> They wanted nothing but the destruction of the Arāqim
>
> They emptied in plain sight our property and our women
> And they thought they would get away with these spoils
>
> Their hordes turned back, like the darkness
> Or the downpour of a high-piled cumulous cloud
>
> We inclined toward them in the Wāʾilī way
> With spearheads and whetted swords
>
> The armies from the Rabīʿa came urgently
> And they turned against the Ṭayy with the striking of skulls
>
> Then the Quḍāʿīs fled, fearing perdition
> Flurrying in the desert like the south wind

[16] This would appear to be another name for Umm Sālim.

The despicable men of Ṭayy fled
While the noble and genteel persevered

If al-Barrāq had remained among them, then they would not have stayed
And they would have surrendered, in a war of contemptuous lions

Says Ibn Nāfiʿ: That night Naṣīr attacked a people of the Banū Dhuhl and killed many of their men. From them he took al-Afras b. Mālik b. Samīr captive, and he left, saying:

O daughter of the Bakrī, ask about us and about them
On the morning we met with commingled spears

The morning they turned back, fleeing, and they surrendered
Their womenfolk who were divided among the clans

Did I not attack with spears, charging on a horse?
Kulayb recoiled cowardly from the falling of swords

And I brought Laylā and, along with her coevals she seemed
Like bright white stars

We attacked them, dispersing their hordes
With an army competing for glory

Their horses came to that with a sounding-cry
About young men of courage, like lions from their lairs

The youth al-Barrāq returned the property of a clan
How honourable he is! How daring and how vengeful!

And when death pulled from us and from them
They left, fleeing with their allies, with soldiers

Men from the Banū Ṭayy turned back, then I
Did not fear other clans like them

Kahlān, I made you acquire up close treachery,
The pleasure of enemies and the dislike of the in-law

Indeed, the sons of my sister were content with us
I will thank them sincerely [in deeds not words]

I will pay them back and show my gratitude
To the offspring of good freewomen

The sons of our sister by their virtue were generous with us
They had pity on us and showed us respect

Says he: When Naṣīr arrived back with his people, he released his two prisoners, and he equipped them well, and bestowed upon them themselves. So, they left and when they had traversed part of the road, they came across al-Barrāq, who was out on a raid with his people. That was because al-Barrāq, when it reached him that Naṣīr had attacked a people of the Banū Dhuhl by night, grew extremely angry and said, 'Was it not enough for him to backbite me and attack my people in my absence? Did he have to attack a people of the Banū Dhuhl by night and kill some and take prisoners? Did he not notice when the horses of the Wāʾil had them surrounded, and I took pity on them out of the goodness of my heart and due to the bonds of kinship?'

Says he: Then the two men led him to one of the hamlets of the Ṭayy. Al-Barrāq set out for it with his people, and they killed some of their men and took captives, and they left. When they were on the road, he released his prisoners and said to them, 'I had no desire to do this. It is just that your people did something for which we had to pay them back in kind.' Then al-Barrāq gathered his people and attacked his maternal uncles. He vowed to them not to come face to face with any one of them unexpectedly, and he said, 'I do not do the likes of what Naṣīr did – taking advantage of absences and opportunities.' He was deeply enraged by Naṣīr due to his back-biting of him, and he swore to himself that he would never gain a victory in this way. When he was on the road, he deputised a group from the houses of the Banū ʿIjl, and he put Nuwayra b. Rabīʿa in charge of them, and said to him, 'You be at the rear of the horses, and go slowly and do not hasten. For maybe there will be a change of fortune against us, then you can take care of us, and you'll have an escape route.' Al-Barrāq advanced with the hordes of Rabīʿa, and they were met by the hordes of Ṭayy, and Naṣīr was at their front, and the two groups met and they fought a fierce fight. The cavalry of the Rabīʿa were defeated, so Nuwayra and those with him took care of them, and the war raged on, and the flag of Nuwayra did not miss any of the defeated men of the Rabīʿa. There was a desperate struggle between the two peoples, and they struck each other with swords until minds were bewildered, and it was almost as if man would strike man without knowing whom he was striking, due to the crowdedness and the bold advancing. It kept on like this until the Ṭayy and the Quḍāʿa were defeated. They left their property and their womenfolk, and the Rabīʿa took it all, leaving not a footed animal nor a hoofed one, not a slave nor a slave-girl, and not a woman. They left with them, and when they were on the way, al-Barrāq became ashamed for the womenfolk of his maternal uncles, so he returned them and their property with them, and he said, 'Tell the family of Luhaym that I did not want what happened. I only wanted to pay them back for what they did.' When that reached them, and when their women and property came to them, they thanked him for that, and they acknowledged his virtue, honour, and generosity towards them. Thus, the schism between him and his maternal uncles was cut off. They were reconciled, and they lived like true friends. They sent him a delegation whom he honoured, and he sent them a delegation whom they honoured.

Says Ibn Nāfiʿ: Then al-Barrāq, after people had left and he was by himself, was overtaken by his love for Laylā, and his sorrows were many, such that he stayed at home and hardly went out. He was keeping it to himself, not telling anyone amongst his brothers or friends, with the exception of Kulayb. Kulayb did not like al-Barrāq's absence and visited him at home and found him in a weak state. This was very painful for Kulayb and was too much for him to bear, so he left al-Barrāq's place and went to his paternal uncle Lukayz and said, 'O uncle, why don't you change your mind and marry Laylā to al-Barrāq, for he is worthier of her than others.' Lukayz replied, 'What a terrible thing! Do you accept the gift of a king and promise a marriage to him and then go back on your word?' Lukayz spoke to his nephew with offensive language. So Kulayb said, 'By God, if you do not agree to what al-Barrāq wants and marry him to Laylā, then I will tell him to take what he wants.' Then he came to al-Barrāq and said to him, 'Do you feel like leaving off the opinion of Lukayz and marrying Laylā?' He said, 'O Kulayb, do you divide the king's gift amongst yourselves and have your father and uncle promise his daughter in marriage, and then, because one man among you is against it, go back on your word, after the Arabs have heard about it all? God curse the man who breaks his promises.' Then he sighed and said:

> 'Patience is a virtue' is one of those sayings
> And one of the most difficult to carry out
>
> And though in the morning I am, because of her
> The most miserable of prisoners, shackled in the fetters of love
>
> Yet loyalty to the pact won't be wrung from me
> Until I use my five fingertips as a pillow
>
> What will the tribal chiefs of Muḍar say
> If Rabīʿa is abundant with falsehoods?

Then he said, 'O Kulayb, for Laylā I have no patience or solace, I will not oppose the plan for her, and the Arabs won't hear of such a thing.'

Says he: Al-Barrāq was overwhelmed by love for Laylā, and he swooned much. Kulayb worried about him immensely, so he called al-Barrāq's father and brothers, informed them of the state he found him in, and consulted with them in the matter. The matter weighed heavily upon them, and his father Rawḥān said, 'O my sons, look for something that will fix your brother and protect our honours from shame.' At that al-Barrāq's brother Junayd spoke and said:

> A precious gift is divided among the tribes of Rabīʿa
> And you want someone of sound opinion – what a thought
>
> From it, relations with my brother were severed
> Out of fear of eternal censure
>
> You protect Abū ʿAmr, for you are informed
> And explain what you want to do with Abū l-Naṣr
>
> Abū l-Naṣr is a victory, in him is any assistance
> And any righteousness, and mankind knows that

Then his brother Naṣīr spoke and said:

> May God cover loyalty with shame, and every people
> Wants loyalty unto death

Give camels to Lukayz
He'll pasture them in the valley of thorny trees

He permits their milking and extends a hand
For fighting and striking

If he accepts our advice, then we'll accept
If not, then there'll be a return to troubles

You strive to noble deeds, O family of my people
But what is the use of a sandal when its strap is gone?

Then Gharsān spoke and said:

Every man has his opinion and his advice
And his ordeal is in what he wills and indicates

There is no young man without affairs
The goals of which he still pursues

And if al-Barrāq wants something, then we
Will hasten to what he desires and fly

And if he doesn't want something, then what is there to say after what you have said?
Here he is, a judge amongst you, and a prince

Says he: So Rawḥān turned to Kulayb and said, 'Do not leave al-Barrāq and do not stop visiting him until you see what will happen.' Then they left, and the tribes from Rabīʿa were secure and dispersed in their lands, which were fertile in that year.

Says Ibn Nāfiʿ: A people of the ʿAkk left their land and took up residence with the Banū ʿIjl, and the Rabīʿa were finding no hospitality. They had resided with the Red Muḍar, who made ample room for them and were kind to their neighbours. Among the Banū ʿIjl was a man named al-Ṣalt, and he was a hunter who watched the watering holes. A riding beast belonging to a man from the ʿAkk got loose, so he went after it and came to the well of Bujayra in its wake. Al-Ṣalt was there, watching over the well, waiting for prey to come to water. When the ʿAkkī man came, he startled the game. The ʿIjlī man got angry, shot him with an arrow, and knocked him down dead. Then the ʿAkk came looking for their fellow tribesman and found him dead, and they were informed of what had happened.

So, they left the vicinity of the Banū ʿIjl, and they caught up with their people. They were sixty horsemen, and they helped themselves to camels and took them, and they killed two slaves, and that was at sunset. When the screaming reached the Banū ʿIjl, they said, 'A man for a man', as they were unaware of the second slave and the camels. They saddled up in their wake, and they found places to lie in wait for them. No sooner did the ʿAkk pass by one of these places than the Banū ʿIjl pounced on them and killed one man, then two, then ten. Of the sixty men, only two made it past the ambush. The two of them went to their people and informed them, and the news spread among the tribes of Muḍar. It was hard for them to bear, and they resolved to wage war against the Rabīʿa. Then the chiefs of Muḍar convened a meeting for consultation at the sanctuary of God the exalted. They met there and consulted each other, and it was the general opinion of the Quraysh that they should gather their armies against the Rabīʿa and wage the fiercest of wars against them. Then Nawfal b. ʿAmr al-Qurashī said, 'If you accept my opinion, don't wage a war against the Rabīʿa, so that you reject them and they reject you, but rather send them the message that they must leave our lands.' Ultimately, they agreed with the opinion of Nawfal, whose words held a lot of sway amongst them, and they sent this message to the Rabīʿa. The matter weighed heavily upon them and they said, 'By God, the cutting of bonds is greater than killing.' Then they left the Muḍar and isolated themselves from them and went to their land in the abodes of the Rabīʿa.

Says he: Meanwhile the chiefs of the Wāʾil came to Lukayz and said, 'There's no excuse for you [not] to marry Laylā to al-Barrāq.' When he saw the majority opinion Lukayz went to al-Barrāq and complained about it to him. Al-Barrāq asked, 'What do you want me to do for you?' Lukayz replied, 'Go out to see King ʿAmr b. Dhī Ṣahbān.' Al-Barrāq said to him, 'Get your people ready and those of your sons who agree with you, and I will ride with you until I get you away from the tribes of Rabīʿa.' So Lukayz and his men and al-Barrāq prepared, and they went on their way, and the Rabīʿa vowed to cut off Lukayz forever. Then Lukayz and his people took up residence with Naʿīm b. Mahla al-Azdī, who was at the borders of King ʿAmr. Naʿīm received Lukayz and honoured him.

Says Ibn Nāfiʿ: There was a man from the Anmār called Karīm Son of the Lame who visited the home of Naʿīm b. Mahla one night as he was on his way to the city of Shahrmayh, the king of the Persians. The tribes of Anmār and Iyād were at the borders of King Shahrmayh and in his lands, and he used to call on their services on certain occasions. Now Naʿīm was busy and did not pay much attention to Karīm Son of the Lame, and he and his friends spent the night hungry. When they got up in the morning, they asked Naʿīm what diverted his attention from them. He replied, 'I have a guest from the Rabīʿa', and he told them about Lukayz and his relationship by marriage to King ʿAmr b. Dhī Ṣahbān. And the Anmārī had heard about Laylā and much description of her virtues and beauty. So, he said to himself, 'By God, I could not present the king with a better gift.' Then he saddled up and rode on his riding beast, urging it along until he came to Shahrmayh's city, and then he requested permission from the gatekeeper to see the king. The gatekeeper went to the king and informed him of his presence. Then the king said, 'Show him to the private hall and offer him a drink.' Then he summoned Burd b. Ṭurayḥ al-Iyādī, who was one of his viziers. Burd invited Karīm to speak, and he told him what he wanted to tell them. So Burd asked, 'How do we obtain her?' Karīm replied, 'The king should send a command to ʿAmr to bring her to him.' He said, 'Very good.' Then he went to the king and informed him of this. The king smiled, laughing, and he was wise and clever and liked to look at beautiful women. Then he said, 'As for her, do not make room for suspicions of us in her soul, and if she is not satisfied and rejects it, do not force her.' The king wrote to ʿAmr b. Dhī Ṣahbān about this. He replied, 'I agree and will let go of her, but I do not know if they will agree to marry her to the king or if they, being Arabs, would not like to marry into Persians. But I will do my utmost in this.'

Says he: With this the king renewed the documents about ʿAmr and his engagement to Laylā. Meanwhile Burd b. Ṭurayḥ dispatched, along with Karīm, his two brothers, al-Rabīʿ b. Ṭurayḥ and al-Ḥunaysh b. Ṭurayḥ, and a great army, and he ordered them to conduct Laylā as a bride to the king. If the Rabīʿa refused, they should kill the men, take the women captive, and bring Laylā as a prisoner.

Says he: They marched in haste, and they were watching who was in front of them and who was behind them, lest they be preceded by a spy. When they arrived at Naʿīm al-Azdī's hamlet and took up residence there, ʿAmr b. Dhī Ṣahbān transferred his engagement with Laylā to King Shahrmayh. Lukayz said to him, 'Is it not enough for you that I left my people, and they left me, and that I denied her to the chief of the Arabs, al-Barrāq b. Rawḥān, for your sake, and that I went back on my word and betrothed her to you? You had to go and tell the king of the Persians about her, and you want to marry her to someone who is unsuitable for her. That will not be. As for you, you have my excuse after what you have done. Her engagement to both of you is null and void.' Then ʿAmr started making excuses to him, saying that he had nothing to do with it, but that it was Karīm the Anmārī who told King Shahrmayh about her. Lukayz said, 'We have heard your excuse. You no longer have any rights with us. And as for them, well they are not in the least welcome.' Now when al-Rabīʿ and al-Ḥunaysh heard Lukayz' words, they attacked his house with the army and extracted Laylā. Then Lukayz and his sons and their neighbourly ally Naʿīm b. Mahla and his people mobilised in five hundred horsemen. War broke out, and fighting was fierce. King Shahrmayh's men got the upper hand, and they took property and captured women – among them Laylā the Chaste. Then Lukayz and his sons and Naʿīm and his sons and horsemen from his people attacked, and they killed al-Ḥunaysh and those around him. Khuzayma b. Lukayz was killed, and the Anmārī guide Karīm 'Son of the Lame' was also killed. Lukayz and his son ʿUqayl were wounded. The soldiers left with the property and the captives.

Says he: So, al-Rabīʿ b. Ṭurayḥ came and asked after Laylā, and one of the women led him to her. Then he himself saddled up a noble camel for her and made it kneel close to her. He then helped her onto its back and said, 'By God, I am not content with this. It is a loathsome thing. The reason for this is only Karīm al-Anmārī, and he got what he deserved. How many a digger falls into his hole!' And it became a proverb.[17] As Laylā rode, tears were running down

[17] This is, indeed, a well-known proverb in Arabic. It is also found in the Old Testament (*Proverbs*, 26:27).

her chest. Then al-Rabīʿ released the rest of the women and all of the property and said, 'This is what the king needs.' Then he turned to face Persia and recited:

> Burd called me to sever ties
> And Burd among us is always obeyed
>
> Our reputations were rising
> Today we have become worthless provisions
>
> And the tribes of the family of Ṭayy and Taghlib
> Did not seek refuge from the fight
>
> But we have done the foulest of deeds to Lukayz,
> Who is praiseworthy by nature
>
> And to al-Barrāq and to the headman Kulayb
> Likewise, to Nuwayra the protector of the abodes

Says Ibn Nāfiʿ: Then Lukayz and his son ʿUqayl took their property and their womenfolk and headed for their people. As for al-Rabīʿ b. Ṭurayḥ, when he came near to King Shahrmayh's city, he sent word to his brother congratulating him on his victory and giving him condolences for their brother. Burd then entered upon the king, and said to him, 'I have brought Laylā to your abode, and I have ordered that her needs be seen to. Do you want me to conduct her to you now? Or should I set aside a place in my home so that you can ride to her?' The king responded, 'You tell me something, and I'll tell you that she is not happy and I won't compel her. Let her stay with you. There is no hurry.' Then he ordered a grand gift for him. Then Burd left, and two slaves of the king came with him, carrying the gift. He entered upon his family in his home and said, 'What have you done with the young girl? The king has given me what you see before you out of desire for her. And we will make her even better. Attire her in the best adornments and dress her in the finest of garments so that she comes to him as a beauty.' His wife replied, 'Where did you get this idea? Does the king want to keep in the company of the dead? My God, she refuses to let us lay an eye on her.' At this he grew anxious and said, 'If she wants favour, I will do as she commands me. Otherwise I will torture her severely.' Then he went to her, threatened her, and tried to make her want the king and long for his blessings. When he had spoken much, she sighed and said:

Just wait, you'll get your comeuppance in no time
For what you have done, without delay and without respite

Is there someone to inform al-Barrāq and his brothers
Lions of the thicket, the worthiest of raids with spears

Al-Iyādī, the vilest of people, has acted
And now Barrāq today is distracted by work from me

O Banū Asad, do not forsake Lukayz over me
And rally the Muḍar – have them come in a hurry

Burd asked, angrily, 'Why did you make the vilest of people the Iyādī when you know that I am related to the Shaybān and the Iyād?' She retorted, 'How could that not be?', and she recited:

If you were related to the Shaybān
You would preserve their branches on every tongue

And you would avoid an abominable deed, O brother of abomination
And you would lower your gaze with bashful eyelids

But your obscenity is still there in your courtyard
And you followed the path of Munawwar b. ʿInān

You will be repaid for the foul deeds you have done
By the family of Wāʾil, the repayment of abjection

O family of Barrāq, valiant in battle
And Nuwayra, the loftiest of horsemen

Saddle up your finest horses and come for me
Prepared to fight the competitors

And when you see the divided forelocks
From every brow of a tall horse

In them are the Banū Muḍar and the family of Rabīʿa
To stab every big man, wont to thrust the enemy

Be firm – may I be bereft of you as an associate! And stand up!
To the angry men from Muḍar and ʿAdnān

For lions of war, whose meeting will not fail
Broad-bladed swords passing like fire

Says Ibn Nāfiʿ: Now I heard that Burd listened patiently to all that poetry and took offence at what she said at the end, 'may I be bereft of you as an associate', and he said, 'Woe be upon you, is Burd b. Ṭurayḥ the son of a she-ass? Are not Iyād and Rabīʿa brothers?' She said, 'True. But you, O son of a Persian woman, do not belong to Iyād. If you did, you would not be content to do this action to a respectable woman of the Rabīʿa. Rather, you are an outsider.' This enraged him further, and he ordered that she be shackled and beaten a painful beating. (Meanwhile the king was not aware of any of this.) Burd's wife asked him to have mercy, but he would not show Laylā any. So Burd's wife went to her and said, 'O my sister, in the matter of your honour, you have an excuse. Take my advice. Now is not the time for chastity. That's for when you are with your own men and your own people.' Laylā replied, 'Torture and killing are easier for me to bear than what he asks from me.' Then she wept and said:

If only al-Barrāq had an eye to see
The agony and distress I endure

My brothers, Kulayb, ʿUqayl
Junayd, help me weep

Woe upon you, your sister has been tortured
Awfully morning and night

They fettered me, shackled me, and beat
My chaste surface with a stick

The Persian deceives whenever he approaches me
And I'm on my last breaths of life

Fetter me, shackle me, do
Whatever agony you [all] will to me

For I abhor your outrage
And the bitterness of death has become sweet

Do you lead a horseman to us,
O Banū Anmār, O people of baseness?

O Iyādīs, you are losers
Blindness confounds Burd's view

O Banū al-Aʿyāṣ, are you not cutting
The cords of hope for the Banū ʿAdnān?

Be patient, stand good stead
Every victory is hoped for after hardship

Say to the ʿAdnān, 'May you be shown the way, tuck up
For retribution from the detested clan

Tie banners in their lands,
Unsheathe your swords, and press on in the forenoon'

O Banū Taghlib, press on until victory
Leave off the inertia and slumber

Beware: shame is at your heels, upon you
As long as you linger in lowliness

Says Ibn Nāfiʿ: When the wife of Burd b. Ṭurayḥ heard her poetry, she went back home, and being certain that a protracted war lay ahead, she transmitted the poetry to a slave-girl of hers and said, 'Recite it to your master Khayr b. Ṭurayḥ.' Subsequently, the slave-girl went to him and recited the poetry to him. Khayr said, 'God curse the judgement of my brother Burd. Hasn't he done enough to cover us in shame with his shackling and beating of her? Does one like us lead women of the Rabīʿa into scandal, or refer to them in scandalous terms, or satisfy himself adulterously with them? This is a despicable act, and he shall reap what he has sown. By God, he has caused us war with the Rabīʿa, and he has reminded us and them of what Time helped us and them to forget of the events of al-Ḥajīb, which annihilated the old and turned the young white-haired, and which cleared us of our homes and property and banished us from the lands of our fathers and grandfathers. By God, the valiant ones of Wāʾil will disdain Laylā's imprisonment, and all the tribes from the sons of ʿAdnān will get angry over her.' Then he left and went to King Shahrmayh and requested permission from his gatekeeper to see him. Khayr informed the king of what his brother had done to Laylā, and he recited her poetry to him in Persian. The king blamed Burd greatly and said, 'He was not content with being a stranger, nor did he shun people. We could have done without her and without the march of her people towards us and their making war against us.' Then he ordered Laylā a home and presented it to her and bestowed honours upon her like he had for no one else. He summoned a diviner and asked him what would happen with Laylā. The diviner said, 'The Arabs will come to the land of the Persians because of Laylā, and there will appear continuous stories about it, and there will be much plundering and imprisonment.'

Says Ibn Nāfiʿ: Meanwhile Lukayz, after his daughter was taken captive, went to her suitor ʿAmr b. Dhī Ṣahbān and asked for help, saying, 'You were the only reason she was taken captive and taken to the land of the Persians. Why don't you extend to me what you can of your armies? Or we'll march together. Perhaps we can rescue Laylā without informing my people, without having them rejoice in my despair – what with what I did by leaving them and cutting off ties with them, and my preferring you over them when it came to Laylā until what happened happened.' ʿAmr replied, 'You are right. I was the reason she was taken captive. If it wasn't for my engagement to her, she would not have left her lands or left your people. However, what prevents me from coming to your aid is that I am an agent of the king, and it would not be appropriate for me to take your side. Moreover, if I offered you a small army which could be hidden from the king, it would not be big enough for you to achieve your aim, because this king has armies that are large enough to fill the universe lengthwise and widthwise. Around him are as many Arabs from my people and yours as there are Persian soldiers.' Then he recited:

How many Arabs this side of Persia
Are people good at meeting and advancing to the front

Without the Persians' soldiers and the weapon for which
The heads of mankind stoop proudly

And if I had the power to break the unity of their hordes
Then I would not have reneged on the deal with my in-law

And if there was meekness in the sons of Nizār
While Barrāq the effective man with [his] army got ready for war

And while Nizār's foot-soldiers and cavalry came running
To give the ʿĪṣ a taste of a loathsome beating

Then I will provide from my horses and my youth
Men who see killing as glory and pride

So, tuck up to your uncles the Banū Murra
And call upon their allies in victory

Says he: When he finished his poetry, he said, 'O Lukayz, go to your people and ask them for support. For I think that they will be sympathetic with you, and I know that they will be ashamed of that and will be angry about it for their own sakes not just yours. For Laylā is one of their respected women, and her violation is upon them. If they resolve to come to your assistance, then I'll extend to you what I can in the way of secret men and horses.' Lukayz replied, 'I am not ignorant of this, and I am not someone who needs to be told to go to his people to ask for help. Rather, I sought sufficient help from you given what had happened with me and my separation from my people, and my preference for you over them, and my desire for my daughter to be away from them. Furthermore, I maintained that you had enough zeal that you would help me with your soldiers. Perhaps that way we could have rescued Laylā without my seeking the sympathy of my people, and without my breaking down before them, and without their *schadenfreude*. If not, then they are a blessed people who give generously and who don't fear calamity, and I hope that they sympathise with me and forgive me the error of my ways and help me in my humiliation and fix my brokenness. If I go to them, then I am not in need of any help from you.' Then he rode away, packed up his possessions, got his family ready to go, and set out for his people. He stopped with the Arāqim, just short of al-Barrāq, and sought their sympathy and broke down before them and apologised to them. They sympathised with him, and Kulayb said, 'This is not the time for rebuke nor for apologies. It's just that you lit the fire and others face the heat.' And it became a proverb. The news of Laylā's capture spread amongst the tribes of Rabīʿa and Muḍar, and they felt shame and grew angry, and the zeal of the Jāhiliyya overtook them. Al-Barrāq felt great concern for Laylā, but he kept the extent of his lovesickness hidden.

Says Ibn Nāfiʿ: When ʿĀmir b. Dhu'ayb al-Arqamī saw how Lukayz' face had changed and what he was going through, it upset him, and he went to al-Barrāq and told him about Lukayz' condition. Then he asked him to stand up with the houses of Rabīʿa. So al-Barrāq said, 'I am one of you. If you stab, I stab. If you thrust, I thrust. If you escape, I turn aside. If you go, I go. And if you stand up, I stand up.' When ʿĀmir heard that, he knew that there was a hidden uneasiness, so he said:

Al-Barrāq composed himself with manly vigour
But between the sides of his ribs he has a palpitation

He has a closed eye and a refreshed eye
And a chest which is ample in what comes from him

I swear the Rabīʿa won't rise after him
And that's from the marvellous action of the hero

Then ʿĀmir left, confounded and perplexed. Then Umm al-Agharr came to her brother Kulayb, and she berated him a lot about the matter of Laylā, blaming him and shaming him, and she said:

I see you heedless about the distracting affair
As if you have escaped, unharmed, from its shame

If a man is sitting back from his match
You will not see him on the heights, standing

Go to Laylā, may you not be reviled on account of her shame
The Arāqim have been scandalised in the matter of Laylā

Says he: So Kulayb shut her up and said to her, 'Go easy on the blame, for we feel it enough already. You will see.' At that moment he got up, along with his brothers and their uncle Lukayz and his sons, and they all came to al-Barrāq and said, 'O Abū Naṣr, we have come to you in a matter that has covered us in shame, and riders have spread news of it, and women have spoken of it.' Then Kulayb recited:

To you we have come seeking assistance
Tuck up, and get ready to raid O Abū Naṣr

If you don't revolt, the family of Wā'il will be cursed
And they will be denigrated among mankind for eternity

People follow one alone
If, in him, is the instrument of glory and pride

Call out and the lions of the family of Wāʾil will answer you
O family of Wāʾil, you have no excuse

Al-Barrāq answered him, saying:

Am I anything but one of the Rabīʿa?
I am weak if they are weak, and their pride is my pride

I am strong when they are noble
And I lose completely in their hour of loss

I will grant you what you know of me
I'll tuck up my robe and climb atop my colt

And I'll summon all my paternal cousins and my brothers
To the homeland of war or the ground of battle

Says Ibn Nāfiʿ: When Kulayb heard al-Barrāq's poetry, he knew what kind of hatred was seething inside him because of Laylā, so he said, 'O Abū Naṣr, this is not the place for rebuke or for hatred, but this is the time to rise up and do something, for this is a catastrophe whose shame infects all. By God, the women have spoken about us in their gatherings, and Umm al-Agharr blamed me until my head turned away from her, and I was incapable of responding. What if the Arabs as a whole blame us? Will you not stand up with the Rabīʿa and reveal their shame and take their revenge on the Banū ʿĪṣ and free Laylā from her captivity and torture?' Al-Barrāq answered, 'O Kulayb, this is not hatred from me, nor even disagreement. It's just that I am not hoisted up for leadership, and I am no match for it. But if you see fit to retire me from the leadership of Wāʾil and to set up one of you, and if my brothers and I and my cousins and people are the first to stab and the last to flee, then do that.' He said, 'O Abū l-Naṣr, we have no chief besides you and no leader in your stead. How can you turn us down when we have answered your call to war against the Ṭayy and Quḍāʿa, and you want to forsake us and clothe us in shame amongst the tribes of the Arabs for the sake of a man whose soul has fallen, and whose purpose has gone, and who desired what kings have, until the affair unfolded as it did, and its fire was ignited and we have borne its shame.'

Says he: When al-Barrāq heard Kulayb's words and knew that he had no excuse for that, he was overtaken by the fiery ardour of the Jāhiliyya, and he responded to him, saying, 'O Kulayb, hold your tongues in calling for invasion, and cast off this matter. For this is not like other matters, because this is a great king whose call all the other kings will answer, and his army is numerous, and he is in fortified cities against which invasion is of no use. Nothing will work but siege with all the expenses that that entails and the widening of the war. If he came to us in open space then it would be easier for us than drinking pure water, but the task is next to impossible. Go to the chiefs of the Rabīʿa and their intellects, and call them for consultation. Then let us head for our brothers the Red Muḍar and ask for their help, even if we wronged them and killed some of their men, perhaps they don't hate us, and they would not punish us through the womenfolk of the Banū ʿIjl.' So Kulayb set out at once and called the chiefs and intellects of the Rabīʿa, and they came to him, so he greeted them with the warmest of greetings. Then he said, 'O cousins, you know what has happened with the abduction of Laylā by the Persians and the news of her that the riders have brought. And the Arabs have learned of our daring and our great courage and that we do not fear great troubles. How could we? For we have been covered in shame like pieces of the night when it darkens, and we have been overwhelmed by a humiliation before which it would have been better for us if we died. So, what do you think?' They said, 'O Abū l-Naṣr, we have been covered by what covers you. We are at your service. Tell us what to do.' He said, 'We want to head to our brothers the Red Muḍar making up for the blood feud that cut us off from them and asking for their help in this grave matter for the likes of which nobody can help us but them. What do you think?' They said, 'Yes to what you have indicated.'

Says he: At that a group of their notables set out for the Muḍar, and at their head was ʿĀmir b. Dhuʾayb. They came to the Muḍar, who received them with the utmost generosity, and ʿĀmir said, 'O cousins, you have learned of what Time has painted us with in terms of the noble maiden Laylā's abduction by the Persians. We have come to you seeking that you forgive us the blood that we owe you and asking your assistance in her rescue. It is right that you forgive us what we ask you to forgive and that you help us after our request for assistance. You know that the Rabīʿa and the Muḍar are like right and left, neither is sufficient without the other. You need no excuse to sympathise with us and help us, so that we can be one hand against the Banū al-Aʿyāṣ.'

Says Ibn Nāfiʿ: Nawfal b. ʿAmr al-Qurashī then spoke and said:

Calamity struck my cousins and we were aggrieved
By God, what happened injured us

But what you did yesterday divided us
As if we were not yesterday neighbourly allies

Blame no one but yourselves, O cousins
You started the matter of tyranny

You killed ʿAkk in oppression and unjustly
As if you were not even brothers

We were patient, and patience was our custom
To the friend, even though he was the first to act unjustly

Then he said, 'As for forgiveness, I don't think that the Banū ʿAkk will forget the blood feud. As for assistance and marching, that could be. But I fear that it will bring together the killer and his seeker. For if the ʿAkk see an adversary from the Banū ʿIjl we cannot be sure that a schism won't break out between us irrespective of the Persians, and then the matter will become even more grave. That is our excuse. Tell it to the sensible people among you.' The delegation from the Rabīʿa turned around until they came to al-Barrāq with what Nawfal had said, and they recited his poetry to him. So, al-Barrāq said, 'Perish the wronging of a friend.' And it became a proverb. Then al-Barrāq gathered his people the Banū Wāʾil and their allies together and he started inciting them, saying:

Oh, woe upon you there is nothing left but meeting them
And the fire-brand of war is the one who finds it and comes to it

Do not have aspirations after it in your people the Muḍar
After this, make their clients their masters!

He amongst you who survives in this has
The glory of life, even if its nights are long

And he who dies, dies excused, and he has
The goodness of praise, enduring, though buried in the earth

If you leave the Wā'il to war, O Muḍar
Then you will be met by what has met them

O you traversing rider, crossing
The rugged ground of lands and at times their deserts

Tell the Banū l-ʿĪṣ about us when you reach them
And the tribe of Kahlān that the army seeks a favour

My people must advance and they have struggled
Over difficult elevations without ladders

As for Iyād, they brought with them evil novelties
In what some committed, even if some others were not satisfied

Says he: Then al-Barrāq and those of his people the Rabīʿa who were with him, and those from the Arab tribes who were with him, conducted a morning raid on the city of ʿUrana, and it was among the abodes of the Arabs that bordered on the king. In it was a commander of the king who led seventy thousand men from the Persians as well as a mix of Arabs from the Anmār and the Kahlān. Al-Barrāq raided them with a small cavalry until they left the city. And al-Barrāq's horses were routed and they drove in their wake until they made them go far. Then al-Barrāq charged at them and killed some of them. They were surrounded, so he took them, and he collected as booty everything that was in the city in the way of gold, silver, weapons and all sorts of luxuries. Then he returned, victorious, with the spoils and said:

Have obstacles stood between me and Laylā?
Soldiers, and a wild ground where ostriches graze

Persians, Arabs, and a remote land
Before her a fortress, dwellings and arrows

Lukayz, in his ignorance, made her go away from me
And no one has yet stood in his way in this matter

He has burdened me with what I cannot bear, since
Our noble brothers, the Banū Muḍar the Red are weak

Indeed, I hope for them and I do not despair
And O people, undoubtedly, I have faith in them

O Laylā, my night has been long after our separation
And my tears have run down my cheeks

How could it be otherwise, since you are in a strange territory
And the ignorant hypocritical old man turned you over

May God smite the one who cast suspicions on the young girl
And he who speaks scandalously in the night

For who will tell Burd al-Iyādī and his people
That I will no doubt exact my revenge

Sharp white swords and spears will help me
And I'll be carried by a stallion that outruns the lean and lank

On a riding beast, difficult to mount, for her sake
Making me rise up for actual misfortunes

Says Ibn Nāfiʿ: When al-Barrāq returned from his raid, the Arab chiefs and important people sent him delegations to congratulate him on his victory. And the Arabs praised him in their poetry. So, he gave them gifts and clothed them and asked for hospitality. Nawfal b. ʿAmr al-Qurashī sent him a delegation congratulating him, and there was affection between them, and he stayed with him. Nawfal apologised to al-Barrāq for not having marched with him and for having remained with the tribes of Muḍar, and he mentioned that the reason for that was the blood feud with the Banū ʿIjl and that their getting together with them would cause a schism. Al-Barrāq accepted his excuse and thought his words were on target. Then he sent a message to his maternal uncles the Ṭayy, seeking their assistance against the Persians. They came to him on every tame and untame horse. Al-Barrāq then gave his uncle Naṣīr the most precious gift from among the booty. Note that the Rabīʿa had become the most generous of Arabs due to everything they gained from the spoils of ʿUrana. Then al-Barrāq sent his uncle Naṣīr to watch the Persians and see what kind of preparations they were making. So Naṣīr rode in a group of his people until he came to the city of Karkhā and entered it. There he met King Shahrmayh, whose army had come to him, defeated. The king had sent the soldiers out to the city of Karkhā because it was the key to his lands. Located there were a hundred thousand fighters from Arabs and Persians. The Iyād, the Anmār and the Kahlān were there, and so they welcomed Naṣīr b. ʿAmr, not realising he was the friend of al-Barrāq, and they received him warmly and held him in high esteem. He stayed with them until he knew what they were up to, then he sought permission to leave, so the king granted him excellent provisions for the road. Then he departed, and Burd b. Ṭurayḥ al-Iyādī was with him. Burd asked him, 'Have you seen the armies and soldiers we have in this city?' He replied, 'Yes.' Burd said, 'If al-Barrāq asks you about that, tell him.' Naṣīr responded, 'Al-Barrāq is not unaware of this.' So Naṣīr and his companions went on their way and came to al-Barrāq and informed him of what they knew. Al-Barrāq said, 'We must set out for them, even if their people are like the people of Tubbaʿ.'[18] Then he called for a raid. So, they prepared and he left with them, and with him was his maternal uncle Naṣīr, with all of Ṭayy and Quḍāʿa. Now Nawfal b. ʿAmr al-Qurashī had been staying with him, so they went out together and travelled by night until they reached a place called Mahda, which was full of water. Al-Barrāq said, 'Make us a plan for tomorrow.' They answered, 'The plan is up to you.' Then he said, 'Know, gentlemen, that these people, if they are holed up in this city with its gates closed, they will tire us out from all the waiting. Thus, the plan is to surround them on the right and on the left and then raid them with a small cavalry. When they see them, they will have ambitions on them due to their paucity, and they will exit the city. Then, when fighting breaks out, they will turn towards us fleeing, and they will charge behind them until they are in open space, at which point every tribe will attack them with all they've got. And we'll cut off their rear-guard from what lies next to the city.' They said, 'Yes, that's the plan.' When they got up the next morning al-Barrāq tied some standards and

[18] Tubbaʿ (pl. Tabābiʿa) is the name used to designate a series of Ḥimyarite dynastic leaders who ruled over southwest Arabia from the third to the sixth century, CE. In the popular imagination they became known for their fantastic exploits. See A.F.L. Beeston, 'Tubbaʿ', *EI*².

flags: he gave Nuwayra b. Rabīʿa a standard and put him in charge of Jusham; he gave Kulayb a standard and put him in charge of the family of ʿIkrima and the Arāqim; he tied another standard for ʿĀmir b. Dhuʾayb and put him in charge of the tribes of Taghlib; he gave another standard to his brother Junayd b. Rawḥān and put him at the head of the Banū Shaybān and the tribes of Bakr b. Wāʾil; another went to his maternal uncle Naṣīr, who was put in charge of Ṭayy and Quḍāʿa. They travelled until they came close to the city – and that was at sunrise. Then al-Barrāq ordered Kulayb and ʿĀmir to take their soldiers to the right of the city, and he ordered Junayd and Naṣīr to take theirs to the left. Meanwhile he went forth with his men from the Banū Asad, and the Banū Yashkur, the Banū ʿIjl, and the Banū Ḥanīfa were in the middle. Al-Barrāq was carrying the flag of leadership and dominion. He said to Nuwayra, 'Advance with your men to the gate of the city and kill whomever you see there, and when fighting breaks out between you turn back towards us in defeat, being overrun and deviating, and do not turn back upon them until you reach us.' Nuwayra did as he was told and set out for the gate. There he found soldiers of the king guarding it, so he struck them with swords and arrows. Yelling arose in the city. King Shahrmayh then came out with his soldiers and tribesmen, and they fought a fierce fight. Nuwayra was defeated, so the king set out in his wake with soldiers like armies of ants. At times Nuwayra would return to fight them only to be defeated again. Suspecting that something was up, Burd b. Ṭurayḥ came to the king and said, 'You do not know the fighting of the Arabs. This is a trick from al-Barrāq. Do not go far, and stick close to the gate of the city.' So, the king held back, and Burd attacked with the soldiers behind Nuwayra. Now when the soldiers of the king came out into the open space, every tribe attacked with everything behind it, and al-Barrāq attacked from the centre of the people and Kulayb and Naṣīr cut off the rear-guard of the soldiers, and the fighting was epic. The Rabīʿa killed frightful numbers of Persians and the Anmār and Iyād who were with them until they wanted to concede defeat but were unable to do so. All the while al-Barrāq was looking at Burd b. Ṭurayḥ and not recognising him, and in every attack, he was calling out, 'Where is Burd, the horseman?' Burd would hear him but not show himself out of fear of him. At that point the king and those who were with him attacked and they fought until night fell down between them. Then the king entered the city in a bad state, and the Rabīʿa spent the night with their fires kindling until morning.

Says he: Under the cover of night, al-Barrāq and Zayd b. Dhuʾayb got up and, donning their swords, went in search of news of Laylā. They entered the city, as its gate was always open, day and night, for the sake of the Arab tribes that were around it. They did not see anyone from whom they could find information, so they set out for the pavilion of Jabr, the brother of Burd b. Ṭurayḥ. There they found no one but a Persian on a bed of silk brocade. So Zayd knocked him off the bed, and he cried out. Then Zayd said, 'Be quiet, or I'll slaughter you. But if you shut up, you'll be safe.' He was quiet, and they took him out of his place, and Zayd had him mount his horse behind him, and they left with him and asked him about Laylā, and they said to him, 'Lead us to her and we'll let you go on your way.' He agreed to that. It turned out that this man was one of the king's high commanders. Al-Barrāq suggested, 'Let's return tonight and seek Nawfal's advice.' Then they went back to Nawfal and, with the Persian in their company, they brought him up to speed. He said to them, 'Be present this coming night, as for tonight, it is over.' So, they shoved the Persian at him, and he turned him over to someone who would keep him until the morning.

Says Ibn Nāfiʿ: When they got up, al-Barrāq saddled up from his place and went close to the city, and branches of his armies were on its right and on its left, and in front of it and behind it. No sooner did they come by a footed or hoofed animal of an Anmārī or an Iyādī than they took it, and no sooner did they come by a man than they killed him. Furthermore, they did not get hold of anyone entering or exiting the city without taking what was with him and killing him. This did harm to the tribes of the Arabs and the Persians, so they came out against them and fought a fierce fight. The Rabīʿa killed a horrific number of them – more than before, and they were still fighting when daylight was almost gone. At that moment the brother of the Persian commander appeared and challenged someone to a duel. So Qarīḥ b. ʿAṣar b. Mālik appeared, and the Persian shot him with an arrow and killed him. He did not stop challenging opponents to duels until he killed twenty-five horsemen with twenty-five arrows. Then al-Barrāq pressed his horse forward and urged him on before he shot the Persian and knocked him down dead. He was upright in the field when another foreigner called Harqal appeared to him. They battled for a while, and al-Barrāq forced him off his mount onto his feet, and he put a rope around his neck and took him away until they arrived at Nawfal b. ʿAmr al-Qurashī, and he handed him over to him. Then he returned to the field and challenged someone to a duel. Another foreigner appeared to him, so he took him captive and had him join his countryman. Then he returned to challenging opponents to appear and did not stop until he had killed ten. Then he called for Burd b. Ṭurayḥ to appear and he said, 'Where is Burd al-Iyādī the horseman and captor of Arab girls?' Burd did not answer him, even though he heard him. Al-Barrāq repeated it three times until all the king's army had heard him. Then he called for an attack. They engaged *en masse* in combat, and they fought the fiercest of fights until darkness descended upon them and they parted ways.

Says he: Then al-Barrāq called Zayd b. Dhuʾayb, who had accompanied him the night before, and they took the Persian prisoners and told them that if they helped to render him victorious of Laylā, then he would let them go on their way. Nawfal advised, 'O Barrāq, take some of your people's horsemen with you, for the roads may be blocked to you upon your return.' Al-Barrāq selected a group of them: Kulayb b. Rabīʿa, Nuwayra, ʿUqayl, and his brother Gharsān b. Rawḥān, and they set out into the night with the three prisoners. The gate of the city was open wide enough to let men in without horses or camels. They would keep the gate open like this due to the mixing of the Persian city-dwellers and the surrounding Arab tribes. Now the Persian prisoners led the way until they arrived at the castle where Laylā was kept. The doorman of the castle was Persian, so the prisoners confided to him, 'These Arabs have taken us prisoner and have promised to release us if we lead them to Laylā, and we have assured them that we would. Do you feel like permitting us?' They persisted in ingratiating themselves until he let them in. They entered the castle and extracted Laylā, and ʿUqayl put her behind him on his horse, and they departed and let the prisoners go free. The doorman cried out when they left. So, the young male slaves of the king, with veiled chests and ornate swords, came and blocked the roads and narrowed the paths, and they projected arrows and stones at them and came down upon them with swords. They recaptured Laylā from al-Barrāq and his men, who escaped after an intense struggle and returned to Nawfal and informed him of what happened. He said, 'Did you not kill the doorman and the prisoners after you got hold of Laylā?' They answered, 'The promise we had granted them prevented us from doing that, and we did not think they would break theirs.' He said, 'That's what happened. You were lucky to get out alive.' They spent the night there until morning, then the people cried out and they fought until the evening when the warring parties separated. Then al-Barrāq called his friend Zayd and said, 'Mount your horse. Let's go look for Laylā, perhaps we can gain her back, but she will not be obtained except through a ruse.' Zayd replied, 'You saw what happened to us last night, and the way to her became difficult, and no one agreed to it.' So, al-Barrāq spent the night with high anxiety, and he felt helpless, and said:

> Have you not seen that between us and Laylā
> Is long fighting, a slow-moving army?
>
> The pelting of stones, the shooting of arrows,
> Lions of war blocking the way?
>
> The dread of the mountain pass, the evil of the road,
> And a tall door with its keeper?
>
> If only I had reached Laylā, then
> I would have ridden to her by my resolve on horseback
>
> But she is under the fear of perdition
> And that worry I fear is long

Says he: When they got up in the morning, the people lined up and fought until the evening. The Persians were defeated and there were many wounded and dead among them. They entered the city and closed its gates, and they left heavy items, furniture, pavilions and mules outside the city. The Rabīʿa took every last item. Then

King Shahrmayh asked all the sons of Japheth from all countries to join his army, and he wrote to the king of the Byzantines seeking assistance. Now this king provided him with Byzantine fighters. So Shahrmayh was fortified in his city, and he had become part of an indescribable force. The Rabīʿa were still surrounding the city on all sides, night and day, and not one of the Persians appeared. So the chiefs of the Rabīʿa gathered round al-Barrāq and said, 'O Abū l-Naṣr, the siege has exhausted us, and killing has depleted our numbers, and our horses are weakened, and we see that the Persians have not been depleted by killing, nor have they suffered wounding, and people are adding to their numbers, so what do you think we should do?' He replied, 'Let us return to our lands and ask our people the Muḍar to take pity on us, and we'll increase the size of our force and return.'

Says Ibn Nāfiʿ: After that they set out, returning to the sanctuary of God the exalted with all the booty that they took, and it was an impressive amount, and al-Barrāq said:

With my men I obliterated the sea, draining its waters
But can anyone drain the sea, O men?

The day we met remained a day of a raging sea
On it dust was stirred and there were storms

And there were painful head-cutting sword strikes
And on it the swift horses advanced slowly

Whenever it was said, 'They have fled in defeat'
They would turn back in the blink of an eye

There remained for them a day gathering a whirlwind
At the horizon, from which a standing roof could be built

The handmill of war churned on, turning the young man grey
Terrifying the intelligent

In it necks pronounce the melody of swords
Eloquent-edged, retaliating, agile

War came back, rousing my father's sons
The proud and noble stirring it up

Says he: Now when Thaʿlaba b. al-Aʿraj, Lukayz' in-law, heard of the march of the Wā'il, he cried out to those of his people the Kahlān who answered his call and he set out, raiding, to assist the Rabīʿa. He came, having missed the Rabīʿa who were travelling in the opposite direction on the road, and he staged a morning attack on the city of Karkhā and fought it fiercely with no one fighting back. Then the Persians surrounded him and his men in great numbers, and he was defeated, and he said:

> By my life, my men showed gallantry and fought
> The tribes of Karkhā which rage like the sea
>
> I met all of them on a battle day with my people
> And on that day another people were not meeting
>
> Had my tribe been joined by the tribe of Rabīʿa
> Then we would certainly have vanquished them

Says he: When Thaʿlaba returned home, he sent a message to al-Barrāq, informing him of what happened and of his readiness to help in all of his advances and asking him not to hide anything from him. Al-Barrāq thanked him for that. Meanwhile Laylā, when she learned about her people's retreat and the length of exile imposed upon her, cried vehemently. She called a man from the Anmār, and she gave him a present, and she sent him to her people the Rabīʿa, and she ordered him to ask them to rescue her and to recite her poem rhyming in *ā*. So, the Anmārī went and stopped with the Rabīʿa and informed them of Laylā's sadness and grief, and he recited to them her poem which begins:

> If only al-Barrāq had an eye to see
> The agony and distress I endure

When he came to the end of the poem and the Rabīʿa had heard it, they were choked up with tears. Kulayb said, 'O people, this is not the time for weeping. Get up and let's go to al-Barrāq.' They came to him with the Anmārī, who recited the poem. Al-Barrāq felt ashamed and was overcome by the fiery ardour of the Jāhiliyya, and he said, 'Set out, O Kulayb, you and your brothers and the son of your paternal uncle Lukayz and take with you a group of your people's chiefs as well as the Anmārī the messenger of Laylā and present yourselves to Ṭayy and Muḍar. Seek their compassion, ask them to forgive the blood feud, ask for their assistance in rescuing Laylā, and recite to them her poetry.' They went with the Anmārī, and the first one who was sent to them was Zayd b. Rabāḥ, and they informed him of the situation and recited her poetry. He felt deeply ashamed and said:

Tell the Rabīʿa that I seek vengeance with them
In the clan of Ḍabba the caller of the people is our caller

And if the Rabīʿa respond then they know
That Wā'il are our clients in this

They have the most excellent horses
They kill on the spot, with spears and swords lighting us up

Advancing upon them in every event
Are those who come to the watering holes of death, unconcerned

Tuck up O sons of Qays in your entirety
To stabbing, for you are still wont to thrust the enemy

I forbid the cousins – do not disgrace the Banū Asad
Do not desist and do not spare our enemies

Says he: Zayd got ready to march and said, 'Present yourselves to your brothers the Muḍar, tell them what has happened, seek their compassion, ask them to forgive the blood feud of the Banū ʿAkk, and recite to them this poetry of mine as well as Laylā's poem that she sent with the Anmārī.' So, they went to the Muḍar, sought their compassion and asked them to forgive the blood feud. Then the Anmārī recited Laylā's poem to them, so when he reached her words:

Say to the ʿAdnān, 'May you be shown the way, tuck up
For retribution from the detested clan

Tie banners in their lands,
Unsheathe your swords, and press on in the forenoon'

They felt great shame and they ran to one another. Then al-Naffāʿ b. ʿAwf al-ʿĀmirī got up amongst the Ghaylān[19] and said:

[19] This is probably a corruption of the tribal name ʿAylān.

What's this forsaking of relations, O sons of Ghaylān?
You have broken off Wā'il my people in public

There's no escape from raiding the Persians, so struggle
Matters will change for them

I have no patience after this for the Banū Asad
Proud people who disdain criminality

O people go on your fine horses to the
Iyād, in a dust-cloud

O people, your mother has no mother
The Banū l-ʿĪṣ thought something far-fetched

Wā'il and I are a bone that cannot be cracked
My glory-filled strongholds, my horsemen

Then Ziyād b. Durayd got up and said:

O family of ʿAmr, Banū l-ʿAlyā' of Muḍar
You are a proud house of the family of Nizār

O family of Mudrika, go, all of you
With troops of horsemen and beardless youths and sharp swords

The Banū l-ʿĪṣ thought something which was their undoing
And they will meet it in hardship after ease

And you have learned that victory is your habit
When you get up it follows your tracks

Says Ibn Nāfiʿ: Now the chiefs of the Muḍar had their passions roused by that and they were overtaken by the fiery ardour of the Jāhiliyya, and they resolved to assist their brothers the Rabīʿa, and they forgave them what was between them of blood and revenge, and they made promises to the sanctuary of God the exalted to undertake the task. Then they went to Kulayb and those of the chiefs of the Rabīʿa who were with him, and they said, 'Welcome, O chiefs of the Rabīʿa, you have our assistance and support against your enemy.' They left them delighted, and they promised to attend with al-Barrāq at the sanctuary and to meet there. The tribes of Muḍar met at the place of the Quraysh, and they came before Nawfal b. ʿAmr al-Qurashī, and he sent for al-Barrāq to come meet his people and his clan. Subsequently, al-Barrāq and all of the chiefs of the Rabīʿa came and met with their brothers from the Muḍar, and they took each other's hands and made peace with one another, and Nawfal received them generously and gave them the good news of their support. Then ʿAmr b. Nawfal got up in preparation for leaving, and he ordered his people to get provisions and get ready, and they set a known time for departure. After that they left to tend to their affairs. Al-Barrāq went away with those in his company joyful and delighted, and he recited:

> The one bringing news and advising spoke the truth
> And preparing for travel was savoury for me
>
> Toward the Aʿyāṣ I have a heart in which
> The troops of longing beat and fly
>
> Banū Isḥāq, shame on you, get ready
> Along with those ever around you and advance
>
> To you are the Rabīʿa and their horses, together with
> The Banū Asad and Ghassān the falcons

Says he: And al-Barrāq sent a message to his in-law Thaʿlaba informing him of the advance of the Rabīʿa and the Muḍar and of what they had agreed to, and he sent a message to him, saying:

> Advancing was pleasant and soothing
> Old men agreeing with the young
>
> Today I enjoyed getting ready for war
> Prepare in haste, Banū Shaybān
>
> Those of you who have been supportive of me and advising
> Let them move forward with swords and spears
>
> Prepare for me urgently with an appointment
> From me, from the Muḍar and from Shahdān
>
> O family of Anmār, you will see them
> With dishevelled forelocks, and eyes bulging
>
> Patience, Banū l-Aʿyāṣ, patience, woe unto you
> Do not become impatient for the troops of horsemen

Says Ibn Nāfiʿ: Now when the Persians heard of the agreement between the Rabīʿa and the Muḍar to advance on the city of Karkhā, they grew anxious about this and feared it. The king's two deputies in Karkhā, ʿAmr b. Dhī Ṣahbān and the chief of the Kahlān, wrote to the king informing him of that and asking him whether he could come to them or prepare an army for them and order the two of them to stay behind for him. The king then ordered the two of them and those Arabs and Persians who were with them to stand up in arms. With the two of them were soldiers like the blackness of a dark night, and the Arab and Persian leaders were at the command of King Shahrmayh.

Says he: Then the Banū Iyād and Anmār moved their womenfolk and their possessions from the borders of the Arabs to the borders of the Persians, and they enjoined themselves to them properly out of fear of the Rabīʿa and the Muḍar, due to what had previously occurred with the Rabīʿa's guidance to Laylā bt. Lukayz, who was their sister and their cousin. The Rabīʿa and the Muḍar advanced, and Naṣīr, the maternal uncle of al-Barrāq, advanced with them, as well as his people the Ṭayy and those who were capable of joining the advance. Thaʿlaba, Son of the Lame, met them, saying:

We came and we advanced with swords and spears
The Banū Muḍar the Red and the sons of Wāʾil

With a dusty, boundary-penetrating army, in large numbers
Hosts followed by hosts

Good chiefs of Ghassān, my people, and others
Dust is raised with dust

With it we are intent on Karkhā and those who encamp around it
From the Iyād and the Anmār, the associates

Says he: Now when the Rabīʿa and the Muḍar and those who followed them from the tribes of Ṭayy and Ghassān descended upon the city of Karkhā, they met countless numbers of soldiers from the Persians and Arabs such as the Iyād, the Anmār and the Kahlān. Every tribe came up against another tribe: the Kahlān attacked their maternal uncles the Ṭayy, and the Banū Shaybān came up against the Iyād, the Taghlib the Anmār, the Tamīm the Japheth, and the

Ghaylān and the Mudrika the Persians. Oh, what a day! No day had raised more dust or horrors. The first to be victorious were the Mudrika and the Ghaylān. Then the soldiers of Karkhā turned back and permitted escape. The soldiers of the Rabīʿa and the Muḍar and those who were with them then entered the city. There they came upon booty that was priceless, and captives from among the women of the Arabs and the Persians who could not be valued. Out of a sense of chivalry and respect for the Arabs, they let the Arab women go free, and they kept the Persian women as slaves. As for the soldiers of King Shahrmayh, they withdrew to the city of Idrīja, and they sent a message to the king informing him that al-Barrāq and his people had conquered Karkhā and that they had fled to Idrīja. That horrified him, and he sent commanders from among his friends and he put them in charge of many armies of Persians, and he ordered them to set up in the city with the defeated, not allowing anyone to enter. At that they set out and caught up with their friends. Meanwhile the Rabīʿa and the Muḍar spent a month in Karkhā waiting for those who would pursue them, but they did not see anyone. Indeed, the awesomeness of the Arabs was great in the hearts of the Persians. Now once the Rabīʿa and the Muḍar were relaxed, and when they had rested their horses and camels, they set out for the city of Idrīja, and when they reached it every people came up against its counterpart. The army of the Persians was very numerous and the Rabīʿa and the Muḍar opposed them, and they fought a fierce fight. The Persians acted patiently that day and a great deal of them were killed. They were defeated, and they withdrew to a city called Rughwa in an attempt to preserve it along with the soldiers who were in it. Meanwhile the Rabīʿa and the Muḍar entered the city of Idrīja, and there they came across more booty than they found in the city of Karkhā. There was gold and silver, silk and linen, brocades, musk, amber, camphor, and all manner of precious goods. They stayed there a month, waiting for someone to come after them, but nobody came. So, they set out for the city of Rughwa, taking their booty with them. When they drew near to it, the armies of the Persians and the Byzantines came out against them. So the Rabīʿa and the Muḍar drew lots to see which of the two would fight the Byzantines, for the Byzantines were stronger than the Persians. The arrow was cast with the Muḍar, so they were opposed to the Byzantines and the Rabīʿa were opposed to the Persians. It was a horrific day. And the Persians did not stand firm against the Rabīʿa, so they were defeated and the Byzantines followed in their wake. Then the Arabs entered the city of Rughwa and conquered it. The Persians turned back upon them, so they spent a difficult night and then in the morning, the two groups met and fought a fierce fight. Then the Persians retreated. They had a lot of property that they had holed up in the city, and due to their numerousness, they did not think that they could be challenged, but the Arabs took the spoils.

Says he: Now the soldiers of the king withdrew to the city of Turāba, and they sent the news to King Shahrmayh. He was horrified by that and got very agitated and sent them even more soldiers than he had the first time, and they joined up with their friends in the city of Turāba. Meanwhile the Rabīʿa and the Muḍar spent a month in the city of Rughwa until they had rested their horses and camels. Then they got ready, packed up their spoils and set out looking for the Persians, and they were on the road when suddenly Nawfal b. ʿAmr al-Qurashī fell ill. They stopped and tended to him for some days until he was restored to health and their souls were satisfied. Then they got ready and set out for the city of Turāba, where they were met by soldiers of the king, and they fought against them a fierce fight. Many of them were killed, and the Persians took the spoils out of their hands. But the Arabs were cautious and waged a perfect campaign. Meanwhile the Persians were excessive in their raid and became distant from the city. The two sides fought a fierce fight. Ultimately victory was with the Arabs, and the Persians were defeated. The Rabīʿa and the Muḍar killed a great number of them, and they took their booty back off their hands. The Persians then turned away seeking their master, and the Arabs entered the city of Turāba. The matter weighed greatly on King Shahrmayh, and he feared for himself and that they would enter upon him in the city where he was located. So, he sent messages asking for help to the kings of Byzantium, India and China. Many soldiers from the sons of Japheth and others gathered around him. He ordered the preservation of look-outs and mountain passes, assigning a people to guard each one, and he stationed his soldiers in his city and made them settle there. As for the Arabs, they entered the city of Turāba where they encountered indescribable spoils. They spent some days there, resting, and they sent what their camels would carry to their people and their lands, sending cavalry with them to guard them. They stayed in the city of Turāba waiting for someone to come to them, but no one dared approach them due to the terror they instilled in the chests of the Persians, until the cavalry that they sent came back. Then they got ready to move on from Turāba. They left the spoils there as well as people to look after them, and they set out for the city of the king, looking for a path they could take. But they did not find one because the city was fortified and at every egress there was a look-out or an arrow-thrower. They encamped behind the look-outs, and they spent ten days waiting for someone to come out to them, but nobody did. Then they mobilised, sending the camels out in front. Their horses and their men were in their wake and interpenetrated among them out of caution against the arrows and stones. Indeed, the soldiers met them with stones and arrows, but they did not return them. Then they attacked them and pushed them out of the first look-out until they went out into a wide land where horses grazed. With that the Persians withdrew to the second look-out, and the Rabīʿa and the Muḍar descended into the open space where there was a lot of water and trees. They stayed there ten days waiting for someone to come out against them but nobody came out. News reached the king that the Arabs had assaulted a look-out, and that horrified him, and he feared he would not be safe from them. After that they got mobilised and advanced on the second look-out, sending the camels before them to protect them from arrows and stones. They assaulted the look-out after fighting and a great effort, and then they went out into a wide land in which horses roamed. They fought some more, and the Persians and the Byzantines were defeated, clinging to the third look-out after which was nothing but the gate of the city. So, the Rabīʿa and the Muḍar descended into a fertile land there waiting for someone to come out to them, but nobody came. News reached the king that the Arabs had arrived at the third look-out, and that horrified him, and he was certain of defeat. Then they got up and advanced on the third look-out, sending the camels out in front as was their habit, and when they came to it, they were overtaken by great hardship and horrific fighting. Arrows and stones rained down upon them. The Rabīʿa and the Muḍar patiently endured what no one had endured before such that they did not reach a bit of land until they killed a thousand Persians and crossed all the look-outs, with nothing remaining but the gate to the city. Fighting was desperate by the gate, and voices were raised, and King Shahrmayh came out and participated in the fighting himself. It was a grim day, and there was no more terrifying day than it. Huge numbers of Arabs and Persians were killed. It stayed like that until the sunset, then the two sides went their separate ways without a victor, and each side spent the night stoking its fire.

Says Ibn Nāfiʿ: And when a portion of the night had passed, al-Barrāq got up and put on his armour and said, 'O Nuwayra, bring me the Zayds of this body of troops: Zayd of the Horsemen, Zayd b. Rabāḥ, Zayd b. Mālik al-Asadī, Zayd b. ʿAmr al-Lakhmī, Zayd b. Naṣīr al-Kinānī, Zayd b. ʿAwf al-Sulamī, Zayd b. ʿĀmir al-Dhubyānī, Zayd b. ʿUbayd al-Hudhalī, Zayd b. Ṣahbān al-Dārimī, Zayd b. Muʿawwad al-Yarbūʿī, Zayd b. Muqātil al-ʿIjlī, Zayd b. ʿAzīz al-Ṭāʾī, Zayd b. Jaʿīd al-Ghassānī, Zayd b. Mufliḥ al-Būqī, Zayd b. Salmān al-ʿAdwānī, Zayd b. Mālik al-Muḥāribī, Zayd b. Manṣūr, Zayd b. ʿAbdullāh al-Ashjaʿī, Zayd al-Lakʿī, Zayd b. al-Arqab al-Qurashī, and Zayd b. Wahb al-Thaqafī.' So Nuwayra rushed to fetch them, and they were dispersed throughout his people, and they attended when a certain portion of the night had passed. Al-Barrāq said, 'I called you here O cousins for an important matter.' They replied, 'We are at your service, and you have learned O Abū l-Naṣr that we do not leave family and homeland except for that which will lift the shame from us.' He said, 'You have learned that the goal of this raid in which heroes have been lost and which has brought its ill to the Arabs and the Persians is Laylā the Chaste. And you have learned that she is under the threat of perdition and that she will not be obtained except through finagling and trickery. Will you support me in her quest? Perhaps we will win her back and rescue her alive or dead. It is our reasoning among the tribes of the Arabs.' They answered, 'We are at your service. We hear your command and we do what you ask.' He thanked them for that, and he travelled with them by night to the city, infiltrating the Persian soldiers. No one suspected them, due to the mixing of Arabs and Persians. They were still spying that night in the abodes of the king, looking for Laylā's pavilion, when they came upon a great pavilion, which was surrounded by other pavilions and leathern tents. In them were great numbers of soldiers. So, they took note of them and revolted against them and surrounded them. Al-Barrāq and his companions struck them with swords and blocked off the roads to them after crying arose from every quarter. They kept killing everyone who came before them and defending their adherents until they had exited through the gate of the city after an extensive effort, and they saw that safety was booty for them.

Says he: When morning broke, the people cried out and the soldiers of the king came out against them. They fought until evening and then parted without a victor. This situation persisted for several days in a row; they would fight from morning until evening at the gate of the city. Whenever the Persians saw victory, they would close the gates and throw arrows at them from the high points on the wall. When the fighting raged blindly and the Arabs wanted to leave the city for the open space, the Persians would return to the gate. This was their custom for a while. This situation was detrimental to the Arab tribes. Their horses weakened, killing diminished their numbers, their provisions lessened, and wounding distressed them. Meanwhile the Persians were only increasing in power, and their numbers were not being depleted by killing. So Naṣīr b. ʿAmr al-Ṭāʾī, al-Barrāq's maternal uncle, got up with his people, and Thaʿlaba Son of the Lame got up with his people the Ghassān, and they travelled that night without informing anyone. As for the broad tribes of the Rabīʿa and the Muḍar, they spent the night there until morning, and soldiers spreading like locusts came out against them, and they fought a fierce fight. The banner of the Persians appeared over the Arabs, and there were many casualties among the Rabīʿa and the Muḍar, but they patiently held up their standards and kept their banners until the evening after they had nearly been defeated. When night came down on them the Persians entered the city and closed the gates, and the Arabs returned to their tents.

Says he: Then the chiefs of the Rabīʿa and the Muḍar gathered around al-Barrāq to seek his counsel. They said, 'O Abū al-Naṣr, this situation has been detrimental for us. It has weakened our horses and taken away our men through killing and wounding. Meanwhile the Persians are only increasing in power. You have seen the casualties we suffered after we were almost defeated. And the tribes have broken away from us. No one remains but us, the sons of the two brothers. We fear that we will set a precedent for us whereby we do not reach the beautiful one and we do not submit from defeat and killing. Will you allow us to go to our families and rest, and rest our horses, and get ready to return another time? God decrees matters that be.' Al-Barrāq wept and said, 'How far your chests have closed and you have feared killing! By the Lord of the Kaaba, as for me, I am not returning without freeing her or I will die. As for you, you do what you need to do.' And al-Barrāq had lost his brother Gharsān, so he asked them to stay that night. But they would not agree, and the opinion prevailed that if they entered upon morning and fought, then the Persians would take them. They called out for leaving, and the Rabīʿa and the Muḍar left, with their booty before them. And there were some among them who did not realise that al-Barrāq had stayed behind, and they travelled as comrades. In every place they would spend a night or two, claiming that al-Barrāq could not endure staying there, and that he was catching up with them on the road. Meanwhile al-Barrāq spent the night where he was, and he got up in the morning and took his brother Gharsān and carried him on his horse to the east of the city, and he was covered with wounds. Lo, he came upon a flowing river, and there was a wall of trees and a lofty abode belonging to a man called Ṣuraym and his brothers and their slaves. Then al-Barrāq approached the river and laid down his brother and washed the blood and the dirt off him. He made him a bed from a silk brocade he had with him, and he laid him upon it, and he put a silk robe over him. Then al-Barrāq took off his armour and his clothing, and he started washing and cleansing himself from the rust of coats-of-mail. Then he got dressed and leant over his brother and kissed him between the eyes and said:

My men turned back with spoils and with wealth
Urging on the camels from Ramlān

They called for departure, but I could not bear
Going back when my brother in battles had vanished

And Kulayb turned away after he was certain that I
Would tarry, my hands not pulling at the reins

Likewise, Abū Zayd went on with his booty
Along with Ibn ʿAbbād and the youth Ibn Abān

And Lukayz the shaykh went protecting a raiding party
Whose horses were emaciated, slimming up for the race

Junayd, too, turned back
He would not be angered by Gharsān's [death]

And so Ẓalīl, al-Rasīl and Sālim
They are horsemen and fighters

Muhalhil, when he left, not ignorant of my affairs,
And certain in his knowledge, announced

That I was staying behind with Gharsān
And that I was not approaching the homelands

Do I return to my mother, healthy and prized,
When Gharsān lies slain in an abode of abjection?

Do I leave someone who was ever obedient,
Following what I ordered with every tongue?

My brother, my helper through adversity, my companion
On all my raids at spearpoint

What gets to me most is that Nuwayra turned back
Ignoring what I had done for him the day that he called me

He called me when al-Muhalhil had thrown spears
At the shoulders of the Banū Badr and every Yemeni

And when he called 'O Abū l-Naṣr' I did not recoil cowardly
And I made accurate my lance and the chest of my stallion

I stabbed with the front of the spear the forehead of Mālik
And I sunk my spear in him forthwith

And I threw down ʿAmmār with the strike of a sword
And I tore apart the army roaming hither and thither

Who will convey my message to Kulayb,
Should he not be assisted in what he desires?

Says he: And when al-Barrāq had finished reciting his poetry and weeping for his brother, he raised his knees and put his forehead on them in order to rest from the extreme fatigue. Nearby was a slave-boy of Ṣuraym al-Iyādī. He saw al-Barrāq, but al-Barrāq did not see him. He heard his poetry and it saddened him. And when al-Barrāq lay on his back, the slave-boy approached Gharsān and uncovered his face. He looked at the beauty of his face, and he could not hold back the tears. Al-Barrāq raised his head and said, 'Who is your master, young man?' He said, 'Ṣuraym al-Iyādī, and he is the owner of these residences.' Al-Barrāq said, 'Tell me about Burd b. Ṭurayḥ – where may I find him?' He answered, 'In the city.' 'Is he in your master's circle of acquaintances?', asked al-Barrāq. 'Yes', he replied. Then al-Barrāq sighed and said:

I have cried for Gharsān, and if my eye cries
For the one slain by the Persians, it is only proper

I have cried for one whose sticks produce fire, a young man of war
Quick to the battle when running

Whenever he mounts a strong and fine horse, setting out spears
Throwing down a Bakrī and shaking a Yemeni

He was murdered in an ugly land
In which a young man, like a sword, outstripped any contender

Al-Barrāq had been in a foreign abode
Separated from his brothers and clients

Cleaving to remoteness, thin-bellied, spilling blood
Repeating tears that rouse the weeping women

Who will inform Karīma, his mother, for me,
So that she may mourn Gharsān, and then Barrāq

Tell Kulayb – may he not stay in his dwelling
And may his deeds never be praised or effective

May the fires of the family of Nuwayra never light up
And may he never bear the standard of the people

Indeed, Lukayz is shame-faced
As he sent the beautiful one away and found himself alone

If only Laylā could see me so as to help me
Make seven pilgrimages, yes, or eight

If only Laylā knew and was aware
She would have come, vying with the windstorms

Does Laylā not know this morning that I
Have excessive grief for Gharsān?

Lukayz has cut off the connection that was between us
With raids that turn the forelocks white

Says Ibn Nāfiʿ: Now when the slave-boy had heard al-Barrāq's words he went to his master to tell him about the state of al-Barrāq and to seek his assistance with preparing and burying his brother. So, the slave-boy informed his master, who said, 'Describe him to me.' The slave-boy said, 'He is the chief of the Banū Wāʾil.' The master knew that it was al-Barrāq and he desired to kill him. He gathered his brothers and his slaves and informed them of his intentions, and they agreed to that and they prepared their finest horses. When the slave-boy saw that, he hurried to al-Barrāq and warned him. Al-Barrāq then saddled up his horse, put on his coat of mail, mounted his horse and said:

You inform me now of a frank word
When I had only wanted to rest

And I am the haughty and brave one who
Would pledge proper allegiance to your master

Perhaps through him I could exact our revenge
And I would quench his thirst with a cup overflowing

Says he: While al-Barrāq was waiting for Ṣuraym and his men, he came to him with his seven brothers – and he was the eighth of them – and his slaves, with weapons and on horseback. He then straightened the heads of his spear between the ears of his horse and prepared for an attack. Now Ṣuraym anticipated the trajectory of the spear, so he got down from his horse and undid his sword-strap and gave it to one of his slave-boys, and he proceeded to run on foot. When he approached al-Barrāq, he called out, 'Hey you! Fate has brought you to our space. Welcome. Tell me who you are.' So, al-Barrāq said:

> Ṣuraym frightens me even if around me
> Are the Banū Asad with sharp swords
>
> And the family of Ḥanīfa and the Banū Luhaym
> And Taghlib with fine spears
>
> And indeed Kulayb, woe unto you, on my right
> Yes, and Nuwayra – the lions of confrontation
>
> Al-Ṣuraym was startled by my being alone
> He got his horses ready to meet
>
> Had al-Ṣuraym more resolve
> He would have remained with me tied to the bond
>
> Will fate not bring me close to Burd
> So that I can stab him where his collarbones are joined?
>
> I would cause a cry in his abodes
> His women I would grant a divorce
>
> The divorce of death – what a divorce
> A divorce after which there is no reconciliation

When al-Barrāq finished with his poetry, he said to Ṣuraym, 'What stopped you from doing what you intended?' He said, 'By God, O chief, I came planning to kill you, but when I set eyes on you, that plan disintegrated. Is there in my people the Iyād or anyone else an equal to you? No, indeed. Now I submit to you. Know that you are safe with me, and I will support you in all your endeavours.' Al-Barrāq said:

> He must help me, this young man in the land of the Shaybān
> For I do not count men like women
>
> How many are the women weeping for Laylā among the Banū Asad!
> How many are the women mourning the death of Gharsān!

How I have grieved for him, he was laid to rest in a coarse territory
There, among fleet horses with swords and spears

And the horses were champing at the bit
And the land was projecting a torrent of intensely red blood

That was the watering-place of my ancient fathers who before me
Battled as young men and old

We do not stretch our necks in bed to look at death, nor
Do we like our family or neighbours to be killed

Return, Ṣuraym, as urgently as you came to me
For your concern, O Qurashī, is not the same as mine

I am of Bakr and Ṭayy whereas from us are mixed
Relations from Ṭayy and ʿAdnān

My mother is from Ṭayy if I obtained a right from her and I
Am truly Abū l-Naṣr Barrāq Son of Rawḥān

And Wāʾil are my relations and I want no substitute
For them, and there is no other people on a par with them

Here you are set up in the domain of the Persians
Like an adherent of falsehood and calumny

Burd's crime was committed, if only the nights
Would render me victorious over him even after some time

Bringer of shame to a noble people
And the status of his people is second-class

Says Ibn Nāfiʿ: When Ṣuraym heard al-Barrāq's poetry, he said, 'May God curse Burd's judgement and face. By God the exalted, if you accept my counsel, you will achieve your intention, for Burd is not among your equals.' Then he gave him a pact attesting to the counsel between them. Suddenly, dust was stirred up. It was the horses of the king's soldiers headed to the city of Turāba, where the Rabīʿa and the Muḍar had left some spoils behind, to uncover news and to look for what remained of the spoils. Al-Barrāq asked, 'What are these horses, O Ṣuraym?' He replied, 'I think amongst them are those who are seeking us.' Al-Barrāq said to him, 'Stay here until I come to you with news of the people.' Then al-Barrāq mobilised his horse until he advanced to them, and he stopped to look at them, and they were Arabs and Persians. He asked, 'Where are you going?' They replied, 'We're headed for the city.' He said, 'This side of the city is the striking of swords and the charging of long-bodied horses.' Then he attacked them and defeated them, but he refrained from killing. Therefore, they thought he had come out of the city and that the Arabs had returned to it, and this is what they told the king. Al-Barrāq returned straight away. Ṣuraym renewed the pact and said, 'O Barrāq, rest assured, you have my word that the matter will stay secret.' Al-Barrāq felt reassured. For the Arabs, when they gave their word, did not go back on it. Al-Barrāq got down off his horse and shook his hand, and put his palm in his palm. Then Ṣuraym gave him his condolences on his brother and ordered his slaves to dig a grave for him. While they hurried to get that done, Ṣuraym went to his house and came back with shrouds of the most precious material he had. He shrouded Gharsān and buried him. And they wept for him. Then Ṣuraym took al-Barrāq to his house and seated him in its guest area, and he laid out a dining cloth of silk, and he ordered that food and fruit be served. Then he sat down and ate with al-Barrāq and promised to help him vanquish Burd b. Ṭurayḥ. Al-Barrāq stayed there all day and all night until daybreak, then he went to his brother's grave, and stood over it and wept fiercely and said:

Morning time brings neither greetings nor words
From a youth, buried, who does not respond to 'hello'

O dweller in the grave where I deposited
Auspiciously for your dust, what includes bones

I wonder if you know, O brother, of my exile
Among the Persians, I stay in their wild land for years

I cry for you, when I cry for you, not shamelessly
For a friendship in blame and not in rebuke

And when the iron-clad sport together for a squadron
Ibn Rawḥān is there out front

I have given evidence on him when war attacked
They struggled and they raise standards to him

Junayd fled when I alighted opposite him
Singly I have been satisfied with staying in his two open spaces

The Banū Asad passed, and the Nuwayra left
And Kulayb did not keep his pledges

And the ʿIjl turned back, and Muhalhil left me
There, and they expressed much spite

And the Ḍubayʿa left, Ḥārith among them,
Out of respect for Kulayb or in honour of him

Have you forgotten, my dear friends, the great favours
I bestowed on you in the past?

Am I not equal to Kulayb, their free man?
And Nuwayra came laughing and smiling

I forget my protection of Ḥārith and Muhalhil
And Lukayz, when he recoiled with the Ghaziyya[20]

The Banū Asad b. Bakr succeeded in pressing ahead
After vying for glory and making connections with kinship bonds

For I am a guest, making a home in exile
Remembering neither family nor people

Sufficing me in your stead is the tomb of my brother
Whenever I visit it in the daylight and the darkness

And perhaps I will free Laylā from being confined
Openly and I will kill a tyrannical possessor

I must be patient and endure a long estrangement
Until I obtain my end and aim

I will kill the Persians in their lands
I will forget my maternal and paternal uncles

If I don't show Laylā the sharpness of my resolve
And make the soul of Shahrmayh taste death

And lead an army in these parts
By myself, and send a weaner to the suckling

[20] Ghaziyya is a tribal name. I am not sure that this is what is meant.

Then I am the lowly one, seeking strength in his disgrace
And I clothe myself in blameworthy and disgraceful shame

O Laylā, wail as long as you remain, and rejoice
In victory, wait here and be safe

Hope for a young man, a firmly-made coat-of-mail, and a thin
Slim-bellied horse, and a sharp sword

Says he: As for the Rabīʿa, when they came to their people with their spoils and al-Barrāq was not with them, the women asked them about him. They did not bring any news of him, but they did have news of the killing of Gharsān and all the casualties of the Rabīʿa and the Muḍar. So, the women wailed from every place. Not a single one of them celebrated the safe return of a husband or a son. As for the women of the Banū Asad, they curtained themselves off from their men, blackened their cheeks, tore their chest coverings, cut their hair, and wailed and wept. Then they put everyone who was slain with al-Barrāq out of their minds, and Umm al-Agharr spoke against her brothers and said:

Cry, noble daughter [Karīma], and do not tire of it
For I shall always wail together with you

May our clan not be safe and sound
If the magnificent Ibn Rawḥān is abroad

If you go and you leave behind Abū l-Naṣr
If you are bereft of him, then may the tribe go nowhere

You took the spoils when you left
And the great booty – may you be wretched! – has gone

You left the loyal commander
Behind you – may the guide lead you astray

Tell Nuwayra and Kulayb, easy now
Stay where you are, for your disgrace is long

Umm al-Agharr also said:

The girls of the tribe cry for an individual from Asad
Who had always protected them

Let go self-restraint and lift your veil in broad daylight
Cry for Abū l-Naṣr, not for anyone else

Says Ibn Nāfiʿ: As for al-Barrāq, he lingered with Ṣuraym, planning his affairs and anticipating his surprise attack on King Shahrmayh. While he was thus engaged, a messenger from Burd b. Ṭurayḥ brought something of a present to Ṣuraym. He said, 'Ride, you and your brothers, for the king has sent his son to the city of Karkhā, and his son has summoned me as a vizier, and he has promised to meet me in a place I know at a certain time.' So Ṣuraym got ready to go and said, 'O Barrāq, make yourself at home until I get back.' Al-Barrāq replied, 'I am not staying behind but rather coming with you on a route other than that of the king, and I will support you in your affairs, and maybe you will lead me to Burd, as you promised me that you would do.'

Says he: Now the son of the king headed to the city of Karkhā and found Byzantine soldiers had taken over the city. They had fought before Ṣuraym's arrival, and the army of King Shahrmayh was defeated. When Ṣuraym and al-Barrāq met them, they were defeated. Al-Barrāq said, 'O Ṣuraym, summon an army of your friends for an attack' – for he wanted their support in defeating Burd. Then Ṣuraym summoned his friends, and he and his brothers and al-Barrāq attacked – and all the while al-Barrāq's heart was busy with Burd b. Ṭurayḥ. Then the Byzantine army was defeated and, with al-Barrāq's help, the king's son was victorious. Al-Barrāq kept looking for Burd among the cavalry, and he asked Ṣuraym about him. Ṣuraym pointed him out, and he was himself busy with a Byzantine foreigner. So, al-Barrāq attacked him and asked, 'Are you Burd?' He replied, 'Yes.' Al-Barrāq said, 'Is this how you treat the girls of the Wāʾil, leading the Persians to them and sending your brothers to them, and you beat Laylā and shackle her and force her to do base things?' Burd responded, 'Woe and humiliation unto thee and unto the girls of Wāʾil.' Then al-Barrāq said, 'Thank God who has let me have you', and he attacked him. The two of them battled each other and struck each other. Al-Barrāq got in first with a fatal blow and Burd fell down dead. Al-Barrāq then returned to Ṣuraym with his thirst for revenge quenched.

Says he: Now the king's son, when he had regained Karkhā and defeated the Byzantine army, made Ṣuraym a vizier. He wrote to his father, congratulating him on his victory, sending his condolences to him for Burd, expressing gratitude to Ṣuraym, and informing the king that he had made Ṣuraym a vizier. Ṣuraym thanked al-Barrāq for what he did and held him in the highest esteem, and he said to him, 'O my master, because of you I have become a vizier.' Then he headed home with al-Barrāq and one of his brothers and ordered that al-Barrāq be honoured. So, he returned to the home of Ṣuraym and he stayed there a couple of days. Then he went out to his brother's grave, sat by it, wept fiercely, and said:

Lukayz thwarted my expectation of giving battle
And dashed my hopes and my desires

With his opinion, he granted every tyrant victory over us
And made me bear its weights and misfortunes

Oh, he has made the antelope disappear among enemies
Prolonging my grief and my weeping

If only I, when deprived of meeting her
Put her aside as neither mine nor my burden

I will carry myself in struggling for your release
And ride in a dreaded place that makes the forelocks white

And I'll live in the land of the Persians for a year
Increasing my days there and my nights

Then he stood over the grave of his brother, wept, and said:

That is sorrow upon sorrow with Laylā
An extreme and never-ending anxiety

Who will convey my greetings to Laylā,
From a sincere intimate broken-hearted friend?

And inform her of what I have come across openly
Of torture and fierce sadness

And that I do not sleep and am all alone
How does one with disturbed sleep rest?

Pleasure left me and my sleep became sweet
And Kulayb made me alone like a vagrant

And had al-Nuwayra desired patience
He would have observed the pacts

Rawḥān, my old man, was not patient with me either,
Our understanding was broken by soldiers

Says Ibn Nāfiʿ: Now Ṣuraym's brother transmitted al-Barrāq's poetry and came with him to the household and ordered that he be treated with honour. He went to the wife of Ṣuraym, al-Raqshāʾ, and recited al-Barrāq's poetry to her and informed her of the good things he had done for them and that he was the one who defeated the Byzantine army and made his brother become a vizier. She asked, 'What are you commanding me to do?' He answered, 'Go to the city and figure out how to enter upon Laylā, and tell her where he is and bring news of her.' She said, 'Check it out with al-Barrāq.' Ṣuraym's brother went to al-Barrāq, who said, 'If she is going to do this, bring her to me.' Al-Raqshāʾ then came to al-Barrāq at some point in the night, and she greeted him and said, 'Tell me what you would like me to do.' He replied, 'Give her my regards and inform her of my whereabouts. Then say to her, "Do not be anxious about the great thing you are pushing him to do, for he is not one who fears portentous events, and do not be deceived by the multitude of soldiers, and do not fear the king, for he will kill him when he sees him."'

Says the narrator: Now al-Raqshāʾ went and entered upon the wife of Burd and asked her about Laylā. She said, 'O sister, what do you want with her?' Al-Raqshāʾ replied, 'I want to visit her.' Burd's wife said, 'She is in the remotest abode of the king, and he has put in her service two slave-girls, and he has installed a guard at the door. No one can reach her except with his permission. By God, when I want to visit her or consult with her about something, she does not speak to me except from behind the curtain. When I asked her if I could come to her she apologised. If you would like to visit her behind the curtain, I can get you someone who will take you to her.' Al-Raqshāʾ said, 'Yes.' So Burd's wife sent a slave-girl with her. When al-Raqshāʾ stopped before the guard, he called Laylā's slave-girl and said, 'Seek permission from your mistress for this woman to enter.' The slave-girl asked, 'Who are you?' She replied, 'Someone from her clan.' Now this slave-girl informed Laylā, who said, 'Bring her to the women's place behind the curtain.' So, she brought her. Laylā greeted her and asked her how she was, and, since none of Laylā's slave-girls knew Arabic, al-Raqshā' recited:

> You have my condolences for Gharsān and that is my news
> And we have among us the chief of the two tribes of Muḍar
>
> The soldiers left him there leaning over
> Him and weeping in the darkness and at daybreak
>
> Due to his exile and to cares that will not leave him
> Tears pour down his cheeks like rain
>
> He cannot overcome his grief, my lady
> And he travels neither to the desert people nor the townsfolk

Says Ibn Nāfiʿ: When Laylā heard al-Raqshā', she trembled on the spot; for she was certain of the truth of the news, and she rejoiced in al-Barrāq's presence, and she was saddened by his exile and the loss of Gharsān. Still, she wanted to verify that it was really al-Barrāq, so she said to the woman, 'Describe him to me if you know him.' She responded, 'Despite his youth, he has the dignity of a mature man and the wisdom of a septuagenarian. As for his physical beauty, he is light-bodied, with a balanced stature, broad-shouldered, with prominent forearms, dark-complexioned,[21] with a round face, his cheeks glisten over the top of his beard, black-eyed, with tight curly hair.' Now Laylā recognised his description and said, 'With what did he send you when he knows that there is no way to get to me?' Al-Raqshā' replied, 'He is expecting to save you and has asked for your assistance in that.' Laylā said, 'Give him my regards and tell him to come with you in women's clothing so that I can see him and ask him how he is and give him condolences on his brother, and after that we'll see what happens.' Then she ordered her some food. Al-Raqshā' ate and drank and chatted with Laylā, and when

[21] Literally, this reads 'green of colour' (أخضر اللون), Ahlwardt 9747, 137 v. 'Green' would seem to connote a range of skin-tones from tawny to brown to black. Lane suggests that the phrase 'green of skin' (أخضر الجلدة) means 'of pure race', because this is the complexion associated with the Arabs. See his *Arabic-English Lexicon, kh-ḍ-r*.

she wanted to leave, Laylā recited a poem to her and asked her to recite it to al-Barrāq on her behalf. It was her poem that goes:

I already had enough grief over Gharsān
And now my anxiety and sadness has increased

What is the situation of Barrāq after me and our clan,
And my parents, uncles and brothers?

This side of me, O Barrāq, lies a struggle
Unceasing in its efforts against misfortunes

How can there be entry and how reuniting, oh what a pity
How wrong I was to imagine it was possible now!

When you were mentioned as on your own my sadness was increased
Until I was about to show openly my distress

Longing settled in my heart and I melted
Like lead melts when it is heated on a fire

For if you saw me with my longings turning me over
You would be surprised, Barrāq, by my patience and my holding back

May Kulayb not thrive due to the day he left
Nor my father Lukayz, nor my horses nor my horsemen

Together Wā'il left Ibn Rawḥān
They left the bearer of all the loads and weights

And their Kulayb had turned aside from knowledge
And the flintstone from Zayd b. Rawḥān failed to produce a spark

They handed over the property and people and they took as booty
Their souls, hovering above heads

Until al-Barrāq, their chief, repairs them
Brother of troops, and until the builder scatters the dust

O eye, cry, and pour forth tears and do not
Weary O heart if you have been afflicted with sorrows

For remembering Barrāq, master of the tribe, from Asad
Makes me forget my life without a doubt and myself

Young man of Rabīʿa, circumnavigator of its places
Valiant knight in war and in the racecourse

Says Ibn Nāfiʿ: When al-Raqshāʾ reached al-Barrāq, she recited the verses to him. He moaned for a while then said, 'O Raqshāʾ, I will not visit her in women's clothing. Either I can meet her in the clothing of heroes, or else you will tell her about me and tell me about her. Perhaps, after that, God will create an opportunity.' Then the Byzantines sent an army to Karkhā and they expelled the king's son from there after much killing and wounding. When they arrived in front of the city, Ṣuraym said to the prince, 'Get down, here, let's rest, then we'll lean on them and expel them from here and go back to the way things were.' He then got down, and Ṣuraym sent for al-Barrāq asking for assistance. Then al-Barrāq rode and charged ahead until he met up with Ṣuraym and his men. Now the Byzantine army lined up for them, and the prince lined up his army. Al-Barrāq called for someone to appear, so a Byzantine foreigner appeared to him, and he struck him dead. He again called for someone to appear, so another appeared to him, and he killed him, too. And it went on like this until he had killed eighteen of their fighters. Then he called for an attack, and the Byzantine soldiers were defeated, and a large number of them were killed. King Shahrmayh's son took control of the city of Karkhā, and he praised Ṣuraym, who had ordered that this man be brought. He said, 'O Ṣuraym, who is this man who brought us victory? Perhaps we should compensate him and let him share in the property – for he is deserving of that.' Ṣuraym replied, 'He is a Bedouin man, known only in the desert.' Then the prince received Ṣuraym very warmly, and he made him a vizier and invested authority in him. So Ṣuraym thanked al-Barrāq and praised him and said:

I walk on my feet as long as I remain among mankind
And as long as the vanquishing ancients preceded me

Earthly matters I manage in my hands
My status is high in the castle

I lift a people when I lower another
And I knot the untied and I untie the roped

And that I obtained through Barrāq b. Rawḥān
He with the brilliant teeth, brother of victory

He mended the flocks and the soldiers with his triumph
And they had been certain of terror and humiliation and defeat

And I have never seen an individual fighter like him
He fights an army like a swollen sea

Who will be so good as to tell al-Raqshā᾽ for me,
That I am a vizier of the sovereign lands, having command?

I am greeted with the greetings of kings and I am feared
As if I am the son of Rawḥān, the father of glory and victory

Says Ibn Nāfiʿ: Now word about al-Barrāq spread in the land of the Persians, but they did not know who he was. So, King Shahrmayh sent a message to Ṣuraym and said, 'Tell me, who is this man who led you to victory and who fought with you until the Byzantine army was defeated? Perhaps we can compensate him.' He replied, 'He is a Bedouin man, and I will tell him what you have said, and I will make him desirous of your virtue. If he wants to join with you, he will be one of the pillars of the kingdom, and if he refuses, I will send him a nice reward.' Ṣuraym then got up and went to al-Barrāq and informed him of what the king wanted to do for him, and that he wanted to make him a participant in his kingdom and put him in charge of his army, and he said, 'O Barrāq, would you like to go to the king and acquire power and free your cousin and attain the highest status with him?' Al-Barrāq replied, 'Kings have their virtue, and they are worthy of it, but I will not humble myself before a king, and I will not ask for his favour. By God, were I to humble myself before an old woman, and sit in front of her, and let her command me and forbid me, and let her unfold her tongue – that would be easier for me than humbling myself before a king and asking for his favour! How could I when they killed Gharsān and took Laylā captive? Are you advising me as if I am someone whose soul has fallen and who has lost his manhood? I will not say otherwise as long as I have a sharp sword, a swift horse, a firm heart, and a sincere clan. I want nothing but to keep the pact that is between you and me. As for me, you have my word that I will not retract it with my hands or with my tongue, and if you want that, and you enable me to take revenge and free my cousin, then I will release you from your pact and leave your house.' So Ṣuraym said, 'I hear and I obey. You have my word that as long as you are in my house, I will not betray your secret or reveal your affair.' Then he bade farewell to al-Barrāq and headed as a vizier to Karkhā with the prince, having instructed his brother and his wife al-Raqshāʾ to treat al-Barrāq and his horse with honour, and having emphasised to them that they should keep his affair a secret. Al-Barrāq stayed there a while, and he did not take off his armour, day or night, and he kept his horse saddled, fearing betrayal. One day, while he was like this, his heart welled up and he remembered his sorrow and his brother and said:

Ask my heart about anxiety and upset
And the tears of my eyes about flowing and pouring

When will I get a cure for my illness with
Known flags and men not unarmed?

By them I will quench my thirst for revenge for my brother and by them
I will return Laylā to the people and the property

Perhaps Rawḥān will come with the Banū Asad
Like a lion of the thicket running with cubs

In an army of Muḍar like the blackness of the night
And the tribe of Ghassān, people of high status

And Kulayb will get up with Nuwayra
And ʿĀmir b. Dhu'ayb and Ibn Ḍahhāl

A people, stirrers of the fire of war, riding into battle,
Who in truth desired from the matter every dread

After that, al-Barrāq went early in the morning to his brother's grave and wept. Then he said:

The weeping that we do is not through our eyes
But through Indian blades and spears

For that, Gharsān, is what I want when my hand
Is victorious, for that to me is the ultimate hope

Do you hear my call when I call? And do
You see one standing there like a solitary camel?

I ask the wind about my people when it shudders
And about Kulayb, who turned away and did not ask

Then he returned to his resting place in the dwelling of Ṣuraym. And the brother of Ṣuraym came to al-Raqshā' and ordered her to show great honour to al-Barrāq and his horse. Ṣuraym's brother then sat with al-Barrāq, and al-Raqshā' brought the two of them food. They ate and they spent the night conversing. Then al-Raqshā' went to al-Barrāq with the idea that she would suggest to King Shahrmayh that he go out with Laylā into the desert for a walk. Then, if he went out, she would inform al-Barrāq and set a certain time for him to look out for him on one of his paths. So, al-Barrāq said, 'Let it be.' Then al-Raqshā' went to Laylā and let her in on her plan. They swore each other to secrecy, and the two of them met with the king, trying to persuade him to go out. They did not let up until he agreed, and he set a date for that. When Laylā learned that he would go out with her, she ordered al-Raqshā' to inform al-Barrāq. She did, and he got ready to leave Ṣuraym's dwelling, and he sent a message to Ṣuraym informing him of that, and saying goodbye to him, and releasing him from the pact that was between them. Then, one morning, al-Barrāq was looking out for the departure of the king from the city when he heard a noise coming from the city gate. He knew this meant that the king had gone out, and he hurried to put on his armour and mount his horse. He stopped opposite the road when the first of the soldiers passed by. Then he asked after the king and they pointed the king out to him, as he did not know what he looked like. Then al-Barrāq urged his horse forward, unsheathed his sword, and came down on the king with a firm blow, and his head flew off his body. Now Laylā was behind him on a fine breed, and with her were three slave-girls on mules. Al-Barrāq said to her, 'Urge on your horse, for I have killed the king.' So, she urged her horse on and it lent with her to the side. Now the slaves sensed something was up with their master, but the pre-dawn darkness confused them, and they did not realise al-Barrāq was heading off with Laylā until he had got away from them. Then some soldiers caught up with him, and he leant against them and repelled them one after the other. They returned to the city, and al-Barrāq went away victorious with Laylā and said:

Hey, ask al-Raqshāʾ, for she knows
About the knight al-Barrāq, the destroyer of knights

Yes, and ask Ṣuraym and his people about me
In the morning we met up on the day of the striking of caps

So that al-Raqshāʾ can tell you all about it
Yes, and Ṣuraym, the day the enemies were snubbed

Did my noble soul not attack in war?
And come with the spoils of the stern-faced and iron-clad?

I killed the little king of the Persians amidst his soldiers
And I took Laylā away with a defiant look

And I was alone from the men of Rabīʿa
And their beautiful sister is the most precious of beings

In revenge for Gharsān, my mother's son, I killed the son of Jurhum
And I rescued Laylā from a Persian's bonds

I retreated to depart, praised, having done the best deed
And having achieved the best life, after an onslaught of inauspicious events

Says Ibn Nāfiʿ: Meanwhile the Rabīʿa, after al-Barrāq was slow to return, and after they had heard no news of him, started worrying about him and blaming themselves, and regretting what they did and cursing each other. Umm al-Agharr came to her brother Nuwayra asking after al-Barrāq. He said, 'Since we came, we have had no news of him.' She then shamed him and blamed him violently. Nuwayra then rode to the Arab tribes seeking their help and support and their willingness to set out in search of al-Barrāq. Now the Rabīʿa, Muḍar, Ṭayy, Quḍāʿa, their maternal uncles the family of ʿAmr and Ibn Luhaym, and King Thaʿlaba b. al-Aʿraj all responded to the call and set out to look for him. At the front was Zayd b. Rabāḥ, and he said:

To al-Barrāq we drive our slender horses
And lions preparing swords for a fight

We responded to al-Barrāq with the best response
We drive to him horses like long-bodied arrows

Upon them squadrons of noble people
There, followed in their march by other people

Then they proceeded, each on his camel and leading his horse at his side. Then they came across a man who was afraid of them and who wanted to get out of their way but could not. He said to himself, 'These are the Rabīʿa and the Muḍar out looking for al-Barrāq.' They called him over and he submitted himself to them. They then asked him for news of al-Barrāq, and he told them about him. They took him and advanced with him. Now the news spread among the tribes of Nizār. Good tidings prevailed and banners were unfurled, and they rejoiced greatly. They clothed the man and bestowed him with blessings and went on their way. At the forefront was Zayd b. Rabāḥ. While they were advancing, they ran into al-Barrāq, and Laylā was with him. When they saw him, they got down off their riding beasts and came to him walking on their feet. Al-Barrāq then got down on his feet and met them. They greeted him, gave him condolences for his brother and congratulated him on his victory. They spent the day and night there until his clan and all the clans of the Arabs had encountered him. Now al-Barrāq thanked them, and they returned to their people pleased and delighted. Good tidings were exchanged among the Rabīʿa. Every tribe came to congratulate al-Barrāq and they raised their weapons and slaughtered camels, and they presented tables and foods. Then they married al-Barrāq to Laylā. She was a virgin; neither Arab nor Persian had vanquished her due to her modesty and her chastity. For this reason, she was called 'the Chaste'. Now the tribes of the Arabs stayed with him for seven days, and he would set up tables for them and serve them food and drink. Then each tribe went back to its own land. Al-Barrāq led an easy life in the best of circumstances. There ends the tale of al-Barrāq and Laylā.

3
The Narrative, Its Components and Its 'Novelisation'

> If the term 'novel' itself is far from being unproblematic, the notion of novelization (or, more accurately, novelizing) may provide a more productive point of entry since it foregrounds the dimension of processuality, indicating both change and progression, without prematurely foreclosing debate. It gives room to non-novelistic narrative as well as to the novel itself. The term denotes the processes of making other narratives look like the novel, but also allows such processes to remain open and unfinished.
>
> Mohamed-Salah Omri[1]

Introduction

Once upon a time, perhaps at the tail end of the seventeenth century, a story circulates in manuscript form about an Arab knight-in-shining-armour rescuing a damsel-in-distress from forced marriage to a Persian king. As I have demonstrated in Chapter 1, over the course of a few centuries, this fictional story evolves and proliferates, accruing Christian elements and entering the framework of history at the same time that it comes to be disseminated through the print media and the published book. In the twentieth century it re-enters the fictional realm through its cinematic and novelistic adaptations. It is my purpose here in this chapter to consider the impact of this

[1] Mohamed-Salah Omri, 'Guest Editor's Introduction', *Comparative Critical Studies* 4.3 (2007), 321.

paradigmatic tale on the history of modern Arabic fiction by analysing its structural characteristics at two moments on its evolutionary scale. First and foremost, I am interested in breaking down the version of the tale which appears in transcription and translation here in this monograph, that is the Christian version found in the Berlin manuscripts, which were copied in 1824 and 1854. Secondly, at the end of the chapter, I analyse ʿĀdil al-Ghaḍbān's 1954 novel *Laylā al-ʿafīfa*, with a view towards comparing its self-consciously novelistic structure with the base from which it is adapted.

When breaking down a narrative – any narrative – into its constituent parts, it is useful to draw on the scholarship of Seymour Chatman. He divides the narrative text, first of all, into story (what is told) and discourse (how it is told). He further divides story into events (actions and happenings) and existents (characters and setting).[2] These categories structure my analysis of the *Tale of al-Barrāq Son of Rawḥān and Laylā the Chaste* below. Under the heading 'discourse', I discuss the quality of the narration, the figure of the narrator and his command of the narration. I then move on to discuss setting, characters, and events, in that order. Informing these discussions, and particularly those about character and setting, is the three-pronged typology set forth by Saʿīd Yaqṭīn in his book *Qāl al-rāwī* (Says the Narrator, 1997) of (1) the Historical/Sourced (*al-Marjiʿī*), (2) the Fictional (*al-Takhyīlī*), and (3) the Fantastical (*al-ʿAjāʾibī*).[3] Subsequently, I focus on a leitmotif that permeates the narrative – the theme of chastity. My narratological analysis determines that the tale may be described as a fictional text whose plot has a 'homophonic' texture. I conclude with an assessment of how the story fits into a generic framework. In other words, I ask how the analysis of its constituent parts places the narrative under the rubric of genre. Is the text a rudimentary novel? A popular epic? An ʿUdhrī love tale? Or is it a singular hybrid, constituting a genre of its own? This leads into a comparison of the text with its

[2] Seymour Chatman, *Story and Discourse: Narrative Structure in Fiction and Film* (Ithaca, NY/London: Cornell University Press, 1978), 19.
[3] Saʿīd Yaqṭīn, *Qāl al-rāwī* (Casablanca: al-Markaz al-Thaqāfī al-ʿArabī, 1997).

twentieth-century novelistic adaptation and a discussion of the implications of the existence of this text for our understanding of the history of the Arabic novel.

Part I: Narrative Characteristics

Discourse or How the Story Is Told

The *Tale of al-Barrāq Son of Rawḥān and Laylā the Chaste* may strike the reader who is unfamiliar with certain conventions of pre-modern Arabic literature as peculiar in a number of respects. None perhaps requires as much explanation as the narration. The narration is for the most part third-person, but it is not the third-person omniscient narration to which we are accustomed. There are, if you will, two levels of narration. The interior narrator, a certain Dhuʾayb b. Nāfiʿ, knows most, though not all, of what is going on. His 'I' first appears in the text at the end of the opening section, after he has presented family trees for the tribes of the Rabīʿa and the Muḍar but then admits that his knowledge is imperfect when he says: 'As for Iyād b. Nizār and his sons, they lived in Bahrain and the lands of the Persians, and I do not have their peoples and tribes memorised' (2:38). This is the first of only two occasions where the narrator inserts his first-person voice into the narrative thread. In the second instance, Ibn Nāfiʿ makes himself the receiver of information, and the insertion of his 'I' into the narrative serves to remind us that he was not present at the events and that he is not omniscient:

> *Says Ibn Nāfiʿ*: *Now I heard* [*balaghanī* or 'it reached me'] that Burd listened patiently to all that poetry and took offence at what she said at the end, 'may I be bereft of you as an associate', and he said, 'Woe be upon you, is Burd b. Ṭurayḥ the son of a she-ass? Are not Iyād and Rabīʿa brothers?' (2:106, emphasis mine)

Then there is the exterior narrator, who is unidentified, who periodically narrates the interior narrator's presence with *qāl*, which means 'he said', and which I have translated in inverted fashion as 'says he' and rendered in italics to distinguish those instances of the word 'to say' from those that occur naturally within the inner narration. This exterior narrator we may equate with the voice of our anonymous author. Or else we may equate the interior narrator, Ibn Nāfiʿ, with the author and the exterior narrator who narrates Ibn Nāfiʿ's words with the redactor or copyist. In any case, the diegetic interruptions of *qāl* serve to punctuate the narrative, hence I have made the interjections of 'says he' coincide with paragraph breaks.[4] Curiously, *qāl* is missing from the opening of the narrative, so that when the 'I' admits that he does not know the genealogy of the Iyād, we do not yet know of Ibn Nāfiʿ's existence – we can only read it retrospectively as his 'I'.

Qāl or 'says he' may be thought of as an echo of an *isnād*, or chain of transmission where all but the last figure in the chain is suppressed. An *isnād* introduces a report or *khabar*, an account which relates either first-hand testimony of an individuated event or a memorisable chunk of text attributed to an authority. The ʿUdhrī love narratives that were set in the Umayyad era and that emerged as textual traditions in the ʿAbbāsid era were built upon these reports or *akhbār*, often leading back in their chains of transmission to an anonymous authority or transmitter. Sometimes, separate *isnād*s introduce different versions of the same event or different redactions of the same poem. So, we have in the frequent interpellations of 'says he' a kind of echo or trace of this earlier kind of structure. But here, in the *Tale of al-Barrāq Son of Rawḥān and Laylā the Chaste*, we have a narrative that is presented entirely consecutively, with no two renditions of the same event, and hardly any overlapping events, apart from an occasional deployment of 'meanwhile'.

Setting

The chain of events that constitutes the narrative is not set against a calendar. There are no dates, years, months, or even days of the

[4] Similarly, Thomas Herzog suggests that the 'naming of the narrator' in the popular epic 'occurs at the narrative's intersection points'. See his 'Orality and the Tradition of Arabic Epic Storytelling', in Karl Reichl (ed.), *Medieval Oral Literature* (Berlin/Boston: De Gruyter, 2012), 645.

week. There are times of day, and days accumulate within the context of one event, but apart from that, time is not measured. It is, as I have said in Chapter 1, what Bakhtin calls 'adventure time'.[5] Hence, in terms of time, there is hardly what one might call a setting. The only indicator of a temporal boundary is the recurrence of the phrase 'the fiery ardour of the Jāhiliyya overtook him'. This situates the narrative in a pre-Islamic setting, though it has to be said that the characters, and particularly the noble ones, speak and sometimes behave as Muslims. This includes al-Barrāq who, whilst he is meant to be a Christian, goes on pilgrimage, yearning for the sanctuary (*ḥaram*) of God. At one point he even says 'By the Lord of the Kaaba' (2:132).

Spatially, too, the boundaries are vague. We are told during the presentation of the Arab family tree at the opening of the narrative that 'The Rabīʿa lived in Greater Nejd and the surrounding land, and the Banū Muḍar lived in Mecca, Tihama, Jidda, and adjacent lands in Yemen, like al-Sullān and Daqqa and such' (2:38). Arabia is the primary setting, then, but few place names orient us more specifically in space. We are told of a battle that takes place at Manwar (منور), which is identified in the epic as a valley (2:63). It is not until the field of action transfers to the Persian sphere of influence – that is after the kidnapping of Laylā – that we begin to familiarise ourselves with place names, most notably the names of the cities that sequentially come under Arab attack: ʿUrana (2:114 and 115), Karkhā (2:115 etc.), Idrīja (2:127), Rughwa (2:127–8), and Turāba (2:128–9, 137). At one point on the road, shortly before they arrive at Karkhā, al-Barrāq and a companion come upon a place called Mahda, which is 'full of water' (2:116). Few other place names are mentioned, and the final city, after Turāba, which comes under Arab attack, the city where the king is located, is known simply as the 'city of the king'. ʿUrana (عرنة), we are told, was among 'the abodes of the Arabs that bordered on the [Persian] king' (2:114). Otherwise the narrative makes no attempt to orient us in space. Moreover, the names of the cities, whilst they seem to correspond with real places,

[5] Bakhtin, *Dialogic Imagination*, 4–5.

do not locate us in the borderlands of the Arabs and Persians, even as they are evocative of an Arabo-Persian milieu. Perhaps the city of Karkhā (كرخا), which is the most frequently mentioned place name in the epic, is the one exception to this rule. For Yāqūt lists a place called Karkh Khūzistān, which he identifies as a 'city' (*madīna*) in Khuzestan, adding that 'most of them say Karkha (كرخة)'.[6] Karkhā and Karkha are virtually phonetically indistinguishable. The word *karkh* itself is derived from the Aramaic *karka*, meaning 'fortified city', and it generally precedes a geographic location;[7] hence Karkh Khūzistān.

Karkhā is stable between the various manuscripts and sources of the legend,[8] but the other place names vary tremendously. For example, the city that is called ʿUrana (عرنة) in the base manuscript appears variously as ʿIzba (عزبة),[9] Ghaziyya (غزيّة),[10] and ʿAzya (عزية)[11] in other sources, whereas what is called 'Idrīja' (ادريجة) in most of the sources appears as Adarbayjān (اذربيجان) in the base manuscript.[12] *Muʿjam al-buldān* by Yāqūt (d. 626/1229) identifies places with the same names as the above locations, but they do not help to orient us geographically. ʿUrana, for example, is the interior of a valley across from Mount ʿArafāt; it is also the name of a mosque in the vicinity.[13] Rughwa, we are told, is 'a body of water on Ajā, one of the two mountains of Ṭayy'.[14] Turāba, according to Yāqūt, is a town in Yemen, or the name of a valley.[15] Idrīja is found in Yāqūt, but it is the name of a village in Upper Egypt.[16]

It may very well be that the names of the cities, like the name of the Persian king, Shahrmayh, are a sign that the tale was meant

[6] Yāqūt al-Ḥamawī, *Muʿjam al-buldān* (Beirut: Dār Ṣādir, 1955–57), 4:449.
[7] M. Streck and J. Lassner, 'al-Karkh', *EI*².
[8] In ʿĀdil al-Ghaḍbān's novel it appears as Karkhāʾ with a *hamza* at the end.
[9] 5984 Adab (72).
[10] Arabe 5833 (22r).
[11] Leiden (169r).
[12] Ahlwardt 9747 (127r).
[13] Yāqūt, *Muʿjam al-buldān*, 4:111.
[14] Ibid., 3:54.
[15] Ibid., 2:20.
[16] Ibid., 1:168.

to be received as fiction; the names are conjured up, rather than corresponding to specific locales. One would think that if the tale was meant originally to be understood as or mistaken for history, then its author would have made more of an attempt to be temporally and geographically precise or at least specific. Even Karkhā, which may or may not be identifiable with the location of Karkh Khūzistān, in a sense evokes a typical city, rather than a specific one, because in essence it means 'fortified city'.

Characters

There is little 'character development' – the lead protagonists end the story just exactly as they began it. This is not to say, however, that there is no psychological depth. The characters feel and express emotion. Generally speaking, their emotions are not narrated – instead, the characters emote in verse. Poems need to be read not so much for their language or their imagery but for their participation in a kind of emotional discourse. Each poem represents a position or a point of view. How these points of view build upon and react with one another is part of the narrative fabric. If a classic western novel tends to alternate between scene and summary,[17] or description and narration, we have in our tale, and in many other prosimetrical tales of its ilk, an alternation of prose and poetry, where the prose narrates the exteriority of events and the poetry narrates their interiority; the prose narrates actions in the external world and the poetry narrates thoughts and emotions of the internal mind.

There are a host of characters, good and bad, that populate the story-world of this tale. The male and female protagonists, al-Barrāq and Laylā, it may be said, are 'all good'. They are not complex but idealised character types, who consistently convey their virtues from beginning to end. At the other end of the spectrum, we have Burd al-Iyādī, who is consistently evil. In between we have a variety of characters who are basically noble but who make some

[17] Chatman, *Story and Discourse*, 75. Chatman attributes this observation to scholars such as Percy Lubbock.

unfortunate decisions. These characters are, in a sense, a little more complicated. Lukayz, Laylā's father, is perhaps the most significant and central of these characters; for he is an honourable man who, in an attempt to secure the material well-being of his tribe, promises his daughter's hand to an Arab king, reneging on a previous commitment to marry her to her beloved cousin, al-Barrāq. By the end of the narrative, he understands the failings of his decision, and he regrets it, and in this way, he exhibits a bit of character development. Then there is the semi-complex villain, King Shahrmayh, who is altogether more sympathetic than Burd al-Iyādī, but whose comeuppance at the end of the story is equally gruesome. His character displays depth not in its development, but rather in the conflicting impulses that define his actions.

As for al-Barrāq's characterisation, it is summed up nicely by Ibn Nāfiᶜ, when he says, 'Al-Barrāq was forbearing, generous, brave, dignified, and knowledgeable despite his young age' (2:38). That his moral integrity is matched by physical beauty is not revealed until much later in the narrative, when Laylā asks the wife of Ṣuraym al-Iyādī, al-Raqshāʾ, to describe the figure who claims to be al-Barrāq so that she can make certain that it is indeed him. Al-Raqshāʾ's description reads as follows:

> Despite his youth, he has the dignity of a mature man and the wisdom of a septuagenarian. As for his physical beauty, he is light-bodied, with a balanced stature, broad-shouldered, with prominent forearms, dark-complexioned, with a round face, his cheeks glisten over the top of his beard, [he is] black-eyed, with tight curly hair. (2:144)

The specificity with which al-Raqshāʾ describes al-Barrāq's physical characteristics stands in marked contrast to the narrator's observation about Laylā, in the midst of an enumeration of Lukayz' three daughters. He states, 'She was called Laylā "the chaste", and she was the youngest of them and the one with the prettiest face, and al-Barrāq loved her' (2:38). Laylā's beauty is, in a sense, symbolic, and taken for granted in the narrative, as it is never elaborated in its prose sections. It is only in the verse of al-Barrāq that we begin to get a proper description. He pines for her:

By God, there is no sickness in my body
Nor insanity,[18] and I have committed no sin

Other than loving one with a beautiful face
And soft, dyed fingertips

And luxuriant hair, as black as the night
In imitation of the raven

Whoever sees her says she is a gazelle of a human being
Or a crescent moon whose brightness parts the clouds (2:52)

Laylā's black hair is the most prominent characteristic that appears in this description. Here it is worth pointing out that her name, like her hair, evokes blackness: *Laylā* is a variant of *laylāʾ*, the feminine of *alyal*. A night which is described with this adjective is long and difficult, and most especially, dark.[19] Apart from this quality in her hair and the moon imagery which implies a white face, her appearance is vague and contrasts with the detailed specificity of al-Raqshāʾ's description of al-Barrāq, where we learn that he is curly-haired (*jaʿd al-shaʿr*), black-eyed, dark-complexioned, broad-shouldered, etc. It is worth pointing out here that al-Barrāq is portrayed as a sex object as much as Laylā, if not more so. His physical beauty is emphasised, and when he is described as having a dark ('green')[20] complexion, his noble Arab lineage is evoked. According to E.W. Lane, the phrase *akhḍar al-jilda* (or 'green of skin') means either 'tawny of skin' or 'of pure race' 'because the complexions of the Arabs are tawny'.[21]

Al-Barrāq's nobility leads us perhaps to the ignoble birth of the primary villain Burd al-Iyādī. Burd belongs to the tribe of Iyād, one of the tribes of Bahrain and the land of the Persians whose family

[18] By affirming that he is neither sick nor insane, al-Barrāq is placing himself in direct opposition to the hero of the ʿUdhrī love narrative.
[19] Ibrāhīm Muṣṭafā et al. (eds), *al-Muʿjam al-wasīṭ* (Istanbul: Dār al-Daʿwa, 1989), 850.
[20] Geert Jan van Gelder tells me that *akhḍar* in classical Arabic does not literally mean 'green': it does not coincide precisely with one of the colours we recognise today. It covers a range of dark hues including green but also brown or dark in general.
[21] Lane, *Lexicon*, *kh-ḍ-r*.

tree our narrator has neglected to memorise. On several occasions, the narrator speaks of the 'mixing' of Arabs and Persians in Persian lands and around Persian towns and cities. Here he is talking about interaction, rather than intermarriage. This phenomenon is, in itself, neutral, and it helps al-Barrāq to pass unnoticed into Persian territory on occasion. However, when it comes to 'mixed marriage' and the births resulting from it, we have a clearly negative perspective. That Burd is the son of a Persian woman, according to Laylā, when she confronts him, is the reason that he is not a genuine Arab and the reason he is apt to abuse her, a woman of Rabīʿa. Just before she recites her 'torture poem', Burd asks her if Iyād and Rabīʿa are not brothers. She responds, 'True. But you, O son of a Persian woman, do not belong to Iyād. If you did, you would not be content to do this action to a respectable woman of the Rabīʿa. Rather, you are an outsider' (2:106). As a result of this insult, Burd subjects her to a painful beating and then she recites 'If Only al-Barrāq Could See'. Whilst Laylā explicitly links Burd's depraved behaviour to his mixed background, this is not to say that the narrative condemns all products of mixed marriages as equally reprehensible. Indeed, Burd's brother Khayr, who presumably but not definitively has the same mother, is appalled by Burd's behaviour. When Laylā's torture poem is recited to him, he says:

> 'God curse the judgment of my brother Burd. Hasn't he done enough to cover us in shame with his shackling and beating of her? Does one like us lead women of Rabīʿa into scandal, or refer to them in scandalous terms, or satisfy himself adulterously with them? This is a despicable act, and he shall reap what he has sown.' (2:107)

Burd's behaviour is condemned by nearly every character in the narrative; he is alone in his infamy. Similarly, al-Barrāq is alone in his heroism. Many characters disapprove of Burd, but only al-Barrāq confronts him.

Shahrmayh, as a villain, is much more nuanced. He is not that bad, in nature. The first description the narrator gives of him is pleasant: 'The king smiled, laughing, and he was wise and clever and liked to look at beautiful women' (2:102). He likes the idea of marrying Laylā, when it is suggested to him, but he specifically discards the idea of marrying her against her wishes. He says, 'As for her, do not make room for suspicions of us in her soul, and if she is not satisfied and rejects it, do not force her' (2:102). However, when he learns of the abuse Laylā suffers at Burd's hands – when Burd's brother Khayr recites to him a Persian translation of her torture poem – he makes the wrong decision. He rightly blames Burd. As the narrator tells us: 'The king blamed Burd greatly and said, "He was not content with being a stranger, nor did he shun people. We could have done without her and without the march of her people towards us and their making war against us"' (2:108). But then, instead of freeing Laylā and returning her to her people, he maintains her captivity:

> Then he ordered Laylā a home and presented it to her and bestowed honours upon her like he had for no one else. He summoned a diviner and asked him what would happen with Laylā. The diviner said, 'The Arabs will come to the land of the Persians because of Laylā, and there will appear continuous stories about it, and there will be much plundering and imprisonment.' (2:108)

It is this unforgivable error, perhaps, that leads to his ignominious ending.

Events

The 'actions' and 'happenings' of the tale unfold in one uninterrupted and continuous causal chain: one event leads directly to the next, and there is only one sphere of action at any particular point in the narrative. It should not be inferred from this that the plot is flat or unidimensional. Together the events create the texture of the plot: this texture is composed of events that repeat themselves, on the one hand, and singular events on the other. If one wanted to compare it to a musical texture, one could say that the tale is 'homophonic' – a 'melody' of singular events informing the plot structure is set against a 'drone' of repeated events. In the *Tale of al-Barrāq Son of Rawḥān and Laylā the Chaste*, the drone consists of battle scenes and the melody of the singular events that inform the knight-in-shining-armour rescues damsel-in-distress paradigmatic plotline. While I would not wish to read too much into the implications of the analogy, it should be noted that much of Arabic music, and especially folk-music associated with storytelling genres, is homophonic in texture: a storyteller or *rāwī* recites a tale melodically against the steady pitch of a particular instrument.[22] Here, our steady pitch is the battle scene. This is not to say that nothing singular ever happens in battle – to the contrary – but that the way the battles are narrated is monotonously repetitive. Breaks or ruptures to that repetitive pattern come as a kind of exquisite relief.

Battles

By far the most numerous of the events in the tale are battles. These battles are often precipitated by unplanned killings that then escalate out of control in cycles of blood vengeance. For the first half of the epic these battles are inter-Arab. Then, after Laylā's kidnapping and, more specifically, after her torture poem circulates, the Arabs forget their differences and unite against the common enemy of the Persians. The battle sequences are very formulaic and repetitive. There seem to be two modes of combat: one-on-one battle and collective battle. In one-on-one battle a strong or heroic figure appears (*baraza*) and calls for someone else – often a specific person – to appear (*nādā bi-l-birāz*). Typically, one gets in his thrust first and knocks the other down dead before calling for someone else to appear. Then there are collective skirmishes where enemy soldiers fight each other *en masse*. The recurring phrase here is *wa-ḥamal al-sawād ʿalā al-sawād*, which I have translated as something like 'they engaged in combat *en masse*', but which could be rendered more literally as 'blackness opposed blackness'. In these confrontations, people die in large numbers, whether serially in duels or in mass combat. Battles often start in the early morning

[22] Descriptions of musical performances of popular Arabic narratives may be found in Connelly, *Arab Folk Epic and Identity*, 53–115; and Pierre Cachia, *Popular Narrative Ballads of Modern Egypt* (Oxford: Clarendon Press, 1989), 96–100. See also Edward William Lane, *The Manners and Customs of the Modern Egyptians* (London: J.M. Dent/New York: E.P. Dutton, 1908), 397–431.

and last all day, breaking up when night falls with no clear victor, only to resume the following morning. Collectively, the battles form the backdrop against which the main storyline is set, or to continue with an earlier analogy, the drone that accompanies the line of melody.

Disputation

The 'melody' that overlays the drone consists of disparate types of events. What marks them as melodic is their common opposition to the battle scenes. Whilst most of the 'events' are described in prose, sometimes the action is propelled through the content of verse. This happens fairly early on in the narrative. After King ʿAmr b. Dhī Ṣahbān has asked for his daughter Laylā's hand in marriage, Lukayz summons his sons and asks them to fetch their paternal uncle, Rabīʿa b. Murra, and his sons as well as their maternal uncle, Rawḥān, and his sons, so that he can garner their opinions about the marriage proposal. Lukayz makes the case for the king, saying that he would be a 'shelter' for them 'when confronting great threats' (2:46). Initially, he receives a uniform response from his kinsmen: 'They all looked down at the ground because they knew of al-Barrāq's desire for Laylā, and they knew that he wanted no one else, and they did not want, on his behalf, any other man near her' (2:46). Then, at Lukayz' prompting, each man speaks in turn, giving his perspective on the matter. Whilst they are all opposed to the marriage, there are subtle differences between their stances, voicing varying degrees of opposition and expressing various amounts of anger and frustration. They also put forward different points. One suggests that Lukayz has been unduly influenced by the king's wealth; another emphasises that al-Barrāq, being the bravest of men, is most worthy of Laylā. Finally, Lukayz invites al-Barrāq to speak. On a surface reading, it would appear that al-Barrāq is graciously giving in to his uncle's wishes to marry Laylā off to King ʿAmr b. Dhī Ṣahbān, and this is certainly how the poem is received by the characters in the narrative. But between the lines, one may read a certain warning and a certain disapproval. This posture of ambivalence can be detected principally in two lines that yield dual interpretations. The first is the opening line:

O seeker who is not granted his wishes
Be patient in what you covet (2:48)

Here there is ambiguity of addressee; for one can read the 'seeker' as al-Barrāq, in which case he is counselling himself to be patient after having been denied Laylā, or one can read it as Lukayz, who wishes to obtain the approval of his kinsmen to marry off Laylā but who does not receive this approval. Likewise, in the middle of the poem, al-Barrāq states:

Lukayz, do not go back on your word (2:49)

We may understand the message in one of two ways – al-Barrāq may be referring to Lukayz' promise to King ʿAmr, as the narrative would suggest that it be interpreted, or al-Barrāq may be referring to the understanding that al-Barrāq and Laylā are engaged. One may read the line, in other words, as 'do not betray ʿAmr', or one may read it as 'do not betray me'. Hence al-Barrāq conveys a sense of dissatisfaction at the same time that he tells Lukayz what Lukayz wants to hear. The whole disputation scene lays out the central conflicts of the narrative.

Ibn al-Dhaʿīr Insults Kulayb; Kulayb Exacts Revenge

Another event in the tale where the action is propelled by the poetry occurs in a peculiar and interesting episode involving scatological imagery. After a battle that ends in stalemate, al-Barrāq utters a poem in which he calls a certain Mālik b. al-Dhaʿīr a scoundrel and a coward. Mālik responds with a poly-thematic ode, complete with an erotic prelude, that singles out not al-Barrāq b. Rawḥān but rather Kulayb b. Rabīʿa for a nasty bit of invective:

Did Kulayb not shrink back in fear
Of my spear, loose-hipped, shitting (2:82)

Ibn Nāfiʿ then tells us that 'when Kulayb heard Mālik b. al-Dhaʿīr's poetry and came upon his words "loose-hipped, shitting", he swore not to eat or to drink to satiety until he met Mālik b. al-Dhaʿīr and humiliated him' (2:82). A curious detail in Kulayb's revenge mission is that he asks al-Barrāq if he may borrow his horse al-Shabūb. Al-Shabūb is a filly of noble lineage – 'her father was a sprightly horse of the Quḍāʿa and her mother a horse of the Banū Shaybān' (2:72). Rawḥān had given al-Shabūb as a gift to his son al-Barrāq to reward him for becoming the chief of his people. It may be that the significance of al-Shabūb here is that, as a young thoroughbred, she is a symbol of purity, and Kulayb, whilst he is astride her, could not look more heroic, and less cowardly, and the image of him being fecally incontinent could not be more absurd. Kulayb, when he confronts Mālik, repeats the scatological imagery, saying, 'O Mālik, where is your spear that loosened the hips of Kulayb such that he shat on his saddle?' Kulayb then knocks Mālik off his horse, wraps his turban round his neck and takes him captive (2:82). Kulayb does not kill his captive but rather releases him back to his people with a message of doom. A battle ensues.

Perhaps the significance of the profanity can be related to Bakhtin's theory about the role of laughter in the novel, as a means to undermine epic 'distance'.

> This is the zone of maximally familiar and crude contact; laughter means abuse, and abuse could lead to blows. Basically this is uncrowning, that is, the removal of an object from the distanced plane, the destruction of epic distance, an assault on and destruction of the distanced plane in general. In this plane (the plane of laughter) one can disrespectfully walk around whole objects; therefore, the back and rear portion of an object (and also its innards, not normally accessible for viewing) assume a special importance.[23]

Kulayb, whilst he is ultimately victorious over Ibn al-Dhaʿīr, nevertheless suffers from a diminishment of his persona as a warrior, in a way that al-Barrāq, as an epic hero, never could. The profane epithet of 'shitting' makes him, momentarily at least, more like a novelistic hero than an epic one.

Pilgrimage

At one point al-Barrāq feels longing for the sanctuary of God and goes on pilgrimage. The narrative does not follow him on this pilgrimage – we are merely told of his departure (2:92) and then of his

[23] Bakhtin, *Dialogic Imagination*, 23.

return (2:93–4), when he falls ill, pining after Laylā on the road. Our attention is drawn rather to what takes place in his absence, and the rituals of the pilgrimage itself elude us. Clearly the fact that he goes on pilgrimage is an indicator of his piety, but what is his religion? In the Christian versions of the tale, where we are told that he learned to recite the Gospels from a monk and that he had the same religion as the monk, then it would necessarily follow that he was going on a Christian pilgrimage, but we are not told where the sanctuary of God for a Christian would be. The sanctuary of God, in a Muslim Arab context would be the Kaaba, but this tale is set in pre-Islamic times, so even if we follow the non-Christian version of the tale, it is not logical that he would be going on a Muslim pilgrimage. On the other hand, that he would be going on a pagan pilgrimage to the Kaaba is unthinkable, as he and all of the other characters for that matter consistently speak as monotheists.

False Accusation of Rape against al-Muhalhil

Whilst al-Barrāq is on pilgrimage, the people around his maternal uncle Naṣīr b. Shabīb try to persuade him to take advantage of his nephew's absence and to attack the Rabīʿa. Naṣīr refuses as he finds such an act dishonourable. So Naṣīr's mother, who is quite keen for Naṣīr to take revenge on them, resorts to her feminine wiles and persuades a slave-girl to accuse al-Muhalhil of rape. The slave-girl, it is specified, is a virgin (2:93). The ruse works, as this proves to be incentive enough for Naṣīr to attack the Arāqim. It may be that the purpose of this event in the narrative, in addition to creating a pretext for the attack on the Rabīʿa in al-Barrāq's absence, is to show up the vulnerability of al-Muhalhil, like Kulayb before him, to having his reputation besmirched. This vulnerability of the two warriors in the narrative whose military prowess rivals al-Barrāq's own, stands in opposition to al-Barrāq's invulnerability.

Kidnapping and Torture

Laylā is taken captive after Lukayz rejects King ʿAmr's proposal to transfer Laylā's engagement to King Shahrmayh. The circumstances of her captivity are not described – we are told only of a battle between Lukayz and his men and the army of Shahrmayh, led by Burd b. Ṭurayḥ's brothers, al-Rabīʿ and al-Ḥunaysh, in which the latter get the upper hand (2:103). Similarly, her detention once they arrive in Persian lands is not the subject of detail in the narrative. All we know is that she is being held, initially, at the home of Burd, and that he is mistreating her. Description and detail of her suffering come rather in the 'If Only al-Barrāq Could See' poem and especially in line 4, where she states:

غلّلوني قيّدوني ضَرَبوا
مَلمس العِفّة مِنّي بالعَصا

> They fettered me, shackled me, and beat
> My chaste surface with a stick (2:106)

The word *malmas*, which I have translated as 'surface', is a noun of place derived from the verb *lamasa* which means 'to touch'; hence 'touching place' would be a more literal translation. 'Touching place of chastity (*al-ʿiffa*)', whilst it could refer to the body in general or any part thereof, would seem to have been understood by Cheikho as the groin area.[24] So they are fettering her, shackling her, and (potentially) beating her groin with a stick. The image of sexual violation is very strong. Indeed, if the narrative did not tell us explicitly that she was a virgin at its end, one would think she had been raped.

From then on, the poem is frequently recited by characters in the narrative. Sometimes it is quoted and sometimes we are merely told about the fact of its recitation. The wife of Burd transmits it to a slave-girl. The slave-girl in turn transmits it to Burd's brother, Khayr b. Ṭurayḥ (2:107). Khayr then recites it, in Persian, to King Shahrmayh (2:107). Then an Anmārī man, sent by Laylā, recites it to the Rabīʿa, and its first line is quoted in the text (2:122). Then the same Anmārī recites it to al-Barrāq (2:122). Then al-Barrāq sends Kulayb and his men and the Anmārī to recite it to the Ṭayy and

[24] See Chapter 1, note 51. Other authors also seem to interpret the 'place of chastity' as the groin. Muḥammad ʿAbd al-Wāḥid Ḥijāzī, in his biographical dictionary of women poets, where he renders the phrase as *mawḍiʿ al-ʿiffa*, rather than *malmas al-ʿiffa*, states: 'In our view, there is nothing uglier or more likely to incite rage than hitting someone on this part of his body.' See his *Nisāʾ shāʿirāt: Dirāsa fī shiʿr al-marʾa al-ʿArabiyya* (Cairo: Maktabat Jazīrat al-Ward, 2010), 88.

Muḍar, whereupon they recite it first to Zayd b. Rabāḥ (2:123) and then to the Muḍar (2:123), where a couple of lines of the poem are quoted. In each case, the poem shames the listener and causes him to take action.

Zayd Raid

In what is perhaps the most fantastical event of the narrative, unlikely and unexplained if still, in some sense, plausible, al-Barrāq decides to conduct a raid into enemy territory – the unnamed city of the king – with everyone he knows named 'Zayd'. He asks his friend Nuwayra to summon no less than twenty-one Zayds:

> *Says Ibn Nāfiʿ*: And when a portion of the night had passed al-Barrāq got up and put on his armour and said, 'O Nuwayra, bring me the Zayds of this body of troops: Zayd of the Horsemen, Zayd b. Rabāḥ, Zayd b. Mālik al-Asadī, Zayd b. ʿAmr al-Lakhmī, Zayd b. Naṣīr al-Kinānī, Zayd b. ʿAwf al-Sulamī, Zayd b. ʿĀmir al-Dhubyānī, Zayd b. ʿUbayd al-Hudhalī, Zayd b. Ṣahbān al-Dārimī, Zayd b. Muʿawwad al-Yarbūʿī, Zayd b. Muqātil al-ʿIjlī, Zayd b. ʿAzīz al-Ṭāʾī, Zayd b. Jaʿīd al-Ghassānī, Zayd b. Mufliḥ al-Būqī, Zayd b. Salmān al-ʿAdwānī, Zayd b. Mālik al-Muḥāribī, Zayd b. Manṣūr, Zayd b. ʿAbdullāh al-Ashjaʿī, Zayd al-Lakʿī, Zayd b. al-Arqab al-Qurashī, and Zayd b. Wahb al-Thaqafī.' (2:130)

The Zayds' names – or nineteen of them in any case – reveal their tribal origins. The *nisba* adjective at the end of each name is derived from the individual Zayd's tribe. Hence Zayd b. ʿUbayd al-Hudhalī hails from the Banū Hudhayl, Zayd b. Mālik al-Asadī comes from the Banū Asad, and Zayd b. al-Arqab al-Qurashī originates from the Banū Quraysh. Their names thus display the great panoply of tribal allegiances that have rallied around the cause of rescuing Laylā. Al-Barrāq and the Zayds infiltrate the city of the king – due to the mixing of Persians and Arabs there – and they locate her pavilion before becoming embroiled in a fight with Shahrmayh's soldiers and then retreating from the city.

This episode of the Zayd raid clearly demonstrates that representatives of various tribal groupings are uniting against a common enemy, but what is the significance of their shared first name? The only explanation I can find is that the name 'Zayd' traditionally serves as a prototypical exemplar in Arabic grammars. Thus, there is a sense in which it represents 'everyone' or 'anyone' like the phrases 'Tom, Dick, and Harry' or 'Joe Schmo' and yet with two further layers of meaning that connote Arabness, on the one hand, and didacticism, on the other. The eighth-century grammarian Sībawayhi used three names as placeholders: Zayd, ʿAmr, and ʿAbdullāh, claiming that these were the most common Arab men's names.[25] Together, these two further layers of meaning ensure that al-Barrāq's summoning of the Zayds or 'Zuyūd' – and it's not every name that has a recognisable broken plural – is received as a lesson on Arab identity and purpose.

Burial of Gharsān

Gharsān is not the first brother of al-Barrāq to die in the course of the narrative; his brother Ẓalīl b. Rawḥān dies from a stab wound, apparently inflicted by one of his maternal uncles (2:84), and al-Barrāq elegises him (2:88–89). But it is the death of Gharsān which highlights al-Barrāq's humanity and the strength of his brotherly affection. Curiously, we are not told of the circumstances of Gharsān's death. It is merely revealed, after the lengthy and costly Arab siege of the city of the king, and after the Arab soldiers come to al-Barrāq and ask him if they might not be able to go home, rest and regroup, that 'al-Barrāq had lost his brother Gharsān, so he asked them to stay that night' (2:132). The Arab soldiers do not stay the night, and they leave al-Barrāq on his own to look after his brother. Al-Barrāq is carrying the body of Gharsān around with him on his horse when he sees a flowing river. Then we have the following description of al-Barrāq's treatment of his brother's corpse:

> Then al-Barrāq approached the river and laid down his brother and washed the blood and the dirt off him. He made him a bed from a silk brocade he had with him, and he laid him upon it, and he put a

[25] Amal E. Marogy, 'Zayd, ʿAmr and ʿAbdullāhi: Theory of Proper Names and Reference in Early Arabic Grammatical Tradition', in Amal Elesha Marogy (ed.), *Foundations of Arabic Linguistics: Sībawayhi and Early Arabic Grammatical Theory* (Leiden/Boston: Brill, 2012), 119 and 129.

> silk robe over him. Then al-Barrāq took off his armour and his clothing, and he started washing and cleansing himself from the rust of coats-of-mail. Then he got dressed and leant over his brother and kissed him between the eyes . . . (2:132)

Al-Barrāq then recites an elegy, and the slave-boy of a certain Ṣuraym al-Iyādī overhears him. He approaches Gharsān and uncovers his face. Then, we are told, the slave-boy is so moved by the beauty of his face that he bursts into tears (2:134). The episode serves to highlight al-Barrāq's gentle and caring nature. It also celebrates the masculine as beautiful; for Gharsān, like Laylā, is said to have a beautiful face.

Deaths of the Villains

The tale's two principal villains each come to an ignominious end, but whereas Burd b. Ṭurayḥ has what is, within the framework of the narrative, an ordinary death, King Shahrmayh experiences an extraordinary one. That is to say that Burd dies in a one-on-one confrontation with al-Barrāq during the course of a battle, whilst King Shahrmayh is 'tricked' into taking an outing and then ambushed by al-Barrāq.

The city of Karkhā, where the Arabs defeated the Persians, has now been taken over by the Byzantines, and the Persians are attempting to wrest it back. In an effort to locate Burd, al-Barrāq decides to fight alongside Ṣuraym al-Iyādī and the Persians to gain back control of the city of Karkhā. Al-Barrāq fights valiantly and secures success for the Persians. But throughout the battle he is aiming to identify Burd and slay him:

> Al-Barrāq kept looking for Burd among the cavalry, and he asked Ṣuraym about him. Ṣuraym pointed him out, and he was himself busy with a Byzantine foreigner. So, al-Barrāq attacked him and asked, 'Are you Burd?' He replied, 'Yes.' Al-Barrāq said, 'Is this how you treat the girls of the Wā'il, leading the Persians to them and sending your brothers to them, and you beat Laylā and shackle her and force her to do base things?' Burd responded, 'Woe and humiliation unto thee and unto the girls of Wā'il.' Then al-Barrāq said, 'Thank God who has let me have you', and he attacked him. The two of them battled each other and struck each other. Al-Barrāq got in first with

> a fatal blow and Burd fell down dead. Al-Barrāq then returned to Ṣuraym with his thirst for revenge quenched. (2:141)

Thus, Burd dies a death much like the vanquished party in one-on-one combat. The language used to describe his death – 'Al-Barrāq got in first with a fatal blow and Burd fell down dead' (2:141) – is similar to previous descriptions of deaths.[26] The only major difference here is that al-Barrāq is ostensibly fighting on the same side as Burd.

By contrast, the king dies an unusual – and an unusually gruesome – death; for his is the only beheading in the narrative. He dies not in battle, but rather in an ambush. As al-Barrāq has pre-arranged with Laylā via a messenger, the king will accompany Laylā on an outing, and then, catching the king unawares, al-Barrāq will kill him. The text tells us:

> He knew this meant that the king had gone out, and he hurried to put on his armour and mount his horse. He stopped opposite the road when the first of the soldiers passed by. Then he asked after the king and they pointed the king out to him, as he did not know what he looked like. Then al-Barrāq urged his horse forward, unsheathed his sword, and came down on the king with a firm blow, and his head flew off his body. Now Laylā was behind him on a fine breed, and with her were three slave-girls on mules. Al-Barrāq said to her, 'Urge on your horse, for I have killed the king.' (2:149)

It is curious that King Shahrmayh, who is altogether a more sympathetic character than Burd b. Ṭurayḥ al-Iyādī, should come to a more horrific end, and under the circumstances of ruse, rather than a straightforward battle. I suppose that although he is less villainous than Burd, as a king he is more powerful in his villainy. Moreover,

[26] Note, for example, 'Then they inclined toward one another, and stabs were exchanged between them. ʿImrān got one in first, and he caused ʿĀmir to fall down dead' (2:64); 'Then he advanced on his horse to ʿImrān, and they charged at each other for a while until stabs were exchanged. Al-Ḥārith got in first and knocked ʿImrān down dead' (2:64); 'So al-Ṣāmit al-Sadūsī appeared to him, and they exchanged blows. Al-Ḥārith got in first and knocked him down [dead] on the ground' (2:84).

he epitomises the Persian 'other'.[27] Perhaps for these reasons, by the logic of the tale, he deserves his fate.

The Leitmotif of Chastity

No theme is more central to the narrative than that of chastity. It recurs throughout the singular events of the narrative, in some sense tying them together. While it crops up first and foremost in the nickname Laylā the 'Chaste' (*al-ʿafīfa*), and while it is expressly linked to her status as virgin at the end of the tale, when she marries al-Barrāq, it would be wrong to see it as a theme relating to women's sexual behaviour alone. Men, too, are expected to exhibit chastity – at least heroic men are. Thus al-Barrāq wards off the advances of the beautiful young, married, servant Ṭarīqa, stating that he only wishes to be her friend and that he has a strong bond with someone else:

> Stop making advances, O Ṭarīqa
> Indeed, you have become a friend to me
>
> Noble, dear and true
> Sympathetic to me in what you have said
>
> It's out of the question, for I have a firm bond
> With the noblest of human beings in all creation (2:53)

[27] If I have read Bruce Masters correctly, it would seem that the Ottoman authorities based their legitimacy in large portions of the Arab world on the fact that the Ottomans and the majority of Arabs fell on the same side of the Sunni-Shiʿi divide. See his *The Arabs of the Ottoman Empire, 1516–1918* (New York: Cambridge University Press, 2013), 21, for example. It may be that the demonisation of Persians in the tale conveniently supported this sectarian bias, even if the tale in no way directly represents this religious schism. With the emergence of Arab nationalism, the anti-Persian rhetoric would perhaps relate to a desire on the part of the Arabs to distinguish themselves culturally from other ethnicities in the Islamic world, but presumably this would be reflected in their attitudes about the Turks as well. Note that in the tale, the alliance of Arab tribes fights against a variety of peoples who assist the Persian king. This includes the sons of Japheth, which may well include Turks. See B. Heller and A. Rippin, 'Yāfith', *EI*².

Chastity, then, is a virtue he exercises in his own life. He also counsels Lukayz to 'wear' his chastity in what he has in mind (البس عفافك في ما كنت تعنيه) (2:48). This occurs in the poem when al-Barrāq responds to Lukayz' decision to marry Laylā off to King ʿAmr b. Dhī Ṣahbān. It thereby suggests that chastity regulates not only personal sexual behaviour, but also contractual relationships. In one way or another, the quality of 'chastity' is related to Lukayz' decision for his daughter. I should point out that, unlike its English counterpart, the Arabic word *ʿiffa* has connotations of excellence and purity that transcend sexuality, as it involves the suppression of all kinds of desires, not just carnal ones.[28] Nevertheless, the sexual connotations are made explicit, especially at the end of the story where we learn that she has earned her nickname by maintaining her virginity against all odds.

Although men, and particularly honourable men, are expected to exhibit chastity – sexual or otherwise – it is a duty particularly incumbent upon women. In a poem addressed to her aunt Umm al-Agharr, Laylā observes that the 'honour [*ʿirḍ*] of a chaste one [*al-ʿafīfa*] is like a woven fabric' (2:54). The simile is meant to convey the precariousness of chastity – how easily it can become unravelled. Hence it is backed up in the poem by images of female powerlessness. Addressing her love for al-Barrāq, Laylā states:

> Indeed, I long for what you mention, only
> The honour of a chaste one is like a woven fabric
>
> What power do I have over what my father thinks?
> Does someone who stands at the bottom reach the heights?
>
> Women are lowly and secluded
> Known for their weak and defenceless opinion (2:54)

Indeed, so powerless are women that one can hardly blame them when their chastity is violated. Burd's wife, ashamed of how her husband has been treating Laylā, counsels her, 'Now is not the time for chastity' (فليس هذا اوان عفة) (2:106). This immediately precedes

[28] One dictionary defines it as follows: ترك الشهوات من كلّ شيء، وغلب في حفظ الفرج مما لا يحلّ Muṣṭafā et al., *al-Muʿjam al-wasīṭ*, 611.

Laylā's 'torture poem' where she specifies that 'they' have beaten her 'chaste surface' (*malmas al-ʿiffa*) with a stick (2:106). This graphic image, which is evocative of rape, epitomises Laylā's victimhood, and if she emerges from this violation with her virginity intact, as the happy ending of the narrative informs us that she does, then perhaps we have to read her virginity as figurative rather than literal. Indeed, she is known as the 'Chaste' by virtue of the strength (*shidda*) of her modesty (*ṣiyāna*) and chastity (*ʿiffa*) (2:151). These are moral, ephemeral qualities, rather than bodily characteristics.

Part II: Considerations of Form and Genre

This part of the chapter represents an assay of sorts; in it I assess the tale's compatibility with certain narrative paradigms, given the above narratological analysis of its components. I compare it to the ʿUdhrī love tale, the popular epic, and the novel in terms of its discourse, setting, characters, and events. I then conclude with a discussion of the epic's novelistic adaptation and the ways in which the novel distinguishes itself from its source text as a means of situating the tale within the tradition of the novel genre.

ʿUdhrī Love Tale[29]

Discursively, the ʿUdhrī love tale takes many forms,[30] but for the purposes of our analysis, I am drawing on the ʿAbbāsid-era

[29] On the ʿUdhrī love paradigm, see R. Jacobi, 'ʿUdhrī Poetry', *EAL*, 789–91; and Jacobi, 'ʿUdhrī', *EI*². See also the aforementioned contributions to Pannewick (ed.), *Martyrdom in Literature*: Renate Jacobi's 'The ʿUdhra: Love and Death in the Umayyad Period', 137–48; and Stefan Leder's 'The Udhri Narrative in Arabic Literature', 162–89.

[30] So strong was the ʿUdhrī paradigm that many narratives that did not begin as stories of this type evolved into them. Examples include the ʿUdhrification of the anecdotal material surrounding the Umayyad poet Laylā l-Akhyaliyya and her lover and subject of her funereal elegies, the brigand-poet Tawba b. al-Ḥumayyir. Some versions of her legend see her die of lovesickness. Another example is the

khabar-based narratives that one may find in a compendium such as the *Kitāb al-Aghānī* by Abū l-Faraj al-Iṣfahānī (d. *c.* 363/972). In these accounts, such as those pertaining to ʿUrwa b. Ḥizām,[31] to Jamīl b. Maʿmar[32] and to Qays b. al-Mulawwaḥ, a.k.a. Majnūn Laylā,[33] individual reports are framed by chains of transmission (leading back to different, sometimes anonymous, transmitters), and reports may overlap and repeat themselves. Hence the texture of the narrative is very different from our tale, where there is one continuous storyline going back to a single narrator. In terms of its discourse, then, the *Tale of al-Barrāq Son of Rawḥān and Laylā the Chaste* in no way resembles the pastiche of the ʿUdhrī love tale.

Character-wise, there is the shared premise that we have first cousins in love. Beyond that, and beyond the protagonists' Arab pedigree, there is little that unites them. Indeed, one may say that al-Barrāq b. Rawḥān, by virtue of his military prowess and his status as a robust warrior, is the opposite of the ʿUdhrī hero, who literally wastes away from lovesickness. Our heroine here, too, differs in one very important respect: whilst the ʿUdhrī beloved guards her chastity, she is not a virgin. To the contrary, she is married off to another man, and it is understood that she has conjugal relations with him. The ʿUdhrī hero is thus more passive than al-Barrāq, and the ʿUdhrī heroine less passive, or at least less untouched, than Laylā.

The setting of the ʿUdhrī love tale is much more bound to historical time and geographical space than is the *Tale of al-Barrāq Son of Rawḥān and Laylā the Chaste*. There is a real sense in which the ʿUdhrī love tale is both born of and set in the Umayyad era. This plays out

evolution of a humorous anecdote about an extremely pious man, ʿAbd al-Raḥmān al-Qass, warding off the advances of a singing slave-girl named Sallāma. While classical *akhbār* detailing the incident, which is also set in the Umayyad era, end simply with a statement of abstention, one twelfth-century version of the anecdote, which had by then been developed into a short story, ends with the male protagonist dying of love. See ʿAbd al-Raḥmān Ibn Naṣr al-Shayzarī, *Rawḍat al-qulūb wa-nuzhat al-muḥibb wal-maḥbūb*, eds David Semah and George J. Kanazi (Wiesbaden: Harrassowitz, 2003), 133–6.

[31] Abū l-Faraj al-Iṣfahānī, *Kitāb al-Aghānī* (Cairo: Dār al-Kutub, 1927–), 24:146–60.

[32] Ibid., 8:90–154.

[33] Ibid., 2:1–96.

on a thematic level, with its emphasis on the Islamic ethos and an attention to permitted and forbidden behaviours. But the setting also leaves its imprint on the plot, such as when ʿAfrāʾ the beloved of ʿUrwa is married off to an Umayyad official and squirrelled away to Damascus. Moreover, the chains of transmission that frame the individual reports that constitute the ʿUdhrī narrative often include identifiable historical figures.

The primary events in our epic differ in one major respect from the ʿUdhrī love narrative for the simple reason that the latter contains few if any battle scenes, whereas the *Tale of al-Barrāq Son of Rawḥān and Laylā the Chaste* consists principally of battle scenes and the causal chains that connect them. Many components of the love story are there: (1) there is an understanding that the girl's father will give her in marriage to the male protagonist; (2) the father then reneges on that promise to marry her off to a wealthy and powerful outsider; (3) the lovers spend an evening alone together saying goodbye before their imminent separation; and (4) the male lover falls physically ill, pining away for his beloved. It should be noted that in the case of al-Barrāq, the lovesickness is extremely short-lived, occurring only as he returns from pilgrimage. As soon as his services are required in battle, he finds himself in robust health. The pilgrimage itself is an event that links our tale to that of the ʿUdhrī love model, as the ʿUdhrī lover often undertakes the hajj as part of the narrative of his demise. One event which characterises the ʿUdhrī love story is that the male protagonist disguises himself or assumes a fake identity to gain access to the harem and sneak a visit with the beloved.[34] Interestingly, al-Barrāq explicitly refuses to don the clothes of a woman when Laylā suggests via a messenger that he do this in order to meet up with her. Al-Barrāq, ever the manly man, announces that he will not meet up with Laylā except in the clothing of heroes.

[34] ʿUrwa, for example, pretends to be from ʿAfrāʾ's husband's tribe, and Majnūn, in Niẓāmī's rendition of the tale, disguises himself as a beggar and a sheep.

Popular Epic[35]

The discourse of the tale, or how it is told, strongly resembles the popular epic or romance. It is one continuous narrative composed in a low register of Arabic, interposed with lengthy passages of poetry, characterised by repetition, and attributed to an elusive figure of the narrator (*al-rāwī*), even if, in our case, that narrator is named. So ensconced in the tradition of the romance is the tale that, for our Christian version at least, the whole introductory section, detailing the genealogy of the Arab tribes and tracing their ancestry back to Nizār b. Maʿadd, seems to have been inspired by a similar passage in the epic of al-Zīr Sālim.[36] The tale's characters, too, as warriors who emote in verse, are reminiscent of the epic heroes. It must be said, however, that Laylā falls somewhat short of the epic heroine. She is utterly passive, unlike the warrior women who populate the folkloric imagination.[37]

One major difference between the *Tale of al-Barrāq Son of Rawḥān and Laylā the Chaste* and the popular epic is in their divergent relationships to history. Whereas the former hardly situates itself in a temporal setting, with no clue as to time-frame other than the phrase 'the fiery ardour of the Jāhiliyya overtook him', the latter often inserts itself into geopolitical history. Take, for example, the *Sīrat Banī Hilāl*, and specifically its fourth cycle, the *Taghrība*, which charts the migration of the Banū Hilāl from Arabia to Egypt and then their conquest of Ifrīqiyya.[38] It references historical events and person-

[35] For an overview of the popular epic, see G. Canova, 'Sīra Literature', *EAL*, 726–7; and P. Heath, 'Sīra Shaʿbiyya', *EI*². See also Reynolds, *Arab Folklore*, 52–67. Important monographs on popular epics include: Lyons, *The Arabian Epic;* Connelly, *Arab Folk Epic and Identity;* Peter Heath, *The Thirsty Sword;* and Reynolds, *Heroic Poets, Poetic Heroes*.

[36] See Anonymous, *al-Zīr Sālim Abū Laylā l-Muhalhil* (Beirut: Dār al-Kutub al-ʿIlmiyya, 1984), 3.

[37] On the prevalence of the warrior woman in the folkloric Arabic tradition, see Remke Kruk, *The Warrior Women of Islam: Female Empowerment in Arabic Popular Literature* (London/New York: I.B. Tauris, 2014). This is not to say that there are no other passive heroines in Arabic epic. ʿAbla, the beloved of ʿAntar, is a prime example.

[38] G. Canova, 'Banū Hilāl, Romance of', *EAL*, 133.

ages such as Muʿizz b. Bādīs, the Zīrid ruler of Tunisia. Moreover, the ahistorical *Sīrat ʿAntar*, a romance about a pre-Islamic Arab poet who participates in the Islamic conquests and even the crusades,[39] is less vague and ambiguous when it comes to its setting/s.

In terms of events, the *Tale of al-Barrāq Son of Rawḥān and Laylā the Chaste* resembles the popular epic in its attention to battle scenes. What we do not have in the former, however, are the fantastical flourishes we often find in the latter. Apart from the Zayd raid, which is at least plausible, fantastical elements are completely absent from our tale.

Novel[40]

This brings us to the novel; to what extent does the *Tale of al-Barrāq Son of Rawḥān and Laylā the Chaste* adhere to the formal and the generic requirements of the novel? If, by 'novel', we mean any lengthy or sustained piece of narrative fiction, and if – and this is a big if – you accept my contention that the tale is straightforwardly fictional, then I would say that it greatly conforms. If you rely on more specific definitions of the novel, it conforms less comfortably.

Let us begin with a dictionary definition. *The Chambers Dictionary* defines novel: ' – *n* a fictitious prose narrative or tale presenting a picture of real life, *esp* of the emotional crises in the life history of the men and women portrayed; (with *the*) such writing as a literary genre'.[41] Discursively, then, we find one major difference; whereas the novel is a *prose* narrative, our tale is a *prosimetrical* narrative; that

[39] G. Canova, 'ʿAntar, Romance of', *EAL*, 93–4.
[40] Much has been written on the Arabic novel, too much to be cited here. For a brief encapsulation of the emergence and early development of the novel in Arabic fiction, see, for example, Roger Allen, *An Introduction to Arabic Literature* (Cambridge: Cambridge University Press, 2000), especially 184–5. For a recent and voluminous collection of astute essays on the topic, see Waïl S. Hassan (ed.), *The Oxford Handbook of Arab Novelistic Traditions* (New York: Oxford University Press, 2017); the two contributions to this book which relate most directly to this work are Waïl S. Hassan's 'Toward a Theory of the Arabic Novel', 19–47, and Roger Allen's 'The Arabic Novel and History', 49–65.
[41] *The Chambers Dictionary* (Edinburgh: Chambers Harrap, 1998), 1109.

is, it is comprised of a mixture of prose and verse. That it presents a picture of 'real life' is evident in the fact that scholars misconstrued it as history. That it presents an emotional crisis in the life history of al-Barrāq and Laylā is also clear. Therefore, our tale meets two of the three criteria one could glean from the *Chambers* definition.

Character-wise, there is little or no development. The characters end the narrative as they began it: virtuous, beautiful, chaste. In this way it is unlike the modern novel, even if it resembles the ancient Greek novel[42] described by Bakhtin in his discussion of 'adventure time'.[43] Likewise, there is no 'psycho-narration' – no exploration, at least on the part of the third-person narrator, of the thoughts and feelings of the characters.[44] Instead the characters express their thoughts and emotions in verse. So, there is psychological depth if not psychological development.

In terms of setting, it is fair to say that modern novels invest a great deal more in spatial and temporal matters than does the *Tale of al-Barrāq Son of Rawḥān and Laylā the Chaste*. If, as Seymour Chatman describes, the novel's texture is often characterised by an alternation of 'scene' and 'summary', we have in our tale instead an alternation between action and utterance, where action is presented in prose with a bare minimum of detail and utterance reveals an emotional take on the action in poetic form.

The events that punctuate the narrative of the tale are like those in many conventional novels in the sense that there is linear causation – one event leads to the next. However, because the events of the tale are mostly battle scenes which are extremely repetitive in nature, there is a circularity to the tale which is alien to the genre, or at least the genre in its high modern formulation.

[42] The ancient Greek novel dates as far back as the second and third centuries, CE. Abrams and Harpham state: 'Typically they dealt with separated lovers who, after perilous adventures and hairbreadth escapes, are happily reunited at the end.' An example is *Aethiopica* or *An Ethiopian Tale* by Heliodorus. See M.H. Abrams and Geoffrey Galt Harpham, 'Novel', in *A Glossary of Literary Terms*, 9th edn (Boston: Wadsworth Cengage Learning, 2009), 226–33.

[43] Bakhtin, *Dialogic Imagination*, 86–110.

[44] On 'psycho-narration', see Dorit Cohn, *Transparent Minds: Narrative Modes for Presenting Consciousness in Fiction* (Princeton: Princeton University Press, 1983).

Conclusion

I would like to conclude this chapter by analysing the narrative structure of the tale with reference to its twentieth-century novelistic adaptation. Highlighting the differences between the pre-modern pseudo-historical text and ʿĀdil al-Ghaḍbān's 1954 historical novel *Laylā al-ʿafīfa* (Laylā the Chaste) will help to accentuate the ways in which the former adheres to the genre and the ways in which it does not. This will lead into a discussion of whether the *Tale of al-Barrāq Son of Rawḥān and Laylā the Chaste* should be considered an early example of the novel, or merely a precursor to it.

The modern Arabic novel, since its inception in the late nineteenth and early twentieth century, has had a complicated relationship to textual traditions. In *Politics of Nostalgia in the Arabic Novel*, Wen-chin Ouyang contemplates the role of intertextuality in the emergence of the novel that projects itself specifically as Arab:

> Tradition, whatever form it takes in the novel's reconstruction of it, comes to be a key building block of the Arabic novel, giving it historical layers and narrative texture. It gives it an inflection unique to each instance of intertextuality, to every new novel that engages intertextually with tradition.[45]

Many Arabic textual traditions, from the *ḥadīth* to the *Arabian Nights*, to the popular epics, to historical annals, inform the modern Arabic novel, helping to distinguish it from the European model. Most of these traditions are either 'medieval' or 'ancient', harking back to the 'golden age' of Arabic literature; others may be more contemporary but originate as folklore. Hence they, too, date back indefinitely in time. ʿĀdil al-Ghaḍbān, in composing his novel *Laylā al-ʿafīfa*, presumably thought he was adapting an ancient, historical text, creating a narrative of historical fiction on the basis of actual recorded events, however distorted they may be by the vagaries of time and transmission. But what if he was, instead, adapting an

[45] Wen-chin Ouyang, *Politics of Nostalgia in the Arabic Novel* (Edinburgh: Edinburgh University Press, 2013), 68.

already fictional text, and one which was not ancient but relatively recent? In other words, what if he was adapting a novel from a novel? Might not a comparison of his text with the text he adapted reveal much about the process of 'maturation' of the novel? Might it not lend us new insights into the novel in its 'formative' stage? Might it not change our thinking about Arabic precedents for the novel and where to look for them?

Discursively, there are three major differences between the one text and the other. The first is that al-Ghaḍbān's novel dispenses, for the most part, with the prosimetrical texture and opts instead for what is primarily a prose narrative. The second is that his 'novel' suppresses the presence of a narrator, creating a narrative in the omniscient third-person voice. The third is that his novel is *authored*, attributable to a named individual, whereas the text from which it is adapted is *authorless* in the sense that it is anonymous.

Al-Ghaḍbān's novel treats space and time quite differently from the text on which it is based. That is to say that it adds boundaries, clarifying different spaces with respect to one another, especially in the Arabian milieu. ʿAmr b. Dhī Ṣahbān is not simply a king, he is the king of Yemen. Familiar place names abound: Nejd, Tihama, Mounts Aja and Salma. Our hero, al-Barrāq, travels at one point to Bahrain. Gone are the obscure and hard-to-identify locales, with the exception of Karkhā, even if a certain ambiguity remains in Persian territory: much is set in the 'capital' of the Persians, a city which remains unnamed. Time-wise, the novel is, like the original tale, vague. We are still very much in adventure time, with days accumulating in the unfolding of particular events but without specific chronological markers. What we do have in the novel is references to historical or semi-historical pre-Islamic figures which would set the narrative in the Jāhiliyya in the century or so before the coming of Islam. For example, in passing it is mentioned that Zuhayr b. Janāb al-Kalbī is the Yemeni governor over Nejd and the peninsula.[46] This Zuhayr is a historical, if 'semi-legendary', figure, one who is said to have led the Quḍāʿa and who flourished in the sixth

[46] ʿĀdil al-Ghaḍbān, *Laylā al-ʿafīfa* (Cairo: Dār al-Maʿārif, 1954), 24 and 39.

century, CE.[47] Interestingly, al-Ghaḍbān, like Cheikho before him, dispenses with King Shahrmayh and replaces him with a historical Sāsānid figure. But this time he opts not for Chosroes or Kisrā, who would set the narrative in the sixth or early seventh century, but rather for the figure of Fīrūz b. Yazdajird, who reigned from 459 to 484, CE, and his brother Balash, whom al-Ghaḍbān mistakenly identifies as Fīrūz' son, and who ruled from 484 to 488.[48] Al-Ghaḍbān also sets the narrative against a backdrop of war between the Persians and the Hephthalites. It would appear that al-Ghaḍbān, assuming he was drawing on Cheikho as a source, was guided more by the death date assigned to Laylā of 483 CE than he was by Cheikho's assertion that she was kept in captivity by the son of Kisrā. Al-Ghaḍbān's adaptation thus grounds the narrative much more tangibly in space and time than does the epic on which it is based.

The characters that populate the novel are by and large the same, though their religious profiles differ. Whereas in the Christian version of the tale, al-Barrāq is identified at the outset as a Christian but later on speaks and behaves as a Muslim, and whereas all the other characters seem to behave and speak like Muslims, too, al-Ghaḍbān's novel, quite logically, as it is set in the pre-Islamic era, has no Muslims. Al-Ghaḍbān explicitly introduces al-Barrāq and Laylā as Christians and references to this fact occur periodically throughout the novel. Other characters are pagan, if they are Arabs, and fire- and star-worshippers, if they are Persian. Thus, we find Laylā's aunt Umm al-Agharr, for example, swearing by the deities Allāt and ʿUzzā rather than by God.[49]

Characterisation in the novel differs from that of the tale in that the narrator gets inside the heads of the characters and shows the reader what they are thinking. In the tale, we only ever get to see what the characters are thinking when they emote in verse, but in the novel, the characters' thoughts and feelings are described

[47] M. Lecker, 'Zuhayr b. D̲j̲anāb', *EI*[2].
[48] M. Morony, 'Sāsānids', *EI*[2]; al-Ghaḍbān, *Laylā al-ʿafīfa*, 89.
[49] Al-Ghaḍbān, *Laylā al-ʿafīfa*, 6.

through various techniques of psycho-narration. Thus, for example, after Laylā learns of her father's plans to marry her off to King ʿAmr b. Dhī Ṣahbān, the narrator speaks of her insomnia as follows: 'As for Laylā, she did not sleep a wink or rest an eyelid all night, she was rolling around on her mattress, tortured and in agony, as if her mattress was stuffed with thorns' (29). Such a simile, were it to appear in the tale, would appear in verse and be uttered in the voice of the character concerned.

The course of events differs tremendously in the novel. Most notably, the novel lacks the endless repetition of battle scenes. Instead we have two: one internecine battle where Arab fights against Arab, and one battle fought between Arabs and Persians. Al-Barrāq, being a Christian, does not go on the hajj – instead he takes a trip to visit the Banū Ḥanīfa in Bahrain. Another discrepancy in the plot is that al-Barrāq does not behead the Persian king, nor does he kill him. (Perhaps this is because the historical King Fīrūz b. Yazdajird was killed by the Hephthalites.) Our hero simply whisks Laylā away astride his horse. But many other events – the false accusation of rape against al-Muhalhil, the recitation of Laylā's torture poem, the burial of Gharsān, and al-Barrāq's pronouncement that he will not meet Laylā in women's clothes – these are all preserved in the novel. And the basic arc of the storyline – particularly as it pertains to the love story between al-Barrāq and Laylā, her engagement to King ʿAmr b. Dhī Ṣahbān, her kidnapping at the hands of Burd b. Ṭurayḥ al-Iyādī, the threat of her forced marriage to the Persian king, and her rescue by al-Barrāq – is identical to the 'original' Christian version of the narrative. Al-Ghaḍbān did not need to create a story arc for his novel – it was already there.

So al-Ghaḍbān was not adapting a historical text – he himself must have detected this on some level, since he had to conjure up a historical framework for his novel as well as erase the tale's ahistorical elements. The question remains, what kind of text was he adapting? At best it was a pseudo-historical text, but this would presuppose that its author, or authors, meant it to be received as history. Why, if that were the case, would the central historical detail be patently fictitious? There was no King Shahrmayh, not even in legend. No, I believe it was composed as fiction and meant to be understood as such. It was a novel, or if you will, a novella. Why was it not recognised for what it was – make-believe?

The answer lies, I think, in the orientalist notion that the pre-modern Arabs *lacked* fiction. Either this notion was by and large accurate, and thus there was no way to categorise the tale, along-side other Arabic texts, except as historical or pseudo-historical, or the notion was inaccurate, hence the existence of this novella, but internalised by scholars such as Cheikho, who failed to catch on to the text's fictitious intent. One wonders how many other sustained fictional narratives – how many proto-novels or proto-novellas – have eluded categorisation as such, simply because we are told they do not exist.

It is tempting to use this specimen of sustained fictional narrative as evidence that we should push the emergence of the Arabic novel back in time, even further than scholars have in recent decades, when it has been acknowledged that too much attention has been paid to Muḥammad Ḥusayn Haykal's 1913 novel *Zaynab* as the tradition's first 'mature' novel.[50] The problem is that, if you reject, as I do, the attribution of the text to ʿUmar b. Shabba, the *Tale of al-Barrāq Son of Rawḥān and Laylā the Chaste* cannot be dated with any certainty, nor can its authors be identified. Perhaps the question we should be asking, then, is not when the novel – as a sustained piece of narrative fiction – emerged in the Arabic tradition but rather what forms did it take? After all the novel does have very early precedents, such as the eleventh-century Ibn Buṭlān's *Daʿwat al-aṭibbāʾ* (The Physicians' Dinner Party) or the twelfth-century Ibn Ṭufayl's *Ḥayy Ibn Yaqẓān* (Alive, Son of Awake). Texts may not have been packaged

[50] Recent studies bearing on the early development of the Arabic novel include: Elizabeth Holt, 'From Gardens of Knowledge to Ezbekiyya after Midnight: The Novel and the Arabic Press from Beirut to Cairo, 1870–1892', *MEL* 16.3 (2013), 232–48; Elliott Colla, 'How Zaynab Became the First Arabic Novel', *History Compass* 7.1 (2009), 214–25; Roger Allen, 'Rewriting Literary History: The Case of the Arabic Novel', *JAL* 38.3 (2007), 247–60; and Samah Selim, 'Novels and Nations', chapter 2 of *The Novel and the Rural Imaginary in Egypt, 1880–1985* (London/New York: RoutledgeCurzon, 2004), 60–90. See also Hassan, *The Oxford Handbook*, mentioned in note 40, above.

as 'novels', so how was the novel or its equivalent packaged? Perhaps it is worth taking a closer look at works such as this one, that have been presented as historical or pseudo-historical texts, to see if they might fit the bill. Indeed, some scholars have already found precedents to the modern novel, and specifically the historical novel, in the *sīra* tradition, on the one hand,[51] and in historical literature, on the other.[52] Robert Irwin has gone so far as to argue that the sixteenth-century Ibn Zunbul, who chronicled the downfall of the Mamlūks and the rise of the Ottomans, is the 'Arab world's first true historical novelist', conforming as he does to the important criterion laid out by Georg Lukacs in his *The Historical Novel* that the characters 'take part in historical events and are changed by them'.[53]

What sets the *Tale of al-Barrāq Son of Rawḥān and Laylā the Chaste* apart is that it is both anonymously-authored and has an overtly ahistorical if not downright fictional status. Whereas other lengthy folkloric narratives purport to unfold against a backdrop of actual events, our tale takes place in a non-chronological and pseudo-geographical realm, based neither on history nor on legend. In this respect it distinguishes itself even from the narratives that, together with our tale, are appended to copies of the anthology of *al-Jamhara*. For these are based on the legends surrounding Kulayb b. Rabīʿa[54] and the War of the Basūs.[55]

It is clearly a fictional narrative, then, but is it an epic or is it a novel? As Lukács asserts: 'It would be superficial – a matter of a mere artistic technicality – to look for the only and decisive genre-defining criterion in the question of whether a work is written in

[51] See, for example, Franz Rosenthal, *A History of Muslim Historiography*, 2nd edn (Leiden: Brill, 1968), 46–7.

[52] For a brilliant discussion of a historical narrative which is novel-like in terms of its characterisation, see Stefan Leder, 'Features of the Novel in Early Historiography: The Downfall of Xālid al-Qasrī', *Oriens* 32 (1990), 72–96.

[53] Robert Irwin, 'Ibn Zunbul and the Romance of History', in Julia Bray (ed.), *Writing and Representation in Medieval Islam: Muslim Horizons* (London/New York: Routledge, 2006), 3. See Georg Lukács, *The Historical Novel*, trans. Hannah and Stanley Mitchell (Lincoln/London: University of Nebraska Press, 1983).

[54] G. Levi Della Vida, 'Kulayb b. Rabīʿa', *EI*².

[55] J.W. Fück, 'al-Basūs', *EI*².

verse or prose.'[56] In any case, since our tale is composed of verse and prose in equal measure, this would not be a decisive criterion; instead what we would have would be half-epic, half-novel. This turns out to be not such a bad characterisation of what we have before us; for whilst, in some respects, the tale exhibits features that Lukács associates with the epic, such as the 'childlike' or 'theodicean' preoccupation with crime and punishment[57] and the symbolic communal agency of the protagonist,[58] in other respects – such as its architectural plotline – it is more reminiscent of the novel. He writes:

> The epic gives form to a totality of life that is rounded from within; the novel seeks, by giving form, to uncover and construct the concealed totality of life. The given structure of the object (i.e. the search, which is only a way of expressing the subject's recognition that neither objective life nor its relationship to the subject is spontaneously harmonious in itself) supplies an indication of the form-giving intention. All the fissures and rents which are inherent in the historical situation must be drawn into the form-giving process and cannot nor should be disguised by compositional means. Thus the fundamental form-determining intention of the novel is objectivised as the psychology of the novel's heroes: they are seekers.[59]

Here I would like to point out that the two different versions of our tale – that is the Christian version and the non-Christian or 'Muslim' version – would fall on opposite sides of the epic/novel divide. The Christian version, with its stronger story arc, and the way that it sets up the love story and presents the protagonists as 'seekers' of a reunion, would fall under the rubric of the novel, whilst the Muslim version, devoting less obvious intentional attention to form and beginning randomly with the slaying of al-Ḥārith b. ʿAbbād, might be seen, rather, as epic in nature. It would thus be very interesting to know for certain which came first. Does the Christian version of the

[56] Georg Lukács, *The Theory of the Novel*, trans. Anna Bostock (London: Merlin Press, 1971), 56.
[57] Ibid., 61.
[58] Ibid., 66.
[59] Ibid., 60.

tale come second – does it represent a 'step forward' on a narrative continuum between epic and novel through a formal accretion, a development toward modernity in the field of Arabic prose fiction? Or does it constitute a precursor of sorts? Did the non-Christian epic version evolve from the Christian novel by suppressing or rejecting some of its novelistic features, thereby helping to disguise its status as fiction? Of this we cannot be sure, but the manuscript sources we have tracked down thus far would suggest that the Christian version comes later. The two Christian manuscripts, Ahlwardt 9747 (Berlin) and Ms. Or. Oct. 1383 (Berlin), date from the nineteenth century, whereas the non-Christian manuscripts – at least those which are dated – namely Arabe 5833 (Paris) and 1194 Adab (Cairo) – were copied in the eighteenth century. Thus, we could say that a text that originates as an epic during the seventeenth or eighteenth century transmutes into a novel in the nineteenth century. Given the vast corpus of Ottoman-era Arabic manuscripts that remains unexplored and unavailable to researchers,[60] one wonders if there are not other supposedly non-existent sustained fictional narratives out there.

[60] Nelly Hanna draws attention to this corpus of manuscripts, stating that those dating from the sixteenth through to the eighteenth century are 'significant in number' and 'diverse in subject matter and genre', adding that manuscripts of the seventeenth and eighteenth centuries are 'in fact much more various and diverse than is generally believed'. See her *In Praise of Books: A Cultural History of Cairo's Middle Class, Sixteenth to the Eighteenth Century* (Syracuse, NY: Syracuse University Press, 2003), 23.

Bibliography

Manuscripts and Published Editions of the Tale

Ahlwardt 9747, Berlin, copied in 1854, 77v–141v. Also, Sprenger 1215.
Arabe 5833, Paris, copied in 1797, 107v–131.
Ms. Or. Oct. 1383, Berlin, copied in early 1824, 87–147.
Or. 2676, Leiden, undated, 155v–231.
5984 Adab, Dar al-Kutub, Cairo, copied in 1927, 2–119. A copy of 1194 Adab.
Anonymous, 'Riwāyat al-Barrāq b. Rawḥān', *Ḥadīqat al-akhbār* 1.39–1.48 (2 October 1858–4 December 1858).
Iskandar Abkāriyūs, 'Ḥarb al-Barrāq', *Tazyīn nihāyat al-arab fī akhbār al-ʿArab* (Beirut: al-Maṭbaʿa al-Waṭaniyya, 1867), 211–300.
Aḥmad ʿAṭiyya (ed.), *Kitāb al-Jamhara fī Ayyām al-ʿArab li-l-ḥāfiẓ ʿUmar b. Shabba al-Baṣrī al-mutawaffā sanat 262 hijrī* (Ismailiyah: Maktabat al-Imām al-Bukhārī, 2015), 69–183.

Archival Materials

British Library, India Office Records, IOR/L/PJ/7/1296.
British National Archives, Colonial Office, CO 323/1421/3.
British National Archives, Foreign Office, FO 371/52594.
Bahīja Ḥāfiẓ, Laylā al-Badawiyya (Alexandria Library, shelfmark 791.4372/VHS 748).
New York State Film Script Archive, State Museum at Albany, File 50803, Box 1335: *Leila la Bedouine*.

Other Sources

Abkāriyūs, Iskandar, *Nihāyat al-arab fī akhbār al-ʿArab* (Marseille: Maṭbaʿat al-Faʿla, 1852).

— *Rawḍat al-adab fī ṭabaqāt shuʿarāʾ al-ʿArab* (Beirut: Maṭbaʿat Bayrūt, 1858).

Abrams, M.H. and Geoffrey Galt Harpham, *A Glossary of Literary Terms*, 11th edn (Stamford, CT: Cengage Learning, 2014).

Allan, Michael, *In the Shadow of World Literature: Sites of Reading in Colonial Egypt* (Princeton and Oxford: Princeton University Press, 2016).

Allen, Roger, 'The Arabic Novel and History', in Hassan (ed.), *Oxford Handbook*, 49–65.

— *An Introduction to Arabic Literature* (Cambridge: Cambridge University Press, 2000).

— 'Rewriting Literary History: The Case of the Arabic Novel', *JAL* 38.3 (2007), 247–60.

Allen, Roger and D.S. Richards (eds), *Arabic Literature in the Post-Classical Period*, Cambridge History of Arabic Literature (Cambridge: Cambridge University Press, 2006).

Anonymous, 'Fī ḥadāʾiq al-ʿArab: Laylā l-ʿafīfa wa-l-Barrāq', *al-Zuhūr* 1.4 (June 1910), 166–8.

— *The Romance of Antar*, trans. Terrick Hamilton, ed. W.A. Clouston (Milton Keynes: Dodo Press, n.d.).

— *al-Zīr Sālim Abū Laylā l-Muhalhil* (Beirut: Dār al-Kutub al-ʿIlmiyya, 1984).

el-Ariss, Tarek, 'Let There Be Nahḍah!', *Cambridge Journal of Postcolonial Literary Inquiry* 2.2 (2015), 260–6.

Armbrust, Walter, 'Audiovisual Media and History of the Arab Middle East', in Israel Gershoni, Amy Singer and Y. Hakan Erdem (eds), *Middle East Historiographies: Narrating the Twentieth Century* (Seattle and London: University of Washington Press, 2006), 288–313.

Asmahān wa-Farīd al-Aṭrash, *Farid & Asmahan* (Baidaphon Beirut compact disc, 1990).

Badawi, M.M., 'Shukrī the Poet – a Reconsideration', in R.C. Ostle (ed.), *Studies in Modern Arabic Literature* (Warminster: Aris & Phillips, 1975), 18–33.

Bakhtin, Mikhail M., *The Dialogic Imagination: Four Essays*, trans. Michael Holquist (Austin: University of Texas Press, 1981).

Baron, Beth, *Egypt as a Woman* (Berkeley: University of California Press, 2005).

Bauer, Thomas, 'In Search of "Post-Classical Literature": A Review Article', *Mamlūk Studies Review* 11.2 (2007), 137–67.
Beeston, A.F.L., 'Tubbaʿ', *EI*².
Bint al-Shāṭiʾ (a.k.a. ʿāʾisha ʿAbd al-Raḥmān), 'Majmūʿāt min al-qiṣaṣ', *al-Ahrām*, 1 March 1955, 5.
Bloch, Howard, *Etymologies and Genealogies: A Literary Anthropology of the French Middle Ages* (Chicago and London: University of Chicago Press, 1984).
Booker, Christopher, *The Seven Basic Plots* (London: Continuum, 2004).
Booth, Marilyn, 'Exemplary Lives, Feminist Aspirations: Zaynab Fawwāz and the Arabic Biographical Tradition', *JAL* 26.1–2 (1995), 120–46.
Cachia, Pierre. *Popular Narrative Ballads of Modern Egypt* (Oxford: Clarendon Press, 1989).
Canova, G., 'ʿAntar, Romance of', *EAL*, 93–4.
— 'Banū Hilāl, Romance of', *EAL*, 133.
— 'Sīra Literature', *EAL*, 726–7.
Çelebi, Kâtip [Ḥājjī Khalīfa], *Lexicon bibliographicum (Kashf al-ẓunūn)*, ed. Gustavus Fleugel, 7 vols (Leipzig, 1835–58).
The Chambers Dictionary (Edinburgh: Chambers Harrap, 1998).
Chatman, Seymour, *Story and Discourse: Narrative Structure in Fiction and Film* (Ithaca, NY and London: Cornell University Press, 1978).
Cheikho, Louis, *Kitāb shuʿarāʾ al-Naṣrāniyya* (Book of Christian Poets), vol. 1 (Beirut: Maṭbaʿat al-Ābāʾ al-Mursalīn al-Yasūʿīyīn, 1890).
— *Riyāḍ al-adab fī marāthī shawāʿir al-ʿArab* (Beirut: Catholic Press, 1897).
Chelhod, J., 'Ḥimā', *EI*².
Chraïbi, Aboubakr, *Arabic Manuscripts of the Thousand and One Nights* (Paris: Espaces & Signes, 2016).
— 'Classification des traditions narratives arabes par "conte-type": Application à l'étude de quelques rôles de poète', *Bulletin d'Études Orientales* 50 (1998), 29–59.
Cohn, Dorit, *Transparent Minds: Narrative Modes for Presenting Consciousness in Fiction* (Princeton: Princeton University Press, 1983).
Colla, Elliott, 'How Zaynab Became the First Arabic Novel', *History Compass* 7.1 (2009), 214–25.
Connelly, Bridget, *Arab Folk Epic and Identity* (Berkeley: University of California Press, 1986).
Dāghir, Yūsuf Asʿad, *Maṣādir al-dirāsa al-adabiyya*, vol. 2: *al-Fikr al-ʿArabī al-ḥadīth fī siyar aʿlāmihi*, part 1: *al-Rāḥilūn (1800–1955)* (Lebanon: Jamʿiyyat Ahl al-Qalam, 1956).

Della Vida, G. Levi, 'Kulayb b. Rabīʿa', *EI²*.
Farès, Bichr, *L'honneur chez les Arabes avant l'Islam* (Paris: Librairie d'Amérique et d'Orient Adrien-Maisonneuve, 1932).
Fawwāz, Zaynab, *al-Durr al-manthūr fī ṭabaqāt rabbāt al-khudūr* (Cairo: Hindāwī, 2012).
Fück, J.W., 'al-Basūs', *EI²*.
al-Ghaḍbān, ʿĀdil, *Layla l-ʿafīfa* (Cairo: Dār al-Maʿārif, 1954).
Grunebaum, Gustave E. von, *Medieval Islam: A Study in Cultural Orientation*, 2nd edn (Chicago and London: University of Chicago Press, 1953).
Hammond, Marlé, '"If Only al-Barrāq Could See . . .": Violence and Voyeurism in an Early Modern Reformulation of the Pre-Islamic Call to Arms', in Hugh Kennedy (ed.), *Warfare and Poetry in the Middle East* (London: I.B. Tauris, 2013), 215–40.
Hammond, Martha Latané, 'The Poetics of S/Exclusion: Women, Gender and the Classical Arabic Canon' (PhD thesis, Columbia University, 2003).
Hanna, Nelly, *In Praise of Books: A Cultural History of Cairo's Middle Class, Sixteenth to the Eighteenth Century* (Syracuse, NY: Syracuse University Press, 2003).
Hārūn, ʿAbd al-Salām (ed.), *Nawādir al-makhṭūṭāt* (Cairo: Maṭbaʿat Lajnat al-Taʾlīf wa-l-Tarjama wa-l-Nashr, 1951–5).
Hassan, Waïl S. (ed.), *The Oxford Handbook of Arab Novelistic Traditions* (New York: Oxford University Press, 2017).
— 'Toward a Theory of the Arabic Novel', in Hassan (ed.), *Oxford Handbook*, 19–47.
Heath, P., 'Sīra Shaʿbiyya', *EI²*.
Heath, Peter, 'Styles in Premodern Arabic Popular Epics', in Bilal Orfali (ed.), *In the Shadow of Arabic: The Centrality of Language to Arabic Culture* (Leiden and Boston: Brill, 2011), 413–31.
— *The Thirsty Sword: Sīrat ʿAntar and the Arabic Popular Epic* (Salt Lake City: University of Utah Press, 1996).
Heller, B. and A. Rippin, 'Yāfith', *EI²*.
Herzog, Thomas, 'Orality and the Tradition of Arabic Epic Storytelling', in Karl Reichl (ed.), *Medieval Oral Literature* (Berlin and Boston: De Gruyter, 2012), 629–52.
— '"What They Saw with Their Own Eyes . . .": Fictionalization and "Narrativization" of History in Arabic Popular Epics and Learned Historiography', in S. Dorpmueller (ed.), *Fictionalizing the Past: Historical Characters in Arabic Popular Epic* (Leuven: Peeters, 2012), 25–43.

Ḥijāzī, Muḥammad ʿAbd al-Wāḥid, *Nisāʾ shāʿirāt: Dirāsa fī shiʿr al-marʾa al-ʿArabiyya* (Cairo: Maktabat Jazīrat al-Ward, 2010).

Hill, Peter, 'Revisiting the Intellectual Space of the *Nahḍa* (Eighteenth-Twentieth Centuries)', *Les carnets de l-Ifpo: La recherche en train de se faire à l'Institut français du Proche-Orient* (Hypotheses.org), 5 June 2014.

Hirschler, Konrad, *The Written Word in the Medieval Arabic Lands: A Social and Cultural History of Reading Practices* (Edinburgh: Edinburgh University Press, 2012).

Holt, Elizabeth, 'From Gardens of Knowledge to Ezbekiyya after Midnight: The Novel and the Arabic Press from Beirut to Cairo, 1870–1892', *MEL* 16.3 (2013), 232–48.

Ḥusayn, Ṭāhā, *Fī al-adab al-jāhilī* (Cairo: Maṭbaʿat al-Iʿtimād, 1927).

Ibn Abī Ṭāhir Ṭayfūr, *Balāghāt al-nisāʾ* (Beirut: Dār al-Ḥadātha, 1987).

Ibn al-Athīr, *al-Kāmil fī l-Tārīkh*, ed. Abū l-Fidāʾ ʿAbd Allāh al-Qāḍī (Beirut: Dār al-Kutub al-ʿIlmiyya, 1987).

Irwin, Robert, 'Ibn Zunbul and the Romance of History', in Julia Bray (ed.), *Writing and Representation in Medieval Islam: Muslim Horizons* (London and New York: Routledge, 2006), 3–15.

al-Iṣfahānī, Abū l-Faraj, *Kitāb al-Aghānī* (Cairo: Dār al-Kutub, 1927–).

Jacobi, R., 'ʿU<u>dh</u>rī', *EI*[2].

— 'ʿUdhrī Poetry', *EAL*, 789–91.

Jacobi, Renate, 'The ʿUdhra: Love and Death in the Umayyad Period', in Friederike Pannewick (ed.), *Martyrdom in Literature: Visions of Death and Meaningful Suffering in Europe and the Middle East from Antiquity to Modernity* (Wiesbaden: Harrassowitz, 2004), 137–48.

Jamil, Nadia, *Ethics and Poetry in Sixth-Century Arabia* (Cambridge: Gibb Memorial Trust, 2017).

al-Jazāʾirī, Saʿīd, *Asmahān: ḍaḥiyyat al-istikhbārāt* (London: Riad El-Rayyes, 1990).

Kaḥḥāla, ʿUmar Riḍā, *Aʿlām al-nisāʾ fī ʿālamay al-ʿArab wa-l-Islām*, 2nd printing, vol. 4 (Damascus: al-Maṭbaʿa al-Hāshimiyya, 1959).

Kāmil, Maḥmūd, *Muḥammad al-Qaṣabjī: Ḥayātuh wa-aʿmāluh* (Cairo: al-Hayʾa l-Miṣriyya l-ʿĀmma li-l-Taʾlīf wa-l-Nashr, 1971).

Kendall, Elisabeth, *Literature, Journalism and the Avant-Garde: Intersection in Egypt* (London and New York: Routledge, 2006).

Kruk, Remke, *The Warrior Women of Islam: Female Empowerment in Arabic Popular Literature* (London and New York: I.B. Tauris, 2014).

Lane, E.W., *Arabic-English Lexicon* (London: Williams & Norgate, 1863–7).
— *The Manners and Customs of the Modern Egyptians* (London: J.M. Dent/ New York: E.P. Dutton, 1908).
Lecker, M., 'Zuhayr b. Dj̲anāb', *EI*[2].
Leder, S., ''Umar b. Shabba', *EI*[2].
Leder, Stefan, 'Features of the Novel in Early Historiography: The Downfall of Xālid al-Qasrī', *Oriens* 32 (1990), 72–96.
— (ed.), *Story-telling in the Framework of Non-Fictional Arabic Literature* (Wiesbaden: Harrassowitz, 1998).
— 'The Udhri Narrative in Arabic Literature', in Friederike Pannewick (ed.), *Martyrdom in Literature: Visions of Death and Meaningful Suffering in Europe and the Middle East from Antiquity to Modernity* (Wiesbaden: Harrassowitz, 2004), 162–89.
Lichtenstaedter, I., 'Folklore and Fairy-Tale Motifs in Early Arabic Literature', *Folklore* 51.3 (1940), 195–203.
Lotman, Yuri M., 'The Notion of Boundary', in *Universe of the Mind* (London: I.B. Tauris, 2001).
Lukács, Georg, *The Historical Novel*, trans. Hannah and Stanley Mitchell (Lincoln and London: University of Nebraska Press, 1983).
— *The Theory of the Novel*, trans. Anna Bostock (London: Merlin Press, 1971).
Lyons, M.C., *The Arabian Epic* (Cambridge: Cambridge University Press, 1995).
Marogy, Amal E., 'Zayd, ʿAmr and ʿAbdullāhi: Theory of Proper Names and Reference in Early Arabic Grammatical Tradition', in Amal Elesha Marogy (ed.), *Foundations of Arabic Linguistics: Sībawayhi and Early Arabic Grammatical Theory* (Leiden and Boston: Brill, 2012), 119–33.
Masters, Bruce, *The Arabs of the Ottoman Empire, 1516–1918* (New York: Cambridge University Press, 2013).
al-Masʿūdī, *Kitāb al-tanbīh wa-l-ashrāf*, ed. Michael Jan de Goeje (Leiden: Brill, 1893).
Meisami, Julie Scott and Paul Starkey (eds), *Encyclopedia of Arabic Literature*, paperback edn (London and New York: Routledge, 2010).
Moosa, Matti, *The Origins of Modern Arabic Fiction*, 2nd edn (Boulder, CO and London: Lynne Rienner, 1997).
Morony, M., 'Sāsānids', *EI*[2].
Muhannā, ʿAbd A., *Muʿjam al-nisāʾ al-shāʿirāt fī al-Jāhiliyya wa-l-Islām* (Beirut: Dār al-Kutub al-ʿIlmiyya, 1990).

al-Musawi, Muhsin, 'The Republic of Letters: Arab Modernity?', parts I and II, *Cambridge Journal of Postcolonial Literary Inquiry* 1.1 (2014), 265–80 and 2.1 (2015), 115–30.
Muṣṭafā, Ibrāhīm et al. (eds), *al-Muʿjam al-wasīṭ* (Istanbul: Dār al-Daʿwa, 1989).
Nallino, Maria, 'Le varie edizioni a stampa della Ǵamharat ašʿār al-ʿArab', *Rivista degli studi orientali* 13.4 (1933), 334–41.
Nāṣif, Malak Ḥifnī, 'al-Marʾa al-ʿArabiyya amsi wa-l-yawm', in Majd al-Dīn Ḥifnī Nāṣif (ed.), *Āthār Bāḥithat al-Bādiya* (Cairo: al-Muʾassasa al-Miṣriyya al-ʿĀmma, 1962), 289–92.
Omri, Mohamed-Salah, 'Guest Editor's Introduction', 'The Novelization of Islamic Literatures: The Intersections of Western, Arabic, Persian, Urdu and Turkish Traditions', *Comparative Critical Studies* 4.3 (2007), 317–28.
Ouyang, Wen-chin, *Politics of Nostalgia in the Arabic Novel* (Edinburgh: Edinburgh University Press, 2013).
Ouyang, Wen-chin and Paolo Lemos Horta (eds), *The Arabian Nights: An Anthology* (London: Everyman's Library, 2014).
Patel, Abdulrazzak *The Arab* Nahḍah*: The Making of the Intellectual and Humanist Movement* (Edinburgh: Edinburgh University Press, 2013).
Pellat, Ch., 'Abū Zayd al-Ḳurashī', *EI*[2].
Pellat, Ch., J.T.P. de Bruijn, B. Flemming and J.A. Haywood, 'Madjnūn Laylā', *EI*[2].
Praz, Mario, *The Romantic Agony*, 2nd edn (Oxford and New York: Oxford University Press, 1970).
Propp, Vladimir, *Theory and History of Folklore*, trans. Ariadne Y. Martin and Richard P. Martin (Minneapolis: University of Minnesota Press, 1984).
Qāsim, Maḥmūd, *Mawsūʿat al-aflām al-ʿarabiyya: 1927–2018*, vol. 2 (London: E-Kutub, 2017).
al-Qurashī, Abū Zayd, *Jamharat ashʿār al-ʿArab* (Beirut: Dār Ṣādir/Dār Bayrūt, 1963).
Reynolds, Dwight F., *Arab Folklore: A Handbook* (Westport, CT and London: Greenwood Press, 2007).
— *Heroic Poets, Poetic Heroes* (Ithaca, NY: Cornell University Press, 1995).
Rosenthal, F., 'Ibn Abī Ṭāhir Ṭayfūr', *EI*[2].
Rosenthal, Franz, *A History of Muslim Historiography*, 2nd edn (Leiden: Brill, 1968).
Sajdi, Dana, *The Barber of Damascus: Nouveau Literacy in the Eighteenth-Century Ottoman Levant* (Stanford, CA: Stanford University Press, 2013).

Selim, Samah, *The Novel and the Rural Imaginary in Egypt, 1880–1985* (London and New York: RoutledgeCurzon, 2004).

Shahîd, Irfan, *Byzantium and the Arabs in the Fifth Century* (Washington, DC: Dumbarton Oaks, 1989).

El-Shamy, Hasan M., *Folk Traditions of the Arab World: A Guide to Motif Classification* (Bloomington and Indianapolis: Indiana University Press, 1995).

al-Shayzarī, ʿAbd al-Raḥmān b. Naṣr, *Rawḍat al-qulūb wa-nuzhat al-muḥibb wal-maḥbūb*, eds David Semah and George J. Kanazi (Wiesbaden: Harrassowitz, 2003).

Sheehi, Stephen, 'Towards a Critical Theory of al-Nahḍah: Epistemology, Ideology and Capital', *JAL* 43.2–3 (2012), 269–98.

Shukrī, ʿAbd al-Raḥmān, *Ḍaw' al-fajr*, 2nd printing (Alexandria: Jurjī Gharzūzī Press, 1914 or 1915).

Slyomovics, Susan, *The Merchant of Art* (Berkeley and London: University of California Press, 1987).

Sprenger, A., 'Notes on Alfred von Kremer's Edition of Wáqidy's Campaigns' (Second Notice), *Journal of the Asiatic Society of Bengal* 25.3 (1856), 199–220.

Starkey, P., 'al-Nahḍa', *EAL*, 573–4.

Streck, M. and J. Lassner, 'al-Karkh', *EI*[2].

Strauss, Johann, 'Who Read What in the Ottoman Empire?', *MEL* 6.1 (2003), 39–76.

Thompson, E.F., 'Politics by Other Screens: Contesting Movie Censorship in the Late French Empire', *Arab Media & Society* (January 2009), 1–23.

Thompson, Stith, *Motif-Index of Folk-Literature* (Copenhagen: Rosenkilde and Bagger, 1958).

al-Udhari, Abdullah, *Classical Poems by Arab Women: A Bilingual Anthology* (London: Saqi, 1999).

Warner, Marina, *From the Beast to the Blonde: On Fairy Tales and Their Tellers* (London: Vintage, 1995).

— *Once Upon a Time: A Short History of Fairy Tale* (Oxford: Oxford University Press, 2014).

Watt, W. Montgomery, 'Idjāra', *EI*[2].

Yamūt, Bashīr, *Shāʿirāt al-ʿArab fī al-Jāhiliyya wa-l-Islām* (Beirut: al-Maktaba al-Ahliyya, 1934).

Yaqṭīn, Saʿīd, *Qāl al-rāwī* (Casablanca: al-Markaz al-Thaqāfī al-ʿArabī, 1997).

Yāqūt, *Muʿjam al-buldān* (Beirut: Dār Ṣādir, 1955–7).
Zaydān, Jurjī, *Tārīkh adab al-lugha l-ʿArabiyya*, vol. 2 (Cairo: Dār al-Hilāl, 1912).
al-Ziriklī, Khayr al-Dīn, *al-Aʿlām*, 2nd printing, vol. 6 (Cairo: al-Muʾallif, 1955).
Zuhur, Sherifa, *Asmahan's Secrets: Woman, War and Song* (Austin, TX: Center for Middle Eastern Studies, 2000).

Appendix: The Arabic Text

إعلم أن أوّل العرب نزار بن معد بن عدنان بن أدّ بن متوم بن تارح بن يعرب بن يشخب بن ثيب بن حمل بن فيداد بن اسماعيل بن إبراهيم الخليل عليهما السلام فأولد نزار ثلاثة أولاد وهم ربيعة ومضر وإياد وكل واحد من الثلاثة أولد وتشعب وكثرت شعوبهم وقبائلهم أما ربيعة فأولد أولادًا كثيرة وشعوبًا شتّى وهم بنو أسد وبنو جديلة وبنو دعيم وبنو هيث وبنو ضبيعة وبنو عجل وبنو يشكر وبنو حنيفة وبنو قاسط وقاسط أبو النمر ووائل ووائل أبو بكر وتغلب وتشعب من بكر بنو عليّ وبنو الصعب وبنو عكابة وبنو ثعلبة وبنو قيس وبنو سعد وبنو سفيان وبنو ذهل وبنو مرة وبنو شيبان وتشعب من تغلب بنو غنم وبنو عمرو وبنو حبيب وبنو جشم وبنو أسد والأراقم وبنو زهير وبنو مالك فهؤلاء كلهم بنو ربيعة بن نزار وأما مضر الأحمر فتشعب منه بنو إلياس وبنو مدركة وبنو خزيمة وبنو كنانة وبنو النضر وبنو مالك وبنو فهر وبنو غالب وبنو لؤي وبنو كعب وبنو مرة وبنو كلاب وبنو قصيّ وبنو عبد مناف وبنو هاشم وبنو مخزوم هؤلاء بنو مضر وأمّا إياد بن نزار وأولاده فكان منزلهم البحرين وأراضي العجم ولا أحفظ لهم شعوبًا ولا قبائل وسكن ربيعة نجد العريض وما يليها من الأرض وسكن بنو مضر مكة وتهامة وجدة وما يليها من أرض اليمن كالسلان ودقة ونحوهما وكان رئيس ربيعة بن نزار الأسد بن بكر بن مرة فأولد روحان أبا البَرّاق وابنة زوّجها من لكَيْز بن مرة فأولد منها خمسة أولاد وهم صاف وعكرمة والأرقم وعقيل وبجير وثلاث بنات وهن سعدى وخولة وليلى زوجة البراق فزوج لكيز ابنته سعدى بالملك ثعلبة الأعرج الغساني وزوج خولة وقيل بل اسمها كاملة بشبيب بن لهيم الطائي خال البراق وبقيت ليلى وكان يقال لها ليلى العفيفة وكانت أصغرهنّ سنًا وأحسنهنّ وجهًا وكان البراق يحبها حبًا شديدًا وكان في صغره يتبع رعاة الإبل ويحلب اللبن ويأتي به إلى راهب حول المراعي فيتعلم منه تلاوة الإنجيل وكان يدين بدينه وكان حليمًا كريمًا شجاعًا وقورًا خبيرًا ومع ذلك لم يبلغ الخمس عشرة سنة حتى جاءت الحرب بين بني ربيعة وبني إياد ولخم فظهر منه من القيام والفروسية ما لم يكن لغيره وذلك ان الربيعة أجدبت بلادهم فافترقوا في طلب الخصب ونزل رجل يقال له نوفل بن سمير من تغلب بفريق من قومه على حجيب بن وارد الإيادي فأنزله وأرعاه في الحما وكان حجيب قد زوج معمر بن سوار بابنته فأقامت عنده مدة من الزمان ثم أرادت زيارة أبيها وإخوتها فوجه بها معمر إليهم ومعها غلمان وقيان وإبل وحفدة فنزلوا على حجيب فقام إجلالاً لإبل الملك وأمر بحفظها ورعيها في الحما فوافقت إبل نوفل فلما رآها عبيد الملك الذين مع الإبل ضربوها ضربًا عنيفًا فقدم نوفل والعبيد يضربون إبله فقال مهلاً نحن نغدو عنكم بإبلنا وأمر رعاته بإخراج إبله من الحما فحثوا بإخراجها فغلبت عليهم لجوعها وخصب المرعى وأعيت الضرب والسوق فأقبل واحد من عبيد الملك وانتضى سيفه وحمل على الإبل فعقر عشر رواحل فلما

رأى نوفل ذلك عقل راحلته بفاضل زمامها وحمل على العبد فقتله وحل عقال ناقته وركبها وصاح برعاته فأعجلوا بإخراج الإبل من الحما وصاحت الغلمان إلى أن بلغ الصراخ الأخنس بن حجيب وكان مجنبًا مع الإبل ومعه رجلان فلما سمع الصياح أغار بالرجلين فوجد العبد قتيلاً فركضوا خلف نوفل فأدركوه فالتفت اليهم نوفل وقال الجار جاركم والعبد عبدكم فقد رأيتم ما صنع وما صنع به والأمر يرجع اليكم فتروع الأخنس واستشار صاحبيه في أمره فقالا هذه فضيحة علينا وحملوا على نوفل وأخذوه على أطراف الرماح وانصرفوا عنه قتيلاً قال ابن نافع فحمله رعاة ابله وأنزلوه عند امرأته الهيفاء بنت صبيح القضاعية وأخبروها بخبره وكان معه عشرة من قومه فأرادوا الغارة لينتصروا لصاحبهم فقالت لهم مهلاً لا يقع منكم أمر الآن تلتقوا بقومكم ولا تعجلوا حتى أرجع اليكم ثم شدت على بعيرها وحملت زوجها عليه وكان عند غروب الشمس (وكانت عارفة منزل حجيب)[1] فأناخت بعيرها بجانب منزل حجيب واستعبرت على زوجها بالبكاء فوثب حجيب (من فوق فراشه)[2] وهو لا يعلم بشيء حتى استرجعت من بكائها فتنفست الصعداء وأنشأت تقول

أبكي وأبكي بإسفار وإظلامِ
على فتى تغلبيّ الأصل ضرغامِ
لهفي عليه وما لهفي بنافعه
إلا تكافح فرسان وأقوام
قل للحجيب لحاك الله من رجل
حملت عار جميع الناس من سام
أيقتل ابنك بعلي يا ابن فاطمة
وتشرب الماء ذا أضغاث احلام
(بالله لا زلت أبكيه وأندبه
حتى تزورك أخوالي وأعمامي)[3]
بكل أسمر لدن الكعب معتدل
وكل أبيض صافي الحد صمصام

[1] Parenthetical remark found in Ms. Or. Oct. 1383 (88v).
[2] Parenthetical remark found in Ms. Or. Oct. 1383 (88v).
[3] Parenthetical line found in Ms. Or. Oct. 1383 (88v). I have added the first-person possessive pronoun to 'paternal uncles'.

فلما فرغت قال لها حجيب مهلاً يا حرة العرب والله قد ساءني عويلك فأخبريني بالخبر فقالت أتسألني وأنت الخبير بذلك فقال والله لو كنت خبيراً ما سألتك فأخبرته بالخبر فقال قتلني الله إن لم أقتل من قتل جاري فقالت دونك جارك فادفنه فقال دعيه فقد صار لي وعليّ فتركته ورحلت هي وقومها إلى بني تغلب وأما حجيب فجهز جاره ودفنه والتمس ابنه الأخنس وصاحبيه فلم يظفر بهم وأخبر أنهم لحقوا بصهرهم معمر بن سوار اللخمي فشد حجيب راحلته وأخذ لأمة حربه وجنب جواده وتوجه الى الملك يريد ولده وصاحبيه فنزل بصهره فاستقبله أحسن استقبال وأكرمه وأقبل يسأله في ولده فقال كلا لا يقتل ولدي جاري وأرغب في حياته بعده فقال الملك لست أسلم اليك جيراني فقال والله إن ذلك لقطيعة بيني وبينك إلى آخر الدهر واغلظ الكلام على الملك وقال أتختار أن تكسوني العار بين ربيعة ومضر وإياد فسلم إليه ولده وصاحبيه وقال أنت أحق بولدك فافعل به ما بدا لك فأخذهم من عند الملك وانصرف بهم حتى أوقفهم على قبر نوفل بن سمير التغلبي وضرب اعناقهم مبتدئًا بولده ثم بصاحبيه ودفنهم بجانب قبر جاره وانصرف الى أبياته فلم يهنه أكل ولا شرب ولا نامت له عين واستلقى فراشه وأنشأ يقول

سرى نومي وأرقني السهاد
وذو الأحزان ليس له رقاد
فلو كان القتيل بيوم حرب
وقد كثر التطاعن والجلاد
لكان مصابه فيه يسيراً
ويؤخذ ثأره ممن يراد
بنيّ فما أردت بقتل جاري
أتصطاد الكماة ولا تصاد
بنيّ قتلت جاري باعتماد
وقتلك يا بنيّ هو اعتماد
فذق مثل الذي جرعت جاري
ومت كمدًا فذاك لك العماد
فابكي يا جميلة لا تملي
فقد انضت قلوصي والمزاد
وخيلي في مرابطها قيامًا

جفاها الكر وانفصم الطراد
فوا أسفًا على ولدي وليتي
جفتني عند مقتله الحداد
على الماضين من سلف كرام
من السادات للسادات سادوا
ومن كان الربيع وكان غيثًا
عطاياه إذا وقع الجماد
أبيت مسهداً يا طول ليلي
كأن العين يحشوها القتاد

قال ابن نافع ولما لحقت امرأة نوفل بقومها أخبرتهم بخبر زوجها فجزعوا وأسفوا عليه شديدًا وشدّت إخوته وأولاد عمه وهم خمسة وعشرون فارسًا وأغاروا على حجيب الإيادي فشد هو وأولاده وقومه والتقوا واطردوا والتقى مالك بن سمير أخو نوفل بزياد بن حجيب وأولاده فحملوا على مالك وقتلوه بأخيهم واقتتل القوم بعد ذلك ساعة وتواردت خيل إياد على فرسان تغلب فكسروهم وقتلوا منهم تسعة رجال وأثخنوا الآخرين بالجراح فعادوا على قومهم على أسوأ حال وصاح صائحهم في أحياء ربيعة كافة فشدوا خيلهم واغاروا على حجيب الإيادي قال ابن نافع فأقبلت بوادر الخيل عند طلوع الشمس فشد حجيب وأولاده وجميع قومه ولقوا الخيل فاقتتلوا ساعة فانكسرت خيل حجيب وولوا هاربين وهرب حجيب وأولاده وبنو أخيه وكان حجيب من أشد إياد وقتل من أولاده وأولاد أخيه سبعة فرسان فعند ذلك رفع بنو تغلب السيوف وانصرفت خيلهم راجعة قال ابن نافع فغضبت قبائل إياد لذلك واجتمعوا الى حجيب بن وارد وعزموا على قتال ربيعة وبلغ ما هم عليه معمر بن سوار صهر حجيب فجند جنوده وأنفق عليهم الأموال الجزيلة وأمرهم بالمسير الى صهره حجيب وقبائل إياد فاجتمعت بيوت ربيعة وتداعت حللهم واستعدوا لقتال إياد وصهرهم معمر بن سوار وكان قد أهمهم حرب الملك معمر وأهالهم أمره ثم إن خيل معمر وجنوده وبني إياد قصدوا (صرم) لكيز بن مرة و(صرم) روحان بن أسد وكانا (صرمين)[4] متجاورين فشدت ربيعة خيلها ولاقت الخيل وكان البراق بن روحان لم يعرف شيئًا من الوقائع لصغر سنه فركب جواده ذلك اليوم وأراد القتال معهم فنهاه أخوه الأكبر خوفًا عليه فلم ينته فقال البراق دعني فإني كنت غافلا والآن انتبهت

[4] These parenthetical insertions are from Ms. Or. Oct. 1383 (90r).

فلما رأى أخوه ذلك نادى أمه أن أوثقي البراق فإنه يريد الخروج إلى الحرب فقالت دعه (أفأتركه يرضع ثدي)[5] فخرج وخرج أبوه روحان وجده شبيب بن لهيم الطائي وحضر البراق تلك الموقعة وهي أول موقعة عرف بها فقاتل قتالاً شديدًا وظهرت منه شجاعة لم تظهر من غيره ولم يزل يقاتل هو وقومه جنود الملك معمر وبني إياد في جميع وقائعهم سبع سنين حتى انصرمت الفتنة وانتصرت ربيعة بالبراق على إياد وصهرهم وسموه أبا النصر وفي ذلك يقول عبيد بن دوران

كسرنا بالفتى البرّاق جندًا
من الأعراب كانوا في وثوب
فكان محملاً للواء قومي
فيا لك من قضاقضة غلوب
ولله الفتى أنّا نصرنا
بابن لابن روحان الحبيب
بأروع من بني أسد شهابًا
مضيئًا للبعيد وللقريب
وكم من سائل عن ابن روح
من المسترفدين ذوي الندوب
رأوه غدوة بالواد صبحًا
على ذي منعة نهد صليب
وان لا ينثني عن ضرب قوم
ولا طعن الأباهر من قريب
إلى أن اورد الرايات جهرا
عيون الماء تعذب للشروب
وكنا قد حمينا الماء حتى
شربنا الماء من تحت الركوب
مخافة أن نولي من عدانا
فنفضح بالمذلة والهروب

[5] Parenthetical insertion is from Ms. Or. Oct. 1383 (90r).

شربنا الماء واندقت رحاهم
وأفلت جند معمر والحجيب[6]

قال ابن نافع وكان البراق مع شجاعته كريمًا سخيًا قال وبلغ من كرمه أن قومًا من عدوان قصدوا قبائل وائل يسترفدونهم في ديون عليهم فوفدتهم ربيعة ثلاث مئة راحلة وقصدوا البراق بن روحان فأكرمهم غاية الإكرام ثم رفدهم إبله وإبل أبيه وأخيه فقال أخوه الجنيد مهلاً انك أسرفت في العطاء فقال أبوه روحان لأنت ولدي والعطاء يعدل ميل اللئام فذكر البراق بذلك في الكرم ومن ذلك ما قال فيه مالك بن سليم العدواني

تساقى وائل كرماً فأذرى
بأجواد الأعارب والملوك
فأنعم بالديات فدته نفسي
فما لابن الكريمة من شريك
وأرفدنا رفود بني أبيه
قلائص مثل قضبان الدريك
فلا زال الحياة لنا ضياءً
من القتمات بالبشر الضحوك

قال فسمعت أخواله طيّ بذلك فأرفدوهم اضعاف رفده وعظمت منزلة البراق في أعين الناس واستهالوا أمره وأثنوا عليه جميلاً وقد ذكرنا أن ليلى العفيفة ابنة لكيز بن مرة قد بقيت في بيت أبيها وكان البراق يهواها لنفسه أن يتزوج بها وكان قد شاع في العرب حسنها وأدبها حتى ذكرت في مجالس الملوك وتحدثت بها الناس وكان أبوها لكيز بن مرة يفد على عمرو بن ذي صهبان فيجزل عطيته ويحسن إكرامه فوفد عليه ذات يوم فأكرمه وأتحفه ثم خطب منه في مجلسه ليلى العفيفة فلم يردد له جواباً واستحى منه لأجل إكرامه له وإنعامه عليه وانصرف من عنده فلبث أياماً ثم جهز إليه عمرو وفداً بالهدايا السنية فقدموا عليه وقدموا ما أتوا به فأنزلهم أحسن منزل وأكرمهم غاية الإكرام ثم خطبوا منه ليلى فقال إني قد زوجت ابنتين لي بغير إذن قومي وأما هذه فلا بد أن أشاورهم في أمرها فإن وافقوني وإلا رجعتم إلى صاحبكم قالوا افعل واختر لابنتك دار القرار قال ابن نافع وانصرف لكيز الى خلوة له وأمر اولاده فحضروا إليه فقال

[6] Ahlwardt 9747 (81r) has (والحليب).

عليّ بعمكم ربيعة بن مرة وأولاده وخالكم روحان وأولاده فجاؤوه بهم وجلسوا بين يديه ثم أخبرهم بخطبة الملك واستشارهم في أمره وأطنب لهم في الثناء عليه وإنه يكون لهم عزًا وكهفًا في عظائم الأمور وكان لكيز سيد قبائل وائل فأطرق كل منهم (في الأرض) لأنهم يعلمون رغبة البراق فيها وأنه لا يريد غيرها وهم لا يريدون له غيره (بقربها)[7] فتكلم ربيعة بن مرة وقال

غربت كاملة وسعدى إنّما
أمراك بيعهما بنقد وافر
وطرائف الأملاك عندك لم تزل
من جرد خيل وثياب حرائر
ولأجل ذلك جئت تشفع وترها
فالشفع ويلك ليس مثل الواتر
فدع الطماعة واسْلُ عن تزويجها
في ملك غسان وملك مناذر[8]
ولئن أبيت بسوء فعلك رأينا
لتعض فيه على بنان الخاسر

فقال لكيز قد سمعت ما عندك والتفت إلى كليب بن ربيعة وقال هات ما عندك فقال

مقالي صواب إن يكن فيك ينجع
وفي بعض هذا ما يضر وينفع
أرانا كأنّا حولتيك ثعالب
وأنت كليب النار لا تتروع
نرى غير براق اذا كان معظم
من الأمر محذور يخاف ويرجع
فإن كان قد اعياك يا عم ما ترى
فيا رب رأس بالصوارم يقطع

[7] Parenthetical insertions from Ms. Or. Oct. 1383 (91v).
[8] Ms. Or. Oct. 1383 (91v) has (مساور), as does Ahlwardt 9747 (82r). As Geert Jan van Gelder has explained to me, this is probably a corruption of (المناذر), poetic licence for (المناذرة), plural of (المنذر), the name of several Lakhmid kings.

وليس الذي أملته أن تناله
ولا في الذي جاءت به الوفد مطمع

قال ابن نافع واشتد غضب كليب للبراق لأنه كان يحبه شديدًا فقال لكيز قد سمعت ما عندك فما ترى يا روحان فقال اعذرني من ذلك فقال لا والله لا بد لك من إظهار رأيك فقال

أخوك وأنت أولى بالصواب
وما عند ابن سؤلة من جواب
سوى أني أميل إلى رضاكم
وأكتم عنكم نجوى الخطاب
اذا ما المستشار أفاض نصحًا
ولم يقبل أفاض إلى العتاب
فكل الرأي أقبله لديكم
ولو فيه عظيمات المصاب
دعوا رأيي فليس له سبيل
ورأيكم المفوض في الصعاب

قال ابن نافع فلما سمع لكيز كلام صهره قال لابن اخيه نويرة أشرْ علينا يا نويرة بما أنت أهله فقال

أشير وهل رأيي يصح ويقبل
ورأيك في ما تدعيه مفضّل
وإنك بالرأي المفوض عارف
وغيرك في هذا يضل ويجهل
لعمري وإن كانت ظنوني كثيرة
فإنك للبراق تأبى وتخذل
وترغب في فضل الملوك لأنهم
لهم في فنون الفضل ما هو أفضل
وإن طالت الأملاك بالنيل والجدى
فإن يد البراق بالروع أطول

وإن تطلب الرأي الذي ليس نافعًا
فليس أخو قول كمن هو يفعل

فقال لكيز قد دعوناكم للمشورة فما بال التهديد والوعيد ثم أعرض عنهم ليسمع ما عند المهلهل وكان أصغر إخوته فتكلم المهلهل وأغلظ لعمه بالكلام وتنفس غضبًا وقال

ما لي وللرأي في ما كنت أجهله
وأنت تعلم ما تهوى وتفعله
بالله ما جئت إلا ما علمت وما
يخفي عليك الذي تنوي وتعقله
لو كنت ترجو بني عم وتأملهم
ما كان يقصاك مما جاء أفضله
فالبس حريرك إني عنه في شغل
لباسي الصوف أرضاه وأقبله
لا ترجون كرامات الملوك ولا
تعجل بأمرك شر الأمر أعجله
أرح فؤادك واردد ما أتوك به
واقنع بعيشك هذا الرأي أجمله
إن الطماعة مولاها أخو فشل
ما ينزل الذل إلا وهو منزله

قال فتبسم لكيز مستهزئًا بالمهلهل ثم أقبل على شريف قومه وقال يا براق ان هذا الملك سبقني بالنعمة وعمني بفضله وكان يظن فيّ ما يظن بالسادات انها مطاعة متبوعة فخطب إليّ في مجلسه وخاصته ووزرائه وقد أنعمت له أملاً فيك وحسن ظن بك إنك غير مخالف وتدبيراً مني بأن يكون هذا الملك فرجًا لشدائدكم وحصنًا في جواركم وذخيرةً لعظائم أموركم وما ظننت أحداً يخالفني غيرك وقد سمعت جوابهم فهل ترضى يا بنيّ أن تكذّب عمك بعد صدقه وتصغّره بعد كبره ولم أقل ذلك إلا بعد علمي بصبرك يا براق على المكروه وشرف نفسك ونخوتك وقلة المخالفة عندك لعشيرتك قال فلما سمع البراق كلام لكيز تنفس وأنشأ يقول

يا طالب الأمر لا يعطى أمانيه
استعمل الصبر في ما كنت تبغيه

والبس لسرك ما تخفيه مجتهدًا
والبس عفافك في ما كنت تعنيه
يا أيها الشيخ والمرجو نائله
ناديت من هو ما يرضيك يرضيه
إني أشير بما تهواه متبعًا
هواك دع عنك ماذا أنت تأتيه
أكرم وفودك والميعاد اوف به
ودع ربيعة في ما قال وابنيه
فصاحب الصدق يجني صدقه حسنًا
وصاحب الشر سوء الشر يحنيه
أنت المعول في أهليك حيث ترى
لثوب عرضك أسباباً تنقيه
فأكرم بناتك وافعل ما أردت بها
من صالحات ومن خير ترجّيه
لكيز لا تغدرن ما كنت موثقه
ومن عناك فإني سوف أعنيه
اتبع مرادك لا تتبع كليبًا فما
يرد قولك لغوًا كان لاغيه
لا تنظرن لسقم حل في جسدي
فصاحب الداء يلقى من يداويه
يا أيها الوفد قد فزتم بحاجتكم
وفد ابن صهبان عمرو نحن نفديه
الواهب المئة الحمراء يتبعها
من وافر النقد آلافًا لراجيه
لا تخبرن عمروًا من قولي بفاحشة
فلست أرضى بذم أن اكافيه
واهد التحية مني لابن مارية
وطيبات سلام سوف أهديه

قال ابن نافع فلما فرغ البراق من شعره قام أبوه وإخوته وربيعة وأولاده مغضبين أشد الغضب وأقبل على لكيز أولاده يلومونه وقالوا يا أبانا إن غضب عمنا وبنيه لشأن عظيم فهل لك أن لا تفعل فقال إن البراق ثمرة فؤادي ولا شيء يفوقه عندي وقد عذروني لذكاء عقله وسعة صدره فكونوا طوع يدي من بعده ثم أمر لهم بجياد الخيل التي أهداها له الملك وقسمها بينهم يريد إرضاءهم بذلك فقالوا نحن راضون بما رضوا ساخطون لما سخطوا فافترقوا وقام لكيز الى الوفد وأخبرهم بما كان فقالوا لا نرى رأياً حتى نخبر الملك بما أنتم عليه وننشده شعر البراق وغيره ثم ودعوه وانصرفوا إلى الملك وأخبروه وأنشدوه أبيات القوم فشكر البراق وأثنى عليه وقال سوف أكافيه على مروءته وحسن أخلاقه قال ابن نافع ولما يئس البراق من ليلى اشتد به الوجد وصبر ذلك اليوم إلى ان جنه الليل فمشى الى ابيات ليلى ودخل عليها وهي نائمة فأيقظها وكانت محجوبة عنه لمظنة خطبته إياها فقالت ما ذاك يا براق فقال جئتك زائرًا ومودّعًا وأخبرها بأن أباها أنعم بها للملك فتنفست الصعداء وتململت وقالت يا لك من غم ما أطوله ثم بكت بكاءً شديدًا وأقبلت على البراق فقالت له إن الحب قد نزل عليّ وعليك والصبر جلباب حسن فأعد من الصبر ما تعطي به هواك وتكتم به داءك فلما رآها البراق على تلك الحالة شفق عليها وبكى لبكائها وهم البراق بالانصراف عنها فقالت له أقم هذا الليل نتمتع من الوداع وسيسدل الحجاب من غدٍ ويطول الفراق بيننا ثم أنشدت

تزود بنا زاداً فليس براجع
  إلينا وصال بعد هذا التقاطع
وكفكف بأطراف الوداع تمتعًا
  جفونك من فيض الدموع الهوامع
الا فاجزني صاعًا بصاع كما ترى
  تصوب عيني حسرة بالمدامع

فأجابها البراق يقول

خدي بالصبر لا تبكي ارتياعًا
  فداعي الشوق أجدر أن يطاعا
وغضي الصوت يا ليلى فإني
  متى أخفيت هذا الصوت ذاعا
ولكني سأعرض عنك جهدي

وابتدل السرايا والرقاعا
واقري طارقي لحمًا غريضًا
وأرفده الوليدات الصناعا
ولست وإن حويت جميع هذا
أتيت به وربكم ابتداعا
وقبلي والدي أسد بن بكر
علا في الناس فخرًا واصطناعا
وروحان أبي وأخي ظليل
فشا في الناس ذكرهما وشاعا
فإن يك اللكيز عليه حكم
فإن لنا احتكامًا وامتناعا
أكوع عن الفراق ورب قرن
غداة الروع عني فيه كاعا

قال وبات البراق يودع ليلى وتودعه الى أخريات الليل فخرج وأتى الى أبيه وإخوته وأمرهم بالرحيل فارتحلوا ونزلوا على بني حنيفة قومهم واجتمعوا في أوطانهم وأخذ البراق يعزي نفسه عن ليلى وهو لا يزداد إلا شوقًا إليها وأنشأ يقول

ما لعيني جنت عليّ عذابا
سال دمعي قرنفلاً ولبابا
زرع[9] الحب في بساتين قلبي
شجراً اينعت بكاءً وانتحابا
كلما قلت قد تسلّى فؤادي
ساح دمعي على الخدود انسكابا
لعن الله من يلوم محبًّا
ولئن ظن في الملام صوابا
حب ليلى وحبنا آل ليلى

[9] Ahlwardt 9747 (85r) has (ذرع), a hypercorrection for (زرع), which appears in Ms. Or. Oct. 1383 (95v).

زاد قلبي صبابة وعتابا
من رآني يقول ذا طيف جنّ
أو سقيم كفى بهذا مصابا
عمرك الله ما بجسمي سقام
وجنون ولا جنيت ارتكابا
غير حب لذات وجه مليح
وبنان رخصٍ يزين الخضابا
واثيث كأنما الليل فيه
حالك اللون بات يحكي الغرابا
من رآها يقول ظبية إنس
أو هلال جلا ضياه السحابا
قد براني وقد بلاني هواها
أوقد الحب في فؤادي شهابا
كل يوم تثور في وسط قلبي
حرقة للهوى تزيد التهابا

وقال أيضاً

قل للتي تركت فؤادي هائمًا
يرعى رياض ديارهم ويروح
حسبي بحبك أن أبيت مسهدًا
والدمع من فوق الخدود سفوح
يا ذات وجه كالهلال إذا بدا
خلق الجمال لديه وهو مليح
منّي بوصلك لا عدمتك مرة
حاشا المحبّ فما المحبّ شحيح
كم بين من يمسي ينام وآخر
يمسي على ظهر الفراش ينوح
فانظر خليلي لا عدمتك بيننا
هل يستوي ذو علة وصحيح

قال وكان للبراق قينة جميلة يقال لها طريقة قد زوجها بغلام له يقال له سريع الاحجف فلما سمع الغلام أبيات مولاه وعلم بشدة شوقه ظنّ انه يريد طريقة فقال لها يا طريقة إني أرى سيدنا يتكلم بالمحبة والشوق وربما كان ذلك من أجلك فأرى أن تتزيني بأحسن زينتك وتلبسي أفخر ثيابك وتذهبي اليه وتكثري من التعريض عليه فان وجدت له رغبةً فيك طلقتك وأثرته بك فلبست طريقة حللها وحليها وانتهت الى سيدها وأكثرت من التعريض عليه فلما علم البراق بمرادها أنشأ يقول

كفي عن التعريض يا طريقة
إنك قد أصبحت لي صديقة
كريمة عزيزة حقيقة
عليّ فيما قلته شفيقة
هيهات عندي عروة وثيقة
لأكرم الناس على الخليقة

قال فقامت من عنده سوداء وجهها فانتهت الى زوجها وقالت له قبح الله رأيك لقد فضحتني ثم أخبرته وأنشدته الشعر فطابت نفسه مما يحاذر قال ثم إن أم الأغرّ أخت كليب بن ربيعة دخلت على بنت عمها ليلى فقالت يا ليلى أما لك أن تجزعي بما فعل أبوك بسيدنا وفارس خيلنا البراق قالت وما ذلك فأخبرتها وقالت

غفلت وما أنت بالغافلة
ولكن لكي تحسبي عاقلة
فما زال عقلك لبًّا عليك
وما زلت مشغولة شاغلة
أيجفو لكيز لبراقنا
جفاءً وكنت له آهلة
وبكر وعجل وشيبانها
ستعقر بينهم الراحلة

فأجابتها ليلى تقول

أم الأغرّ فضحتني لا تعجلي

إني أبين القول عندك فاعقلي
براق سيدنا وفارس خيلنا
وهو المطاعن في مضيق الجحفل
وهو الضياء والبرق والقمر الذي
عم الكواكب بالضياء الأطول
وعماد هذا الحيّ في مكروهه
ومؤمّل يرجوه كل مؤمّل
إني أحنّ لما ذكرت وإنّما
عرض العفيفة كالنسيج المفتّل
ما حيلتي فيما يراه أبي وهل
يأتي المعالي واقف في الأسفل
إنّ النساء أذلة مستورة
يعرفن بالرأي الضعيف الأعزل

قال ابن نافع ثم إن البراق لحقه من فراق ليلى سقم واصب وكتم أمره عن كل أحد وفي أثناء ذلك زاره كليب بن ربيعة ذات يوم لينظر ما هو عليه فسأله عن حاله وكان يعلم أنه لا يصبر على فراق ليلى وكان صديقًا له لا يكتم عنه أمرًا فأفاض اليه بسره وشكا اليه وجده عليها فاغتم كليب لذلك غمًا شديدًا وقال إن لم أنفع البراق بصداقتي مع الرحم الذي بيني وبينه فلا حاجة به إلى ذلك ثم خرج من عنده لا يرد جواباً وانصرف إلى أبياته ودعا إخوته وإخوة البراق وأولاد عمه لكيز فحضروا وجلسوا بين يديه فأخبرهم بحال البراق واستشارهم في أمره وكان أول من تكلم عقيل بن لكيز أخو ليلى فقال

الأمر فيه إليك يا ابن ربيعة
فاحكم بما أحببت في الإنجاز
واترك لكيزًا والذي يختاره
ليس اللكيز إذا حكمت بغاز

ثم تكلم صافي بن لكيز وقال يا كليب اقض ما أنت ما قاض في أختنا فنحن لا نريد به بدلاً ولو كان قليل المال فكيف وهو سيد العشيرة وغاية كل طلب ثم أنشأ يقول

اصدع برأيك يا ذا الرأي والأدب
والخيل والسمر والهندية القضب
هذا أخونا ومولانا وسيدنا
نرضى رضاه ولا نرضى برأي أبي
لا تركنن إلى الأملاك إنهم
أهل الطرائف والعقيان والذهب
ونحن أهل الفلاة لا نفارقها
ولا نبالي من العلياء والرتب
فاصدع برأيك لا تخفيه مشترگا
فأنت أولى بنا من سائر العرب

ثم تكلم عكرمة بن لكيز وقال الرأي عندك يا كليب ولعله من دون كل أحد مردود إليك ثم أنشأ يقول

دفعنا إليك الرأي يا ابن ربيعة
فدبر بما تختار خير مفوض
ولا تترك البراق في غمراته
وشمر له من قبل إلحاح مبغض
فبراق مولانا وفارس خيلنا
وصاحب طعن السمر وضرب أبيض

ثم تكلم بجير بن لكيز فقال والله ما أدري ما أشير به فإن وافقت أبي هلك أخي وإن وافقت أخي غضب أبي فيا لك من أمرين شديدين ثم أنشأ يقول

عليّ لكم في مثل هذا التجنب
فقد غرب الرأي الذي كنت أطلب
عليّ لبراق إخاء وذمة
وشيخي له عتب متى شاء يعتب
وما لي في هذا مقال وإنني
متى رمت في هذا المشورة أتعب
أشير بما لا أستطيع وإنما

أخاف مقالي أن يرد فأكذب
فإن كان ما جئتم به تقدرونه
فإني معكم قادر ومسبب
وإن كان صعبًا فالمشية فيكم
إذا وعد الإنسان فالوعد يطلب

ثم تكلم أرقم بن لكيز وقال إن البراق قرة أعيننا ودعامة أمرنا فامض برأيك وأنشأ يقول

لعمرك ما البراق عنّا بشاسع
ولا تارك أثقالنا في المقاطع
ولكن جلا همّ العشيرة بعدما
أتتهم من الأعداء كل الفجائع
فأرضوا لكيزًا باللقاح حلائبًا
وسوقوا إليه صافنات الجرائع
مدّوا[10] على البراق واستجلبوا له
فمستجلب الأشياء غير مسارع
ولا تستضيفوا بعدها الملامة
ويعذركم منها مقالة وادع
وأنتم بنو عم جميعاً وإخوة
لليلى التي فيها جميع البدائع

ثم تكلم نويرة بن ربيعة وقال إنكم أطول الناس باعًا وأشدهم امتناعًا وأمّا لكيز فاذا جدنا له بالعطاء لا يحتاج الملوك بعدها ولا يخاف الفقر ثم أنشأ يقول

إذا ما اجتمعنا في صلاح أمورنا
فمن ذا الذي في ما بنيناه يهدم
فنحن بنو عم وإخوتها الألى
يجر لهم ذاك الخميس العرمرم

[10] Ahlwardt 9747 (97r) and Ms. Or. Oct. 1383 (98v) have (امدّوا).

فسيروا إلى ليلى لإصلاح شأنها
فكلكم فيما ترون المحكّم
فعندي لعمي بعد سبعين بكرة
ثمان لقاح مثلها الخيل تقلم
وعند كليب مثلها ومهلهل
فقوموا إليه مسرعين وقدموا

ثم تكلم مهلهل بن ربيعة وقال إنكم احسنتم وأسأتم وأصبتم وأخطأتم فحكموا كليبًا وسلموا إليه الإبل فقال كليب قد أصاب المهلهل فقدموني على ذلك وأعطوني موعدًا لا يخلف فقالوا اللهم نعم وتواعدوا إلى ثلاثة أيام لاستتمام ما تفاوضوا به قال ابن نافع ثم إن الملك عمرو بن ذي صهبان أعدّ هدية حسنة من أفخر ما يكون من الحلي والحلل والفرش واليواقيت والخيل والدروع والسيوف ووجه بها مسلمة بن مالك الغساني في وجوه حضرته فما شعروا إلا و مسلمة قد نزل بربيعة بن مرة أبي كليب وقسم هدية الملك بين القوم وخص البراق بأحسنها وأفضلها قال ففسخت الهدية رأي كليب وأصحابه وحلت من عزائمهم وجدد مسلمة ومن معه الخطبة للملك فاستسلمهم ربيعة بن مرة إلى أجل معلوم بينهم وانصرفوا إلى الملك مبتهجين بما انعقد على أيديهم قال ابن نافع وفي تلك الأيام ورد بإبل عباد الضبعي غلام له يقال له معمر بن سوار وولده الحرث على عين قويرة يسقيانها فوردت عليهما إبل عمران بن نبيه السدوسي وكان ذا ثروة في المال والولد وكان معها ابن له يقال له الفضيل وغلام له فاصطدمت الإبل وتضايق الغلامان فاقتتلا وأخذ غلام الطائي حجراً فضرب به رأس غلام الوائلي فقتله فرماه الحرث بسهم فقتله وصرعه بين يدي مولاه وكان من رماة العرب فأقبل الفضيل على الحرث فقال الحرث ارجع إنما قتلته إذ قتل غلامي فأقدم فنهاه فلم ينته فرماه الحرث بسهم آخر فأتبعه بغلامه وانقلب إلى إبله فساقها عطاشًا إلى منازل أبيه عباد وإخوته فقالوا ما وراك فأخبرهم بقصته وأنشأ يقول

قتلت ابن عمران الفضيل وعبده
بقتل غلامي معمر بن سوار
وما رمت قتلاً للفضيل وإنما
أردت ذمامي إذ أخذت بثاري
رميت به سهمًا فعجل حتفه

وذلك شيء لم يكن بخياري
ألا فأسعدوني للوقيعة والبلى
وإضمار خيل قربت لمغار

قال فتفل أبوه في وجهه وقال لا أهلاً بك ولا سهلاً إذن والله أسلمك إلى عمران بن نبيه فيقتلك بولده ولا أبعث على قومي حرب سدوس فقال ولده ليس عمران يقتلني بولده ولا تسليمك إياي يدفع عنك حرب سدوس وقد وقعت في البلاء فالبس له جلبابًا قال وبلغ الصريخ إلى عمران بن نبيه فأغار فيمن حضر حتى وافى ولده مقتولاً فاحتمله على يديه وأنشأ يقول

يا عين جودي بدمع منك هتان
على الفضيل السدوسي ابن عمران
فمن لعين بكت مما أضر بها
ومن لقلب كثير الشجو حران
جنت ضبيعة[11] أمرًا لا تطيق له
أفٍّ لها من سحيق عرضه دان
بالله ما الثأر في حرث ووالده
ولا أخيه ولكن في ابن روحان
أعني الفتى السيد البراق فارسهم
أو في كليب فذاك الفارس الثاني
يا طيّ عدي جياد الخيل واحتملي
بيض السيوف فإني ثائر عان
أضحت سدوس من الميعاد قد تئمت
من ليث غاباتها أو ليث فتيان
لهفي عليه وما لهفي بنافعه
إلا تكافح فرسان بفرسان
لا بد من غارة شعواء يقدمها

[11] Ahlwardt 9747 (88v) has (ربيعة). Ms. Or. Oct. 1383 (100r), Arabe 5833 (107v), 5984 Adab (3) and Or. 2676 (155v) all have (ضبيعة).

نصر وجبر ومسعود بن فينان
وفارس الورد منصور وإخوته
من كل معتقل بالرمح طعان
ثأرًا لأروع ذي مجد وذي حسب
معلل المجد من بكر وكهلان
والله لا رقدت عيني ولا أغفلت
حتى أرى الخيل تجري في الدم القاني

قال ذؤيب بن نافع واجتمعت إلى عمران بن نبيه قبائل سدوس وقالوا الرأي إليك فمر بما شئت فقال لهم ليس في ضبيعة كفؤ لولدي ولست أرضى إلا بكليب بن ربيعة او البراق بن روحان فقالوا ليس هذا برأي أيقتل ابنك الحرث بن عباد وتريد التقاضي بكليب والبراق هذا هو البغي الصريح فخذ فيما لا ينكر عليك ودع الظلم والجناية واعلم ان حرب بني ضبيعة سيجني عليك حرب كليب وقومه الأراقم والبراق وقومه بني حنيفة وسائر بني شيبان ولا تستخف بذلك فانه سيكون فأنشد عمران يقول

يا خليليّ قربا لي جوادي
وقناتي دنا أوان الطراد
قربا صارمي ورمحي فإني
عاد ثأري على وضيع العباد
شر هذا الأنام خلقًا وخلقًا
ورضيع اللئام نسل عباد
الجبان النفور في حومة الحر-
ب أذل الفرسان يوم الجلاد
ليت ثأري على ابن روحان كفؤي
فأشتفي[12] منه علة الأكباد
لست أرضى بحيّ آل عباد

[12] (فاشتفي) is found in Ms. Or. Oct. 1383 (100v). Ahlwardt 9747 (89r) has (فاشتفت). Arabe 5833 (108r), 5984 Adab (4) and Or. 2676 (156r) all have (فاروي).

ليس فيهم كفايتي ومرادي
قبح الله حيَّهم بئس حيّ
جاء فيه القضاء بالمرصاد
يا سدوسا أليس فيكم رشيد
ثاقب الرأي صادق الميعاد
كيف يرضى نصر بقتل فضيل
ما له لا يقود شعث الجياد
ما لنصر كذا وما بال جبر
أشتكي الصمت منهما وأنادي
أوحداني وكنت غير وحيد
يوم ضرب الظبي وطعن الصعاد

قال فلما سمعه الرجلان أتيا إليه وهما نصر بن مسعود وجبر بن طورة وقالا أنت سيدنا ونحن قد سلمناك أمرنا فافعل بما شئت قال تأهبوا للغارة قالا على من تغير قال على كليب وقومه الأراقم فقالا لا نوافقك على ذلك بل نغير على أصحاب ثأرنا بني ضبيعة فوافقهما على ذلك مكرهًا قال وبلغ بني ضبيعة كلام عمران بن نبيه وكراهته التقاضي منهم بولده فأنفوا من ذلك واغتاظوا شديدًا وقال عباد في ذلك

حضر السهاد وغاب طيب رقادي
لسمو عمران على الأجواد
وأرى ابن مرة لا يزال مخالفًا
بالقول يسمو شامخ الأطواد
بالله لا نرضى بفعلة حارث
ولنأتينّ به على ميعاد
ولأحقنن دماءنا ودماءكم
في ما جنى الجاني بغير مراد
ولئن رجعت الى اللجاجة في اللقا
وطعان فرسان بيوم طراد
فلنشربن بكأس حرب مرة

كأسًا دهاقًا قاطع الأكباد
يا أيها المغرور بالحرب التي
فيها فنا الأرواح والأجساد
قد جانى القول الذي قد قلته
قول اللئام مورث الأحقاد
فاقبل وخذ قودًا ودع عنك البلى
وتكافحا بذوابل وحداد
واحذر على نصر وجبر واذخر
كل العشيرة إنني لك هاد

قال ابن نافع ثم إن عباد الضبعي وأكابر قومه وجهوا إلى عمران بن نبيه يعتذرون إليه من قتل ولده وإنهم غير راضين بذلك وسألوه أن يحكموه في الدية وأن يسلموه قاتل ولده فيقتله به فلما جأته رسالتهم بكى على ولده وقال لا أقتل الحرث بولدي ولست أقتل إلا كليبًا أو البراق وأنشأ يقول

لعمري ما ثأري بعباد وابنه
ولكن ثأري في كليب بن وائل
أو الفارس البراق سيد قومه
فذاك نظير الفضل عند الفضائل
ولكن قومي ما تساعد إنني
إليكم على وشك بأخذ النوازل
فنقتل قومًا منكم بقتيلنا
ونثني صدور الخيل ردف القبائل
أأقتل ضبعًا من ضبيع بأروع
سلالة أبطال كميّ حلاحل
وتسمع كهلان بأقبح سمعةٍ
فكلا ورب الواقعات اليعامل
ليعترفن أبناء ضبيعة وقعها
بكل رديني من السمر عاسل

وكل سدوسي تعود في الوغى
إذا التقت الأبطال قطع الكواهل
ولولا رجال لم تساعد مقالتي
لما كان ثأري في ضبيع الأراذل
ولكن وشيكًا يا ضبيعة أبشري
بكل طويل الباع ندب منازل
بفتيان صدق من سدوس أعزة
مغاوير في الهيجا ثم قواتل
إذا ما رأونا فوق قب مغيرة
وفوق قطاها فتية بالمناصل
فلا تطمعوا أن يرجع القوم بأسنا
ولكن من ينعيه صوت الثواكل
لأنا أناس قد سمعتم بفضلنا
لنا الطول في الهيجا على كل طائل

قال ابن نافع ولما رجعت رسل بني ضبيعة بجواب عمران شمرت للفتنة وأخذوا في إسراج الخيل واستحداد السيوف ونفض الدروع وأجاب الحرث بن عباد يقول

أرى ابن نبيه قد سما فوق قدره
ومستهزئًا بالأكرمين الأطاول
فاقسم بالبطحا ومن حل حولها
وأكرام قومي الماجدين الأفاضل
ليعترفن عمران رؤوس خيولنا
إذا ما التقينا بالرماح العواسل
فقل لسدوس إن أردتم نزالنا
فيا رب مكتوب على الخد مائل
ولم أبتغي قتل الفضيل ابتداءة
ولكنه لم يستمع قول قائل
كذا ابن نبيه لا يزال مخالفاً

إلى أن يرى منا صدور الجحافل
ويصبح منكبًا على الخد راغما
وتنهشه طلس السباع العواسل
ويرحل مذمومًا وترحل بعده
سراة رجال عن أذاه عوادل
فلا تنوِ يا عمران ما لا تطيقه
لغير الذي ألفيت أخذ الحبائل
ومن كان من قومي وقومك غافلاً
فليس بعيد اليوم عنا بغافل
وأنت إلى البراق في الروع مسرع
فيا لك من قرنين عند التنازل
سيشهدها البراق وشكا بقومه
ومشتملاً فيه كليب بن وائل

قال ابن نافع ثم اجتمع هؤلاء وهؤلاء والتقوا بمنور وهو واد كثير الماء فاقتتلوا حتى مال الضحى وافترقوا فعند ذلك نزل عمران بن نبيه وكان أشد قومه بأسًا ونادى بالبراز فبرز إليه نويرة بن عباد وكان فارسًا شجاعًا فاقتتلا ساعة وظفر عمران بنويرة فجدله صريعًا ونادى بالبراز فبرز إليه عامر بن عباد وكان أفرس إخوته فاقتتلا ساعة وافترقا على سلامة ثم تعاطفا فاختلفت بينهما طعنتان كان السابق فيهما عمران فأرداه صريعًا وتواترت خيل أولاد عباد على عمران فأتبع بعضهم بعضًا وكانوا تسعة رجال فلم يبق منهم إلا الحرث وهو أصغرهم سنًا فلما نادى عمران بالبراز حرك الحرث جواده وأراد الخروج إليه فزجره أبوه وقال مهلاً يا بنيّ دعني وفارس سدوس أنا أبرز إليه فإنه لم يبق من إخوتك غيرك وإنني بعد اليوم لضنين بك فقال الحرث يا أبي دعني وإياه لآخذ منه بدم إخوتي أو ألحقهم فما للعيش بعدهم لذة وركض بجواده على عمران واطردا ساعة فاختلف بينهما طعنتان كان السابق فيهما الحرث فألقى عمران قتيلاً وجال في الميدان ونادي بالبراز فبرز إليه مالك بن عمران فاقتتلا ساعة ثم حمل عليه الحرث فأتبعه بابيه عمران ونادى بالبراز فبرز إليه ابو الأسود بن عمران فاعتركا ساعة ثم أتبعه بهما وتواردت عليه أولاد عمران رجلاً بعد رجل فأتبع بعضهم بعضًا وكانوا تسعة وأبوهم العاشر وقيل عشرة وأبوهم الحادي عشر فكرت الخيل على الخيل واقتتلوا قتالاً شديدًا إلى غروب الشمس وحمل عقيل الضبعي على جماعة سدوس فقتل في تلك الحملة خمسة عشر فارسًا

وعاد إلى سبيله فالتقاه نصر بن مسعود فأخذه نصر أسيرًا وكان نصر رجلاً حليمًا فاستبقى عقيلاً ولم يقتله وحمل منصور بن طلحة السدوسي على بني ضبيعة فالتقاه حمل وكان قد خيم الظلام عليهم فافترقت الخيل وراح نصر بن مسعود بعقيل بن مروان أسيرًا وكان عقيل سيد بني ضبيعة فأنشأ نصر يقول

سائل ضبيعة عنا يوم معركة
والخيل تبعد أحيانًا وتقترب
إن لم تلاقوا بنا جهداً فقد شهدت
فرسانكم أنني للشوص أغتصب
أليس عندي عقيل في سلاسله
على المذلة والتصغير مرتقب
نحن الكماة بنو الهيجاء تعرفنا
نثني الكفاح إذا ما معشر ركبوا
ما زال واحدنا كالآلاف إن عطفوا
وإن أغاروا وهبنا كل ما كسبوا
لا تحسبوا قتل عمران يفوت لكم
كلا وعندي جياد الخيل والقضب
والسابقات ولدن الخط مذّخراً
وسادة قادة معروفة نجب
لأقتلنّ بعمران سراتكم
حتى نكون كنار أكلها الحطب
فترجعون عبيدًا إلى بني أمة
وتحملون الذي لا تحمل العرب
لا تعجبون لما أفنت صوارمنا
وإن أصابوا فتى في جهلهم عجبوا
يا ويل أمكم ما تصنعون إذا
غشيكم من سدوس ويحكم كتب
أترجعون من الموتى فنعذركم
او تصبرون لحرب بردها لهب

فأجابه الحرث بن عباد يقول

سائل سدوس التي أفنى كتائبها
طعن الرماح التي في رؤسها شهب
إن لم تلاقوا بنا جهدًا فقد شهدت
فرسانكم أنني بالصبر معتصب[13]
يا ويل أمكم من جمع سادتنا
كتائباً كالدبا[14] والقطر ينسكب
أبا عقيل فلا تفخر بسادتكم
فأنتم أنتم والدهر ينقلب
فإن سلمنا فإنّا سائرون لكم
بكل هندية في حدها شطب
وكل جرداء مثل السهم يكنفها
من كل ناحية ليث له حسب
لا تحسبوا أننا يا قوم نفلتكم
او تهربون إذا ما أعوز الهرب
كلا ورب القلاص الراقصات ضحى
تهوى بها فتية غر إذا انتدبوا

وقال عباد مجيبًا له

ستشرب كأس الحتف يا نصر فاصطبر
لطعن سنان أو لضرب صقيل
ومهلاً فلا تعجل وإن رحت سالماً
ستلقى لنا حرباً بأسر عقيل
سنقتل أسراكم فلا تسلموا لنا
أسيراً ولا تستعجلوا لقتيل

[13] Ms. Or. Oct. 1383 (103r) has (محترب).
[14] After Ms. Or. Oct. 1383 (103r). Ahlwardt 9747 (92r) has (كالرنى).

قال ابن نافع ثم إن بني ضبيعة بعد أسر سيدهم عقيل بن مروان استبدلوا به الحرث بن عباد وهو ابن ثلاث عشرة سنة وأقاموه مقام عقيل عندهم فأمرهم بشد الغارة على سدوس فأغاروا وأخذوا إبلاً لهم فشدت سدوس خيلها وأغاروا خلف إبلهم فقتل في أول خيلهم كثير من الفرسان فعند ذلك وقفت سدوس أولها لآخرها حتى اجتمعوا وطلبوا الإبل فأدركوا القوم وانقسم بنو ضبيعة فمنهم من لقي الخيل ومنهم من ساق الإبل ولما رأت سدوس ذلك انقسموا فمنهم من قاتل ومنهم من لحق الإبل فاقتتلوا قتالاً شديدًا وتطاردت الخيل فحمل نصر بن مسعود على عباد الضبعي فطعنه طعنة سقط بها قتيلاً ثم حمل على ابنه الحرث فالتقاه الحرث ومال عليه بطعنة فأرداه قتيلاً بأبيه عباد واقتتلوا إلى آخر النهار ثم افترقوا على غير غلبة قال وإن الخيل التي غارت خلف الإبل استنقذتها ورجعت بها فوافقها الحرث ومن معه فأخذوا الإبل ولما علم ابن نصر بن مسعود بقتل أبيه أسرع إلى أسيره عقيل بن مروان فقتله ولم يشعر به أحد ولما علم قومه بذلك لاموه لومًا عنيفًا لأنهم يذمون قتل الأسير بعد مكثه في السجن عندهم وكان أشدهم لومًا جبر بن طورة قال ولما بلغ ضبيعة قتل سيدهم عقيل شدوا خيلهم وأغاروا على سدوس وكان بنو سدوس بعد قتل عقيل بن مروان قد علموا أن بني ضبيعة لا بد أن يغيروا عليهم فاستعدوا وحذروا فوافتهم ضبيعة حذرين والتقت الخيلان فاقتتلوا قتالاً شديدًا وحمل جندل بن عقيل على جبر بن طورة فطعنه طعنة قتله بها والتفت مسعود بن منصور إلى معمر وأخبره بقتل جبر بن طورة فحمل معمر وحمل معه مسعود على جندل والحرث بن عباد والتقوا فاعتركوا شديدًا وطعن مسعود جندلاً فاستنقذته ضبيعة وحمل الحرث على معمر فضربه ضربة قتله بها ثم افترقوا وعاد الحرث بن عباد يجر قناته وهو يقول

لقد شهدت حقًّا سدوس بأنني
أنا الفارس المعتاد قطع الحناجر
تلقيت نصرًا والمعمر بعده
وأرديته كرهًا برغم المناخر
وسوف يرى المنصور منا عجائبًا
يعدد ذكري في جميع المحاضر
ولا بد من غير يتابع غيره
ويتبع أولاها وشيكًا بآخر
ظلمتم سدوس إذ قتلتم والدي
وتسعة إخواني أمدوا بعاشر

فهلا علمتم ان حولي فتية
تصول على بيض السيوف البواتر

قال ابن نافع واجتمعت بعد ذلك سدوس وآل الجراح وبنو جديلة وأغاروا على بني ضبيعة وقتلوا منهم مقتلة هائلة وأخذوا أموالهم وسبوا حريمهم ولم يبقوا فيهم بقية وبلغ الصراخ إلى كليب وإخوته وسائر رهطه الأراقم وإلى قومهم بني جشم فشدوا وأغاروا على كل صعب وذلول وأغارت عشائر تغلب كل من سمع الصوت ولحقوا بالقوم في أريطة فاقتتلوا قتالاً شديدًا واستنقذوا أموال قومهم وحريمهم ولم يذهب لهم شيء ثم تطاردت الخيلان فلما تباعدوا حمل منصور بن طورة أخو جبير على صافي بن لكيز فقتله وحمل منصور بن رباح البجيري فأتبعه به وحملت فرسان جديلة على كليب وحمل أخوه نويرة وأولاد عمه ثم حمل الجراح وحملت الأراقم ثم حمل آل بجير وحمل الحيّ من جشم ثم حملت سدوس وحملت ضبيعة فاقتتلوا قتالاً شديدًا حتى حجز بينهم الليل فانصرف كل منهم وأنشأ نويرة يقول

لقد طمعت فرسان آل جديلة
وفرسان جراح بقومي مطمعا
أغاروا بجمع يشبه الليل عرضه
وساقوا السبايا والقلائص أجمعا
فثرنا على الخيل العتاق نشدها
بأكبادها شدًا فأقبلن شرعا
إلى أن لحقنا في أريطة جمعهم
ودارت رحى الحرب العوان تتبعا
فأقصدت منصورًا وعفرت خده
وأرديت جبارًا وأرديت مسمعا
ونلت مرادي من سدوس وغيرها
وغادرت ماحلوه بالأمس بلقعا

فأجابه مالك بن الذعير يقول

ألم تر قومي في الكفاح كأنهم
أسود الشرى تعدو فلا تتروع

بأيديهم بيض رقاق صوارم
بها الهام منكم والأكفّ تقطع
ولولا ظلام الليل نجاك لم تكن
إلى أمك القرنا نويرة[15] ترجع
فصبرًا إلى ما تعطف الخيل عطفة
وتصبح بيض الهند في الهام تقرع
عجلت علينا يا نويرة فاصطبر
ليوم ترى فيه الأسنة تلمع

قال ابن نافع وتعاظمت الفتنة بين الحيين واتسعت واعي التدبير في الصلح بينهما حتى لحق شرها من كان معتزلاً عنها كالبراق بن روحان فإنه كان قد اعتزل في قومه بني حنيفة وشبيب بن لهيم الطائي فإنه كان معتزلاً أيضًا هو وأولاده واجتمعت قبائل طي ونزلت على شبيب وأرادوا قيامه فيهم لأجل قطع الأرحام بينه وبين وائل فكره شبيب ذلك واستحى ولم تغدره طي فقال ويحكم إنما نصبتموني لتعظيم الفتنة بين الحيين منا ومنهم ووالله لا أفعل ذلك فقالوا قد رأينا ذلك ولا بد منه وليس بنا قلة ولا ذلة وإنما أردنا رئاستك ومشورتك فأجابهم الى ذلك مكرهًا واتفقت قبائل طي وأحلافهم قضاعة على فتنة ربيعة وانضم بعضهم إلى بعض وتجاورت حللهم قال ابن نافع فلما بلغَ ربيعة ما اتفقت عليه طي وأحلافهم وقيام شبيب الطائي فيهم كبر عليهم ذلك واجتمع إلى البراق كليب وإخوته ورهطه الأراقم وسائر قبائل ربيعة وقالوا قد جل الخطب فلا قرار لنا عليه وكان البراق معتزلاً بقومه بني أسد وبني حنيفة لرغبة لكيز بابنته ليلى عن البراق وإنعامه بها للملك عمرو بن ذي صهبان ولما أقبلوا على البراق رأوه في ناد عظيم من قومه فسلموا عليهم وقال البراق هل من علم يا بني العم فأقبل عليه كليب وقال يا براق إن قبائل طي وقضاعة قد اجتمعت على حربنا وأبيات ربيعة متفرقة وأنتم تعلمون أننا نخشى سابقة علينا وعليكم فاجعل لنا أمرًا نكون عليه فأنشد البراق أبياتًا طويلة منها قوله

وهل[16] أنا إلا واحد من ربيعة
أعز اذا عزوا وفخرهم فخري

[15] Ahlwardt 9747 (93v) has (تويرة).
[16] Reading (وهل), after Abkāriyus, *Tazyīn* (235); Ahlwardt 9747 (94r) and Ms. Or. Oct. 1383 (105v) have (وان).

أعز اذا كانوا كرامًا أعزة
وأضر كل الخسر في ساعة الخسر

ثم قال يا كليب أنا رجل منكم غير أن لكيز بن مرة زعيم بيوت ربيعة وهو المعروف فيهم بالقيام وأنا رجل منهم فأشفق كليب من ذلك إشفاقًا عظيمًا وعلم أن ربيعة انصرفت عن لكيز من وقت قيام البراق فيهم في حرب إياد وعرفت فضله على رؤساء ربيعة قال فانصرفوا من عنده ولم يوافقهم على القيام فيهم ولما بلغ شبيبًا الطائي اجتماع ربيعة إلى ابن أخته البراق وأنهم أرادوا قيامه فيهم فامتنع من ذلك لرغبة لكيز بابنته عنه أرسل يطلب خروجه إليه وأنشأ يقول

ألا ابلغ البراق مني نصيحة
بانّا إليكم أجمعين نسير
قبائل طيّ كلها قد تجمعت
وأحلافها جاءت لهن نفير
فهل لك تأتينا سريعًا مسلمًا
فإني لكم ذو نصرة وظهير
ألم تذكروا لما جفاكم لكيزكم
واعرض عنكم والكلام كثير
هلمّ إلينا كي أزوجك ابنة
لها شرف في طيها وطهور
ودع عنك إهمالاً هناك فإنهم
أقاطيع أرحام وانت نصير

فلما بلغت الأبيات الى البراق دفعها الى أبيه روحان وقال له أجب صهرك فقال يا بني الخطاب إليك والجواب عليك فأجبه بما أنت أهله فأجاب البراق خاله يقول

لعمري لست أترك آل قومي
وأرحل عن فنائي أو أسير
بهم ذلي إذا ما كنت فيهم
على رغم العدا شرف خطير

وإني ما أقمت معًا وأهلي
فلي مجد ولي خطر كبير
أأنزل بينهم إن كان يسر
وارحل إن ألم بهم عسير
وأترك معشري وهم أناس
لهم طول على الدنيا يدور
ألم تسمع أسنتهم لها في
تراقيكم وأضلعكم صرير
فكف الكف عن قومي وذرهم
فسوف يرى فعالهم الضرير

قال ابن نافع فلما أتم الأبيات وثب أبوه روحان فقبل بين عينيه وقال الآن تكاملت فيك الرئاسة وبالله إنك شريف قومك وكان يظن أنه يلحق بأخواله لفعل لكيز ثم أمر بمهرته الشبوب ووهبها له وكانت من جياد خيله أبوها جافل من خيل قضاعة وأمها من خيل بني شيبان فعند ذلك زالت الشكوك عن كليب وإخوته وقومه واجتمع إلى البراق كليب وأبوه وإخوته وسائر قومه الأراقم وهم واحد وثلاثون فارسًا وقالوا يا براق أزل ما في نفوسنا من المظنة بالمسير إلى أبيات ربيعة والقيام فيهم فقد أجابوا داعيك في حرب إياد وغيرهم وأقروا بفضلك وإننا نخشى من سابقة تكون علينا تتحدث بها الأمم الى آخر الأبد قال فعند ذلك قام إلى إخوته وأمرهم بالركوب إلى أبيات ربيعة حيث كانوا يستصرخون قبائلهم وأحلافهم فقال أبوه روحان هل تأمر إخوانك وتترك غلمانك فقال

أما العبيد فلا تدعى من الرسل
فما يجيب بنو شيبان بالأسل
إلا لأولادك الغر الكرام إذا
جاءت ترامي بهم مهرية الإبل
واستقبلوا آل ذهل بالصريخ ضحىً
وآل عجل إليك اليوم في عجل
وآل عمران والرسلان قاطبة
تأتيك في عجل منهم بلا مهل

قال ابن نافع ولما فرغ البراق من إنشاده كسر قناته وأعطى كل واحد من إخوته كعبًا منها وقال اركبوا وحثوا أفراسكم وقلدوا نجائبكم قلائد الخيل وكانت العرب تفعل ذلك في عظائم الأمور يريدون بذلك إظهار الجزع في الاستنصار لقومهم فامتثلوا رأيه وافترقوا في أحياء ربيعة فكان كل واحد منهم يقدم بكعب من قناة أخيه وراحلته مقلده فجزعت ربيعة لجزع البراق وجاءت قبائل ربيعة من كل ناحية وتجاورت حللهم ثم نزلت سادات ربيعة بالبراق فاستقبلهم بأحسن القبول وأكرم وأعطى وكسا وقرى وعقدوا الرئاسة له وسلموه أمرهم ونهيهم وبينما هم كذلك إذ وردت رسل شبيب بن لهيم الطائي يحذرهم وينذرهم ويقول قد اجتمعت إليّ قبائل طيّ وقضاعة وخص البراق بأبيات يقول فيها

أقروا سلامي على البراق من رجل
زاكي العمومة من قوم ذوي كرم
هذي قبائل طيّ مع قضاعتهم
قد اشعلوا الحرب إذ قامت على قدم
حلوا السهولة والغيطان واعتقلوا
من الرماح بأعلى الشم في الأكم
فوطن النفس يا براق منتظرًا
هذي الكتائب إذ تأتيك من أمم
يا ويح أمك من حشر الجنود ومن
خفق البنود ومن سفك الدماء بدم
فليس يأتيك إلا كل منتخب
واري العزيمة في الهيجاء كالضرم
وكل لدن يرى ضوء السنان به
كلمع برق إذا ما لاح في الظلم

فأجابه البراق يقول

لقد وجدتك في بعض الكلام عمي
إذ رحت تأخذ في حرب لمنتقم
مخوفًا لي بجند لست أحسبهم

في كل أصيد من عرب ومن عجم
فما لديّ سوى قوم ذوي حسب
ربيعة الشم إذ قاموا على قدم
خلوا شبيبًا ووادي الراس واجتمعوا
اليّ بالمال والأهلين والحرم
فاستقدموا طيّ ذي شيبان قاطبة
وتغلب وسراة الحي من جشم
والوائليون قد قاموا بأجمعهم
من كل منتخب يأتيك عن أمم

قال ابن نافع وبعد ما رد البراق جواب خاله وانصرف رسوله نادى في قومه وقال يا بني ذهل يا بني عجل يا بني مرة يا بني الأزد يا بني ضرار يا بني لخم يا بني يشكر يا بني ضبيعة يا بني الحرث يا بني جشم يا بني نمر يا بني قسم يا بني عبس يا بني مالك يا بني بهران يا بني مروان يا بني عمران يا بني علي يا بني الجراح قد علمتم كثرة قبائل طي وشدة بأسهم ونجدتهم فشدوا بنا الخيل وابدأوهم بالغارة فشدوا وأغاروا وفي أولهم نويرة بن ربيعة وفي آخرهم البراق وكليب وهو يحث البراق على فتنة اخواله طي ثم سائر طي وقضاعة وقال يا براق ناشدتك الله والرحم لا وأخذت بجرم رجل قد غاب عن رشده وسقطت نفسه وغره ما عند الملوك من الزي والمال فانصح قومك ولا تخذلهم فقد أجابوا داعيك وأرادوا ضيعك وأقروا بفضلك فلما أكثر قال البراق يا كليب أنت نصيحي وصديقي وصاحب سري فاعلم أني ما صرخت في عشائري وأنا أريد عليهم غلبًا واعلم أني أفتن قبائل طيّ أشد الفتنة وأمتحن قضاعة أشد المحنة إلا رجلاً القاه من أخوالي فإني أبقي عليه وآمر صاحبي بذلك فلما سمع كليب كلام البراق أشفق من ذلك إشفاقًا عظيمًا وأتهم البراق بقلة النصيحة لأن أخوال البراق هم أشد طي باسًا وليس من أكفائهم غير بني أخيهم البراق وإخوته وبني عمه وكليب وإخوته ورهطه الأراقم وبني حنيفة وأما سائر القبائل فتكل عن لقائهم قال ثم تنفس كليب الصعداء وأنشأ يقول

إذا كانت قرابتكم علينا
مقومة أعنتها الينا
فأنتم يا بني أسد بن بكر
تريدون الطعان فمن يقينا

وأنتم يا بني أسد عماد
لهذا المعشر المتعصبينا
نعيت إليهم وصرخت فيهم
فجاؤوا بالحرائم أجمعينا
وحلوا يا بني أسد عليكم
وجاؤوا للوغى مستصبحينا[17]
وصرتم يا بني أسد وأنتم
لإخوتكم هبلتم خائنينا
إذا اكثرت قرابتكم علينا
بأخلاس الحديد ملبسينا
فما يجري مسيركم وأنتم
كلابكم عليّ يعسعسونا
أبا نصر ابن روحان خليلي
علمنا أنكم تتخيلونا
أبا نصر ابن روحان خليلي
أقيلت بيعة المتبايعينا
أبا نصر ابن روحان خليلي
اذا خضنا الوغى لا تحملونا
أبا نصر ابن روحان خليلي
أراك العز رهطك مستهينا
أبا نصر ابن روحان خليلي
كفى شرا فماذا تفعلونا
ألم تترك ربيعة لا تقدها
تزيدهم المذلة والمنونا
تكون هدية لجميع طي

[17] Ahlwardt 9747 (97r) and Ms. Or. Oct. 1383 (108r) have (مستصجينا). The other manuscripts are unclear.

وكنتم بالسلامة رائحينا
على شأن لكيز وشأن ليلى
أردتم أن تكونوا خاذلينا
بني أسد أراكم من هواكم
تريدون القطيعة جاهلينا
بني أسد أردتم آل عمي
قطيعتنا وكنتم واصلينا
بني أسد تحثكم ليوث
وأنتم في اللقا متخلفونا
بني أسد تبارزنا رجال
وأنتم في المكرة واقفون
بني أسد عشيرتكم قتلتم
بهذا الرأي هلا تعرفونا
بني أسد بن بكر كيف تغدو
تطاعنكم وأنتم تنظرونا
بني أسد وكيف لكم وقوف
إذا خر ابن عمكم طعينا
بدا لي من خليلي ما بدا لي
كأن لهم على البراق دينا
بدا لي من خليلي ما بدا لي
فنون من فنون الأبعدينا
بدا لي من خليلي ما بدا لي
كأنا لم نكن متجاورينا
ألا ابلغ خليلي الصدق عني
رجال بني حنيفة مصطلينا

قال ابن نافع فلما فرغ كليب من شعره وقضى من عتاب البراق وطره انثنى إلى أبيه وإخوته فاعتزل بهم عن البراق وأما نويرة والمهلهل فكانا قد جازا بطائفة من رهطهما مع البراق والحرث بن عباد معهما وهو كالهائج من الإبل يذود الناس عن أيمانهم وشمائلهم وأنشأ البراق يقول

أقول لنفسي مرة بعد مرة
وسمر القنا في الحيّ لا شك تلمع
أيا نفس رفقًا في الوغى ومسرة
فما كأسها إلا من السم ينقع
إذا لم أقد خيلاً إلى كل ضيغم
فآكل من لحم العداة وأشبع
فلا[18] كسبت كفي من الخيل أدهما
ولا عشت محمودًا وعيشي موسع
ولا قدت من أقصى البلاد طلائعًا
ولا صارمًا عضبًا من البيض يلمع
إذا لم أطأ طيّاً وأحلافها[19] معًا
قضاعة بالأمر الذي يتوقع
فسيروا إلى طي لتخلي ديارهم
وتصبح من سكانها وهي بلقع
ولا تتركوا شيخًا لطي ولا فتى
ولا امراة تمشي ولا الطفل يرضع

قال ابن نافع فلما قرب القوم نادى البراق وقال يا قوم إن مكان كليب ومن معه من إخوته وقومه الأراقم مفتوح لا يسده غيره وقد حضرني رأي في إصلاح شأنكم فقالوا الرأي إليك فقال انتخبوا من جياد خيلكم واحملوا عليها من خفاف رجالكم وقدموهم أولاً فإذا توسطوا من حلل طيّ وقضاعة وضعوا فيهم السيوف والرماح فإذا ارتجت الناس وارتفع الصراخ ثنوا إلينا أعنّة خيلهم ونحن متأهبون فإذا جاءت خيل القوم في أثرهم حملنا عليها من كل جانب فقالوا نعم الرأي وحملوا خفاف رجالهم على جياد خيلهم وأمروهم بالغارة على حلل القوم فأغاروا ووضعوا فيهم السيوف وعلت الأصوات وتبادرت إليهم الناس فانقلبت خيل البراق كما أمرهم وأغار القوم على أعقابهم وهم سواد عظيم وصاح فيهم خال البراق شبيب وقال هذا مكر ابن

[18] Reading (فلا) after Abkāriyus, *Tazyīn* (239) and Ms. Or. Oct. 1383 (109r), instead of (فلو), which is present in Ahlwardt 9747 (97v).
[19] Reading (احلافها) after Abkāriyus, *Tazyīn* (239) and Ms. Or. Oct. 1383 (109r), instead of (اجلافها), which is present in Ahlwardt 9747 (97v).

أختكم فلا تغيروا فوقف من سمع الصياح ومن لم يسمع استمر في غارته حتى توسطوا قبائل ربيعة فحملت عليهم كل قبيلة بما يليها فاعتركوا ساعة وولت طي وقضاعة بعد قتلة مريعة وأتبعهم البراق ومن معه وخيل بني ربيعة إلا بني جشم وسائر رهط البراق فإنهم ساروا تحت لوائه في آخر الناس قال ابن نافع فلما رجعت خيل طيّ وقضاعة مهزومة وخلفها خيل ربيعة حمل شبيب الطائي وأخوه عمرو في السواد وعطفت الخيل والتحمت الناس واقتتلوا قتالاً شديدًا وقتلت ربيعة قتلة شنيعة حتى حمل البراق ومن معه فاعتركوا ساعة الى آخر النهار ثم افترقوا عن غير غالب بعد قتل وجراح قال ابن نافع وأقبل عمرو بن لهيم الطائي على أولاده وقال يا بني لم أعدكم إلا لأمر يسرني وتعرفون به بين قبائل العرب واعلموا أن بني أختكم أشد ربيعة وفرسانها بأسًا وقد جاءتكم أولاد أختكم بفتية كالأسود تهابهم داهية العرب وهم البراق وجنيد وظليل وسالم وعمرو وأبوهم روحان فأنت يا ولدي نصير كفوءٌ للبراق وأنت يا ولدي غنم كفوء جنيد وأنت يا سالم كفوء سالم وأنت يا جبر كفوء عمرو وأنت يا طوس كفوء ظليل ومصعب وحبيب وعامر لنويرة وكليب والمهلهل فلما بلغ البراق وصية عمرو لأولاده وتحريضه لهم على قتال البراق وإخوته خاصة نادى إخوته جميعًا وقال قد علمتم شأن هذا الرجل ووصيته لأولاده وتحريضه لهم علينا فإذا نادى أحد منهم بالبراز[20] فلا يبرز إليه احد منكم فأنا أولى به لعلي أرده سالمًا ولا نفجع أمّنا بقتل أحد من إخوتها فيكثر عويلها ويطول حزنها وهي غريبة بيننا فإذا دعاني خالي نصير الى البراز فليست الفرافصة ولا اخوته يتاخرون عنه وهم سبعون فارساً فاذا حملوا بعده فاحملوا بعدي ولا يحمل غيركم يا بني أسد فإذا حملت بعدهم سدوس يحمل بعدكم بنو حنيفة قال ولما كان في اليوم التقى القوم فلما تقابل الحيان قام عمرو بن لهيم ونادى ولده نصيرًا وقال ابرز الى ابن أختك البراق فقد مكنتك الفرصة منه فبرز نصير وطلب براز البراق فبرز اليه وهو يقول

دعاني نصير إلى المكرمات
لرفع السيوف ووضع القناة
فيا أيها الخال ما شاقني
سواك وأبغضت طول الحياة

[20] Ahlwardt 9747 (98v) has (بالبراق). This must be an error.

رويدك أخبر[21] وأنت الخبير
ألست المجرب حرب الكماة

فأجابه نصير

ما الذي قد رأى أبو النصر مني
وأبي عمرو لا يخيب ظني
أكرم السابقين كرّا وفرّا
فأكرم الرمح يا ابن أختي مني
فعلى ما قضيت إني أقضي
وعلى ما بنيت إني أبني

قال فلما سمع البراق كلام خاله تبسم وأقبل عليه فتعاطفا فرسيهما ولم يضمر كل منهما لصاحبه شرًا وعزما أن يفترقا على سلامة وبينما هما كذلك إذ حملت الفرافصة على البراق فحملت إخوته وبنو أسد ولما اطردت الخيل حملت سدوس بأجمعهم وحمل بنو حنيفة وحمل عمرو بن لهيم على صهره روحان فاعترضه نويرة بن ربيعة وأرداه بطعنة أتبعه منها ولم يضره بشيء فاستنقذه بعض أولاده بعد ضرب وطعن شديد وحمل السواد على السواد واقتتلوا إلى غروب الشمس وراح الكل منهم على غير غلبة وأنشأ البراق يقول

دعاني سيد الحيين منا
بني أسد السميدع للمغار
يقود إلى الوغى ذهلاً وعجلاً
بني شيبان فرسان الوقار
وآل حنيفة وبنو ضبيع
وأرقمها وحيّ بني ضرار
وشوسًا من بني جشم تراها
غداة الروع[22] كالأسد الضواري

[21] This wording is from Ms. Or. Oct. 1383 (110r). Ahlwardt 9747 (99r) has (رويداخبر).
[22] Abkāriyus, Tazyīn (243) has (الروح).

وقوم بني ربيعة آل قومي
تهيّت للتحية والمزار
إلى أخوالهم طي فأهدت
لهم طعنًا بسمر الخطّ واري[23]
صحبناهم على جرد عتاق
بأسياف مهندة قواري
ولولا صائحات أسعفتهم
جهارًا بالصراخ المستجار
لما رجعوا ولا عطفوا علينا
وخافوا ضرب باترة الشفار
فيا لك من صراخ وافتضاح
ونقع ثائر وسط الديار
على قب مسومة عتاق
مقلدة أعنتها كبار
تعطف بالقنا في كل صبح
وتحمل في العجابة والغبار
وقد زرنا الضحاة بني لهيم
فأحدرناهم في كل عار
فيممت السنان لصدر عمرو
فطاح مجندلا في الصف عاري
وقد جارت يداي على خميس
بضربة باتر الحدين فار
وأفلت فارس الجرّاح مني
لضربة منصل فوق السوار
فقل لابن الذعير الندل هلا

[23] Ahlwardt 9747 (99v) has (الى اخوالهم طي فاهدوا لهم طعناً من العنوان واري). The above wording comes from Arabe 5833 (113r) and 5984 Adab (30).

تصبر في الوغى مثل اصطباري[24]
ألم أدعوه في سبق فولى
كمثل الكبش يأذن بالخوار[25]
أنا ابن الشم من سلفي نزار
كريم العرض معروف النجار
وحولي كل أروع وائليّ
سديد الرأي مشدود الإزار

فأجابه مالك بن الذعير يقول

تبدت علوة خلف الستار
غداة تحملت بين الجواري
بوجه مثل ضوء البرق طلق
وشعر كالدجى تحت الخمار
ومقلة جودر من وحش نجد
وثغر مثل ساطعة الدراري
تنسمنا فتات المسك منها
يفوح من المعذر والعذار
فدع عنك الهوى بجمال خود
مضت لسبيلها بعد المزار
ولكن هاك مقربة جيادًا
مولدة مهارًا من مهار
تعادي في ربيعة عاديات
بأيام المغار على نزار
تعللها لبان الحمر حتى
ترى الألوان حمرًا باصفرار

[24] Ahlwardt 9747 (100r) has (اصطبار). The first-person possessive suffix is found in Ms. Or. Oct. 1383 (111r), Arabe 5833 (113v), 5984 Adab (31), and Or. 2676 (171r).
[25] Abkāriyus, *Tazyīn* (244) has (بالحذار).

قريناها ربيعة يوم جاءت
إلينا طالبات أخذ ثار
وظلت تطرق البراق جهرًا
فكيف نويرة ولد الحمار
مضى في النقع منهزمًا حقيرًا
كمثل الماء ويحك في القرار[26]
ويجبر والديه وأي حيّ
أحق لوالديه بكل عار
ألم يرجع كليب رُدَّ خوفًا
لرمحي راخي الوركين خار
وخالفه الأراقم مع لكيز
لخوف الطعن والعضب الغرار

قال ابن نافع ولما سمع كليب شعر مالك بن الذعير ووقف على قوله راخي الوركين خاري آلى على ان لا يأكل شبعًا ولا يشرب ريًّا حتى يلقى مالك بن الذعير ويهين العزيز منهم فعند ذلك انتهى الى البراق يعتذر إليه من رجوعه عنه وما كان من مخالفته له فقال البراق يا كليب ليس يذهب بالذي بينك وبيني ذاهب ثم انه طلب منه عارية فرسه الشبوب الذي وهبه له أبوه ولم يكن في خيل قومه أسبق منه فأسلمه إليه ولم يكن يعلم ما يريد به فشد كليب على الشبوب ولبس لأمة حربه وتوجه إلى مالك ولم يعلم به أحد من قومه حتى انتهى إلى صرم بني جديلة في شيء من الليل فسأل بعض الرعاة فدله على خباء مالك فتقدم ونادى يا مالك فأجابه بقوله من قال رجل من أحلافك قضاعة غزيت هذه الليلة وبات أولادي على الطوى فشد مالك ولبس سلاحه وركب فلما برح به عن الصرم وكانت ليلة مقمرة ورآه مالك لا يقف ولايسمع أنكره وقال ليس هذا الفرس من خيل قضاعة وتاالله أخشى أن يكون كليبًا وهذا الفرس أبوه من خيلنا وأمه من خيل بني اسد ولعله الشبوب فاستأخر مالك وفقد كليب وقع الفرس فثنى إليه عنان فرسه وقال لعلك أدركت للإبل حسًا قال ولكن تنبهت بالشبوب وصورت بين عيني كليبًا قال أنا والله هو فاحذر لنفسك وحمل عليه وقال يا مالك أين رمحك الذي أرخى وركي كليب حتى سلح في سرجه ثم أنزله عن جواده وجعل عمامته في عنقه وراح به سيرًا وترك جواده فرجع إلى

[26] Abkāriyus, *Tazyīn* (245) has (القرار). Ahlwardt 9747 (100r) has (الفرار) or (الغرار).

قومه ولما وصل الجواد إليهم في ليلته أيقنوا أن مالكًا قد قتل وأن الذي دعاه وائلي فصاحوا في الناس بالغارة وقصدوا إلى طي وقضاعة على الصعب والذلول وأما كليب فإنه جاز بأسيره إلى آخر ليلته حتى أضاء عليه الصباح وإذا به ينظر عجاج الخيل فعلم أنه خيل قومه وكان أخواه نويرة والمهلهل قد افتقداه وأخبرا البراق فعلم أنه يريد بالفرس أن يهجم على مالك في دار قومه فشد فرسه وصاح فشدوا وأغاروا يلتمسون كليبًا فعند ذلك خلى كليب سبيل مالك وقال ارجع إلى قومك وأخبرهم إنما أضرمتها أنت وتولى حرها غيرك فرجع مالك وأخبر قومه بالذي كان من كليب وأنذرهم بالخيل فاستحوا من الرجوع ثم التقى القوم فاقتتلوا قتالاً شديدًا إلى آخر النهار وافترقوا بعد قتل وجراح وبرز عامر بن الذعير ونادى ببراز كليب فبرز إليه فالتقى الرجلان واقتتلا ساعة طويلة حتى تعجب الناس من إقدامهما وامتناعهما وعجل بنو الذعير فحملت إخوة مالك على كليب وهم ستة عشر من واحدة وستة من أخرى ولما حملوا على كليب (حمل)[27] ربيعة بن مرة وولداه نويرة والمهلهل ولكيز وأولاده على بني الذعير وحمل القوم من الطرفين واطردت خيل بني الذعير والجديلين وخيل بني مرة والأراقم واعتركوا مليًا ولما وقع الطراد حمل نويرة على مقاتل ابن الذعير فطعنه فأرداه جريحاً واستنقذته إخوته حتى استوى على جواده وتعاودت الحملة فحمل خزيمة على مالك ابن الذعير فأرداه جريحًا واستنقذته إخوته ايضًا حتى اعادوه الى متن جواده وحمل نويرة على جراح بن الذعير فطعنه فأرداه جريحًا وحمل مروان بن الذعير على لكيز بن مرة فأرداه بطعنة فاستنقذه أخوه ربيعة وابنه كليب حتى استوى على جواده وحمل عمار بن الذعير على المهلهل فأرداه صريعًا فاستنقذه أخوه نويرة وابن عمه خزيمة بن لكيز حتى استوى على جواده وحملت خيل بني جديلة وخيل الأراقم واقتتلوا ساعة طويلة وحمل نويرة على الحرث بن الذعير فأرداه قتيلاً واشتعلت الحرب بين الحيين واقتتلوا قتالاً شديدًا وافترقوا وبرز الحرث بن عباد ونادى بالبراز فبرز إليه الصامت السدوسي فاختلفت بينهما ضربتان وكان السابق فيهما الحرث فأرداه صريعًا ونادى بالبراز فبرز إليه أخو المقتول ياس وكان أشجع من أخيه فاعتركا ساعة ثم أتبعه الحرث بأخيه وتواترت خيل سدوس على الحرث بن عباد وهم عشرون فارسًا فأهلكهم بالبراز وكانوا أشد سدوس وحمل السواد على السواد واقتتلوا حتى كادت الشمس تغيب فبرز عمرو بن لهيم الطائي جد البراق لأمه ونادى ببراز روحان بن أسد إليه فبرز وقال يا عمرو ما كفاك ما ترى بين الحيين حتى تدعو ببرازي خاصة ثم حمل كل واحد منهما على صاحبه فاختلفت بينهما طعنتان كان الأسبق فيها

[27] Parenthetical word from Ms. Or. Oct. 1383 (112v).

روحان فأرداه جريحًا وحملت أولاده كافة على صهرهم فأشرعوا إليه الرماح وكان درعه حصينًا لا تنفذه الأسنة فألقوه على وجه الأرض فعندها حمل البراق وإخوته وأخذوا أباهم روحان وحملوا جدهم عمرا على جواده وردوه على أولاده سالمًا قال ابن نافع وكان ظليل بن روحان قد أصيب بطعنة كانت منيته بها فلما علم البراق أن أخاه لا ينجو من تلك الطعنة برز بين الصفين وقال يا بني عمرو أما والله لقد فجعتم أختكم بقتل ولدها ولا تبرد فجعتها إلا بقتل كفؤه منكم ثم نادى ببراز خاله مصعب بن عمرو بن لهيم فبرز وحمل عليه البراق حملة منكرة وقد قلص عن شفتيه فأرداه قتيلاً وحمل نصير بن عمرو على البراق وقد قلص ايضًا عن شفتيه ولم يكن لنصير كفؤ في فرسان ربيعة إلا كليب والبراق فاعتركا ساعة ثم حملت خيل الفرافصة خلف أخيها وحملت خيل بني أسد خلف البراق فاقتتلوا شديدًا وحملت خيل سدوس وحملت خيل بني حنيفة ثم حمل السواد على السواد وقاتل نويرة قتالاً شديدًا وكان شجاعًا فاقتتل القوم يومهم إلى أن حجز بينهم الليل وراح الكل منهم على قفاه وأنشأ نويرة يقول

لقد شهدت فرسان طي براعتي
وأني الهمام الأرْيَحِيّ الحلاحل
وقد شهدت ابنا جديلة أنني
صدقتهم بالضرب والنقع شامل
سناني لساني إن نطقت وإنما
يصدق قولي إنني له فاعل
وما الحر إلا ان يصدق قوله
بأفعاله حقًا إذا هو قائل
اما شهدت ابنا الذعير مكرتي
وما لك مقصوص الجناحين ناكل
أرى ابن الذعير لا يكف مقالة
عن النطق بالبهتان إذ هو جاهل
وإني لأنهى النفس عن ادعائها
مواطن مجد قد حوتها الأفاضل
أقصرها عن طول مالا تناله
لعمري ما يجدي عليها التطاول
فغض عن الأعراض مالك والذي

تحاوله لا يحتويه الحاول
ظننت كليبًا تاركًا لك عرضه
فوافاك جهرًا لم تهله الهوائل
وقدنا جياد الخيل تقرع بالقنا
تعادي بفرسان الوغى وتحامل
عليها رجال من ضبيعة تعتزي[28]
ببيض رقاق أخلصتها الصياقل
تجيب ندا البراق عند ندائه
ويظفر فيما يبتغيه ويأمل
وإن الفتى البراق سيد قومه
تقر له يوم اللقاء القبائل
دعا دعوة بابني ربيعة فاحتوى
عليها في الراحتين الأنامل
وصبحكم شعث النواصي مغيرة
تبادر بالفتيان قب هياكل
كتائب من أبناء ربيعة لم يزل
شعارهم يوم التنازل وائل
تجاذب عمرًا ثم صعبًا وراجحًا
ولم ينج منهم راجح ومقاتل
قضاعة خلف عصبة وائلية
وعاين منها ما يهول الأجادل
وكم من جريح راح قد سدّ جلده
من السمر عسال المعاطف ذابل

قال ابن نافع وأراد مالك أن لا يرد جوابًا على نويرة لشأن ما أصابه من كليب فقالت له إخوته أجب الرجل ونحن دونك فلا تخش عاقبة وكان مالك فصيحًا فأنشأ يقول

[28] Ahlwardt 9747 (103r) has (تفتري). (تعتزي) is found in Arabe 5833 (114v) and 5984 Adab (38).

لقد جحدت طيّ مكان نويرة
وما عرفت معروفه في التنازل
ولكن سل الشم العرانين في الوغى
صناديدهم من آل بكر ووائل
عن الضيغم الجراح والعمرو والعلا
خلاصة قوم في حصون العواسل
فهل عاينت عيناك فعل نصيرنا
وإخوته ما أنت عن ذا بغافل
أما درج الدراج تحت لوائه
بأبيض ماض للجماجم فاصل
أراك كمن لا يحضر الجمع يا فتى
فسلني تجدني عارفًا بالخصائل
أنبيك عن قومي الكرام وفضلهم
ودونهم أحسابهم بالذوابل
على كل طاوي الكشح محتبك القرى
ولوج إذا استوليت في كل نازل
وقد علمت ابنا ربيعة أننا
نكر غداة الروع تحت القساطل
ونضرب بالبيض الجماجم في الوغى
بذا شهدت عنا جميع القبائل
إذا ما التقى الجمعان منا ومنكم
رأيت لكيزًا موثقًا بالمفاصل
وظل ظليل بالدماء ولم يكن
دعاه على الأرواح قوم بطائل
ولو برق البراق في الجد ساعة
لما كان في الروحان منه بقاتل

قال ابن نافع وأراد نويرة بن ربيعة أن يجيبه فكفه أخوه كليب وقال مهلاً وقال نصير يرثي أخاه مصعبًا

عين جودي بمدمع منك يجري
للفتى فارس السدوس ابن عمرو
فارس الجحفلين منا ومنكم
ومنيع الذمام في كل عصر
كنت في رقدة فايقظني الآ-
ن مصاب الفتى شقيقي وذخري
إن براق قد بداني جهارًا
بقتيل سميدع غير غمر
شمروا للحروب آل لهيم
يا أبا النصر سوف تعرف نصري
بسدوس جميعها وجديل
سترى الذل في صناديد بكر
أرقت للطعان عيني رويدًا
سيعود الكرى وأقضي وتري
ويرى الوائليّ منا طعانًا
وضرابًا كمثل إضرام جمر
من جديل وآل جراح قومي
وسدوس وسنبس آل نصر
سوف تأتيك كالمرامي سراعًا
في دجى الليل وبساطع فجر
وعليّ الوفا لقولي وعهدي
وترى فيهم تمامًا لنذري

فأجابه البراق راثيًا أخاه ظليلاً

عين تجود وقلب واله كمد
لما ثوى في الثرى الضرغامة الأسد
غاب الكرى وتقضي النوم وانصرمت
حبل التواصل لما إن دنا السهد
يا عين إن تدمعي لا تقتفي ولها

إن الشفاء جياد الخيل تطرد
فتلك فيها عزاء عن أخي ولكم
فيها العزاء ومنكم ينقص العدد
فإن تسيروا إلينا من حبائلكم
وإن وقفتم فإنا نحوكم نرد
ولست أحتم أني غالب لكم
والله يعلم بالانسان ما الأمد
وكل حي يقضي بعض حاجته
من تلك والدهر لا يبقى به احد
عجل نصير لنقضي بعض حاجتنا
وان وقفت فهذي[29] خيلنا تفد
واقدم بخيلك هذي[30] خيلنا صفن
شعثاء تنزع عن أقطائها اللبد
فإن تسيروا إلينا ترفدوا عجلاً
ضربًا يظل على هاماتكم يقد
وإن وقفتم فإنا سائرون لكم
يا آل خالي بجرد الخيل تنجرد

قال ابن نافع واجتمع الكل وصار بعضهم على بعض والتقوا بدومة وهي حدود بلاد أنمار واقتتلوا قتالاً شديدًا وبرز نصير بن عمرو ونادي ببراز البراق فأجابه من فوره وكانا كفوئين كريمين فتحاملا ساعة ولم يظفر أحدهما بالآخر وحملت إخوة نصير على البراق وحملت إخوة البراق حوله والتقى سالم بن روحان وغرسان بن عمرو بن لهيم الطائي واتفقت بينهما ضربتان فوقع سيف غرسان على سيف سالم فقطعه نصفين وحملت خيل بني فرفص وهم سبعون فارسًا وحملت خيل بني اسد واطردت الخيل وتكافح نصير والأحجف وتضاربا بالسيوف فسبقه نصير بضربة أرداه بها قتيلاً فحمل البراق على الأهمس ابن عم نصير فقتله بابن عمه الأحجف وحمل السواد على السواد واقتتلوا قتالاً شديدًا وراح الكل منهم على غير غلبة وقال نصير في ذلك

[29] Ahlwardt 9747 (104r) has (هذه), which is unmetrical. (هذي) occurs in Ms. Or. Oct. 1383 (114v).
[30] See above.

أتاني من بني روحان قول
كمثل الماء في البحر الغزير
تشب النار في أرجاء يوم
ربيعي خريفي مطير
أبا النصر بن روحان رويدًا
إذا ما الحرب تلهب بالسعير
إذا ما تستبين بليث غاب
ضواربه قضاقضة هصور
لهيمي سدوسي مجيب
دعاة الحرب في الرد العسير
ستلقى وقعها بأسًا شديدًا
تنادي بالمذلة والثبور
فيا ابن كريمتي الحسنى رويدًا
توقع عدوة الأسد الجسور
ولا تجعل علينا يا ابن أختي
ستأتي الخيل أمثال الصقور
تهادى بالأسنة مشرعات
إلى الهيجاء مولى من نصير
عليها من سراة الحي غلب
ضراغمة كآساد الجفير
سراعًا يا بني أسد إليكم
ففيكم غاية الحتف المثير
ظننتم يا بني أسد ظننتم
بنا ظن الركيك أو الحقير
بغيتم حين لم نبغى عليكم
ولم نهتك لكم بعض الستور
وأصبحنا تنازعنا رجال
قصار الباع عن خير وضير

بغيتم يا بني روحان هلكًا
كهلك أبيكم الشيخ الكبير
فقل لكريمتي تبكي عليكم
بكا المتقطعين من العمور

فأجابه البراق يقول

أتاني من نصير قول سوء
ركيك مثل تغليل الصدور
ألم تشهد لواءكم كسيرًا
بها ولواؤنا غير الكسير
دعوتم حربنا فقد استجبنا
منادي الحرب بالسمر السمير
كتائب وائل سارت اليكم
ببيض الهند يا لك من مسير
صبحناكم بها ضربًا نثيرًا
وطعنًا ناظمًا غير النثير
وإلجامًا وإفحامًا عليكم
وإقدام المغير على المغير
كورنا إذ كورتم واستقمنا
لعمر أبيك بالطعن العسير
نصير في بلادك أنت طلق
فزرنا وجه صبح مستنير
ونحن إذا حملنا لم تكونوا
بشيء عند تحريض الأمور
نصير منك أرماح دقاق
وأسياف فيا لك من نصير
وقب يرتمين إذا برزتم
بفتيان كأمثال الصقور

توقرنا نصير فسر الينا
لنشفي منك غلات الصدور
ألا سيروا ألا سيروا إلينا
فيا نعما لقومي بالمسير
أنا ابن الشم من سلفي نزار
رؤوس المجد والحسب الخطير
يخوفني نصير صيام يوم
فسل عني ألم تك بالخبير
كفينا من يغيب إذا حضرنا
ومن قد غاب عنا كالحضور
وكم خيل لقيناها بخيل
منحناكم بها ظعن الثغور
وإنك يا فتى لبنا خبير
فكيف سؤال ذي علم بصير

قال ابن نافع ثم إن نصيرًا جمع بني طيّ وقضاعة وغزا بهم ديار ربيعة وتطرقت خيله الى محل رجل من بني جشم وأخذت ابلاً فارتفع الصراخ وشدت قبائل ربيعة خيلها وأغارت خلف الإبل وكان أول من لحق القوم البراق وإخوته واسترجعوا الإبل من نصير وقومه بعد قتل وجراح وجاءت كتائب وائل مثل كراديس النمل والتقت الخيل واقتتلوا قتالاً شديدًا ثم افترقوا على غير غلبة قال وإن البراق بعد هذه الوقعة اشتاق إلى حرم الله فتجهز وتخلف على ربيعة كليب فلما سمع نصير بن شبيب خال البراق بنهوض البراق إلى الحج وغيابه عن قومه وشاع ذلك في أحياء طي اجتمع بأكابر قومه وأقبلوا عليه يحثونه وقالوا يا نصير اغتنم الفرصة في بيوت ربيعة بعد أن غاب فارسهم وسيدهم فإنه لا يمكنك فرصة مثلها فقال واسؤتاه أتأمروني أن أغتاب البراق وأخلفه في قومه شر خلافة لا يبلغه ذلك عني أبدًا قال وإن البراق عند رجوعه من الحج اشتد به حب ليلى العفيفة وشوقه إليها ولحقه مرض في أثناء الطريق من أجلها فأقام برهة من الأيام وهو لا يشعر بمراودة طي لنصير بالغارة على بيوت ربيعة وكانت أم نصير قد أخذت تعيره بقتل ولدها وتحثه على حرب ربيعة بعد البراق وهو يأبى ذلك ويقول والله لو كنت أنا الغائب ما سمع البراق فيّ كلامًا ولا غزا أحدًا من قومي وإنما تريدون أن تكسوني العار ولست أحمل كلامًا ولا أخلفه إلا خلافة حسنة قال ابن نافع وكانت بيوت وائل قد أضربها الاجتماع فلما بلغتهم كراهة نصير لاغتياب سيدهم البراق وغلبته على ما

يأمر به القوم شكروه على ذلك ورغبوا في الانفساخ والتراخي حتى يأتي البراق واستشاروا بعضهم على ذلك وعزموا عليه فزجرهم كليب ونهاهم فلم يسمعوا قال وكانت أم نصير لم تزل تراوده على اغترار البراق في قومه وهو لا يقبل فلما رأت اصراره على مخالفته لها مالت الى كيد النساء وقالت والله لأ كيد له مكيدة تنقصه وتضع من قدره وهو لا يشعر بها ثم إنها شدت لقينة لها على جمل سرًا عن ولدها وقالت لها تقدمي نحو ربيعة ثم أقبلي فاذا كنت بحيث يستمع الداعي فاصرخي ولا تشكي لمن لقيك شيئًا حتى تري مولاك نصيرًا فإذا قال ما لك فقولي له ركبت لزيارة مولاتي كريمة فلقيني المهلهل واستنزلني عن جملي وافتضني وكانت القينة عذراء وقال امضي وأعلمي مولاك نصيرًا وقولي له لنصنعن بأمه مثلما صنعنا بك ولا سلمت له بعد اليوم[31] حرمه فإنه قد جبن عن حربنا وأطمع العرب في قومه وإذا علم مولاك ذلك فإنه سيأنف منه ويغير على المهلهل وإخوته وتكون النكاية فيهم اشد فمضت القينة وجاءت فاستقبلت القوم وصرخت فجاءتها الغارات من كل جانب ولم تخبر بشيء حتى جاء مولاها فأنشأت الزور والبهتان على المهلهل فغضب نصير لذلك غضبًا شديدًا وقال إذا كان ذلك منهم ركبت عليهم وسبيت حريمهم وفضحتهم أشد الفضيحة وأغار من ساعته على الأراقم وكانت قد اجتمعت إليه خيل من طيّ وقضاعة فتقدم صرم بن شبيب وهو يقول

هلم على الثارات من آل أرقم
وقتل كليب ثم قتل المهلهل
متى نظرت عيني كليبًا أجبته
على فعله من حد أبيض فيصل

قال ابن نافع وسار نصير بطيّ وقضاعة وصبح بهم الأراقم رهط كليب فاقتطعوا من أموالهم وسبوا نساءهم وكانت فيهن ليلى العفيفة صاحبة البراق وكان ذلك عند وصول البراق من الحج ثم إن الصراخ ارتفع في قبائل ربيعة فشدت على كل صعب وذلول وأغار نويرة في بعض الخيل في أثر المال والحريم وكليب في آخر الخيل وكان البراق قد ضعف عن الركوب للمرض والتعب وقل أكله وشربه فوصل إلى أهله وقد زاد مرضه حتى كاد لا يستطيع الركوب وإذا به يسمع الخبر فأمر بشد فرسه ولبس لأمة حربه وركب جواده وأغار وهو يقول

[31] The original manuscript, Ahlwardt 9747 (106v), has (بعد اليومه).

لأفرجنّ اليوم كل الغمم
من سبيهم في الفجر بيض الحرم
صبراً إلى ما ينظرون مقدمي
إني أنا البراق فوق الأدهم
لأرجعن اليوم ذات المبسم
الواضح المنضد المنتظم
بنت لكيز الوائلي الأرقم

قال وترامى جواد البراق في عنانه حتى أدرك القوم وقد افترقوا عن قتل وجراح فنادى في قومه فأحاطوا به ثم نادى يا كليب استقم بمن معك من الجمع وأنا احمل بمن معي خلف المال والحريم فاستقام كليب ومن معه وحمل البراق وإخوته وبنو عمه وسائر قومه على طرف من الخيل واشتغل نصير بأواخر الخيل يقاتل كليبًا ومن معه ثم إن البراق أدرك المال والسبايا وكان معها أربعة آلاف عنان ونويرة مشتغل بهم فحمل عليهم البراق وقتل فرسانًا منهم واسترجع ظعائن قومه وأموالهم وأمر من يسير بها إلى منازلهم وأغار قصد كليب وعشائره فوافق الجندين مفترقين وبعض الخيل تطرد بالرماح وتأمل وإذا بلكيز وشبيب صهره قد تنازلا بالسيوف وصرم بن شبيب قريب منهما ينتظر غفلة من لكيز وكان أولاده قد غفلوا عنه فنادى بأخيه وإذا به قد أقبل وحمل على شبيب فطعنه أرداه قتيلاً ثم إن إخوته أحاطوا به وهم الجراح وعاملة وسرعة فثبتوا بيوت ربيعة ولم يولوا ولما (عاين)[32] البراق صبر أخواله واستقامتهم للجميع أشفق عليهم وتنحى وكف فرسه وأمر رهطه وسائر قومه بذلك (وأمرهم بالوقوف عن القتال)[33] فلما رأى نويرة ذلك أقبل على البراق وهو يؤنفه ويقول هذا والله ما كان يخشى كليب من خديعتك يا براق وإغرارك بقومك وعدم نصيحتك لهم أتريد ان تبقى على صناديد طيّ وقد اغتابوك في قومك ولم يراعوا لك ذمة ولم يرحمونا وقتلوا رجالنا وأخذوا أموالنا وسبوا حريمنا فازدجر البراق وأنف من كلام نويرة وحافظ نصير بمن معه بقية يومه إلى الليل وانصرف الكل منهم وأنشأ نويرة يقول

[32] Parenthetical word from Ms. Or. Oct. 1383 (118r).
[33] Parenthetical remark from Ms. Or. Oct. 1383 (118r).

خليلي من أبناء بكر هديتما
قفا فاسألا الأطلال عن أم سالم
نسائلها عن نعم أين تحللت
وأترابها الغيد الحسان النواعم
عقائل من أبناء تغلب ضحوةً
سبتها جيوش الأفضلين الأعاصم
قد اجتمعت طيّ وجمع قضاعة
وأحلافها فوق الجياد الشياظم
وجاؤوا بجيش لا تعد جموعه
ولم يتبغوا إلا هلاك الاراقم
فخلّوا جهارًا مالنا وحريمنا
وظنوا بأن ينجوا بتلك الغنائم
وولوا كأمثال الظلام جموعهم
وأمثال صوب العارض المتراكم
عطفنا عليهم عطفة وائلية
بسمر القنا والمرهفات الصوارم
وجاءت جيوش من ربيعة معجلاً[34]
فمالت على طيّ بضرب الجماجم
فولى القضاعيون خوفًا من الردى
يشيلون في البيداء مثل النعائم
وقد فر من طي لئام رجالها
وحافظت الأشراف أهل المكارم
ولو بقي البراق فيهم لما بقوا
ولا سلموا من حرب شوس ضياغم

[34] Ahlwardt 9747 has (تغتري) or (تفتري). (معجلاً) is found in Arabe 5833 and 5984 Adab.

قال ابن نافع ثم إن نصيراً أغار من ليلته وبيت قومًا من بني ذهل فقتل منهم رجالاً كثيرة فاستأسر منهم الأفرس بن مالك بن سمير وانصرف وأنشأ يقول

سلي يا ابنة البكري عنا وعنهم
غداة التقينا بالرماح الشواجر
غداة تولوا هاربين وأسلموا
حريمهم يقسمن بين العشائر
ألم أحمل الخيل المغيرة بالقنا
وخام كليب عند وقع البواتر
وجئت بليلى وهي تبدو كأنها
وأترابها بيض النجوم الزواهر
حملنا عليهم حملة فتفرقت
جموعهم بالجحفل المتنافر
فجاءت لهذا بالصريخ جيادهم
بفتيان صدق كالأسود الخوادر
ورد الفتى البراق مال عشيرة
فأكرم به من مستغير وثائر
ولما استجر القتل منا ومنهم
مضت هربًا أحلافهم بالعساكر
فولت رجال من بني طي ثم لم
أكن قط أخشى مثلها من عشائر
فأكسبتكم كهلان غدرًا بقربكم
سرور الأعادي ثم رغم المصاهر
وإن بني أختي قد احتسبوا بنا
سأشكرهم بالصدق من غير شاكر
سأجزيهم يا صاح شكرًا بمثلها
جزاء لنسل الطيبات الحرائر
بنو أختنا جادوا علينا بفضلهم
وأبقوا علينا طيبات العناصر

قال فلما وصل نصير إلى أهله فك أسيريه وجهزهما جهازًا حسنًا ومنّ عليهما بنفسيهما وانصرفا فلما جاوزا بعض الطريق إذا هما بالبراق في غارة من قومه وذلك إن البراق لما بلغه ان نصيرًا بيت قومًا من بني ذهل غضب غضبًا شديدًا وقال أولم يكفه اغتيابي في قومي وإغارته عليهم بعدي حتى يبيت قومًا من بني ذهل ويقتل منهم ويستأسر أما كان له أذن وأعين[35] وقد أحاطت بهم خيل وائل فأبقيت عليهم تطولاً وصلة للرحم قال ثم إن الرجلين دلاه على حلة من حلل طي فوجه البراق إليها بقومه فقتلوا منهم رجالاً وأسروا وانصرفوا فلما كان في بعض الطريق أعتق أسراه وقال لهم لم تكن لي بذلك إرادة إلا إذا فعل قومك فعلة جازيناهم بمثلها ثم إن البراق جمع قومه وأغار على أخواله وقدم النذر إليهم أن لا يلاقي احدًا منهم على غرة وقال إني لا أفعل كما فعل نصير أتبع الغيبات والفرص وكان قد حنق على نصير حنقًا شديدًا لاغتيابه له وآلى على نفسه لينتصرن بمثلها فلما كان في بعض الطريق انتدب من بيوت بني عجل وجشم والنمر وتغلب جماعة وجعل عليهم نويرة بن ربيعة وقال كن أنت من خلف الخيل واتئد ولا تعجل فربما تكون الدائرة علينا فتعطفون علينا ولا يفوتكم مهرب وسار البراق بجموع ربيعة فلقيتهم جموع طي ومقدمهم نصير فالتقى الجمعان واقتتلوا قتالاً شديدًا فانهزمت خيل ربيعة فعطف عليها نويرة ومن معه واستقامت الحرب ولم يفت لواء نويرة كل من انهزم من ربيعة والتحم القوم بالقوم وتجالدوا بالسيوف حتى ذهلت العقول وكاد الرجل يضرب الرجل وهو لا يعرفه من التضايق والإقدام وما زالوا كذلك حتى انهزمت طي وقضاعة وخلوا عن الأموال والحرم فأخذتها ربيعة ولم تترك لهم خفًا ولا ظلفًا ولا عبدًا ولا أمة ولا امراة وانصرفوا بها فلما كانوا في أثناء الطريق استحى البراق من حريم أخواله فردهن ورد المال معهن وقال أبلغوا آل لهيم أنني لم يكن لي إرادة بما كان ولكن أردت أن أجازيهم بمثل ما فعلوا فلما بلغهم ذلك وجاءت اليهم نساؤهم وأموالهم شكروه على ذلك وأقروا له بالفضل والشرف والطول عليهم وانصرمت الفتنة بينه وبين أخواله واصطلحوا وتصافوا ووفدوا عليه فأكرمهم ووفد عليهم فأكرموه قال ابن نافع وإن البراق بعد انصراف الناس وخلوه بنفسه اشتد به حب ليلى وتكاثرت شجونه حتى لزم بيته واقتصر عن الخروج وهو كاتم ما عنده لا يبوح به إلى أحد من إخوته ولا خواصه إلا إلى كليب وإن كليبًا أنكر غيبة البراق فزاره إلى منزله فوجده في حال ضعيفة فشق عليه ذلك وساءه أشد ما يكون فخرج من عنده إلى عمه لكيز وقال يا عم ما لك لا ترجع عما في نفسك وتزوج البراق بليلى فهو أحق من غيره فقال لكيز واسوء فعلاه أتأخذون هدية الملك

[35] Ahlwardt 9747 (108v), has (واعيه).

وتعدونه بالزواج ثم تنكثون وتكلم لكيز على ابن أخيه بكلام فاحش فقال كليب والله لئن لم توافق البراق على مراده وتزوجه بليلى لأبلغنه ما في نفسه ثم أتى إلى البراق وقال له هل لك ان تدع رأي لكيز وتتزوج بليلى قال يا كليب اتقسمون هدية الملك ويعده أبوك وعمك بالتزويج ثم يختلف عليه رجل منكم بعد أن سمعت العرب بذلك قبح الله وجه رجل يعاهد ويخلف ثم تنفس الصعداء وأنشأ يقول

الصبر أحزم من بعض الأقاويل
ومن فظائع هاتيك الأفاعيل
إني وإن كنت أصبحت الغداة بها
أشقى أسير بقيد الحب مغلول
فليس عندي وفاء العهد منتزعًا
حتى اوسّد خمسات الأناميل
ماذا تقول سراة الحي من مضر
إذا ربيعة فاضت بالأباطيل

ثم قال يا كليب ما لي عنها صبر ولا سلوة ولا أعارض فيها ولا تسمع العرب بذلك قال وإن البراق جاش به حب ليلى وهاج عليه وكثر غشيانه وأشفق عليه كليب اشفاقًا عظيمًا فدعا بأبي البراق وإخوته وأخبرهم بما رأى منه وشاورهم في أمره فعظم عليهم الأمر وقال أبوهم روحان يا أولادي التمسوا ما يكون فيه صلاح أخيكم وسلامة أعراضنا من العار فتكلم ولده جنيد وأنشأ يقول

تقسم في احيا ربيعة تحفة
وتبغي سديد الرأي يا لك من فكر
تقطعت الأنساب منها الى أخي
مخافة ذم دائم أبد الدهر
تجير أبا عمرو فإنك مخبر
وصرح بما أحببته في أبي النصر
أبو النصر نصر فيه أي معونة
وأي صلاح والأنام به تدري

ثم تكلم اخوه نصير وأنشأ يقول

لحى الله الوفاء وكل قوم
يريدون الوفاء على الهلاك
أفيضوا باللقاح إلى لكيز
يرتعهن في وادي الأراك
يبيح لبانها ويشد باعًا
قويًا للضراب وللصكاك
فإن يقبل مشورتنا قبلنا
وإلا فالمعاد إلى المحاك
تريدون المكارم آل قومي
وكيف النعل من بعد الشراك

ثم تكلم غرسان وأنشأ يقول

لكل امرء رأي له ومشورة
ومحنته فيما يشا ويشير
وما من فتى إلا له من أموره
مقاصد فيها لا يزال يسير
فإن يرد البراق شيئًا فإننا
نسارع فيما يشتهي ونطير
وإن لم يرد شيئًا فما بعد قولكم
وهاهو فيكم حاكم وأمير

قال فالتفت روحان الى كليب وقال لا تفارق البراق ولا تدع زيارته إلى أن ترى ما يكون وافترقوا عنه ثم إن القبائل من ربيعة أمنت وتفرقت في أراضيها وكانت مخصبة في تلك السنة قال ابن نافع وإن قومًا من عك رحلوا من أرضهم ونزلوا على بني عجل وكانت ربيعة مجدبة وقد نزلت على مضر الحمراء فأوسعوا لهم وأحسنوا جوارهم وكان رجل من بني عجل يقال له الصلت صيادًا يرصد الموارد فشردت لرجل من عك راحلة فسار في طلبها وورد عين بجيرة على أثرها وكان الصلت راصدًا عليها ينتظر ورود الصيد فلما ورد العكي فزع القنص فغضب العجلي وأطلق به سهمًا فأرداه قتيلاً فاقتفى عك صاحبهم فوجدوه قتيلاً وأخبروا بخبره فرحلوا عن جوار بني عجل ولحقوا بقومهم وكانوا ستين فارسًا فتطرفوا إبلاً وأخذوها وقتلوا غلامين وكان ذلك عند

غروب الشمس فبلغ الصريخ إلى بني عجل فقالوا رجل برجل فما بال الثاني والإبل وشدوا في أثرهم ولزموا عليهم المراصد فكانوا لا يمرون بمرصد إلا وثبوا عليهم فيقتلون الرجل والرجلين والعشرة ولم ينفذ من الستين إلا رجلان فقدما على قومهما وأخبراهم وفشا ذلك في قبائل مضر فشق عليهم وعزموا على فتنة ربيعة فتواعدت رؤساء مضر إلى حرم الله تعالى للمشورة ثم اجتمعوا وتشاوروا وأطبق أمر قريش أن يجمعوا لربيعة جموعًا ويفتنوها أشد الفتنة فقال نوفل بن عمرو القرشي إن قبلتم رأيي فلا تفتنوا ربيعة فتنبذوها وتنبذكم ولكن ابعثوا إليهم يرتفعوا من بلادنا فاتفقوا على رأي نوفل وكان مطاعًا فيهم مسموع الكلام وبعثوا الى ربيعة بذلك فعظم الأمر عليهم وقالوا والله القطيعة أعظم من القتل ثم ارتحلوا عن مضر واعتزلوهم ونزلوا بأرضهم في ديار ربيعة قال ثم إن رؤساء وائل أقبلوا على لكيز وقالوا لا عذر لك من أن تزوج البراق بليلى فلما رأى الغلبة قدم على البراق وشكاهم إليه فقال البراق ما تحبه[36] أفعله لك قال الخروج إلى الملك عمرو بن ذي صهبان فقال له شد بأهلك ومن وافقك من أولادك وأنا أركب معك حتى أخرجك من قبائل ربيعة فتجهز لكيز ومن معه والبراق وخرج إلى سبيله وآلت ربيعة على مقاطعة لكيز أبداً ثم إن لكيز نزل بأهله على نعيم بن مهلة الأزدي وهو في حدود الملك عمرو فأنزله وأكرمه قال ابن نافع وإن رجلاً من أنمار يقال له كريم ابن الأعرج ألم بدار نعيم بن مهلة الأزدي ذات ليلة وكان متوجهًا إلى مدينة شهرميه ملك الفرس وكانت قبائل أنمار وإياد عند الملك شهرميه في حدوده وأراضيه وكان يستعين بهم على خدمته في بعض الأحوال فاشتغل نعيم عن كريم ابن الأعرج وبات تلك الليلة طاويًا هو وأصحابه فلما أصبح القوم سألوا نعيمًا ما الذي أشغله عنهم فقال عندي رجل من ربيعة وأخبرهم به (ومصاهرته الملك عمرو بن ذي صهبان)[37] وكان الأنماري قد سمع عن ليلى بوصف كثير من المحاسن والجمال فقال والله لا جئت الملك بأحسن من هذه التحفة ثم شد وركب راحلته وحث في سيره حتى قدم الى مدينة شهرميه واستأذن الحاجب في الدخول وصار الحاجب إلى الملك فأعلمه فقال قدمه إلي خلوة سرة ورفع الشراب إليه ثم دعا ببرد بن طريح الإيادي وكان وزيرًا عنده فاستنطقه فتكلم بما عنده فقال برد وكيف الرأي في تحصيلها فقال يكتب الملك الى عمرو أمرًا بوصولها إليه فقال أحسنت وخرج إلى الملك فأخبره بذلك فتبسم ضاحكًا وكان حكيمًا حاذقًا يشتهي نظر الحسان وقال أما هي فلا توسع لنا في نفسها بريبة وإذا لم ترض بذلك وكرهته فلا تكرهها

[36] This wording comes from Ms. Or. Oct. 1383 (121v). Ahlwardt 9747 (111v) has (ترده).

[37] Parenthetical remark from Ms. Or. Oct. 1383 (122r).

ثم إن الملك كتب إلى عمرو بن ذي صهبان بذلك فأجاب إني أوافقك على ذلك وأترك بها غير أني لا أعلم هل يوافقون هم على مصاهرة الملك أم تكره العرب مصاهرة العجم ولكنني أبلغ في ذلك حد اجتهادي قال فجدد الملك المواثيق على عمرو في خطبة ليلى وأرسل برد بن طريح مع كريم أخويه الربيع والحنيش ابني طريح بعسكر عظيم وأمرهما أن يزفا ليلى إلى الملك فإن منعت ربيعة يقتلون الرجال ويسبون الحريم ويأتونه بليلى سبية قال فساروا سيراً حثيثاً وكانوا ينظرون من يتقدم او يتأخر خوفًا أن يسبقهم نذير فلما وصلوا الى حلة نعيم الأزدي ونزلوا عليه جدد عمرو بن ذي صهبان خطبة ليلى على الملك شهرميه فقال له لكيز أما يكفيك أني هجرت قومي وهجروني ومنعتها عن سيد العرب البراق بن روحان لأجلك ووقفت عند قولي وإنعامي بها إليك حتى ترفع خبرها إلى ملك الفرس وتريد تزويجها بمن لا يوافقها ذلك لا يكون وأما أنت فلنا عذر بعد ما كان منك وقد بطلت الخطبة عن كليكما فأخذ عمرو يعتذر إليه بأن ليس له من ذلك خبر وإنما السبب فيه كريم الأنماري وهو الذي رفع خبرها إلى الملك شهرميه فقال لكيز أما أنت فقد بلغنا من لدنك معذرة ولم يبق لك حق علينا وأما هؤلاء فلا اهلاً ولا سهلاً بهم فلما سمع الربيع والحنيش كلام لكيز هجما على داره بالعسكر واستخرجا ليلى فعند ذلك ركب لكيز وأولاده وجارهم نعيم بن مهلة بقومه وكان يركب في خمسمائة فارس وانتشبت الحرب بين القوم واشتد القتال فاستظهرت أصحاب الملك شهرميه وحلوا الأموال وسبوا النساء وفيهن ليلى العفيفة فحمل لكيز وأولاده ونعيم وأولاده وفرسان من قومه فقتلوا الحنيش ومن معه وقتل خزيمة بن لكيز وقتل الدليل كريم بن الأعرج الأنماري وانجرح لكيز وابنه عقيل وراحت الجند بالأموال والسبايا قال فتقدم الربيع بن طريح وسأل عن ليلى فدلته بعض النساء عليها فشد لها بنفسه على جمل من نجائب الإبل وأناخه قريبًا منها فأولاها ظهره وقال والله ما رضيت هذا وإنه على الأشد المكروه وإنما كان السبب فيه كريمًا الأنماري وقد كان جزاءه ما كان فرب حافر حفرة وقع فيها فراحت مثلاً وركبت ليلى ودموعها تتحدر على صدرها وأطلق الربيع بقية النساء وجميع الأموال وقال هذه حاجة الملك وتوجه إلى دار فارس وأنشأ يقول

دعاني للقطيعة منه برد
وبرد عندنا أي المطاع
وكنا في النمو وفي المعالي
فصرنا اليوم من سقط المتاع
وما كانت قبائل آل طي

وتغلب تستعيذ من القراع
ولكن في لكيز شر فعل
فعلنا وهو محمود الطباع
وفي البراق والساعي كليب
كذا ونوير الحامي الرباع

قال ابن نافع ثم إن لكيزًا وابنه عقيلاً أخذا أموالهما وحريمهما وتوجها إلى قومهما وأما الربيع بن طريح فإنه لما قرب من مدينة الملك شهرميه أرسل إلى أخيه برد يهنيه بالظفر ويعزيه بأخيه ثم إنه دخل على الملك وقال له قد حصلت ليلى في دارك وقد أمرت بإصلاح شأنها أفأرفعها إليك أم أخلي لها خلوة في داري وتركب إليها أنت قال إنك تخبرني بشيء وأنا أخبرك أنها لا ترضى وأنا لا أكرهها فتأنّ في أمرك ولا تعجل ثم أمر له بعطية جزيلة فخرج من عنده وقدم معه غلمان الملك يحملونها فدخل على أهله في داره وقال ما صنعتم بهذه الجارية فإن الملك أعطاني ما ترون رغبة فيها وسوف نزداد بها خيرًا فحلوها بأحسن الحلي وألبسوها أفخر الملبوس لتأتيه جميلة فقالت له زوجته هيهات أين منك هذا الحديث أوكان الملك يرغب في معاشرة الموتى فوأيم الله لقد منعتنا نظرها فاغتم لذلك وقال إن أرادت الصنيعة فعلت ما تؤمر به وإلا فلأعذبنها عذابًا شديدًا ثم قام إليها وتهددها ورغبها في الملك وشوقها إلى نعيمه فلما أكثر عليها الكلام تنهدت وأنشأت تقول

اصبر ستجزي الذي أسلفته في عجل[38]
بما فعلت بلا ريث ولا مهل
هل مخبر لي براقًا وإخوته
أسد العرين أولى الغارات بالأسل
صنع الإيادي شر الناس كلهم
هيهات براق عني اليوم في شغل
لا تخذلوا لي لكيزًا يا بني أسد
واستعصبوا مضرًا يأتون في عجل

[38] Ahlwardt 9747 (113v) has (من ذلل). (في عجل) is found in Ms. Or. Oct. 1383 (123v), Arabe 5833 (120r), 5984 Adab (64), and Or. 2676 (167v).

فقال برد لما جعلت الإيادي شر الناس وأنت تعلمين أني منتسب الى شيبان وإياد قالت وكيف لا يكون ذلك وأنشأت تقول

لو كنت منتسبًا إلى الشيبان
لحفظت فرعهم بكل لسان
وعرضت عن فعل الخنا أخا الخنا
وغضضت طرفًا مستحي الأجفان
لكن خناؤك في فنائك لم يزل
وسلكت طرق منوّر بن عنان
فلك الجزاء بكل ما أسلفته
في آل وائل من جزاء هوان
يا آل براق السميدع في الوغى
ونويرة العالي على الفرسان
شدوا جياد الخيل وأتوني بها
مشدودة لتكافح الأقران
وإذا رأيت نواصيًا مفروقة
من كل جبهة شيظم وحصان
فيها بنو مضر وآل ربيعة
لطعان كل غضنفر مطعان
فاثبت عدمتك من قرين واستقم
للشوس من مضر ومن عدنان
لأسود حرب ليس يفشلها اللقا
بصفايح يمضين كالنيران

قال ابن نافع بلغني أنه صبر على الشعر كله وأنف من قولها في آخره عدمتك من قرين فقال ويحك أبرد بن طريح ابن أتان أليس إياد وربيعة إخوان قالت صدقت ولكنك يا ابن الفارسية لست لإياد ولو كنت لهم ما رضيت في حرمة ربيعة هذا الفعل ولكنك زنيم فازداد غيظًا وأمر

بها فقيدت (وغُلّت)[39] وضربت ضربًا اليمًا والملك لا يشعر بشيء من ذلك وسألته زوجته الشفاعة فلم يشفعها فأقبلت عليها وقالت يا أختاه قد بلغت في عرضك عذرًا فاقبلي نصيحتي فليس هذا أوان عفة لكن ذلك لو كنت في رجالك وعشيرتك فقالت العذاب والقتل أهون عليّ مما يطلبه مني ثم بكت وأنشأت تقول

ليت للبراق عينًا فترى
ما أقاسي من بلاء وعنا
يا كليبًا يا عقيلاً إخوتي
يا جنيدًا أسعدوني بالبكا
عذبت أختكم يا ويلكم
بعذاب النكر صبحًا ومسا
غللوني قيدوني وضربوا[40]
ملمس العفة مني بالعصا
يكذب الأعجم ما يقربني
ومعي بعض حشاشات[41] الحيا
قيدوني غللوني وافعلوا
كل ما شئتم جميعًا من بلا
فأنا كارهة بغيتكم
ومرير الموت عندي قد حلا
أتدلون علينا فارسًا
يا بني أنمار يا أهل الخنا
يا إياد خسرت صفقتكم
ورمى المنظر من برد العما
يا بني الأعياص أما تقطعوا
لبني عدنان أسباب الرجا

[39] Parenthetical word from Ms. Or. Oct. 1383 (124v).
[40] Ahlwardt 9747 (114v) has (واضربوا).
[41] Ahlwardt 9747 (114v) has (حساسات). (حشاشات) is found in Arabe 5833 (120v), Or. 2676 (168r), and 5984 Adab (66).

فاصطبارًا وعزاء حسنًا
كل نصر بعد ضر يرتجى
قل لعدنان هديتم[42] شمروا
لبني مبغوض تشمير الوفا[43]
واعقدوا الرايات في أقطارها
واشهروا البيض وسيروا في الضحى
يا بني تغلب سيروا وانصروا
وذروا الغفلة عنكم والكرى
واحذروا العار على أعقابكم
وعليكم ما بقيتم في الدنا[44]

قال ابن نافع فلما سمعت امرأة برد بن طريح شعرها رجعت إلى بيتها وأيقنت بالفتنة الطويلة وروت الشعر لقينة لها وقالت أنشديه مولاك خير بن طريح فانتهت إليه وأنشدته الشعر فقال قبح الله رأي أخي برد أما كان له كفاية بما أغشانا من العار عن تقييدها وضربها أمثلنا يدل على حريم ربيعة أو يشير إليهن ويرضى فيهن الفواحش إن ذلك لبئسما فعل وسيذوق ثمرة ما جناه بيده وتالله لقد ألقح علينا حرب ربيعة وذكرنا وإياهم ما أنسانا وأنساهم الدهر من وقائع الحجيب التي أفنت الكبير وشيبت الصغير وأخلتنا من ديارنا وأموالنا ونفتنا عن ديار آبائنا وأجدادنا فوالله لتأنفن لسبي ليلى صناديد وائل ويغضب لها جميع القبائل من ولد عدنان ثم إنه خرج إلى الملك شهرميه فاستأذن حاجبه عليه وأعلمه بفعل أخيه مع ليلى وأنشده شعرها بالفارسية[45] فلامه الملك لومًا شديدًا وقال ما رضي بالغربة ولا تحاشى من الأهل ولقد كان لنا عنها غنى وعن مسير قومها إلينا ومحاربتهم إيانا ثم أمر لها بدار وأقدمها إليها وأجرى لها من المكارم ما لم يجره لغيرها ثم أمر بإحضار كاهن وسأله عمّا يكون في أمر ليلى فقال الكاهن ستطأ العرب بلاد العجم في شأن ليلى وتظهر فيها قصص متصلة ويكثر النهب والسبي قال ابن

[42] Ahlwardt 9747 (114v) has (فديتم). (هديتم) is found in Arabe 5833 (120v), 5984 Adab (67), Or. 2676 (168r), and Ms. Or. Oct. 1383 (124v).
[43] Ahlwardt 9747 (114v) has (لبني الاعجام تشمير الوحى). (لبني مبغوض تشمير الوفا) is from Arabe 5833 (120v) and Ms. Or. Oct. 1383 (124v).
[44] Ahlwardt 9747 (114v) has (الورى). (الدنا) is from Arabe 5833 (120v), 5984 Adab (67), Or. 2676 (168r), and Ms. Or. Oct. 1383 (124v).
[45] Ms. Or. Oct. 1383 (125r) has (بالعبرانية): 'in Hebrew'.

نافع وأما لكيز فإنه بعد سبي ابنته ليلى سأل صهره عمرو بن ذي صهبان النصرة وقال إنما أنت كنت السبب في سبيها ووصولها الى أرض العجم فهل لك أن تمدني بما تقدر عليه من الجيوش أو تسير معنا لعلنا نستنقذ ليلى دون اطلاع قومنا فيشمتون بنا مع ما فعلته من هجري إياهم ومقاطعتي لهم وإيثارك بليلى دونهم حتى كان ما كان فقال عمرو صدقت إني كنت السبب في سبيها ولولا مصاهرتي ما خرجت من ديارها ولا هجرت قومك غير أنه يمنعني من نصرتك أني من عمال الملك ولا تليق بي المكاشفة والمظاهرة معك ولو مددتك بجيش قليل أخفيه عن الملك لم يكن لك فيه كفاية ولا تقضي به وطرًا لأن هذا الملك عنده جيوش تملأ الفضاء طولاً وعرضًا وحوله من العرب من قومنا وقومكم ما يساوي جنود العجم ثم أنشأ يقول

وكم دون أرض الفرس من آل يعرب
أناسًا يجيدون اللقا والتصدرا
بغير جنود العجم والشوكة التي
تطأطئ لها رؤوس الأنام تجبرا
ولو كنت أقوى فض شمل جموعهم
لما كنت عن صهري إذن متأخرا
فإن كان في ابنا نزار بشاشة
وشمر براق الهمام وعسكرا
وجاءت نزار رجلها وخيولها
لتطعم آل العيص ضربًا منكرا
فإني سأوفي من خيولي وفتيتي[46]
رجالاً يرون القتل مجدًا ومفخرا
فشمر إلى الأعمام منك بن مرة
وناد إلى أحلافهم منتصرا

قال ولما فرغ من شعره قال يا لكيز اذهب إلى قومك واطلبهم للنصرة فإني أرجو العطف منهم لك وأعلم أنهم يأنفون لذلك ويغضبون منه لحق نفوسهم لا لحق نفسك فليلى حرمة من نسائهم وفضيحتها عليهم فإن عزموا على المسير لنصرتك فإني أمدك بما أقدر عليه من خيل

[46] Ahlwardt 9747 (116r) has (وفتنتي). (وفتيتي) is from Ms. Or. Oct. 1383 (125v).

ورجال خفية[47] فقال لكيز أنا ما أجهل ذلك ولست ممن تأمره بالمسير إلى قومه وطلبه النصرة منهم وإنما قصدت الكفاية منك بحيث ما كان مني وهجري لقومي وإيثارك دونهم ورغبتي بابنتي عنهم وقد زعمت أن فيك حميّة فتنصرني بجندك لعلنا نستنقذ ليلى دون استعطافي لقومي وانكساري لهم وشماتتهم بي وإلا فهم نعم القوم يهبون الكريمة ولا يهابون العظيمة وأرجو أنهم يعطفون علي ويغفرون زلتي وينصرون ذلي ويجبرون كسري واذا سرت إليهم فلست محتاجًا إلى نصرتك ثم ركب وشد بأمواله وأهله وتوجه إلى قومه فنزل بالأراقم دون البراق واستعطفهم وانكسر إليهم واعتذر لهم فعطفوا عليه وقال كليب (ليس)[48] هذا وقت عتاب ولا اعتذار إنما أضرمتها أنت وتلقى حرها غيرك فسارت مثلاً وشاع خبر سبي ليلى في قبائل ربيعة ومضر فأنفوا من ذلك وغضبوا ولحقتهم حمية الجاهلية وأشفق البراق على ليلى إشفاقًا عظيمًا (إلا أنه أسر ما عنده من الوجد)[49] قال ابن نافع وإن عامر بن ذؤيب الأرقمي لما رأى تغير وجه لكيز وما هو عليه ساءه ذلك وانتهى إلى البراق وأخبره بحال لكيز وسأله القيام في بيوت ربيعة فقال أنا رجل منكم إن طعنتم طعنت وإن كورتم كورت وإن فررتم عطفت وإن رحلتم رحلت وإن اقمتم اقمت فلما سمع عامر ذلك علم أن هناك خبيّة مطوية على غير رضى فأنشأ يقول

قد اجتمع البراق في حال حادث
له بين أحناء الضلوع وجيب
له عين إغماض وعين قريرة
وصدر على ما جاء منه رحيب
وأقسم لا قامت ربيعة بعده
وذلك من فعل الهمام عجيب

[47] Ms. Or. Oct. 1383 (126r). Ahlwardt 9747 (116r) has (حفية).
[48] Parenthetical word from Ms. Or. Oct. 1383 (126r).
[49] Parenthetical remark from Ms. Or. Oct. 1383 (126v).

ثم خرج عامر وقد داخله أمر مريب من ذلك وجاءت أم الأغر إلى أخيها كليب وتكلمت عليه كلامًا كثيرًا في شأن ليلى ولامته وعيرته وأنشأت تقول

أراك عن الأمر المشتت غافلاً
كأنك ناج من خزاياه سالم
وإن امرؤ عن مثله كان قاعدًا
فلست تراه في العلى وهو قائم
فسيروا لليلى لا شتمتم بعارها
لقد فضحت في شأن ليلى الأراقم

قال فسكتها كليب وقال لها قلي من اللوم فإن الذي بنا يكفينا وسوف ترين ثم نهض من ساعته هو وإخوته وعمهما لكيز وأولاده وقدموا على البراق وقالوا يا أبا النصر جئناك لأمر غشانا عاره وذهبت به الركبان وتحدثت به النساء وأنشأ كليب يقول

إليك أتينا مستجيرين للنصر
فشمر وبادر للمغار أبا النصر
فإن لم تثر سبت بها آل وائل
وعيبوا بها بين الأنام مدى الدهر
وما الناس إلا تابعون لواحد
إذا كان فيه آلة المجد والفخر
فناد تجبك الصيد من آل وائل
وليس لكم يا آل وائل من عذر

فأجابه البراق يقول

وهل أنا إلا واحد من ربيعة
أهون إذا هانوا وفخرهم فخري
أعز إذا كانوا كرامًا أعزة
وأخسر كل الخسر في ساعة الخسر
سأمنحكم مني الذي تعرفونه
أشمر عن ساقي واعلو على مهري

وأدعو بني عمي جميعًا وإخوتي
إلى موطن الهيجاء او مرتع الكر

قال ابن نافع فلما سمع كليب شعره علم ما هو منطو عليه من الاحقاد (لشأن ليلى)[50] فقال يا أبا النصر ما هذا مكان عتاب ولا حقد ولكنه وقت القيام والاهتمام فهذه مصيبة عم الجميع عارها وأيم الله لقد تحدثت بنا النساء في مجالسها ولامتني أم الأغر حتى نكست رأسي عنها وعجزت عن جوابها فكيف إذا لامتنا العرب قاطبة فهلا تقوم في ربيعة وتكشف عارها وتأخذ ثأرها من بني العيص وتستخلص ليلى من أسرها وعذابها فقال البراق يا كليب ليس هذا حقدًا مني ولا خلافًا غير أني لست منتصبًا للرئاسة ولا كفوًا لها فإن رأيتم أن تقيلوني من رئاسة وائل وتقيمون واحدًا منكم وأكون أنا وإخوتي وبنو عمي وقومي أولكم طعنًا وآخركم فرارًا فافعلوا قال يا أبا النصر ليس لنا رئيس غيرك ولا سائس سواك فكيف تتخلى عنا وقد أجبنا داعيك في حرب طي وقضاعة وتريد أن تخذلنا وتكسونا العار في قبائل العرب من أجل رجل سقطت نفسه وذهبت همته ورغبه ما عند الملوك حتى كان من أمره ما كان شب نارها وحملنا عارها قال فلما سمع البراق كلام كليب وعلم أنه لا عذر له من ذلك أخذته حمية الجاهلية وأجاب الى سؤاله ثم قال يا كليب كفوا ألسنتكم عن التشييع بالغارة واطرحوا هذا الأمر فليس هذا كغيره من الأمور لأن هذا ملك عظيم تجيب دعوته جميع الملوك وعسكره كثيرة وهو في مدائن محصنة لا تفيد فيها الغارة ولا يفيدنا الا المحاصرة وبذل الأموال لطول الإقامة وتوسع الفتنة فلو كان يسير إلينا في الفضاء لكان أهون علينا من شرب الماء القراح ولكن دونه خرط القتاد في الليلة الطحناء فامضوا الى رؤساء ربيعة وعقلائها وادعوهم للمشورة فنوجه إلى إخوتنا مضر الحمراء ونستنصرهم وإن أسانا إليهم وقتلنا رجالهم فعسى أن لا يعقوا فينا ولا يؤاخذونا بجرائم بني عجل فانطلق كليب من ساعته ودعا رؤساء ربيعة وعقلائها فجاؤوا من حينهم وقدموا عليه فحياهم بأحسن التحية ثم قال يا بني الأعمام قد علمتم ما كان من سبي ليلى عند العجم وما ذهبت به الركبان من أمرها وقد علمت العرب جرأتنا وعظم بأسنا وإننا لا نهاب العظائم فكيف وقد غشانا من العار كقطع الليل إذا عسعس واعترانا من الذل ما لو متنا قبله لكان خيرًا لنا فما يكون عندكم من الرأي فقالوا يا أبا النصر قد غشينا ما غشاك فيا لبيك بذلك والرأي إليك قال نريد أن نوجه إلى إخواننا مضر الحمراء ونستوهبهم الدماء التي قطعت بيننا وبينهم ونستنصرهم لهذا الأمر المهم الذي لا يعيننا على مثله إلا هم فما ترون قالوا نعم ما أشرت به قال فوجهوا إلى مضر

[50] Parenthetical remark from Ms. Or. Oct. 1383 (127r).

جماعة من أشرافهم ورئيسهم عامر بن ذؤيب فقدموا على مضر فأكرموهم غاية الإكرام وقال عامر يا بني الأعمام قد علمتم ما دهانا به الدهر من سبي كريمتكم ليلى عند العجم وقد جئنا نستعطيكم الدماء التي لكم علينا ونستنصركم في استنقاذها بحق عليكم تعطونا بعد استعطائكم وتنصرونا بعد استنصاركم وقد علمتم أن الربيعة ومضر يمين وشمال ليس لإحداهما غنى عن الأخرى فلا عذر لكم أن تعطفوا علينا وتنصرونا ونكون يدًا واحدة على بني الأعياص قال ابن نافع فتكلم نوفل بن عمرو القرشي وأنشأ يقول

ناب المصاب بني عمي فأشجانا
وقد أضر بنا والله ما كانا
لكن فعلكم بالأمس فرقنا
حتى كأن لم نكن بالأمس جيرانا
فلا تلوموا بني الأعمام غيركم
إذ كان منكم بدء الأمر طغيانا
قتلتم عك طغيانًا ومظلمة
كأنكم لم تكونوا قط إخوانا
وقد صبرنا وكان الصبر عادتنا
على الصديق ولو بالظلم بادانا

ثم قال اما العطاء فلا اظن بني عك يسمحون بدمائهم واما النصرة والمسير فقد يكون لك غير اني اخشى انه يجمع بين القاتل وطالبه فاذا رات عك غريماً من بني عجل لا نامن ان تقع الفتنة بيننا دون العجم فيأول الامر الى اعظم من ذلك هذا عذرنا فاعرضوه على عقلائكم فانقلب وفد ربيعة حتى وصلوا الى البراق بما قال نوفل وانشدوه الشعر فقال تعست الجناية على الصديق فسارت مثلاً ثم ان البراق جمع قومه بني وائل واحلافهم وجعل يحرضهم وقال

لم يبق يا ويحكم إلا تلاقيها
ومسعر الحرب لاقيها وآتيها
لا تطمعوا بعدها في قومكم مضر
من بعد هذا فولوها مواليها
فمن بقي منكم في هذه فله
فخر الحياة وان طالت لياليها

ومن يمت مات معذورًا وكان له
حسن الثناء مقيمًا إذ ثوى فيها
إن تتركوا وائلاً للحرب يا مضر
فسوف يلقاكم ما كان لاقيها
يا أيها الراكب المجتاز ترقل في
حزن البلاد وطورًا في صحاريها
أبلغ بني العيص عنا حين تبلغهم
وحي كهلان أن الجند عافيها
لا بد قومي أن ترقى وقد جهدت
صعب المراقي بما تأبى مراقيها
أما إياد فقد جاءت بها بدعًا
في ما جنى البعض إذ ما البعض راضيها

قال ثم إن البراق أغار بمن حضر من قومه ربيعة ومن معه من قبائل العرب وصبح مدينة عرنة وهي في حدود الملك من ديار العرب وكان فيها قائد للملك في سبعين الفًا من الفرس وأخلاط العرب من أنمار وكهلان فاستغارهم بخيل قليلة حتى خرجوا من المدينة فانكسرت خيل البراق وساقوا في أثرها حتى أبعدوا فعطف عليهم البراق وقتل فيهم وكانت الدائرة عليهم فأخذهم وغنم جميع ما في المدينة من الذهب والفضة والسلاح وأنواع الطرائف ورجع غانمًا ظافرًا وأنشأ يقول

امن دون ليلى عوقتنا العوائق
جنود وقفر ترتعيه النقانق
وعجم وأعراب وأرض سحيقة
وحصن ودور دونها ومغالق
وغربها عني لكيز بجهله
ولما يعقه عند ذلك عائق
وقلدني ما لا أطيق إذ ونت
بنو مضر الحمرا الكرام الشقائق
وإني لارجوهم ولست بآيس

وإني بهم يا قوم لا شك واثق
أليلى استطالت ليلتي بعد بيننا
وقد بات دمعي وهو في الخد دافق
فكيف وقد أصبحت في دار غربة
وأسلمك الشيخ الجهول المنافق
رمى الله من يرمي الكعاب بريبة
ومن هو بالفحشاء في الليل ناطق
فمن مبلغ برد الإيادي وقومه
بأني بثأري لامحالة لاحق
ستسعدني بيض الصوارم والقنا
وتحملني القب العتاق اللواحق
على مركب صعب المراقي لأجلها
وتنهضني للمعضلات الحقائق

قال ابن نافع ولما رجع البراق من غزوته وفدت عليه رؤساء العرب وأكابر الناس يهنئونه بالظفر ومدحته العرب بالأشعار فأعطى وكسا وأقرى ووفد عليه نوفل بن عمرو القرشي يهنيه وكان بينهما مودة وأقام عنده واعتذر إليه عن المسير معه بقبائل مضر وذكر له أن سبب ذلك دماء بني عجل وأن اجتماعهم بهم يهيج الفتنة فقبل عذره ورأى كلامه صوابًا وبعث البراق إلى أخواله طي يستنصرهم على العجم فأقبلوا إليه على كل صعب وذلول وحبا خاله نصيرًا من تلك الغنائم بأسنى العطية وكانت ربيعة قد صارت أوسع العرب خيرًا لكثرة ما حازوا من غنائم عرنة ثم إن البراق وجه خاله نصيرًا يراقب العجم وينظر ما هم عليه من الاستعداد فركب نصير في جماعة من قومه حتى ورد مدينة كرخا ودخلها فوافق الملك شهرميه وقد جاءه عسكره منهزمًا وكان قد أخرج الجنود إلى مدينة كرخا لأنها مفتاح بلاده وفيها من العرب والعجم مئة الف مقاتل وفيها إياد وأنمار وكهلان فرحبوا بنصير بن عمرو ولم يعلموا أنه صاحب البراق وقبلوه قبولاً حسنًا ورفعوا منزلته فأقام عندهم حتى عرف ما هم عليه ثم استأذن في الخروج فأجازه الملك جائزة حسنة وخرج من عنده ومعه برد بن طريح الإيادي فقال له أرأيت ما في هذه المدينة من العساكر والجنود قال نعم قال إن سألك البراق عن ذلك فأخبره فقال إن البراق لا يجهل ذلك وسار نصير وأصحابه وجاؤوا إلى البراق وأخبروه فقال لا بد من قصدهم ولو كان قومهم كقوم تبع ثم نادى بالغارة فشدوا وسار بهم ومعه خاله نصير بجميع طي وقضاعة وكان نوفل

بن عمرو القرشي قد مكث عنده فخرج معه وساروا حتى نزلوا بموضع يقال له مهدة كثير الماء فقال اجعلوا لنا رأيًا نكون عليه غدًا فقالوا الرأي إليك قال اعلموا أيها السادات أن هؤلاء القوم إن تحصنوا في المدينة وغلقوا أبوابها اتبعونا بطول الإقامة فالرأي أن نحيط بهم يمينًا وشمالاً ونغير عليهم بخيل قليلة فإذا رأوها طمعوا فيها لقلتها فيخرجون من المدينة فإذا انتشب القتال بينهم انقلبوا إلينا هاربين فلعلهم يغيرون خلفهم حتى يصيروا في الفضاء فتحمل عليهم كل قبيلة بما يليها ونقطع ساقتهم مما يلي المدينة فقالوا نعم الرأي ولما أصبحوا عقد البراق الرايات والألوية وأعطى نويرة بن ربيعة راية وقدمه على جشم وأعطى كليبًا راية وقدمه على آل عكرمة والأراقم وعقد راية أخرى لعامر بن ذؤيب في قبائل تغلب وراية أخرى لأخيه جنيد بن روحان وقدمه على بني شيبان وقبائل بكر بن وائل وأخرى لخاله نصير في طي وقضاعة وساروا حتى انتهوا إلى قرب المدينة وكان ذلك عند طلوع الفجر فأمر كليبًا وعامرًا أن يأخذا بجنديهما ميمنة المدينة والجنيد ونصيرًا بجنديهما ميسرتها وأقام هو ومن معه من بني أسد وبني يشكر وبني عجل وبني حنيفة في الوسط وعليه لواء الرئاسة والملك وقال لنويرة تقدم أنت ومن معك إلى باب المدينة واقتلوا من تنظرون به فإذا اشتبك القتال بينكم انقلبوا إلينا بانهزام تحيزًا وانحرافًا ولا تولوهم الأدبار حتى تصلوا الينا فأجاب نويرة إلى ذلك وقصد الباب فوجد عسكر الملك يرصده فوضع فيهم السيوف والرماح فقام الصراخ في المدينة فخرج الملك شهرميه ومن معه من جنوده وقبائل فاقتتلوا قتالاً شديدًا وانهزم نويرة فخرج الملك بأثره بعساكر ككراديس النمل وصار نويرة يرجع تارة يقاتلهم وتارة ينهزم فأقبل برد بن طريح على الملك وقال أنت تجهل قتال العرب وهذه خديعة من البراق فلا تفرط بالخروج والزم باب المدينة فانعطف عنهم وأغار برد بالجنود خلف نويرة فلما نزحت جنود الملك الى الفضاء حملت كل قبيلة بما يليها وحمل البراق من وسط القوم وقطع كليب ونصير ساقة الجنود والتحم القتال وقتلت ربيعة من العجم ومن معهم من أنمار وإياد قتلة شنيعة حتى تمنوا الانهزام ولم يمكنهم وكان البراق يتشوف إلى برد ابن طريح وهو لا يعرفه وهو في كل حملة ينادي أين برد فارس الخيل وبرد يسمعه ولا يبرز إليه خوفًا منه وعند ذلك حمل الملك ومن معه فاقتتلوا إلى أن حجز بينهم الليل فدخل الملك المدينة بسوء حال وباتت ربيعة تشب نيرانها إلى الصباح قال ولما جن الليل نهض البراق وزيد بن ذؤيب متشحين بسيفيهما يلتمسان خبر ليلى فدخلا المدينة وكان بابها لا يزال مفتوحًا ليلاً ونهارًا لأجل قبائل العرب التي حولها فلم يريا من يلتمسان الخبر منه فقصدا مضرب جبر أخي برد بن طريح فلم يجدا فيه إلا أعجميًا على فراش من الديباج فأنزله زيد عن فراشه فصاح فقال زيد اسكت وإلا ذبحتك وإن سكت فلك الأمان فسكت واستخرجاه

من موضعه وأردفه زيد وخرجا به فسألاه عن ليلى وقالا له تدلنا عليها ونخلي سبيلك فوافقهما على ذلك وكان من أجلاء قواد الملك فقال البراق نرجع الليلة ونستشير نوفلاً وانقلبا الى نوفل فأخبراه والأعجمي معهما فقال لهما كونا في الليلة المستقبلة وأما هذه فقد انقضت فدفعا اليه الرجل فسلمه الى من يحفظه إلى الصباح قال ابن نافع فلما أصبحوا شد البراق من موضعه ونزل بالقرب من المدينة وفرق جيوشه في ميامنها ومياسرها وأمامها وخلفها وصاروا لا يظفرون بخف ولا ظلف لأنماري أو إيادي إلا أخذوه ولا برجل إلا قتلوه ولا يتمكنون من داخل الى المدينة أو خارج منها إلا أخذوا ما معه وقتلوه فأضر ذلك بقبائل العرب والعجم فخرجوا عليهم وقاتلوهم قتالاً شديدًا وقتلت منهم ربيعة قتلة شنيعة أعظم مما قبلها ولم يزالوا يقتتلون إلى أن كاد يزول النهار فعند ذلك برز أخو القائد الأعجمي وطلب البراز فبرز اليه قريح بن عصر بن مالك فرماه بسهم فقتله ولم يزل يدعو للبراز حتى قتل من الفرسان خمسة وعشرين فارسًا بخمسة وعشرين سهمًا فاحتفز البراق جواده وعاجله قبل أن يرميه فأرداه قتيلاً واستقام في الميدان فبرز إليه علج آخر يقال له هرقل فاعتركا ساعة وانتزعه البراق من سرجه أسيرًا وجعل الحبل في عنقه وأقبل به حتى وصل الى نوفل بن عمرو القرشي فسلمه إياه ورجع إلى الميدان ونادى بالبراز فبرز إليه علج آخر فاستأسره وأضافه الى صاحبه وعاد الى البراز فلم يزل حتى قتل عشرة ثم نادى ببراز برد بن طريح وقال أين برد الإيادي فارس الخيل سابي بنات العرب فلم يجبه وهو يسمعه فكررها ثلاثًا حتى يسمعه جميع عسكر الملك ثم نادى بالحملة وحمل السواد على السواد فاقتتلوا أشد القتال حتى خيم عليهم الظلام فافترقوا قال ثم إن البراق نادى زيد بن ذؤيب الذي صحبه في الليلة الماضية وأخذ أسرى العجم وطلب منهم أن يظفروه بليلى ويخلي سبيلهم فقال نوفل يا براق خذ معك رجالاً من فرسان قومك فربما تلزم عليك الطرق عند الإياب فانتدب البراق جماعة منهم كليب بن ربيعة ونويرة وعقيل وأخوه غرسان بن روحان وساروا والأسرى الثلاثة معهم وكان باب المدينة مفتوحًا منه ما يسع دخول الرجال دون الخيل والإبل وكانوا يفعلون ذلك لاختلاطهم فسارت بهم أسرى العجم حتى وصلوا الى القصر الذي فيه ليلى وكان بواب القصر أعجميًا فناجته الأسرى بأن هؤلاء من العرب قد أسرونا ووعدونا إن ظفرناهم بليلى يخلون سبيلنا وقد ضمنا لهم ذلك فهل لك أن تأذن لنا ولم يزالا يتلاطفان به حتى أذن لهم فدخلوا القصر واستخرجوا ليلى واردفها عقيل خلفه وانصرفوا وخلوا سبيل الأسرى فصاح البواب عند رجوعهم فجاءت غلمان الملك في صدورهم الحجب والسيوف المزخرفة ولزموا عليهم الشوارع وضيقوا عليهم المسالك ورشقوهم بالنبال والحجارة ونازلوهم بالسيوف فاستنقذوا منهم ليلى وأفلتوا بعد جهد جهيد حتى انتهوا الى نوفل فأخبروه فقال هلا

قتلتم الحاجب والأسرى بعد أن ظفرتم بليلى فقالوا منعنا من ذلك العهد الذي أخذوه علينا وما ظننا أنهم ينكثون قال قد كان ذلك فسلامتكم غنيمة وباتوا إلى الصباح فتصايح القوم واقتتلوا الى المساء ثم افترقوا فنادى البراق بصاحبه وقال اركب جوادك نلتمس ليلى لعلنا نظفر بها فإنها لا تنال إلا بالحيلة فقال قد رأيت ما جرى علينا البارحة وقد تعذر السبيل إليها ولم يوافقه أحد على ذلك فبات ليلته على هم شديد وضاق ذرعه فقال

ألم تر من دون ليلى لنا
ضرابًا طويلاً وزحفًا ثقيلا
وحذف الحجار ورمي النبال
وآساد حرب تسد السبيلا
وهول المضيق وسوء الطريق
وبابًا لحاجبه مستطيلا
ولو كنت أدركت ليلى إذن
ركبت إليها بعزم[51] الخيولا
ولكنها تحت روع الهلاك
وذلك هم أراه طويلاً

قال ولما أصبحوا اصطف القوم واقتتلوا إلى المساء فانكسرت العجم وكثرت فيهم النكاية والقتل ودخلوا المدينة وغلقوا أبوابها وتركوا الأثقال والفرش والمضارب والبغال خارج المدينة فأخذتها ربيعة عن آخرها ثم إن الملك شهرميه استجاش ولد يافث من جميع البلدان وكتب إلى ملك الروم يستنصره فأمدّه بقوم من الروم فتحصن في المدينة وصار في قوة لا توصف ولم تزل ربيعة محاصرة للمدينة من جميع أقطارها أيامًا وليالي فلم يظهر أحد منهم فاجتمعت رؤساء ربيعة إلى البراق وقالوا يا أبا النصر أتعبتنا الإقامة ونقص عددنا القتل وضعفت خيلنا ونرى العجم لم ينقصهم القتل ولم تضرهم النكاية وهم يزدادون قومًا على قومهم فما ترى في أمرنا فقال نرجع إلى ديارنا ونستعطف قومنا مضر ونزداد قوة ونعود قال ابن نافع فانقلبوا راجعين إلى حرم الله تعالى بجميع الغنائم التي أخذوها وكانت جانبًا عظيمًا وأنشأ البراق يقول

[51] Ahlwardt 9747 (123r) has (بعزمي). (بعزم) is from Ms. Or. Oct. 1383 (132r).

عفوت بقومي البحر أنزف ماءه
وهل ينزفن البحر يا قوم نازف
ويوم التقينا ظل يوم غطمطم[52]
وفيه غبار ثائر وعواصف
وضرب يقد الهام بالبيض موجع
وفيه الجياد السابحات زواحف
إذا قيل قد ولت هزيمًا فإنها
بقدر لحاظ الطرف منك عواطف
وظل لها يوم يجمع هبوة
بها يبتني سقف من الأفق واقف
ودارت رحى الحرب المشيبة للفتى
وهالت ذوي الألباب تلك المواقف
بها نغم الأسياف تنطق بالطلى
فصيحات حد ثائرات خفائف
فآبت إلى ما يستثير[53] بني أبي
وينهضها الشم الكرام الغطارف

قال وكان ثعلبة بن الأعرج صهر لكيز لما سمع بمسير وائل صرخ فيمن يجيب دعوته من قومه كهلان وأغار لينصر ربيعة فأتى وقد خالفته ربيعة في الطريق فصبح مدينة كرخا وقاتلها قتالاً شديدًا لم يقاتله أحد وتكاثرت عليه العجم فانهزم وهو يقول

لعمري لقد أبلت رجالي وقاتلت
قبائل كرخا وهي كالبحر تزخر
ولاقيتهم يومًا جميعًا بمعشري
وليس يلاقي ذلك اليوم معشر

[52] Ahlwardt 9747 (123v) has (عمطمط). (غطمطم) is from Ms. Or. Oct. 1383 (132v).
[53] Ahlwardt 9747 (124r) has (يستشير).

ولو أدركت قومي رجال ربيعة
لكنا عليهم لا محالة نظفر

قال ولما رجع ثعلبة إلى منزله بعث الى البراق يعلمه بما وقع وبعده بالنصرة في كل مسيره ويسأله أن لا يخفي عليه شيئًا من أمره فشكره على ذلك وإن ليلى لما علمت برجوع قومها وطول الغربة عليها بكت بكاءً شديدًا ودعت رجلاً من أنمار وبذلت له العطية وأرسلته إلى قومها ربيعة ومضر وأمرته أن يستنجدهم وينشدهم قصيدتها المقصورة فمضى الأنماري ووقف على ربيعة وأخبرهم بحزن ليلى وجزعها وأنشدهم قصيدتها التي تقول فيها

ليت للبراق عينًا فترى
ما أقاسي من بلاء وعنا

فلما أتى على آخرها وسمعتها ربيعة خنقتهم العبرة فقال كليب يا قوم ما هذا أوان البكاء قوموا بنا إلى البراق فقدموا عليه ومعهم الأنماري فأنشده الشعر فأنف البراق ولحقته حمية الجاهلية وقال توجه يا كليب أنت وإخوتك وابن عمك لكيز وخذ معك جماعة من سادات قومك والأنماري رسول ليلى واقدموا على طي ومضر واستعطفوهم واستوهبوهم الدماء واستنجدوهم وانشدوهم شعر ليلى فمضوا ومعهم الانماري وكان اول من وفدوا عليه زيد بن رباح[54] فاخبروه وأنشدوه شعرها فأنف من ذلك أنفًا عظيمًا وأنشأ يقول

أبلغ ربيعة أني ثائر معهم
في آل ضبة داعي القوم داعينا
فإن ربيعة ردت فهي عالمة
بأن وائل في هذا موالينا
وعندهم من جياد الخيل أجودها
والزعف والخط مع بيض يلألينا
والمقدمون بهم في كل حادثة
والواردون المنايا لا يبالونا
فشمروا يا بني قيس بأجمعكم

[54] Ahlwardt 9747 (124v) has (رياح). (رباح) is found in Ms. Or. Oct. 1383 (133v) and Arabe 5833 (123v).

إلى الطعان فما زلتم مطاعينا
أنهي بني العم لا تخزوا بني أسد
ولا تكفوا ولا تبقوا أعادينا

قال واستعد زيد للمسير وقال اقدموا على إخوتكم مضر وأخبروهم واستعطفوهم واستوهبوهم دماء بني عك وأنشدوهم شعري هذا وشعر ليلى الذي بعثت به مع الأنماري فقدموا على مضر واستعطفوهم واستوهبوهم الدماء وأنشدهم الأنماري شعر ليلى فلما وصل الى قولها

قل لعدنان هديتم[55] شمروا
لبني مبغوض[56] تشمير الوفا
واعقدوا الرايات وايتوني بها
واشهروا البيض وسيروا في الضحى

أنفوا من ذلك أنفًا شديدًا وسعى بعضهم الى بعض فقام في غيلان النفاع بن عوف العامري وأنشد يقول

كم القطيعة يا أبناء غيلان
قطعتم وائلاً قومي بإعلان
لا بد من غارة للعجم فاجتهدوا
فسوف يبدلهم شأن من الشان
لا صبر لي بعد هذا عن بني أسد
شم العرانين مما قد جنى الجاني
يا أيها الناس سيروا بالجياد إلى
إياد في قسطل مستعزم[57] بان
يا أيها القوم لا أم لأمّكم
ظنت بنو العيص ظنًا ليس بالداني

[55] Ahlwardt 9747 (125r) has (فديتم). (هديتم) is from Ms. Or. Oct. 1383 (133v).
[56] Ahlwardt 9747 (125r) has (الاعجام). (مبغوض) is from Ms. Or. Oct. 1383 (133v).
[57] Note that I cannot work out a meaning for this word and have left it untranslated.

أنا ووائل عظم لا انفصام له
معاقلي وذوي مجدي وفرساني

وقام زياد بن دريد وأنشأ يقول

يا آل عمرو بني العلياء من مضر
أنتم لآل نزار بيت مفتخر
يا آل مدركة سيروا بأجمعكم
بالجرد والمرد والهندية البتر
ظنت بنو العيص ظنًا وهو مخلفهم
وسوف يلقونه عسرًا من اليسر
وقد علمتم بأن النصر عادتكم
إذا نهضتم ويقفوكم على الأثر

قال ابن نافع وهاجت رؤساء مضر عند ذلك واضطربوا واخذتهم حمية الجاهلية وعزموا على نصرة إخوتهم ربيعة وتركوا لهم كل ما كان بينهم من دم وثأر وتواعدوا إلى حرم الله تعالى للمشورة ثم أقبلوا على كليب ومن معه من سادات ربيعة وقالوا مرحبًا يا سادات ربيعة لكم النصرة منا والنجدة على عدوكم فانصرفوا من عندهم مسرورين وتواعدوا أن يحضروا إليهم مع البراق الى الحرم فيجتمعون هناك واجتمعت قبائل مضر عند قريش وكانوا يقدمون نوفل بن عمرو القرشي فبعث الى البراق يحضر في قومه وعشيرته فأتاهم البراق ورؤساء ربيعة كافة والتقوا بإخوانهم من مضر وتصافحوا وتسالموا وأكرمهم نوفل وبشرهم بالنصر والقيام ثم قام عمرو بن نوفل في أهبة المسير وأمر قومه بالزاد والاستعداد ووقتوا للمسير وقتًا معلومًا وانصرفوا لإصلاح شأنهم وراح البراق بمن معه فرحًا مسرورًا وأنشأ يقول

لقد صدق المخبر والمشير
وطاب لي التجهز والمسير
ولي قلب إلى الأعياص فيه
جنود الشوق تخفق أو تطير
بني اسحق ويحكم تهيوا
ومن حوليكم أبداً وسيروا

اليك ربيعة بالخيل معها
بنو أسد وغسان الصقور

قال وأرسل البراق إلى صهره ثعلبة يخبره بمسير ربيعة ومضر وما اتفقوا عليه وبعث إليه يقول

طاب المسير وقرت[58] العينان
بكهول اتفقت مع الشبان
اليوم طاب لي التجهز للوغى
فتجهزوا عجلاً بني شيبان
من كان منكم لي معينًا ناصحًا
فليسع بالأسياف والمران
فتجهزوا عجلاً إليّ بموعدٍ
مني ومن مضر ومن شهدان
يا آل أنمار لسوف ترونها
شعث النواصي شخص الأعيان
صبرًا بني الأعياص صبرًا ويحكم
لا تجزعوا لكتائب الفرسان

قال ابن نافع ولما بلغ العجم اتفاق ربيعة ومضر على المسير إلى مدينة كرخا جزعوا لذلك واستهالوه وكتب إلى الملك مقدماه بكرخا عمرو بن ذي صهبان ورئيس كهلان يخبرانه بذلك وسألاه إما إن يسير إليهما أو يجهز إليهما عسكرًا ويأمرهما بالتأخر إليه فأمرهما ومن معهما من العرب والعجم بالإقامة وكان معهما جنود كسواد الليل المظلم وكانت الملوك من العرب والعجم تحت أمر الملك شهرميه قال ثم إن بني إياد وأنمار رفعوا حريمهم وأموالهم من حدود العرب إلى حدود العجم وانضموا إليها انضمامًا صحيحًا خوفًا من ربيعة ومضر لما سبق من دلالتهم على ليلى بنت لكيز وهي أختهم وابنة عمهم وسارت ربيعة ومضر وسار معهم نصير خال البراق وقومه طي ومن استطاع المسير ولقيهم ثعلبة بن الأعرج وهو يقول

[58] Ahlwardt 9747 (126r) has (وقرن). (وقرت) is found in Ms. Or. Oct. 1383 (134v), Arabe 5833 (124r), Or. 2676 (171r), and 5984 Adab (84).

أتينا وسرنا بالقواضب والقنا
بني مضر الحمراء وأبناء وائل
بأعفر ولاج الثغور عرمرم
جحافل جيش أردفت بجحافل
بهاليل من غسان قومي وغيرها
قساطلها موصولة بقساطل
نريد بها كرخا ومن حل حولها
إيادا وأنمارا أهالي الدلائل

قال ولما نزلت ربيعة ومضر ومن والاهم من قبائل طي وغسان حول مدينة كرخا صادفوا فيها جنودًا لا تحصى من العجم والعرب إياد وأنمار وكهلان ولقيت كل قبيلة قبيلة أخرى فواقعت كهلان أخوالها طي ولقي بنو شيبان ايادًا وتغلب انمارًا وتميم يافث وغيلان ومدركة الفرس فيا له من يوم ما كان أكثر غباره وأشد هوله وكان أول من انتصر مدركة وغيلان ثم تولت عساكر كرخا وأذنت بالفرار ودخلت عساكر ربيعة ومضر ومن معهم المدينة فوافقوا فيها من الغنائم ما لم يعرف له ثمن ومن السبايا ما لم يعرف له مقدار من نساء العرب والعجم فخلوا سبيل العربيات كرامة للعرب ومروءة منهم وأخذوا العجميات سبايا تحت الرق وأما عساكر الملك شهرميه فإنهم استأخروا إلى مدينة إدريجة[59] وأرسلوا إلى الملك يخبرونه أن البراق وقومه قد حازوا كرخا وأنهم هربوا إلى هناك فهاله ذلك وأرسل قوادًا من أصحابه وقدمهم على عساكر كثيرة من العجم وأمرهم أن يقيموا داخل المدينة مع المنهزمين ولا يدخل عليهم أحد فساروا ولحقوا بأصحابهم وأقامت ربيعة ومضر شهرًا في كرخا ينتظرون من يقصدهم فلم يروا أحدًا وعظمت هيبة العرب في قلوب العجم ولما استراحت ربيعة ومضر في نفوسها وأراحت خيلها ونجائبها نهضوا إلى مدينة إدريجة فلما بلغوها لقي كل قوم أصحابهم وكان عسكر الفرس قد كثر عديدهم فالتقتهم ربيعة ومضر واقتتلوا قتالاً شديدًا فصابرت العجم ذلك اليوم وقد قتل منها خلق كثير ثم انكسرت واستأخرت إلى مدينة يقال لها رغوة ليحفظوها مع العساكر التي فيها ودخلت ربيعة ومضر إلى المدينة فوافقوا فيها غنائم أكثر مما وجدوا في مدينة كرخا من الذهب والفضة والخز والبز والديباج والمسك والعنبر والكافور وأنواع الطرائف النفيسة وأقاموا

[59] Ahlwardt 9747 (127r) has (ادربيجان).

فيها شهرًا ينتظرون من يقصدهم فلم يقصدهم أحد فنهضوا إلى مدينة رغوة وغنائمهم معهم فلما قربوا منها خرجت عليهم جيوش العجم والروم فاستهمت ربيعة ومضر على العجم والروم من منهما يكافي الروم لأنها أقوى من العجم فوقع السهم على مضر فتلقت الروم وربيعة تلقت العجم فكان يومًا عظيمًا ولم تثبت العجم لربيعة فانهزمت وولت الروم على أثرها ودخلت العرب مدينة رغوة فحاذوها وعطفت عليهم العجم فباتوا بليلة شديدة إلى الصباح فالتقى الجمعان واقتتلوا قتالاً شديدًا فادبرت الأعاجم وكان لهم أموال كثيرة قد حصنوها في المدينة ولم يظنوا أنهم يطاقون لكثرتهم فاغتنمتها العرب قال واستأخرت عساكر الملك إلى مدينة ترابة ووجهوا بالخبر الى الملك شهرميه فهاله ذلك واضطرب اضطرابًا شديدًا وبعث إليهم بعساكر أكثر من الأولى ولحقوا بأصحابهم في مدينة ترابة وأقامت ربيعة ومضر شهرًا في مدينة رغوة حتى أراحوا خيلهم ونجائبهم ثم شدوا وحملوا غنائمهم وساروا طالبين الأعاجم حتى كانوا في بعض الطريق فمرض نوفل بن عمرو القرشي فأقاموا عليه أيامًا حتى عوفي وطابت نفوسهم فشدوا وساروا إلى مدينة ترابة فالتقاهم عسكر الملك وقاتلهم قتالاً شديدًا فكثر فيهم القتل وأخذت العجم غنائمهم من بين أيديهم فتحامت العرب وحملت حملة صادقة وقد أفرطت العجم في الغارة وبعدت عن المدينة فاقتتلوا قتالاً شديدًا وكانت النصرة للعرب فانكسرت العجم وقتلت منهم ربيعة ومضر قتلة هائلة واسترجعت غنائمها من أيديهم فولوا يطلبون صاحبهم ودخلت العرب إلى مدينة ترابة وعظم الأمر على الملك شهرميه وخاف على نفسه أن يدخلوا عليه في مدينته التي هو فيها فأرسل يستنصر ملوك الروم والهند والصين فاجتمع اليه من ولد يافث وغيرهم جنود كثيرة فأمر بحفظ المراصد والمضايق وثبت بعساكره في مدينته وجعلها له قرارًا وأقام على كل مرصد ومضيق قومًا يحفظونه وأما العرب فإنهم قد دخلوا مدينة ترابة فأصابوا فيها ما لا يوصف من الغنائم فأقاموا بها أيامًا يستريحون ووجهوا بما حملته ابلهم إلى اهلهم وديارهم وأرسلوا معها خيلا تحفظها وأقاموا في مدينة ترابة ينتظرون من يقدم عليهم فلم يجسر أحد أن يقربهم لما عظم من هيبتهم في صدور الأعاجم حتى جاءت نعمهم وخيلهم التي أرسلوها ثم شدوا من ترابة وتركوا فيها غنائم وخلفوا عندها من يحفظها وتوجهوا إلى مدينة الملك والتمسوا لها مسلكًا يسلكونه فلم يجدوا لأنها حصينة وعلى كل منفذ منها أرصاد أو رماة بالنبال فخيموا من وراء الأرصاد وأقاموا عشرة أيام ينتظرون من يخرج إليهم فلم يخرج أحد فشدوا وقدموا الإبل بين أيديهم وخيلهم ورجلهم في أثرها وفي أثنائها متخللة حذرًا من النبل والحجارة فلقيتهم العساكر بالحجارة والنبال فلم يردوهم وهجموا عليهم ودفعوا عن المرصد الأول حتى خرجوا إلى أرض وسيعة حيث تجول الخيل فاستأخرت الأعاجم إلى المرصد الثاني

ونزلت ربيعة ومضر في تلك الأرض الفسيحة وكانت كثيرة الماء والشجر فأقاموا بها عشرة أيام ينتظرون من يخرج إليهم فلم يخرج أحد وبلغ الملك أن العرب تعدت مرصدًا من المراصد فهاله ذلك وخاف أن لا ينجو منهم وبعد ذلك شدوا وضايقوا المرصد الثاني وساقوا الإبل بين أيديهم للنبل والحجارة فتعدوه بعد قتال وجهد عظيم وخرجوا إلى أرض فسيحة تجول فيها الخيل فاقتتلوا وانهزمت الأعاجم والروم ولزمت المرصد الثالث الذي لم يكن بعده إلا باب المدينة فنزلت ربيعة ومضر في أرض مخصبة هناك تنتظر من يخرج إليها فلم يخرج أحد وبلغ الملك أنهم وصلوا الى المرصد الثالث فهاله ذلك وأيقن بالغلبة ثم قاموا وضايقوا المرصد الثالث وساقوا الإبل على عادتهم ونالهم عند قدومهم عليه شدة عظيمة وقتال مريع وارتكمت عليهم النبل والحجارة مثل المطر وصابرت ربيعة ومضر على ما لم يصبر عليه أحد حتى إنهم لم يبلغوا شيئًا من الأرض حتى يقتلوا ألفًا من الأعاجم إلى أن جاوزوا المراصد كلها ولم يكن إلا باب المدينة فالتحم القتال لدى الباب وعلت الأصوات وخرج الملك شهرميه وباشر القتال بنفسه وكان يومًا عبوسًا لم يكن اهول منه وقتل من العرب والعجم خلق كثير وما زالوا كذلك إلى غروب الشمس فافترقوا عن غير غلبة وبات الكل منهم يشب ناره قال ابن نافع ولما كان شيء من الليل قام البراق ولبس لأمة حربه وقال يا نويرة عليّ بزيود هذه السرية زيد الفوارس وزيد بن رباح وزيد بن مالك الأسدي وزيد بن عمرو اللخمي وزيد بن نصير الكناني وزيد بن عوف السلمي وزيد بن عامر الذبياني وزيد بن عبيد الهذلي وزيد بن صهبان الدارمي وزيد بن معود اليربوعي وزيد بن مقاتل العجلي وزيد بن عزيز الطائي وزيد بن جعيد الغساني وزيد بن مفلح البوقي وزيد بن سلمان العدواني وزيد بن مالك المحاربي وزيد بن منصور وزيد بن عبد الله الأشجعي وزيد اللكعي وزيد بن الأرقب القرشي وزيد بن وهب الثقفي فأسرع نويرة في طلبهم وكانوا متفرقين في كل قومه فحضروا وكان قد ذهب جانب من الليل فقال البراق دعوتكم يا بني العم لأمر مهم فقالوا نحن طوع يديك وقد علمت يا أبا النصر أننا لم نفارق الأهل والوطن إلا لما يكشف عنا العار قال قد علمتم أن المطلوب من هذه الغزوة التي ذهبت فيها الأبطال والتحق سوءها بالعرب والعجم هو ليلى العفيفة وعلمتم أنها تحت روع الهلاك ولا تنال إلا بالتلطف والاحتيال فهل فيكم نجدة للقيام معي في طلبها لعلنا نظفر بها ونستنقذها حية او ميتة فهو عذرنا بين قبائل العرب فقالوا نحن طوع يديك نسمع ما تأمر ونفعل ما تريد فشكرهم على ذلك وسار بهم في تلك الليلة ودخل بهم إلى المدينة يتخلل عساكر الأعاجم ولم ينكرهم أحد لاختلاط العرب بالعجم فلم يزالوا ليلتهم يتجسسون في ديار الملك عن مضرب ليلى وبينما هم كذلك وقفوا بمضرب عظيم حوله مضارب وقباب فيها عساكر عظيمة فانتبهوا بهم وثاروا عليهم

واحاطوا بهم فوضع البراق واصحابه فيهم السيوف وقد ضيقوا عليهم الطرق بعد أن قام الصريخ من كل جانب فلم يزالوا يقتلون كل من يقدم عليهم ويدافعون اللاحقين بهم حتى خرجوا من باب المدينة بعد جهد بليغ ورأوا أن السلامة مغنم لهم قال ولما أصبح الصباح تصايح القوم وخرجت عليهم عساكر الملك فاقتتلوا إلى المساء وافترقوا عن غير غلبة وما زالوا على هذه الحال ايامًا متصلة يقتتلون من الصباح إلى المساء عند باب المدينة وكلما رأت الأعاجم الغلبة أغلقت الأبواب ورشقتهم بالنبال من شوارف السور وإذا اقتحم القتال وأرادت العرب أن تنزح خارج المدينة إلى الفضاء رجعت الأعاجم إلى الباب وكان هذا دأبهم برهة من الزمان فأضرت بقبائل العرب هذه الإقامة وضعفت خيلهم ونقص عددهم القتل وقل زادهم وأثخنتهم الجراح والعجم لا تزداد إلا قوة ولا ينقص القتل منهم عددًا فنهض نصير بن عمرو الطائي خال البراق بقومه وثعلبة بن الأعرج بقومه غسان وسارا من ليلتهما ولم يخبرا أحدًا وأما الحيان العريضان ربيعة ومضر فباتوا إلى الصباح وخرجت عليهم جنود كالجراد المنتشر فاقتتلوا قتالاً شديدًا وظهرت راية العجم على العرب وكثرت النكاية في ربيعة ومضر فصابرت على ألويتها وحافظت على راياتها إلى المساء بعد أن كادوا ينهزمون ولما جنهم الليل دخلت العجم المدينة وأغلقت الأبواب ورجعت العرب الى خيامها قال ثم ان رؤساء ربيعة ومضر اجتمعوا إلى البراق للمشورة وقالوا يا أبا النصر إن هذه الإقامة قد أضرت بنا وأضعفت خيلنا وأذهبت رجالنا بالقتل والجراح والأعاجم لا يزدادون إلا قوة وقد رأيت ما حل بنا من النكاية بعد أن كدنا ننهزم وتفسخت القبائل عنا ولم يبق إلا نحن أبناء الأخوين وإنا نخشى من سابقة تكون علينا فنكون لا أدركنا الحسنى ولا سلمنا من الهزيمة والقتل فهلا تدركنا بالرحيل إلى أهالينا ونستريح ونريح خيلنا ونستعد للرجوع مرة أخرى ويقضي الله امرًا يكون فبكى البراق وقال هيهات ضاقت صدوركم وخفتم القتل ورب الكعبة أما أنا فلست براجع دون فكاكها أو أموت وأما أنتم فشأنكم وأنفسكم وكان البراق قد فقد أخاه غرسان فسألهم المبيت تلك الليلة فلم يروا ذلك رأيا وغلبوا الظن إن أصبحوا وقاتلوا تأخذهم العجم فنادوا بالرحيل ورحلت ربيعة ومضر وغنائمها بين يديها ومنهم من لم يعلم بتخلف البراق وكانوا يسيرون رفقاء وكل مكان يبيتون الليلة والليلتين ويزعمون أن البراق لا يصبر على الإقامة وأنه يلحق بهم في الطريق وكان البراق قد بات ليلته إلى الصباح فأخذ أخاه غرسان واحتمله على جواده وخرج به إلى شرق المدينة وكانت قد أدنفته الجراح وإذا هو بنهر جار وعنده حائط جامع للأشجار ودار مشيدة لرجل من إياد يقال له صريم ولاخوته وعبيدهم فدنا البراق من النهر وأنزل أخاه وغسله من الدم والتراب وفرش له فراشًا من ديباج كان معه وألقاه عليه وجعل فوقه ثوب خز ونزع البراق درعه ولباسه وجعل

يغتسل ويستنقي من صدأ الدروع ثم لبس أثوابه وانعكف على أخيه وقبله بين عينيه وأنشأ يقول

تولت رجالي بالغنائم والغنى
مزجين للأجمال من رملان
ونادوا نداءً بالرحيل فلم أطق
إيابا وصنوي في المعارك فان
وولى كليب بعد أيقن أنني
سأمكث لا تثني يداي عناني
كذاك أبو زيد مضى بغنيمة
مع ابن عباد والفتى ابن أبان
وراح لكيز الشيخ يحمي سرية
مضمرة قد ضمرت لرهان
ألا وجنيد قد تولى ولم يكن
ليغضبه ما كان من غرسان
كذاك ظليل والرسيل وسالم
أولئك فرسان وأهل طعان
وأذن منا حين راح مهلهل
بعلم صحيح ليس يجهل شاني
بأني مع غرسانه متخلف
وأني إلى الأوطان لست بدان
أأوب إلى أمي سليما مكرما
وغرسان مقتول بدار هوان
أأترك من لا يترك الدهر طاعتي
ملب لما أدعو بكل لسان
أخي ومعيني في المضيق وصاحبي
بكل إغاراتي بحد سنان
وأكثر ما بي أن تولى نويرة
وأنكر ما أسلفت يوم دعاني

دعاني وقد ألقى المهلهل بالقنا
بنو بدر مكتوفًا وكل يماني
فلما دعاني يا أبا النصر لم أخم
وقومت عسالي وصدر حصاني
طعنت بأولى الرمح جبهة مالك
وغيبته فيه بغير توان
وجندلت عمارا بضربة صارم
ومزقت شمل الجند بالجولان
فمن مبلغ عني كليبا رسالة
ألم يك في ما يشتهي بمعان

قال ولما فرغ البراق من شعره وبكى على أخيه ثم نصب ركبتيه ووضع جبهته عليهما ليستريح من شدة النعاس وكان بالقرب منه غلام لصريم الإيادي فرأى البراق وهو لا يراه وسمع شعره فأحزنه ولما استلقى البراق على قفاه دنا الغلام من غرسان وكشف وجهه فنظر إلى صورة حسنة فلم يملك الغلام عبرته دون أن بكى فرفع البراق رأسه وقال من مولاك يا غلام قال صريم الإيادي وهو صاحب هذه المنازل قال أخبرني عن برد بن طريح أين هو قال في المدينة قال أهو من خواص مولاك قال نعم فتنفس البراق وأنشأ يقول

بكيت لغرسان وحق لناظري
بكاء قتيل الفرس إن كان باكيا
بكيت على واري الزناد فتى الوغي الـ-
ـسريع الى الهيجاء إن كان عاديا
إذا ما علا نهدًا وعرض ذابلا
وقحم بكريًا وهز يمانيا
فأصبح مغتالاً بأرض قبيحة
عليها فتى كالسيف فات المجاريا
وقد أصبح البراق في دار غربة
وفارق إخوانًا له ومواليا
حليف نوى طاوي حشًا سافحًا دماً

يرجع عبرات يهجن البواكيا
فمن مبلغ عني كريمة أمه
لتندب غرسانًا وبراق ثانيا
(وقل)[60] لكليب لا أقام بداره
ولا كان محمود الأفاعيل ماضيا
ولا أومضت نيران آل نويرة
ولا كان يومًا في لواء القوم لاويا
ألا ولكيز غير العار وجهه
كما غيب الحسنى وأصبح خاليا
فليت لليلى نظرة فتعينني
بها حججًا سبعًا نعم او ثمانيا
ولو علمت ليلى وكانت خبيرة
لجاءت تباري العاصفات الذواريا
أما اختبرت ليلى الغداة بأنني
أزيد على غرسان هما كما بيا
لقد قطع الوصل الذي كان بيننا
لكيز بغارات تشيب النواصيا

قال ابن نافع فلما سمع الغلام كلام البراق انقلب إلى مولاه ليخبره بحال البراق ويستعينه على جهاز أخيه ودفنه فأخبره فقال صفه لي قال هو سيد بني وائل فعلم أنه البراق وطمع في قتله فأحضر إخوته وعبيده وأخبرهم بما في نفسه فوافقوه على ذلك وشدوا جياد خيلهم فلما رأى الغلام ذلك أسرع الى البراق فأنذره فقام البراق إلى جواده مسرجًا ولبس لأمة حربه وركب وأنشأ يقول

لتخبرني الآن قولاً صريحًا
فإني أردت بأن أستريحا

[60] (وقل) is from Ms. Or. Oct. 1383 (139v), 5984 Adab (95), and Arabe 5833 (126v). Ahlwardt 9747 (132r) has (وكل).

وإني الكمي الأبي الذي
أبايع مولاك بيعًا صحيحا
لعلي به أقتضي وترنا
وأسقيه كأسًا دهاقًا طفوحا

قال وبينما البراق ينتظر صريمًا ومن معه إذ قدم عليه في إخوته وهم سبعة هو ثامنهم وعبيده بالسلاح على الخيل فقوم سنان رمحه بين أذني فرسه واستعد للكرة فتوقع صريم مكان الرمح من صدره فنزل عن جواده وحل حمائل سيفه ودفعه إلى بعض غلمانه وأقبل يسعى على قدميه فلما دنى من البراق قال أما أنت يا هذا فقد ضمك المقدور إلى فنائنا فأهلاً وسهلاً بك فأخبرني من أنت فقال البراق

يخوفني صريم وان حولي
بني أسد بأسياف رقاق
وآل حنيفة وبني لهيم
وتغلب بالمثقفة الدقاق
وان كليب ويحك عن يميني
نعم ونويرة أسد[61] التلاق
لقد عجب الصريم من انفرادي
فشد الخيل منه لكي يلاقي
فلو كان الصريم أشد عزمًا
لظل لدي مشدود الوثاق
أما يدني القضاء مني لبرد
فأطعنه بمجتمع التراقي
وأجعل في منازله صياحًا
وفي نسوانه أمضى الطلاق
طلاق الموت يا لك من طلاق
طلاق لا يعقب بالتلاقي

[61] Ahlwardt 9747 (133r) has (اسد اسد).

ولما فرغ البراق من شعره قال لصريم ما منعك أن تمضي ما في نفسك قال والله يا سيدي ما جئت إلا طامعًا فيك فلما نظرتك ذهب ذلك الطمع وهل في قومي إياد وغيرها نظير لك كلا وها أنا قد أسلمت إليك فامنن علي بالسلامة وأكون عونًا لك على جميع أمورك فأنشأ البراق يقول

عوني عليه فتى في أرض شيبان
فما أعد رجالاً مثل نسوان
كم باكيات لليلى في بني أسد
ونادبات بحسرات لغرسان
لهفي عليه ثوى في موطن خشن
بين الجياد بأسياف ومران
والخيل تقرع عرضًا في أعنتها
والأرض تقذف سيلاً من دم قان
فذاك مشرع آباي الألى سلفوا
بين المعارك من شيب وشبان
لا نشرئب إلى موت الفراش ولا
نرضى المصارع من أهل وجيران
ارجع صريم كما أقبلتني عجلاً
فليس شأنك يا قرشي من شاني
أنا لبكر وطي حيثما اختلطت
منا المناسب من طي وعدنان
أمي لطي إذا أحققتها وأنا
حقًا أبو النصر براق بن روحان
ووائل نسبي لا أبتغي بدلاً
منهم ولا في سواهم معشر ثاني
وأنت في الفرس محتل بساحتها
شبه اللصيق على زور وبهتان
جرت جريرة برد ليت تظفرني
به الليالي ولو من بعد أحيان

الكاسب العار في قوم ذوي حسب
ومنزل أهله في المنزل الثاني

قال ابن نافع فلما سمع صريم شعر البراق قال قبح الله رأي برد وقبح وجهه وبالله العظيم إن قبلت نصيحتي لتدركن مرادك فليس برد من أكفائك وأعطاه عهدًا وميثاقًا على النصيحة بينهما وإذا بغبار ثائر وكانت خيل من جنود الملك طالبة مدينة ترابة التي خلفت ربيعة ومضر غنائمها بها لتكشف الخبر وتلتمس ما بقي من الغنائم فقال البراق ما هذه الخيل يا صريم قال أظن فيهم من يطلبنا فقال له البراق أقم مكانك حتى آتيك بخبر القوم وحرك البراق جواده حتى تقدمهم ووقف ينظر إليهم وإذا هم عرب وعجم فقال أين تريدون قالوا نريد المدينة قال دون المدينة ضرب القواضب وكر السلاهب وحمل عليهم فهزمهم وكف عن القتل فظنوا أنه خرج من المدينة وأن العرب قد عادت إليها فأخبروا الملك ورجع البراق من ساعته وجدد صريم العهد وقال يا براق طب نفسًا وقر عينًا ولك الأمان على كتمان الأمر فاطمأنت نفس البراق وكانت العرب إذا حلفت لا تنكث فنزل البراق عن جواده وصافحه ووضع كفه بكفه وعزاه صريم بأخيه وأمر عبيده باحتفار قبر له فسارعوا إلى ذلك وانقلب إلى داره فأتى بأكفان من أفخر ما عنده من اللباس وكفنه ودفنه وبكوا عليه ثم ركب صريم بالبراق إلى داره وأنزله في أعلاها وفرش له فرشًا من الديباج وأمر بإحضار الأطعمة والفواكه وجلس يأكل مع البراق ووعده أن يظفره ببرد بن طريح فلبث البراق يومه وليلته إلى طلوع الفجر ثم عهد قبر أخيه فنزل عليه وبكى بكاءً شديدًا وأنشأ يقول

ليس الغداة تحية وكلاما
لفتى ثوى ما يرد سلاما
يا صاحب الجدث الذي ضمنته
سعدًا لتربك ما يضم عظاما
أتراك تدري يا أخي بتغربي
في الفرس أثوي قفرها أعواما
أبكيك إذ أبكيك لا متفحشًا
لصداقة لومًا ولا لواما
وإذا الكماة تداعبوا لكتيبة
كان ابن روحان هناك إماما

ولقد شهدت عليه إذ هجم الوغى
جهدوا وقد نصبوا له أعلاما
ولى جنيد واحتللت حذاءه
فردًا رضيت بساحتيه مقاما
ومضى بنو أسد وراح نويرة
وكليب ما حفظوا لدي ذماما
وتدابرت عجل وراح مهلهل
عني هناك وأكثروا الإرغاما
وضبيعة راحت وفيها حارث
إجلالة لكليب أم إكراما
أنسيتم صحبي الكرام أياديا
مني عليكم قد سلفن جساما
أولم أكن أكفي كليبًا حرها
وأتى نويرة ضاحكًا بساما
أنسى حفاظي حارث ومهلهل
ولكيز لما بالغزية[62] خاما
أنهى بني اسد بن بكر يشمخوا
بعد الفخار ويوصلوا الأرحاما
فأنا الثوي بغربة مستوطنا
لا ذاكرًا اهلاً ولا أقواما
حسبي بكم عوضًا ضريح أخي إذا
ما زرته الإبكار والإظلاما[63]
ولعل ليلى أن أفك حصارها
جهرا وأقتل مالكًا غشاما
لا بد من صبري وطول تغربي

[62] Arabe 5833 (128r) and 5984 Adab (102) have (بالعريسة).
[63] Ahlwardt 9747 (134v) has: حسبي بكم عوضا ضريح اخي الذي اذ داره الابكار والاظلاما
The wording in the text above is drawn from 5984 Adab (102).

حتى أنال مآربًا ومراما
ولأقتلن الفرس في أوطانهم
ولأنسين الخال والأعماما
إن لم أري ليلى مضاء عزيمتي
وأذيق مهجة شهرميه حماما
وأقود في تلك المسالك جحفلاً
وحدي وأبعث للرضيع فطاما
فأنا الوضيع المستعز بخزيه
وكسيت عارًا مخزيًا وملاما
يا ليلى نوحي ما بقيت وأبشري
بالفتح وانتظري هنًا وسلاما
وارجي فتى وحصينة[64] ومضمرًا
طاوي الحشا ومثقفًا وحساما

قال وأما ربيعة فإنهم لما قدموا على أهلهم بغنائمهم وليس البراق معهم سألتهم النساء عنه فلم يأتوا عنه بخبر وأخبروا بقتل غرسان وجميع القتلى من ربيعة ومضر فأعولت النساء من كل مكان وما فرحت منهن امرأة بسلامة زوجها ولا ولدها وأما نساء بني أسد فضربن الستور دون رجالهن وسودن خدودهن وشققن جيوبهن وقطعن شعورهن وأعولن بالبكاء ونسين كل قتيل مع البراق وتكلمت أم الأغر على إخوتها كلامًا شنيعًا وأنشأت تقول

ألا فابكي كريمة لا تملي
فلي بعويلكم أبدا عويل
فلا سلمت عشيرتنا وعادت
إذا غرب ابن روحان الأصيل
إذا رحتم وخلفتم هبلتم
أبا النصر فلا راح القبيل

[64] Ahlwardt 9747 (134v) has (وحصيفة). (وحصينة) is found in Ms. Or. Oct. 1383 (141v), Arabe 5833 (128r), and 5984 Adab (103).

فرحتم بالغنائم حين رحتم
وبان تعستم الغنم الجليل
تركتم ذا الحفاظ وذا السرايا
وراءكم أضلكم الدليل
فقل لنويرة وكليب مهلاً
أقيما إن خزيكما طويل

وقالت أم الأغر أيضًا

يبكين فردًا بنات الحي من أسد
قد كن يحمين منه دائم الأبد
دعن التجمل وارفعن الحجاب ضحى
على أبي النصر لا تبكي على أحد

قال ابن نافع وأما البراق فإنه أطال المكث عند صريم وهو يدبر أمره ويتوقع فتكه بالملك شهرميه فبينما هو كذلك إذ جاء رسول من قبل برد بن طريح إلى صريم بشيء من الهدية وقال اركب أنت وإخوتك فالملك قد أخرج ولده إلى مدينة كرخا واستوزرني ولده وواعدني باللقاء إلى موضع أعرفه في يوم معين فأخذ صريم في التجهز للمسير وقال يا براق أقم على الإعزاز والإكرام إلى رجوعي فقال لست متخلفًا عنك ولكني أسير معك في غير طريق الملك وأكون لك عونًا على أمورك وربما تدلني على برد فإنك قد وعدتني بذلك قال وإن ابن الملك كان قد توجه إلى مدينة كرخا فوجد عسكر الروم قد ملك تلك المدينة فاقتتلوا قبل وصول صريم فانكسر عسكر الملك شهرميه والتقى صريم والبراق به منهزمًا فقال البراق يا صريم ناد بالعطفة في عسكر أصحابك يريد نصرتهم ليظفر ببرد فنادى صريم بالعطفة وحمل هو وإخوته والبراق وقلبه مشغول ببرد بن طريح فانكسر عسكر الروم وانتصر ابن الملك بالبراق فلم يزل البراق يطلب بردًا في أطراد الخيل وهو يسأل صريمًا عنه فغمزه عليه وهو مشتغل بنفسه مع علج من الروم فحمل عليه البراق وقال أنت برد قال نعم قال أما كان لك سعة عن بنات وائل حتى تدل الفرس عليهن وترسل لهن أخويك وتضرب ليلى وتقيدها وتكرهها على البغاء فقال تبًا وذلاً لك ولبنات وائل فقال البراق الحمد لله الذي مكنني منك وحمل عليه فتهاجما وتضاربا فسبقه البراق بطعنة أرداه بها قتيلاً ورجع الى صريم وقد شفى غليله قال وإن ابن الملك لما ملك كرخا وانهزم عسكر الروم استوزر صريمًا وكتب إلى أبيه يهنيه بالظفر ويعزيه ببرد ويشكر صريمًا ويعلمه أنه

استوزره وشكر صريم البراق على فعله واستعلى أمره به وقال يا مولاي بك أصبحت وزيرًا ثم وجه مع البراق ببعض إخوته إلى داره وأمر بإكرامه فعاد إلى دار صريم وأقام بها يومين ثم خرج إلى قبر أخيه فنزل عليه وبكى بكاء شديدًا وأنشأ يقول

لكيز عن الهيجاء عاق رجائيا
وعوق آمالي بها والأمانيا
وأظفر منا كل طاغ برأيه
وحملني أثقالها والدواهيا
فيا لك عما غيب الريم في العدى
وطول أحزاني معا وبكائيا
فيا ليت أني إذ حرمت وصالها
تجنبت عنها لا علي ولا ليا
سأحمل نفسي في فكاكك جاهدًا
وأركب محذورًا يشيب النواصيا
وأسكن في أرض الأعاجم حجة
وأزداد أيامًا بها ولياليا

ثم وقف على قبر أخيه فبكى وأنشأ يقول

وذا أسف على أسف بليلى
وهم بالغ أبد الأبيد
فمن لي مبلغًا ليلى سلامًا
لخل ناصح صب عميد
ويعلمها بما لاقيت جهرًا
من التعذيب والأسف الشديد
وإني لا أنام ولا أحيّى
وكيف ينام ذو نوم طريد
مضى عني السرور وطاب نومي
وأوحدني كليب كالشريد
ولو كان النويرة رام صبرًا

لكان محافظًا رعي العهود
ولم يصبر معي روحان شيخي[65]
وأخلفت المظنة بالجنود

قال ابن نافع وإن أخا صريم روى شعر البراق وقدم به المنزل وأمر له بالقرى وأكرمه وقام إلى زوجة صريم الرقشاء وأنشدها شعر البراق وأخبرها بما له من اليد الحسنة عليهم وأنه هو الذي كسر عسكر الروم ومكن أخاه من الوزارة قالت فما الذي تأمرني به قال تمضين إلى المدينة وتحتالين في الدخول على ليلى وتخبرينها بمكانه وتأتين بخبرها قالت أعرض عليه ذلك فأعرضه فقال إن كانت فاعلة لذلك فجئني بها فجاءت الرقشاء إلى البراق في شيء من الليل فسلمت عليه وقالت اوصني بما شئت قال اقريها سلامي وأخبريها بمكاني وقولي لها لا تشفقي من عظيمة تدفعينه إليها فليس ممن يهاب العظائم ولا تغرك كثرة الجنود ولا تهابي الملك فإنه يقتله إذا نظره قال الراوي فمضت الرقشاء ودخلت على امرأة برد فسألتها عن ليلى فقالت يا أختاه وما تريدين منها قالت أريد زيارتها قالت إنها في أقصى دار الملك وقد أقام لخدمتها قينتين وجعل على الباب حاجبًا لا يدع أحدًا يصل إليها إلا بإذنها وبالله إني إذا أردت زيارتها ومشاورتها في شيء لا تكلمني إلا من وراء الحجاب ولقد سألتها التقدم إليها فاعتذرت فإن أردت زيارتها من خلف الستر أنفذت معك من يوصلك إليها قالت نعم فوجهت معها قينة فوقفت على الحاجب فنادى بقينة ليلى وقال استأذني مولاتك لهذه المرأة قالت القينة من تكونين قالت من عشيرتها فأخبرت تلك القينة ليلى فقالت قدميها إلى موضع النساء خلف الستر فتقدمت بها وحيتها بالسلام فسألتها عن حالها ولم يكن من قيناتها من تعرف العربية فأنشدت الرقشاء

لك العزاء بغرسان وذا خبري
وعندنا سيد الحيين من مضر
قد روح الجند عنه وهو منعكف
عليه يبكي لدى الظلماء والسحر
لغربة وهموم لا تفارقه
سح الدموع من الأجفان كالمطر

[65] Ahlwardt 9747 (136v) has (ولم يصبر ابي روحان ايضا). (ولم يصبر معي روحان شيخي) is found in Ms. Or. Oct. 1383 (143r), Arabe 5833 (129r), 5984 Adab (107), and Or. 2676 (176r).

لا يستفيق من الأحزان سيدتي
ولا يسير إلى بدو ولاحضر

قال ابن نافع فلما سمعتها ليلى تزلزلت عن مكانها وأيقنت بصدق الخبر وفرحت بالبراق واغتمت لغربته وفرقة غرسان وأرادت تحقيق خبر البراق فقالت للمرأة صفيه لي إن كنت تعرفينه قالت فيه وقار الكهل على صغر سنه وحلم الشيخ الذي جاوز السبعين وأما صفة حسنه فإنه خفيف الجسم مستوي القامة عريض المنكبين غليظ الساعدين أخضر اللون صافيه مستدير الوجه قد تلألأ عارضاه على أول لحيته أدعج العينين جعد الشعر فعرفت ليلى صفته وقالت بماذا أرسلك وقد علم أنه لا سبيل إليّ قالت إنه متوقع خلاصك وقد سألك الموازرة في ذلك فقالت اقريه سلامي وقولي له يأتي معك في زي النساء لأنظره وأسأله عن حاله وأعزيه بأخيه والرأي يكون بعد ذلك ثم أمرت لها بطعام فأكلت وشربت وتحدثت عندها ولما أرادت الانصراف أنشدتها قصيدة وأمرتها أن تنشد البراق إياها وهي قولها

قد كان بي ما كفى من حزن غرسان
والآن قد زادني همي وأحزاني
ما حال براق من بعدي ومعشرنا
ووالدي وأعمامي وإخواني
قد حال دوني يا براق مجتهدًا
من النوائب جهد ليس بالفاني
كيف الدخول وكيف الوصل وا أسفا
هيهات ما خلت هذا وقت إمكان
لما ذكرت غريبًا زادني كمدي
حتى هممت من البلوى بإعلان
تربع الشوق في قلبي وذبت كما
ذاب الرصاص إذا أصلّى بنيران
فلو تراني وأشواقي تقلبني
عجبت براق من صبري وكتماني
لا در در كليب يوم راح ولا
أبي لكيز ولا خيلي وفرساني

عن ابن روحان راحت وائل كثبًا
عن حامل كل أثقال وأوزان
وقد تزاور عن علم كليبهم
وقد كبا الزند من زيد بن روحان
وأسلموا المال والأهلين واغتنموا
أرواحهم فوق قب شخص أعيان
حتى تلافاهم البراق سيدهم
أخو السرايا وفض[66] القسطل الباني
يا عين فابكي وجودي بالدموع ولا
تمل يا قلب إن تبلى بأشجان
فذكر براق مولى الحي من أسد
أنسى حياتي[67] بلا شك وأنساني
فتى ربيعة طواف أماكنها
وفارس الخيل في روع وميدان

قال ابن نافع وإن الرقشاء لما وصلت الى البراق أنشدته الأبيات فتأوّه ساعة ثم قال يا رقشاء ما أزورها في زي النساء فإن استطعت أن القاها في زي الأبطال وإلا فبلغيها عني وبلغيني عنها لعل الله يحدث بعد ذلك أمرًا ثم إن الروم وجهوا إلى كرخا عسكرًا وأخرجوا ابن الملك منها بعد قتل وجراح فلما وصلوا إلى قدام المدينة قال صريم لابن الملك انزل هنا نستريح ثم نعطف عليهم ونخرجهم منها ونرجع على عادتنا فنزل وأرسل صريم الى البراق يسأله النصرة فركب البراق وأغار حتى وافى صريمًا ومن معه واصطف لهم عسكر الروم وصف ابن الملك عسكره ونادى البراق بالبراز فبرز إليه علج من الروم فأرداه قتيلاً ونادى بالبراز أيضًا فبرز إليه آخر فقتله ولم يزل كذلك حتى قتل ثمانية عشر من مقاتليهم ثم نادى بالحملة فانهزمت جنود الروم وقتل منهم خلق كثير وحاز ابن الملك شهرميه مدينة كرخا وأثنى على صريم الذي أمر بإحضار هذا الرجل وقال يا صريم من هذا الرجل الذي نصرنا به لعلنا نكافيه ونشركه في الملك فإنه

[66] Ahlwardt 9747 has (وكشف). (وفض) is from Arabe 5833 (129v) and Or. 2676 (176v).
[67] Ahlwardt 9747 (138r) has (حيوتي). (حياتي) is found in Ms. Or. Oct. 1383 (144r), Arabe 5833 (129v), 5984 Adab (111), and Or. 2676 (176v).

حقيق بذلك قال رجل بدوي لا يعرف إلا في الفلاة ثم إن ابن الملك أقبل على صريم قبولاً حسنًا واستوزره ورفعه على سرير ملكه فشكر صريم البراق وأثنى عليه وأنشأ صريم يقول

أسير على الأقدام ما دمت في الورى
وما قدّموني الأوّلون ذوو القهر
أمور البرايا في يدي أديرها
(على الرتبة العليا مكاني في القصر)[68]
(وأرفع قومًا حين أخفض غيرهم)[69]
وأعقد منقوضًا وأنقض ذا مر
وذاك ببراق بن روحان نلته
بأروع براق الثنا يا أخي نصر[70]
تلا في الرعايا والجنود بنصره
وقد أيقنوا بالرعب والذل والكسر
وقاتل فردًا ما رأيت كمثله
يقاتل جندًا مثل طامية البحر
فمن مبلغ الرقشاء عني بفضله
بأني وزير للممالك ذو الأمر
أحيّى تحيات الملوك وأتقى
كأني ابن روحان أبو المجد والنصر

قال ابن نافع وشاع ذكر البراق في أرض العجم إلا أنهم لا يعرفونه فأرسل الملك شهرميه إلى صريم وقال أخبر لي من الرجل الذي نصرتم به وقاتل معكم حتى كسر عسكر الروم لعلنا نكافيه قال هو رجل بدوي وأنا سأبلغه ما تقول وأرغبه في فضلك فإن شاء أن يضم نفسه إليك كان قطبًا من أقطاب المملكة وإن أبى بعثت إليه بجائزة حسنة ونهض صريم إلى البراق وأخبره بما عند الملك من الرغبة فيه وأنه يريد أن يشاركه في ملكه ويستأمره على عسكره وقال يا براق هل لك

[68] Parenthetical hemistich from Ms. Or. Oct. 1383 (144v).
[69] Parenthetical hemistich from Ms. Or. Oct. 1383 (144v).
[70] The wording of the second hemistich is from Arabe 5833 (130r), 5984 Adab (112), Or. 2676 (177r), and, with a minor variation, Ms. Or. Oct. 1383 (144v). Ahlwardt 9747 (138v) has (بأروع براق الثنا باذح الفخر).

أن تصل إلى الملك وتكسب ملكًا وتخلص ابنة عمك وتبلغ عنده أعلى منزلة فقال إن الملوك لهم فضل وهم أهله غير أني لا أتواضع لملك ولا أطلب نواله وبالله إن أتواضع لعجوز هرمة أقعد بين يديها وأقوم تأمرني وتنهاني وتبسط عليّ لسانها أهون عليّ من أن أتواضع لملك وأطلب نواله وكيف وقد قتلوا غرسان وسبوا ليلى أتشير عليّ بمشورة من سقطت نفسه ووهنت مروءته وإني لا أبالي ما بقي لي سيف قاطع وجواد سابق وقلب ثابت وعشيرة صادقة ولا أريد إلا حفظ العهد الذي بيني وبينك وأما أنا فلك أن لا أنقضهم بيدي ولا بلساني فإذا أردت ذلك ومكنت الفرصة من أخذ ثأري وخلاص ابنة عمي أنبذ إليك عهدك وأرحل عن منزلك فقال صريم سمعًا وطاعة لك ما دمت في داري أن لا أفشي لك سرًا ولا أكشف لك أمرًا وودع البراق وتوجه إلى كرخا وزيرًا مع ابن الملك وأوصى أخاه وامرأته الرقشاء بإكرام البراق وجواده وحرضهما على كتم أمره فأقام البراق مدة من الزمان وهو لا يخلع لأمة حربه ليلاً ولا نهارًا وجواده مشدود دائمًا خوفًا من الغدر وبينما هو ذات يوم جاش فؤاده وتذكر شجوه وأخاه فأنشأ يقول

اسأل فؤادي عن همّ وبلبال
ودمع عيني عن سجم وتهطال
متى أنال شفا دائي بألوية
معلومة ورجال غير أعزال
بها أروي غليلي عن أخي وبها
أرد ليلى إلى الأهلين والمال
لعل روحان يأتي في بني أسد
كليث[71] غاب إذا يعدو بأشبال
في فيلق كسواد الليل من مضر
وحيّ غسان أهل المنصب العالي
ويستتفيق كليب مع نويرته
وعامر بن ذويب وابن ضهال
قوم مساعير حرب راكبين وغى
راموا من الأمر حقًا كل أهوال

[71] (كليث) is found in Arabe 5833 (130v), 5984 Adab (114), and Or. 2676 (177r). Ms. Or. Oct. 1383 (145r) and Ahlwardt 9747 (139v) have (كليب).

وبكر البراق بعد ذلك إلى قبر أخيه وبكى ثم قال

ليس البكاء الذي نبكيه بالمقل
لكنه بظباء الهند والأسل
فذاك غرسان ما أرجوه ان ظفرت
كفي فذلك عندي غاية الأمل
هل تسمعنّ دعائي ان دعوت وهل
ترى مقيمًا كمفرود من الإبل[72]
أسائل الريح عن قومي إذا خفقت
وعن كليب الذي ولّى ولم يسل

ثم انصرف إلى منزله في دار صريم وتقدم إلى الرقشاء أخو صريم وأمرها تزيد في إكرام البراق وجواده وجلس إليه فقدمت إليهما الطعام فأكلا وباتا يتحدثان ثم إن الرقشاء تقدمت إلى البراق بمشورة أنها تريد أن تشير على الملك شهرميه أن يخرج بليلى إلى الصحراء يتنزهان فإذا خرج أخبرت البراق وجعلت له وقتًا معلومًا يرصده فيه على بعض مسالكه فقال البراق يكون ذلك ومضت الرقشاء إلى ليلى وبثت إليها بما في نفسها وتعاهدتا على كتم سرهما واجتمعتا على استخراج الملك ولم تزالا به حتى وافقهما وضرب لذلك يومًا معلومًا فلما علمت ليلى خروجه بها أمرت الرقشاء أن تخبر البراق فأخبرته وتجهز من دار صريم وأرسل إلى صريم يخبره بذلك ويودعه وينبذ إليه العهد الذي كان بينهما وما زال البراق راصدًا خروج الملك من المدينة إلى أن كان في صبحة يوم فسمع ضجة خارج باب المدينة فعلم أن الملك قد خرج فأسرع إلى لأمة حربه وركب جواده ووقف حذاء الطريق إذ مر به أول العسكر فسأل عن الملك فأشاروا إليه وكان جاهلاً به فاحتفز البراق جواده وجرد سيفه وأهوى عليه بضربة ثابتة فأطار رأسه عن جسده وكانت ليلى خلفه على نجيب ومعها ثلاث قينات على البغال فقال لها حثي نجيبك فقد قتلت الملك فحثت نجيبها ومال بها إلى جانب وأحس الغلمان بسيدهم وأدهشهم غلس الصباح ولم يعلموا أن البراق توجه بليلى حتى اعتزل عن القوم فلحقه بعض الجند فعطف عليهم وردّ أوّلهم على آخرهم فرجعوا إلى المدينة وراح البراق بليلى منصورًا وأنشأ يقول شعرًا

[72] In 5984 Adab and Arabe 5833, this hemistich reads as (انّي مقيم كمقروح من الإبل).

ألا استخبرا[73] الرقشاء فهي خبيرة
عن الفارس البراق مردي الفوارس
نعم واسألا عني صريمًا ورهطه
غداة التقينا يوم ضرب القلانس
تخبركما الرقشاء ما كان عندها
نعم وصريم يوم رغم المعاطس
ألم تحمل النفس الكريمة في الوغى
وتأتي بأسلاب الكماة العوابس
قتلت مليك الفرس وسط جنوده
ورحت بليلى روحة المتشاوس
وكنت وحيدًا من رجال ربيعة
وأختهم الحسناء خير النفائس
قتلت بغرسان ابن أمي ابن جرهم
وأنقذت ليلى من وثاقات فارس
وأدبرت محمودًا بخير صنيعة
وأطيب عيش بعد سور المناحس

قال ابن نافع وإن ربيعة بعد أن أبطأ البراق ولم يأتهم عنه خبر أشفقوا عليه ولاموا انفسهم وندموا وتشاتموا بينهم وأقبلت أم الأغر على أخيها نويرة تسأله عن البراق فقال مذ أتينا لم نسمع عنه خبرًا فعيرته ولامته لومًا عنيفًا فركب نويرة في قبائل العرب يستنجدهم ويطلبهم إلى النصرة والمسير في طلب البراق فأجابوا إلى ذلك جميع ربيعة ومضر وطي وقضاعة وأخواله آل عمرو وابن لهيم والملك ثعلبة بن الأعرج وساروا في أوائلهم زيد بن رباح[74] وهو يقول

نقود الى البراق خيلاً شوازبا
واسدًا أعدت للقراع قواضبا

[73] This *alif* is not found in the manuscripts, but evidence from lines 2 and 3 suggests that the imperative verb should be conjugated in the dual.
[74] Ahlwardt 9747 (141r) has (دياح). (رباح) is found in 5984 Adab (118) and Or. 2676 (178r).

أجبنا إلى البراق خير إجابة
نقود إليه كالقداح السلاهبا
عليها من القوم الكرام كتائب
هنالك تقفو في المسير كتائبا

ثم صاروا كل على راحلته مجنبًا جواده فصادفوا رجلاً فأشفق منهم وأراد أن يعتزل عن الطريق فلم يطق وفكر في نفسه فقال هؤلاء ربيعة ومضر سائرون في طلب البراق فطلبوه فاستسلم لهم فاستخبروه عن البراق فأخبرهم بشأنه فأخذوه وتقدموا به وشاع الخبر في قبائل نزار وقامت البشائر ونشرت الرايات وفرحوا فرحًا عظيمًا وكسوا الرجل وانعموا عليه وساروا وفي مقدمتهم زيد بن رباح[75] وبينما هم سائرون إذ لقيهم البراق ومعه ليلى فلما رأوه ترجلوا وأقبلوا يسعون على أقدامهم وترجل البراق والتقاهم فسلموا عليه وعزوه بأخيه وهنأوه بالظفر وأقاموا نهارهم وليلهم هناك حتى وافته عشيرته وعشائر العربان فشكرهم وانقلبوا إلى أهلهم فرحين مسرورين وقامت البشائر عند ربيعة وأقبلت كل قبيلة تهني البراق ورفعوا السلاح وعقروا الجزور وقدموا الموائد والأطعمة وزوجوا البراق بليلى وكانت عذراء لم يظفر بها عربي ولا عجمي لشدة صيانتها وعفتها ولهذا لقبت بالعفيفة وأقامت عنده قبائل العرب سبعة أيام وهو ينصب الموائد ويقدم الأطعمة والأشربة ثم انصرفت كل قبيلة إلى أرضها وأقام البراق في أرغد عيش وأحسن حال وهذا ما انتهى إلينا من أخبار البراق وليلى

[75] Ahlwardt 9747 (141r) and Ms. Or. Oct. 1383 (146v) have (دياح). (رباح) is found in Arabe 5833 (130v), 5984 Adab (118), and Or. 2676 (178r).

Publishers' Note

The pages that follow contain the Arabic text of the tale, which begins on the final page of the book. These pages are numbered A1 to A100.